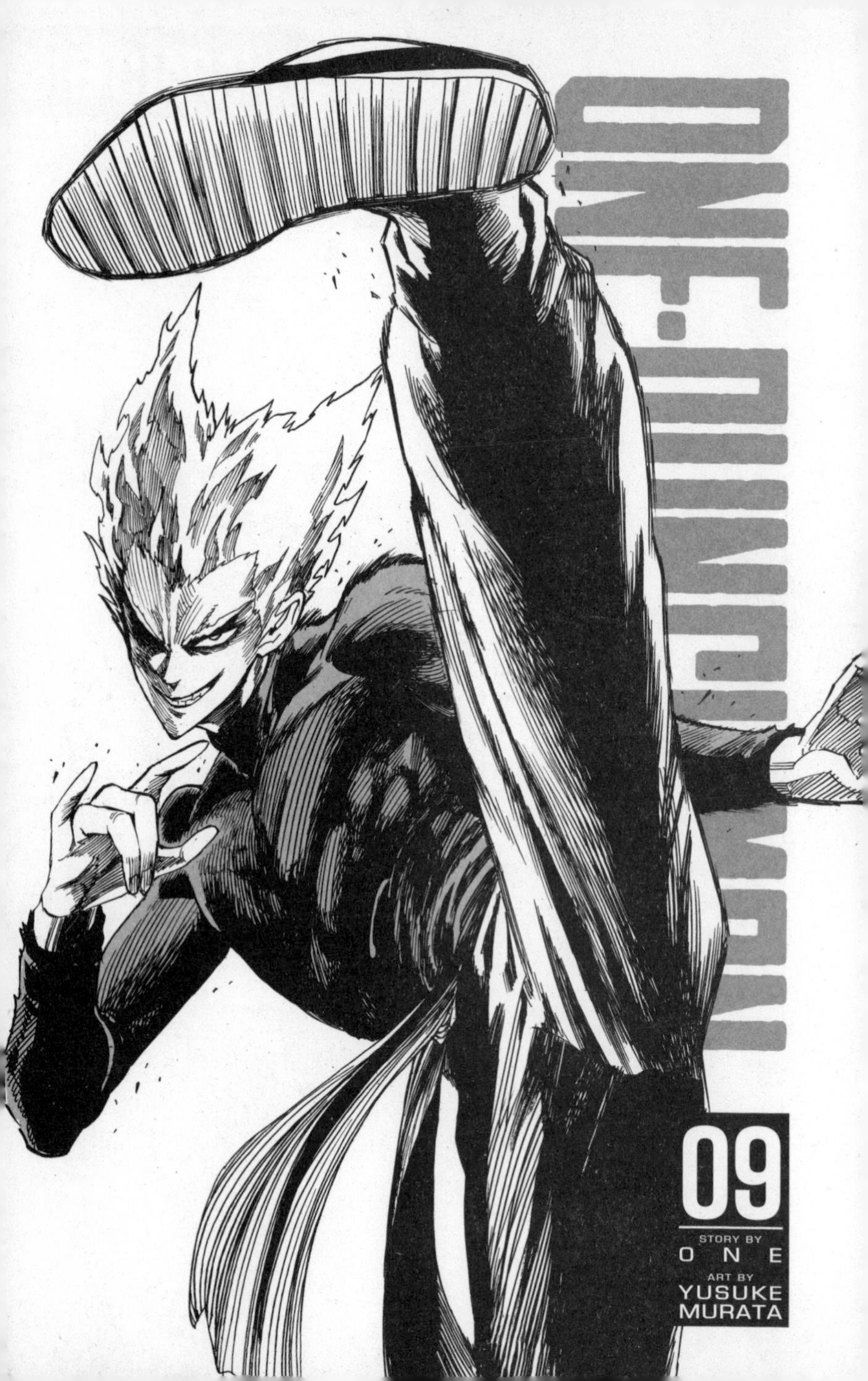
09
STORY BY
O N E
ART BY
YUSUKE
MURATA

CHARACTERS

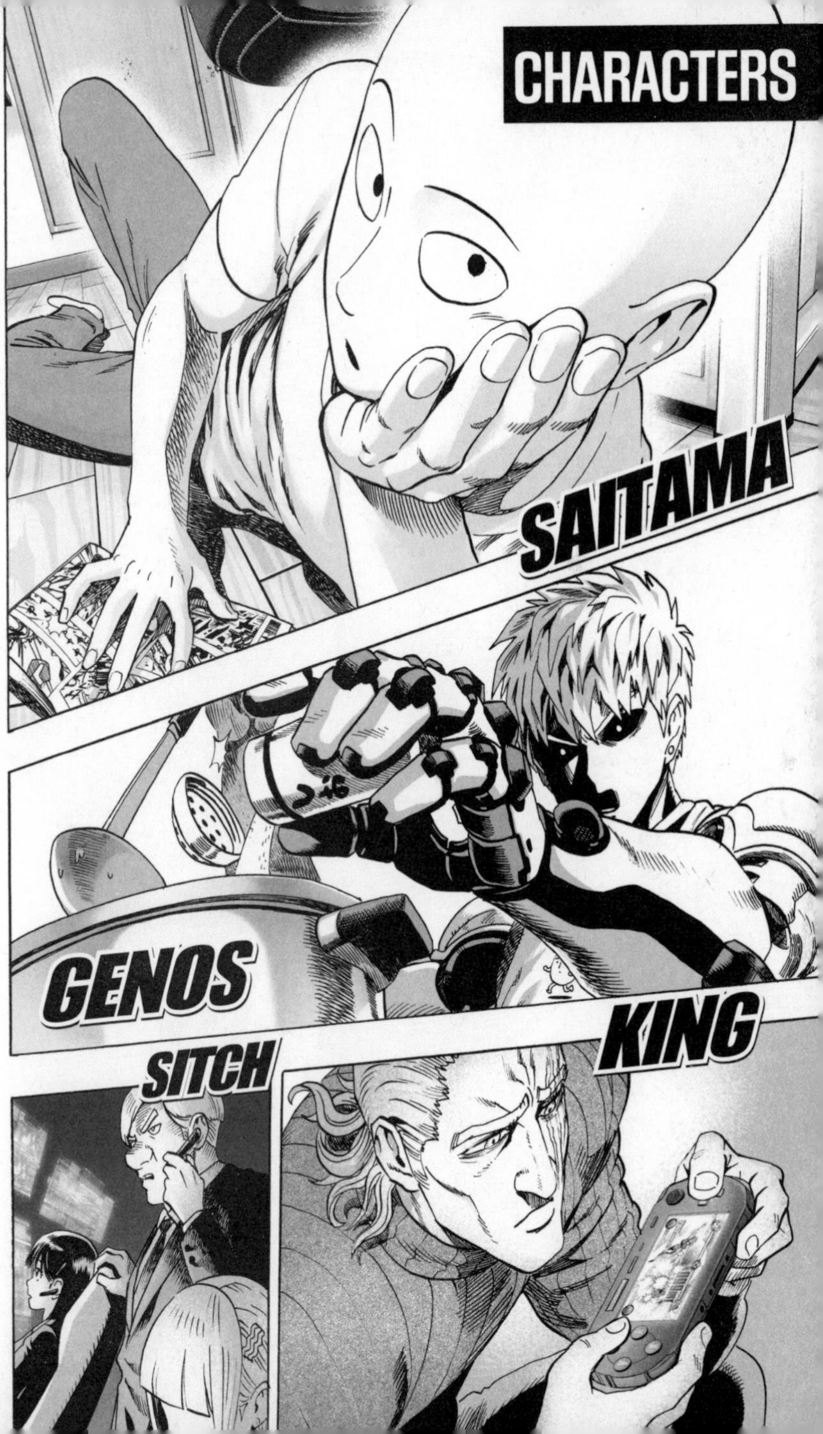
SAITAMA
GENOS
KING
SITCH

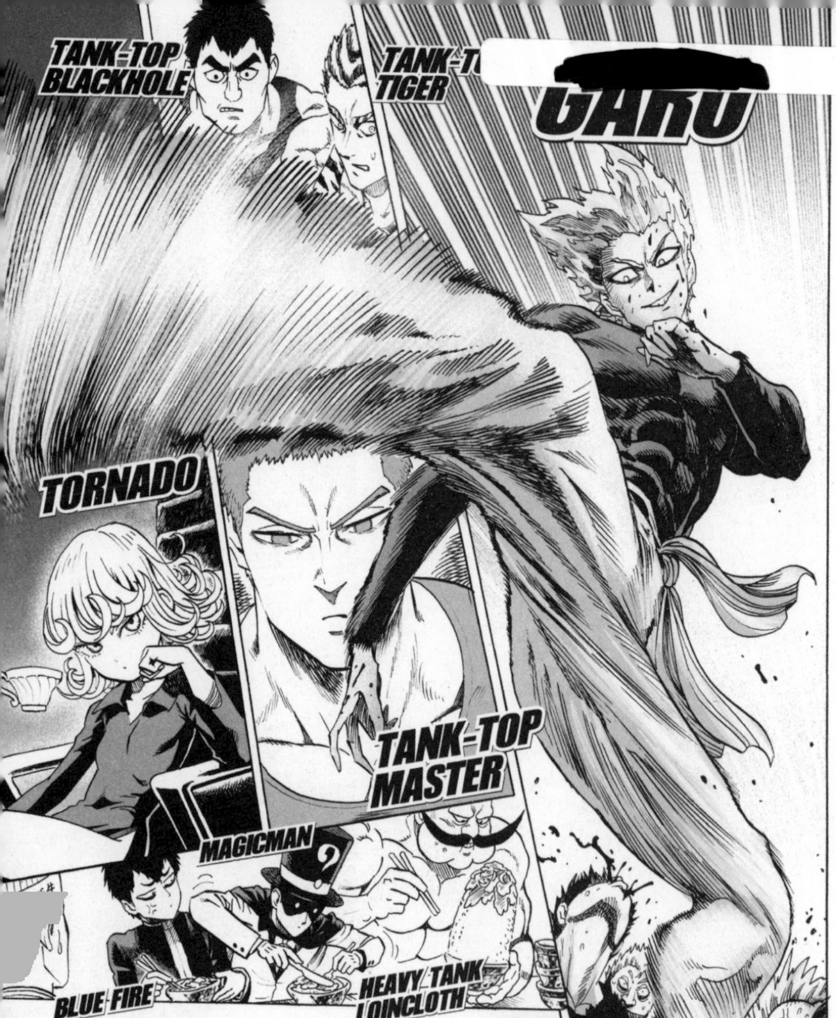
[redacted]
GARO
TANK-T
TIGER
TANK-TOP
BLACKHOLE
TANK-TOP
MASTER
TORNADO
HEAVY TANK
LOINCLOTH
MAGICMAN
BLUE FIRE

STORY

A single man arose to face the evil threatening humankind! His name was Saitama. He became a hero for fun!

With one punch, he has resolved every crisis so far, but no one believes he could be so extraordinarily strong.

Together with his pupil, Genos (Class S), Saitama has been active as a hero and risen from Class C to Class B.

One day, a seer predicts a great danger to Earth and dies. Immediately after, a group of interstellar bandits attacks Earth. Class-S heroes and Saitama defeat the attack, but City A is destroyed. Later, the Hero Association erects a fortress where the city once stood, and a man named Garo, who admires monsters, shows up...

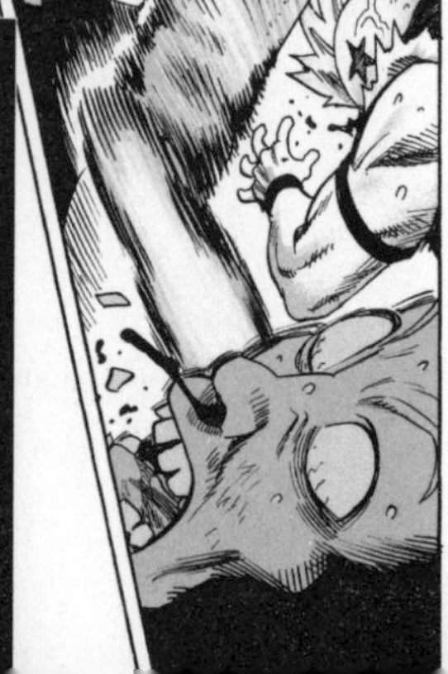

Anti-Monster Measures
HERO ASSOCIATION
TEA

CONTENTS

ONE-PUNCH MAN VOLUME NINE

09

DON'T DIS HEROES!

ONE-PUNCH MAN

ONE + YUSUKE MURATA

My name is Saitama. I am a hero. My hobby is heroic exploits. I got too strong. And that makes me sad. I can defeat any enemy with one blow. I lost my hair. And I lost all feeling. I want to feel the rush of battle. I would like to meet an incredibly strong enemy. And I would like to defeat it with one blow. That's because I am One-Punch Man.

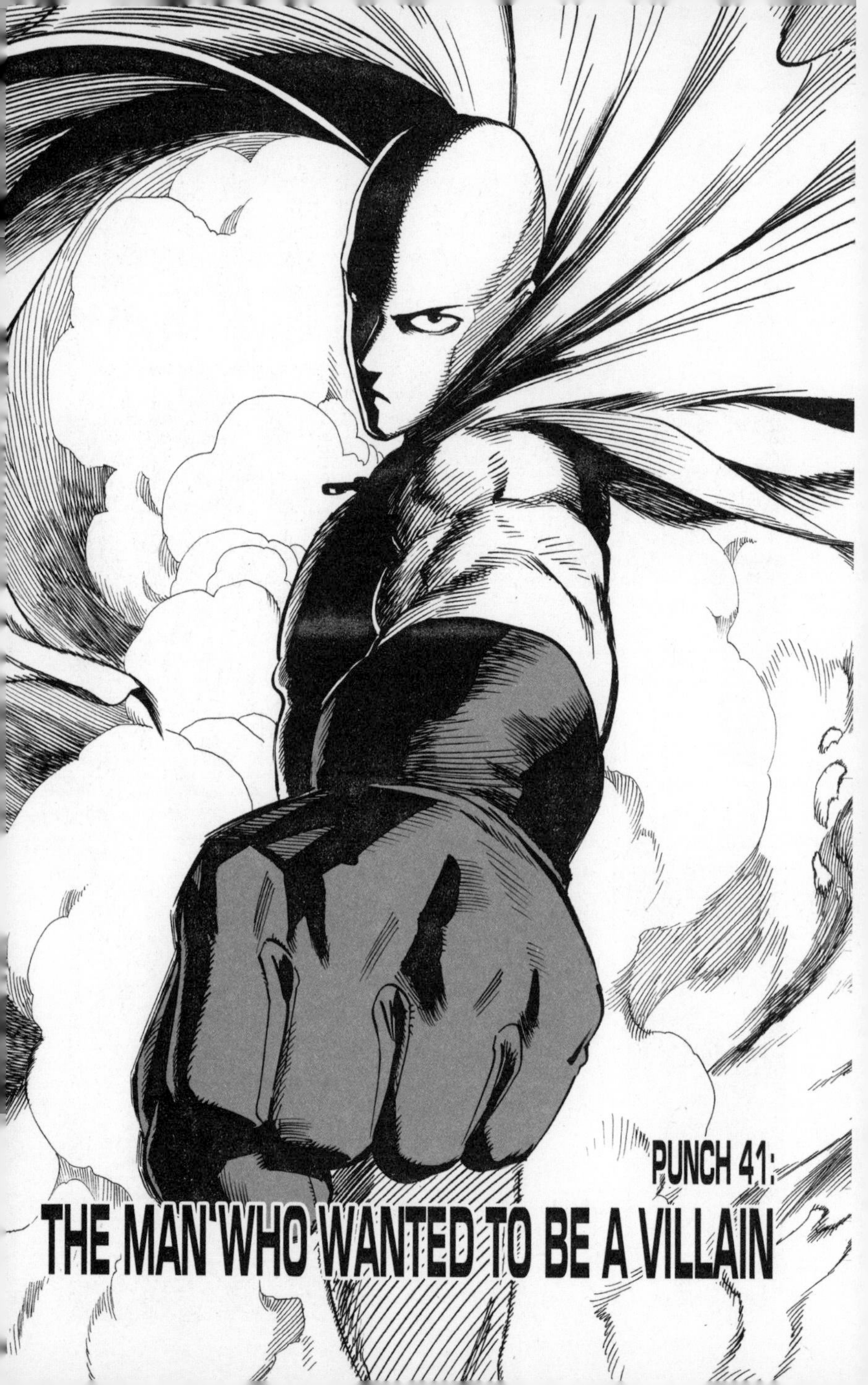
PUNCH 41:
THE MAN WHO WANTED TO BE A VILLAIN

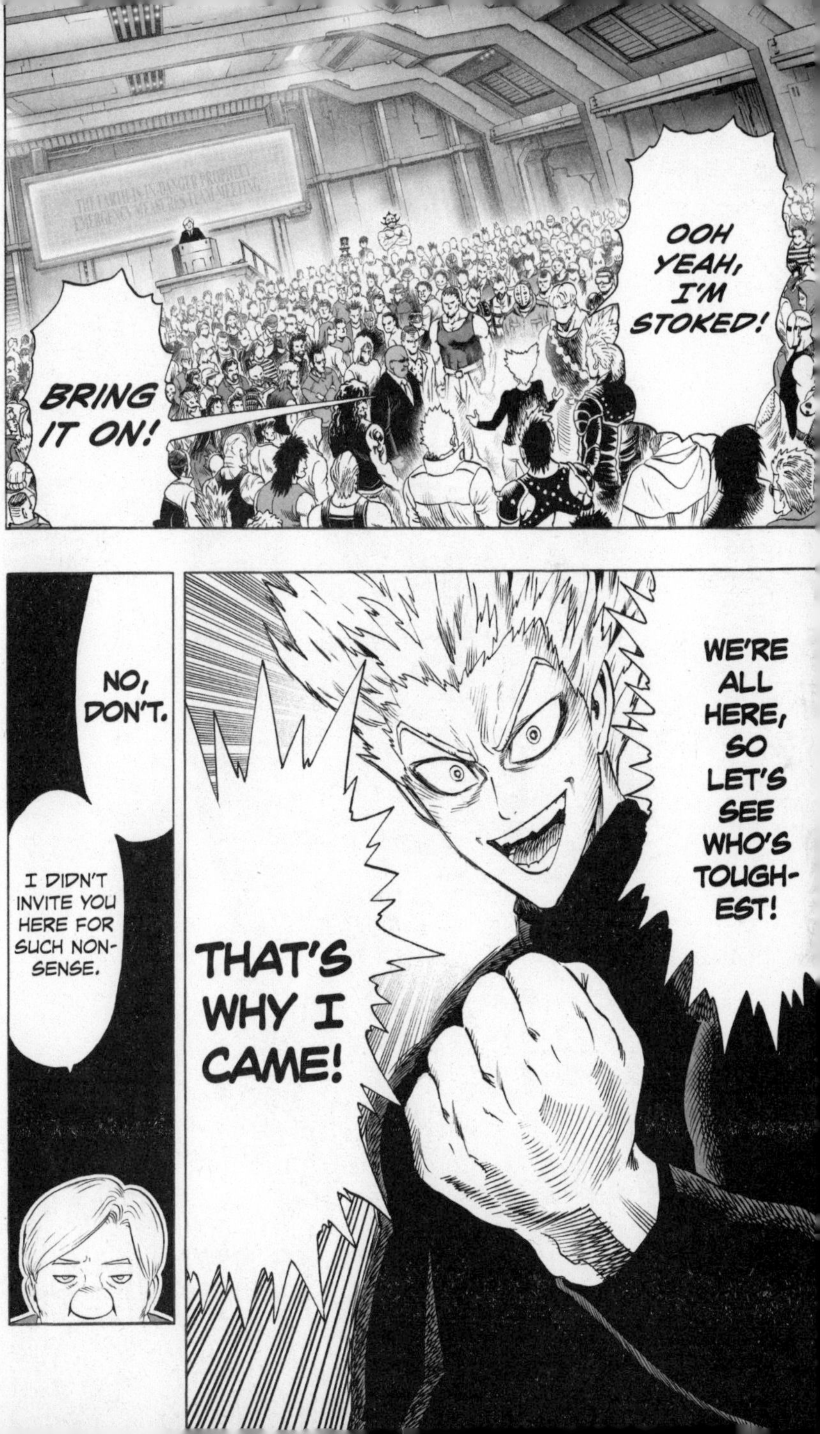
OOH YEAH, I'M STOKED!
BRING IT ON!
WE'RE ALL HERE, SO LET'S SEE WHO'S TOUGH-EST!
THAT'S WHY I CAME!
NO, DON'T.
I DIDN'T INVITE YOU HERE FOR SUCH NON-SENSE.

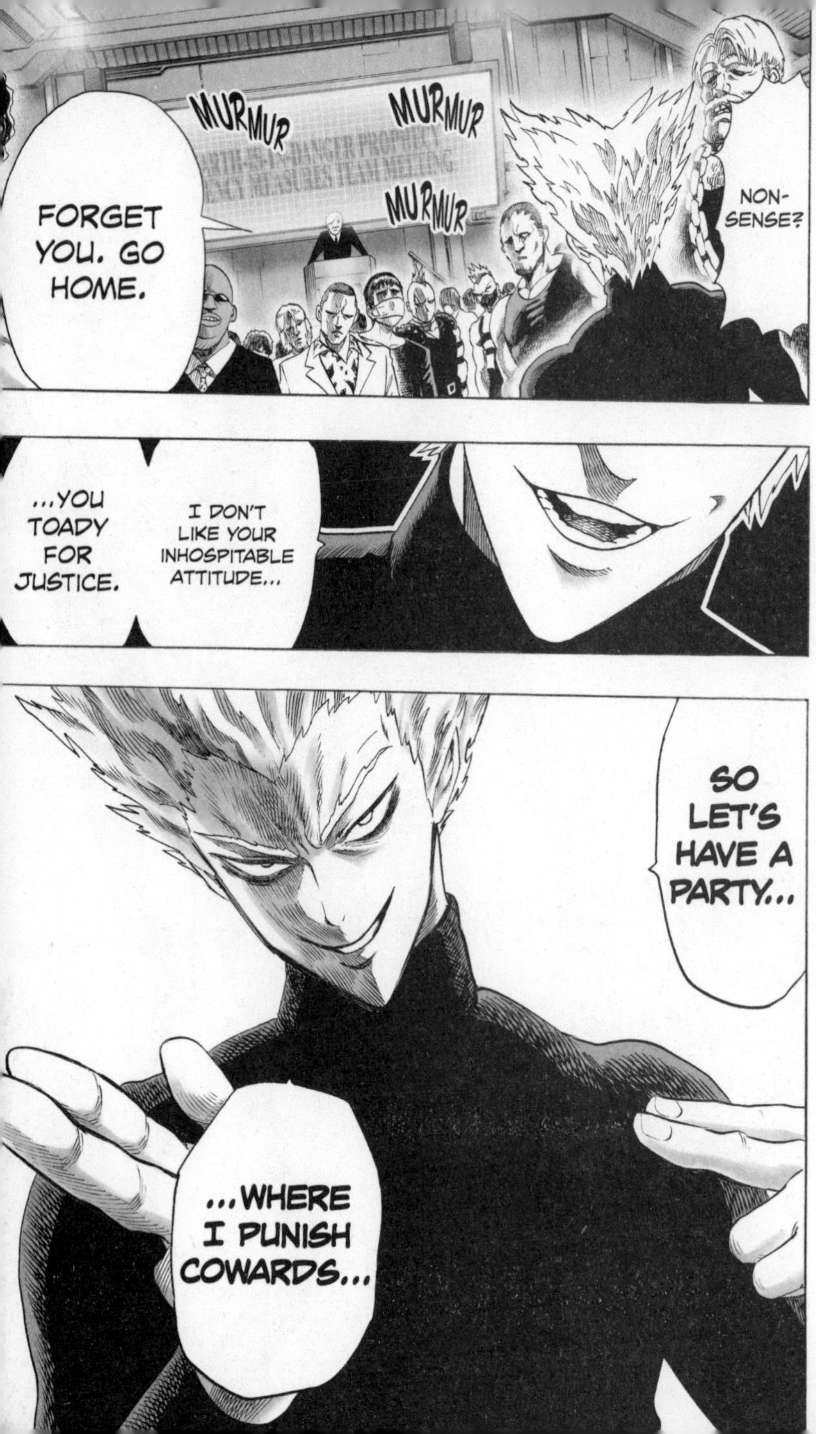
NON-SENSE?
MURMUR
MURMUR
MURMUR
FORGET YOU. GO HOME.
I DON'T LIKE YOUR INHOSPITABLE ATTITUDE...
...YOU TOADY FOR JUSTICE.
SO LET'S HAVE A PARTY...
...WHERE I PUNISH COWARDS...

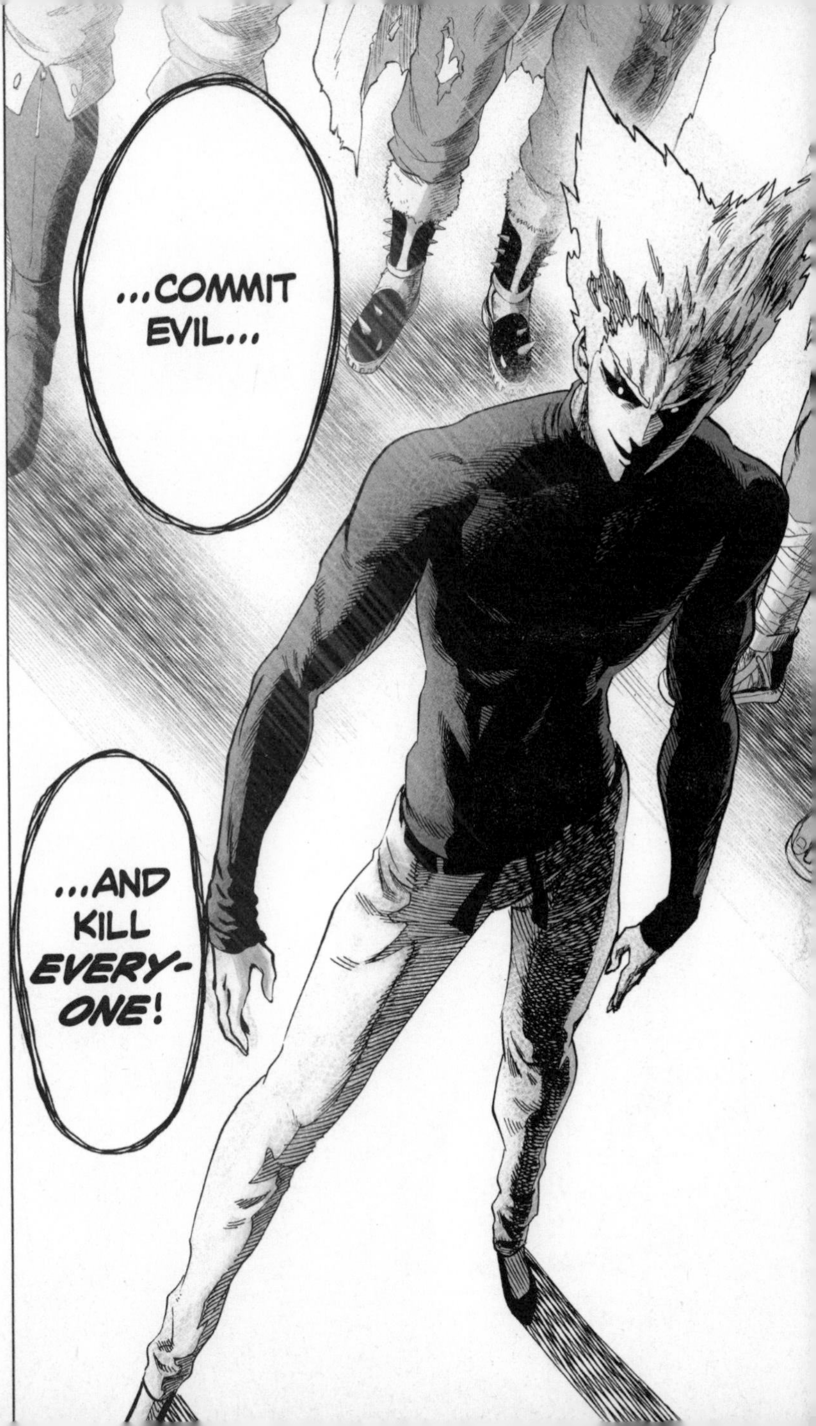
...COMMIT EVIL...
...AND KILL EVERY-ONE!

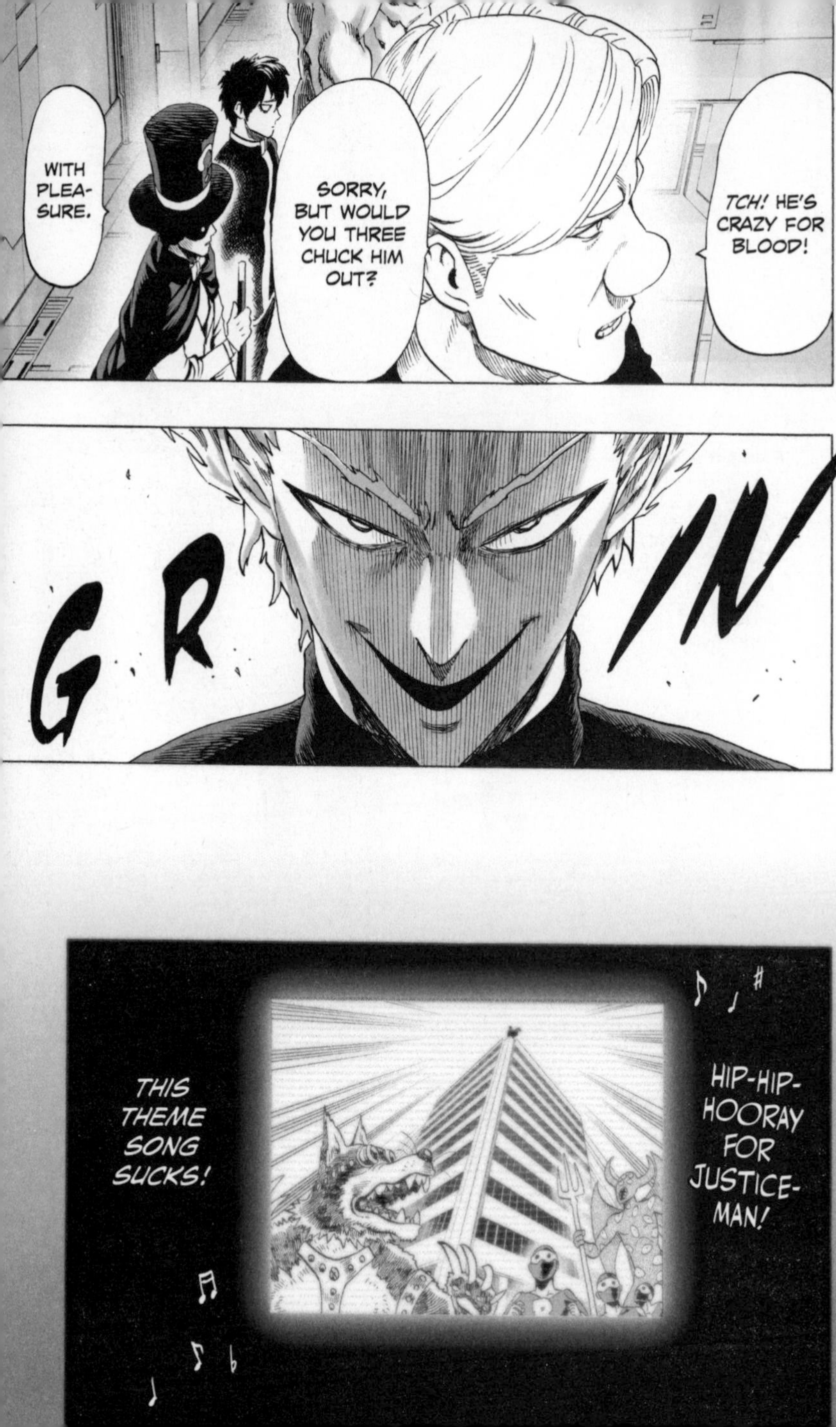
TCH! HE'S CRAZY FOR BLOOD!
SORRY, BUT WOULD YOU THREE CHUCK HIM OUT?
WITH PLEASURE.
GRIN
HIP-HIP-HOORAY FOR JUSTICE-MAN!
THIS THEME SONG SUCKS!

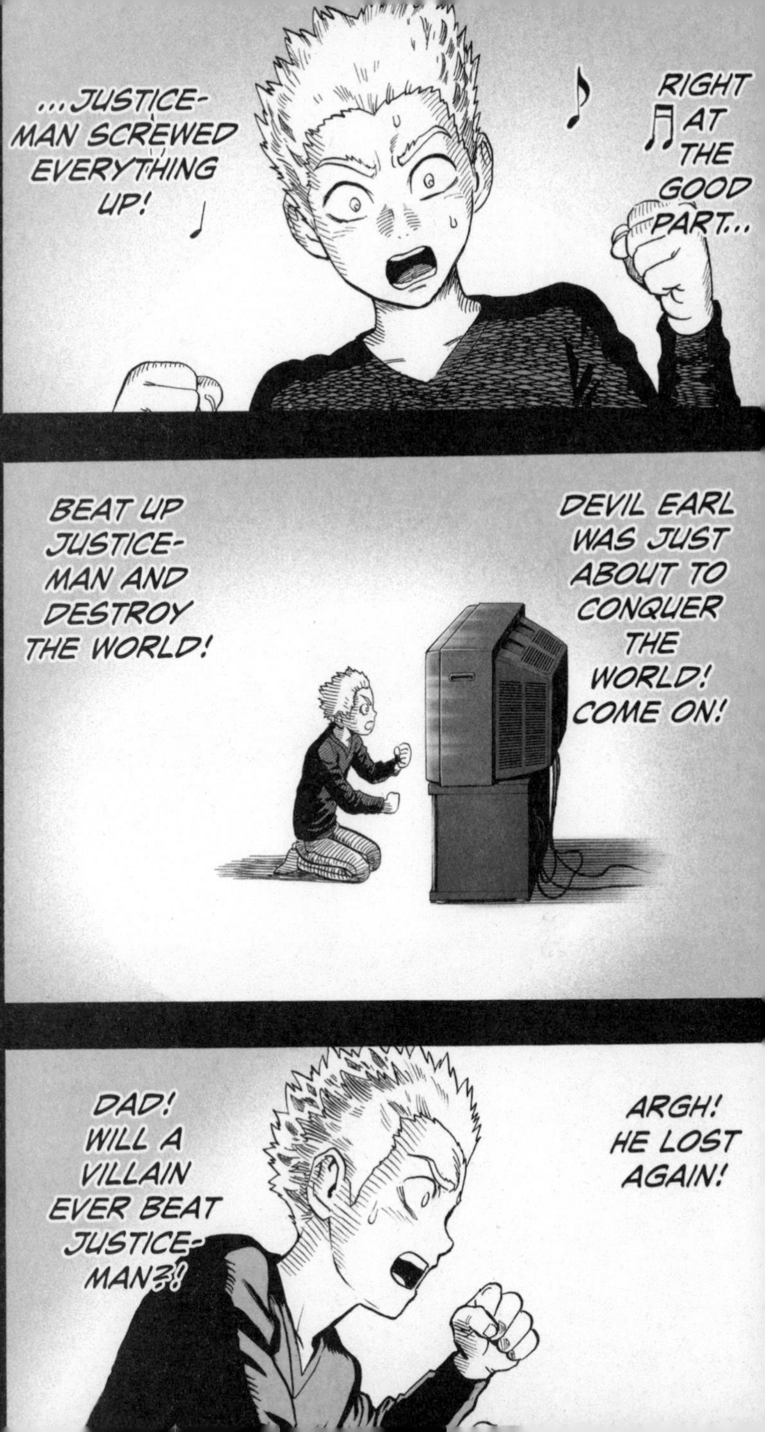
RIGHT AT THE GOOD PART...
...JUSTICE-MAN SCREWED EVERYTHING UP!
DEVIL EARL WAS JUST ABOUT TO CONQUER THE WORLD! COME ON!
BEAT UP JUSTICE-MAN AND DESTROY THE WORLD!
ARGH! HE LOST AGAIN!
DAD! WILL A VILLAIN EVER BEAT JUSTICE-MAN?!

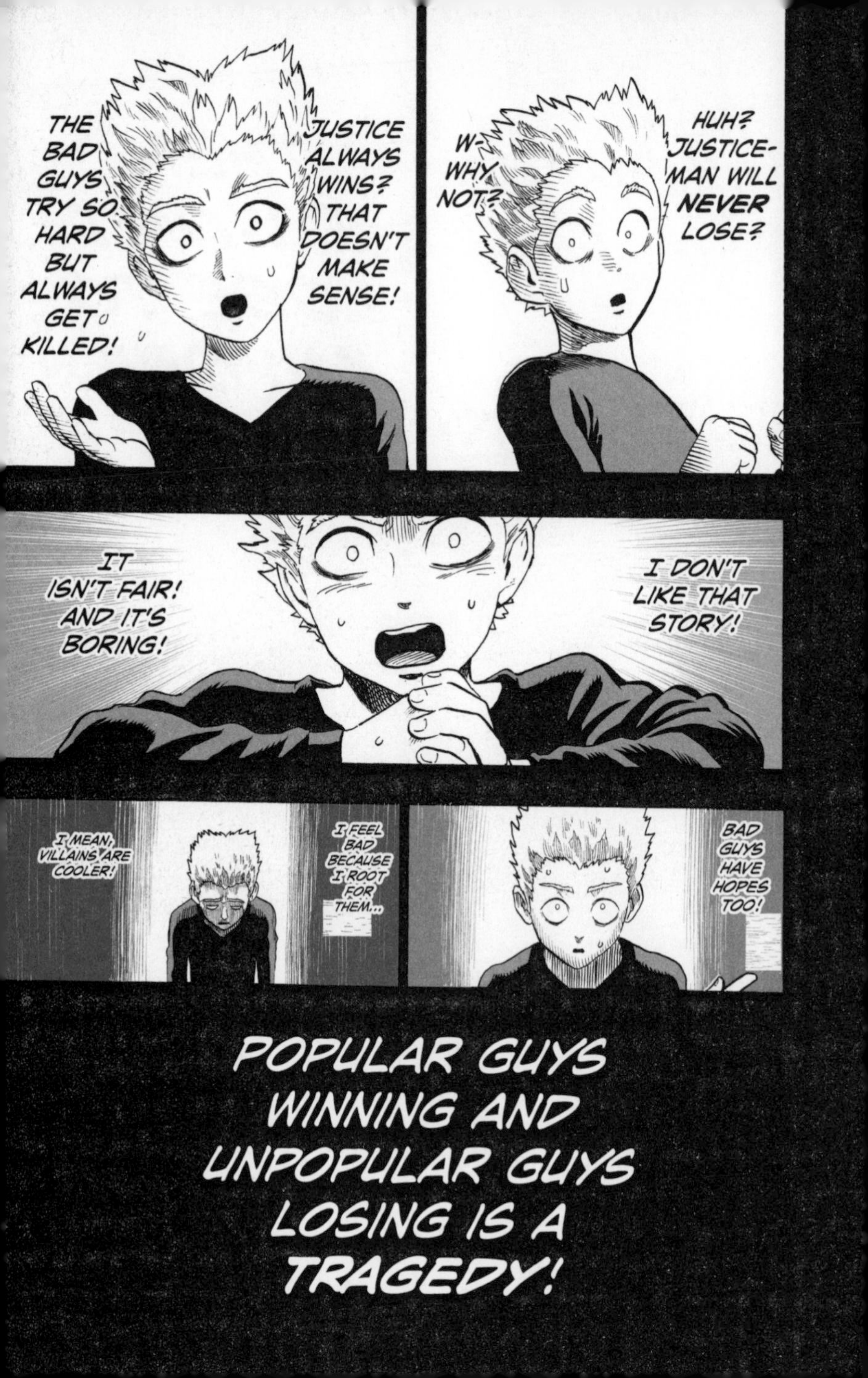
HUH? JUSTICE-MAN WILL NEVER LOSE?
W-WHY NOT?
JUSTICE ALWAYS WINS? THAT DOESN'T MAKE SENSE!
THE BAD GUYS TRY SO HARD BUT ALWAYS GET KILLED!
I DON'T LIKE THAT STORY!
IT ISN'T FAIR! AND IT'S BORING!
BAD GUYS HAVE HOPES TOO!
I FEEL BAD BECAUSE I ROOT FOR THEM...
I MEAN, VILLAINS ARE COOLER!
POPULAR GUYS WINNING AND UNPOPULAR GUYS LOSING IS A TRAGEDY!

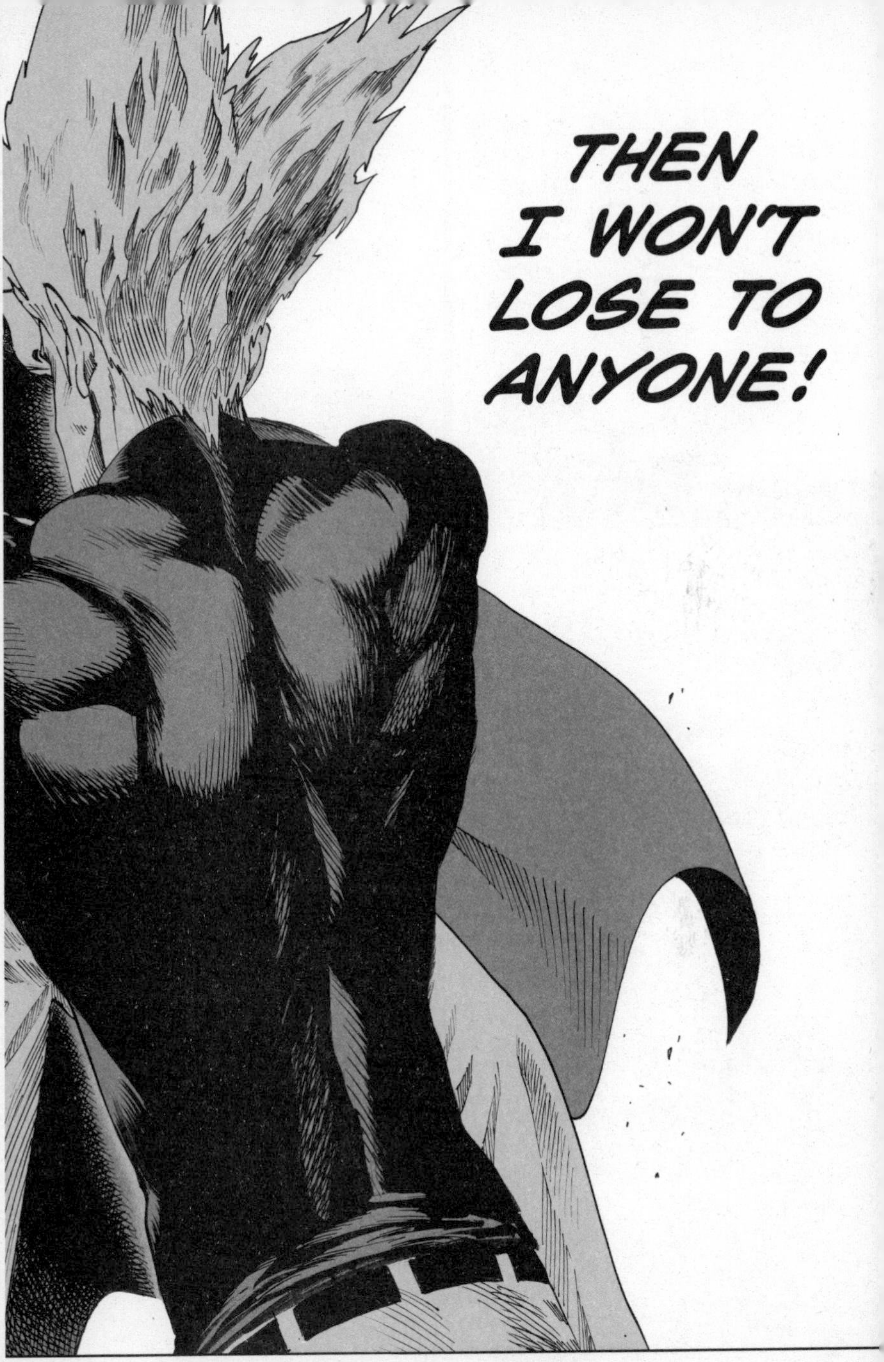
THEN I WON'T LOSE TO ANYONE!

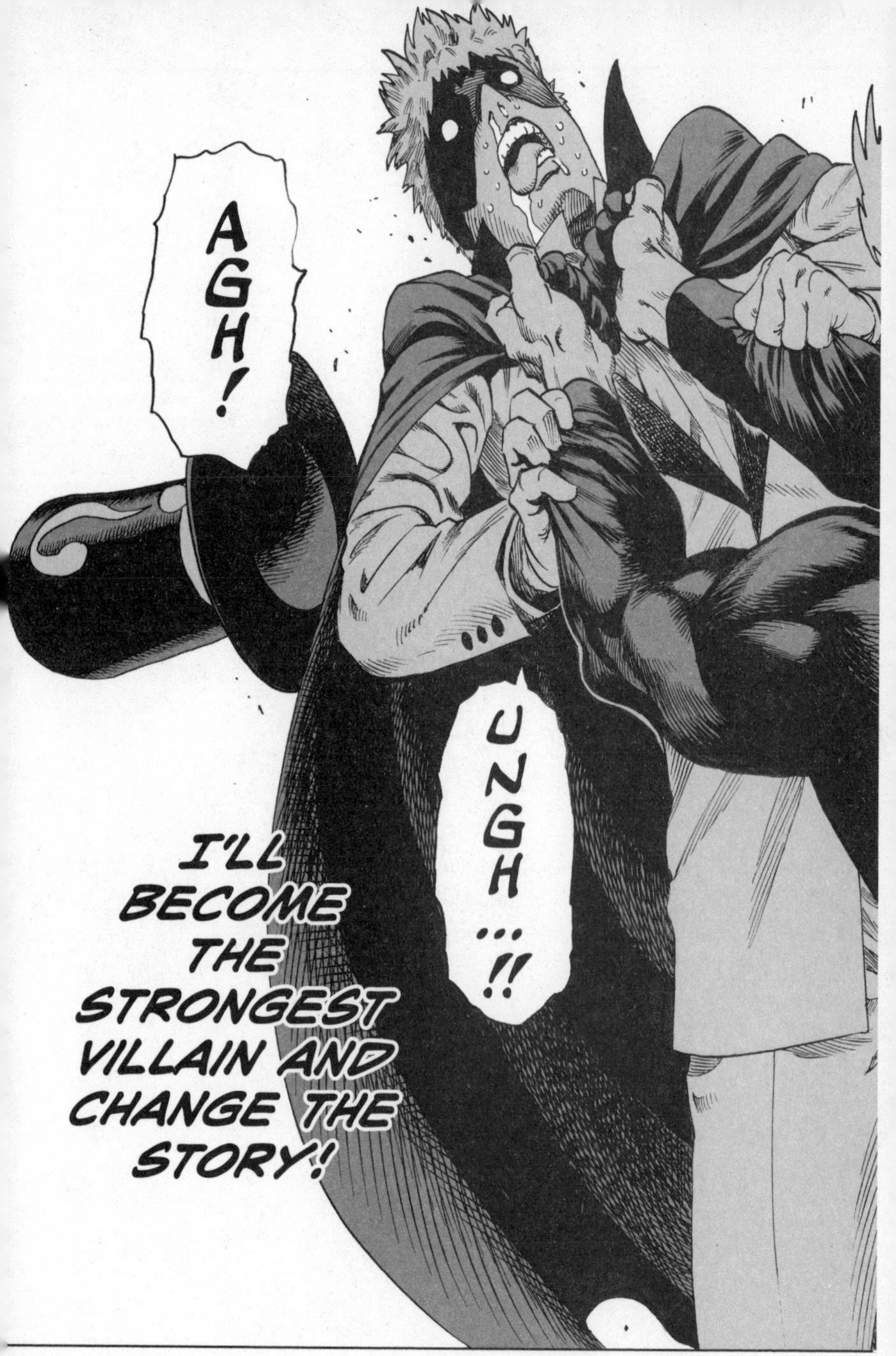
AGH!
UNGH...!!
I'LL BECOME THE STRONGEST VILLAIN AND CHANGE THE STORY!

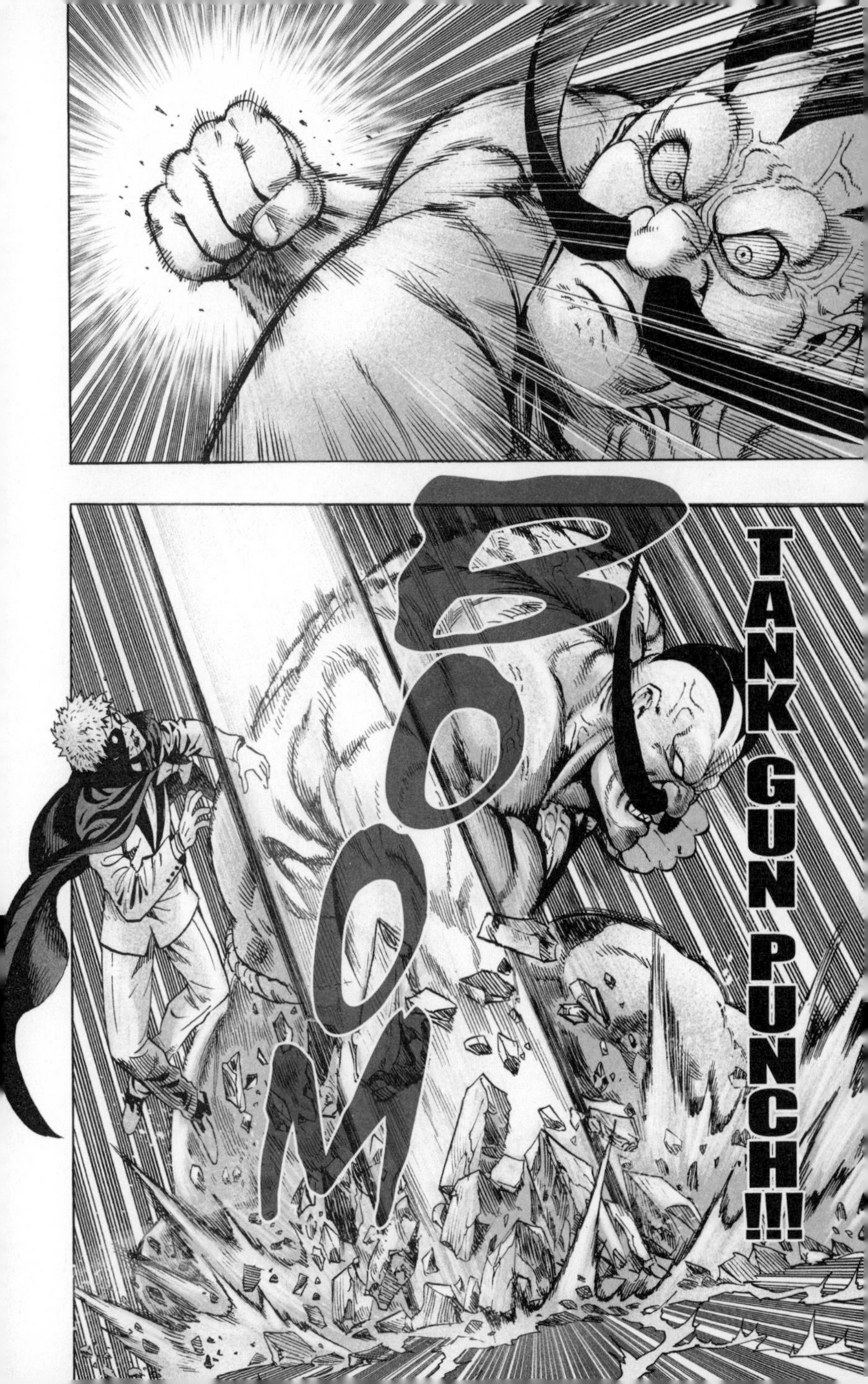
TANK GUN PUNCH!!!
BOOOM

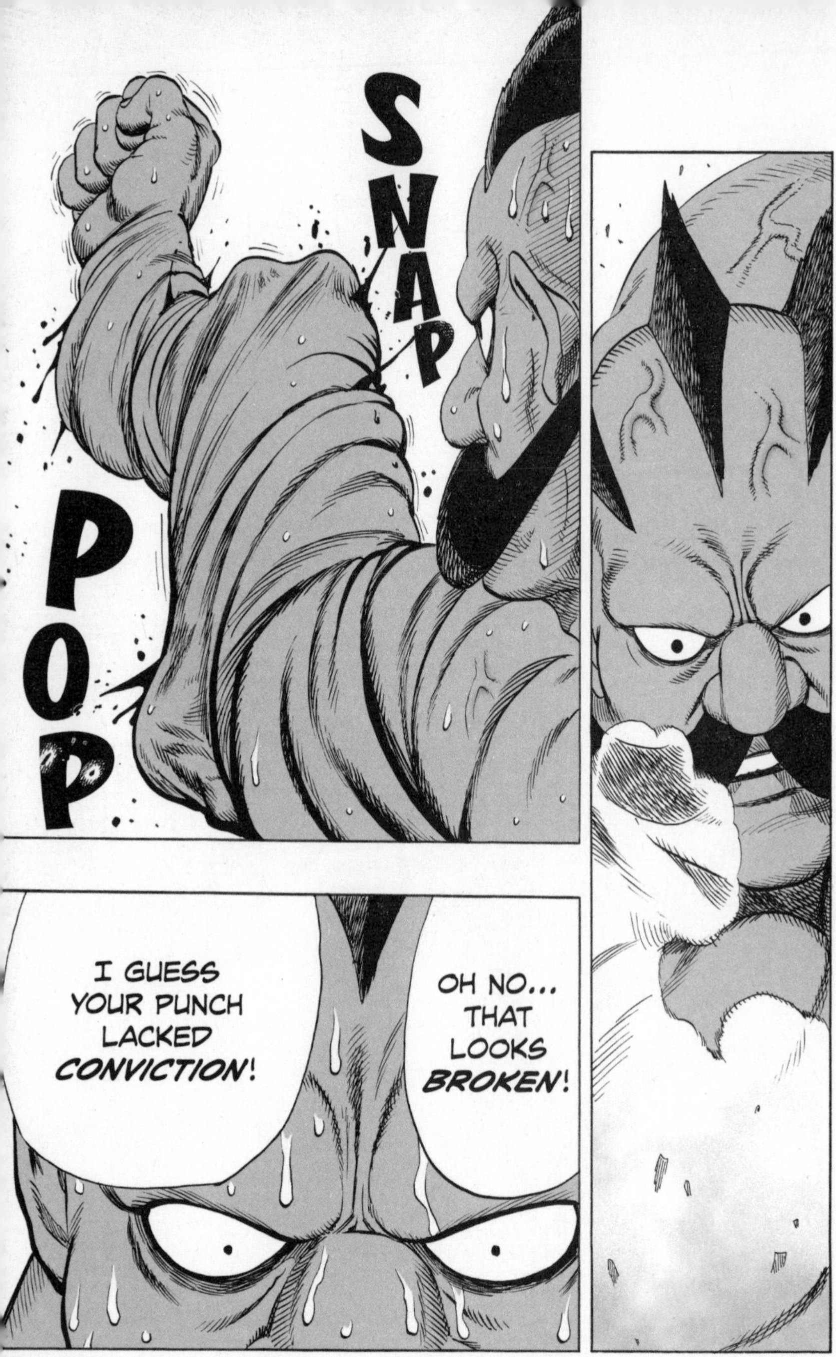
SNAP
POP
OH NO... THAT LOOKS BROKEN!
I GUESS YOUR PUNCH LACKED CONVICTION!

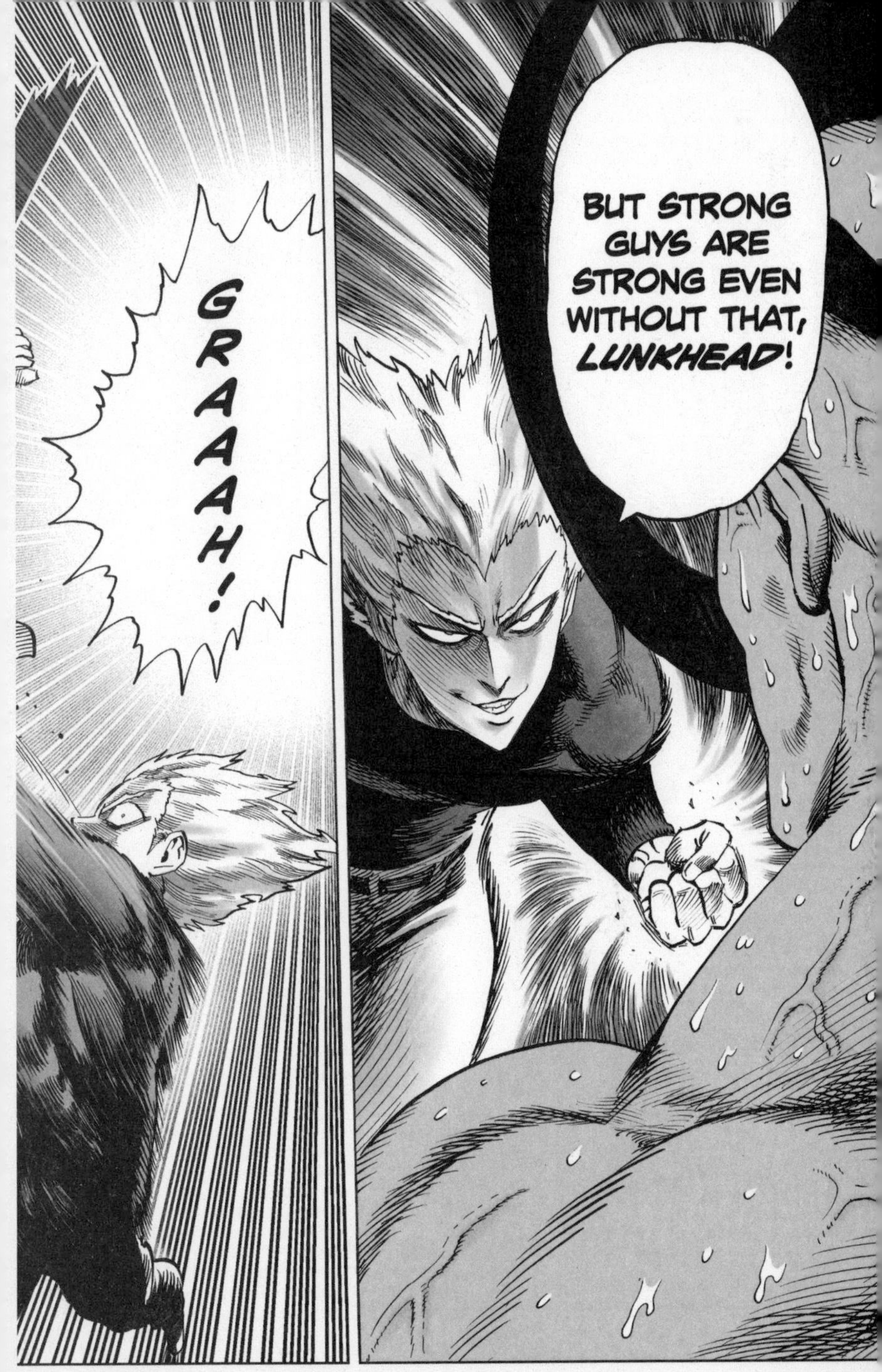
BUT STRONG GUYS ARE STRONG EVEN WITHOUT THAT, ***LUNKHEAD!***
GRAAAH!

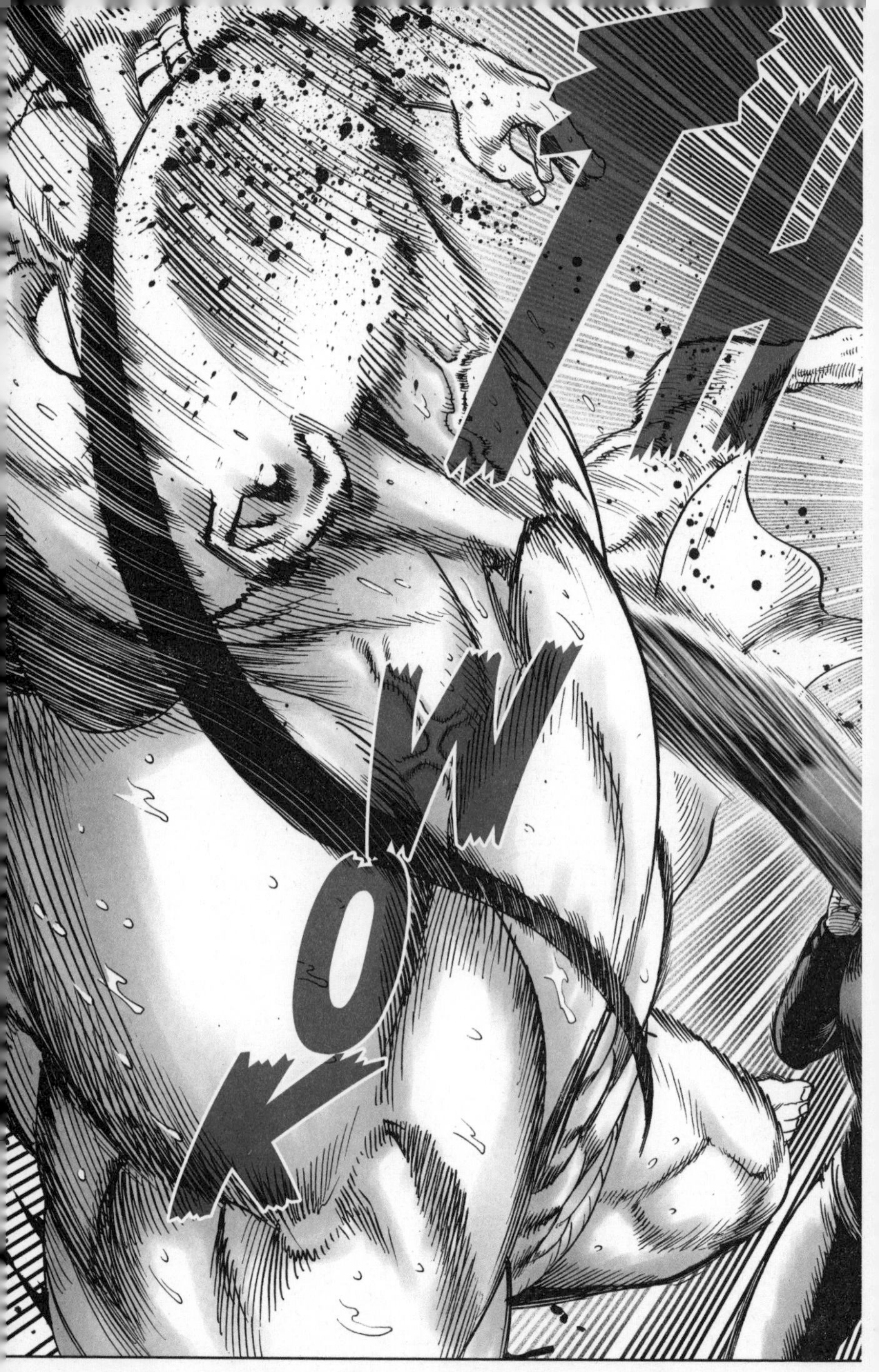
KOWM

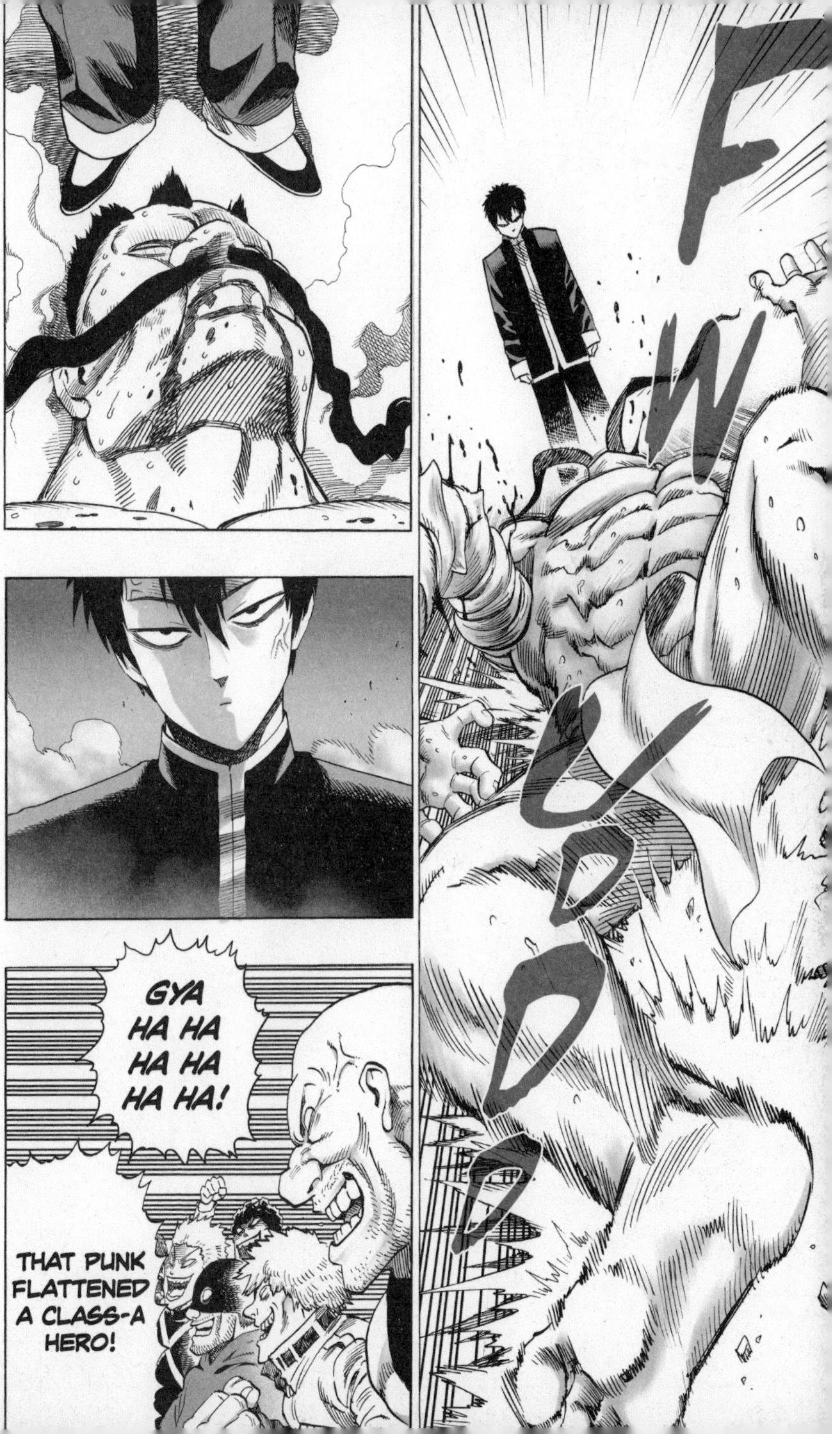
GYA HA HA HA HA HA HA!
THAT PUNK FLATTENED A CLASS-A HERO!

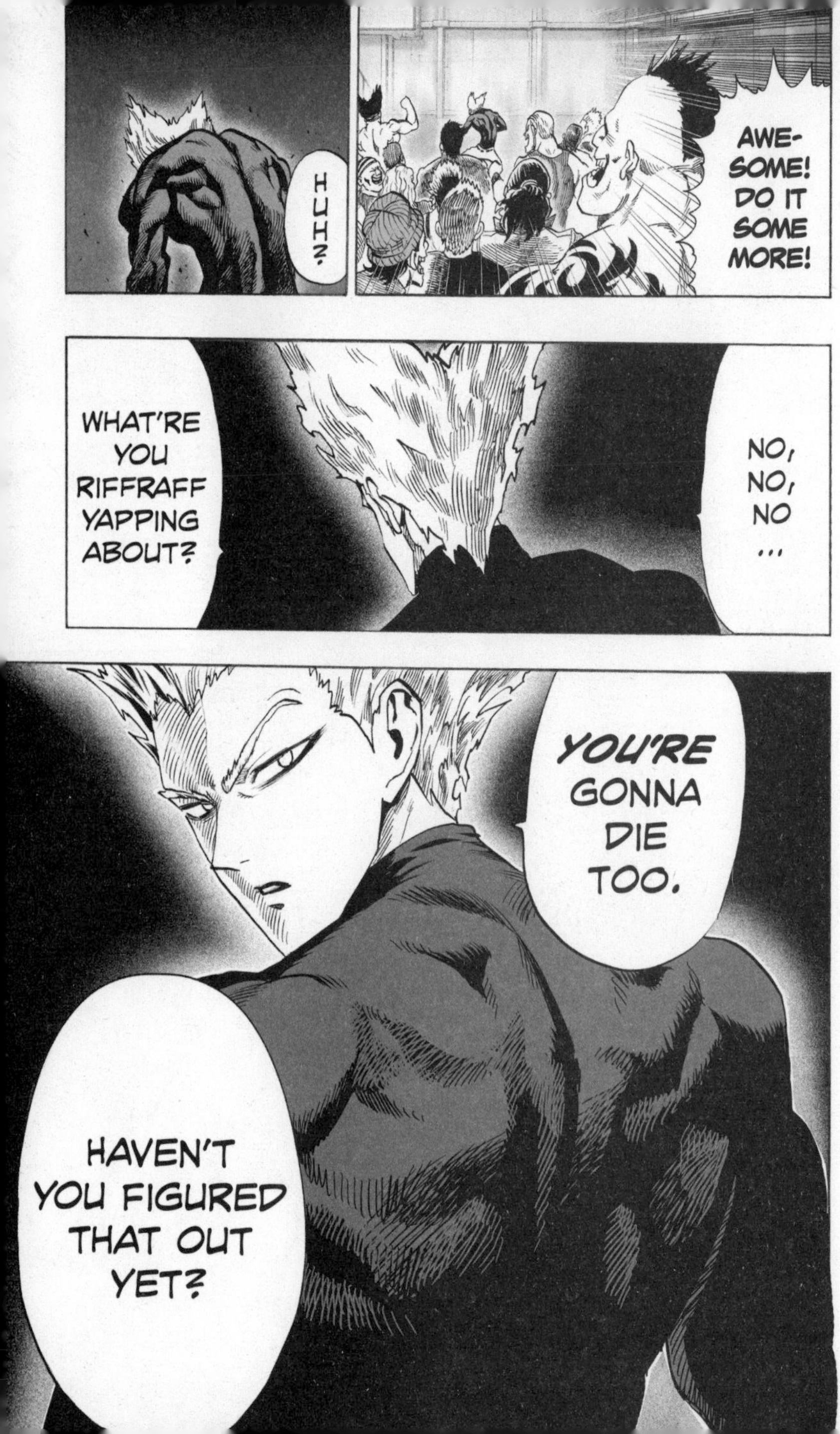
AWE-SOME! DO IT SOME MORE!
HUH?
NO, NO, NO ...
WHAT'RE YOU RIFFRAFF YAPPING ABOUT?
YOU'RE GONNA DIE TOO.
HAVEN'T YOU FIGURED THAT OUT YET?

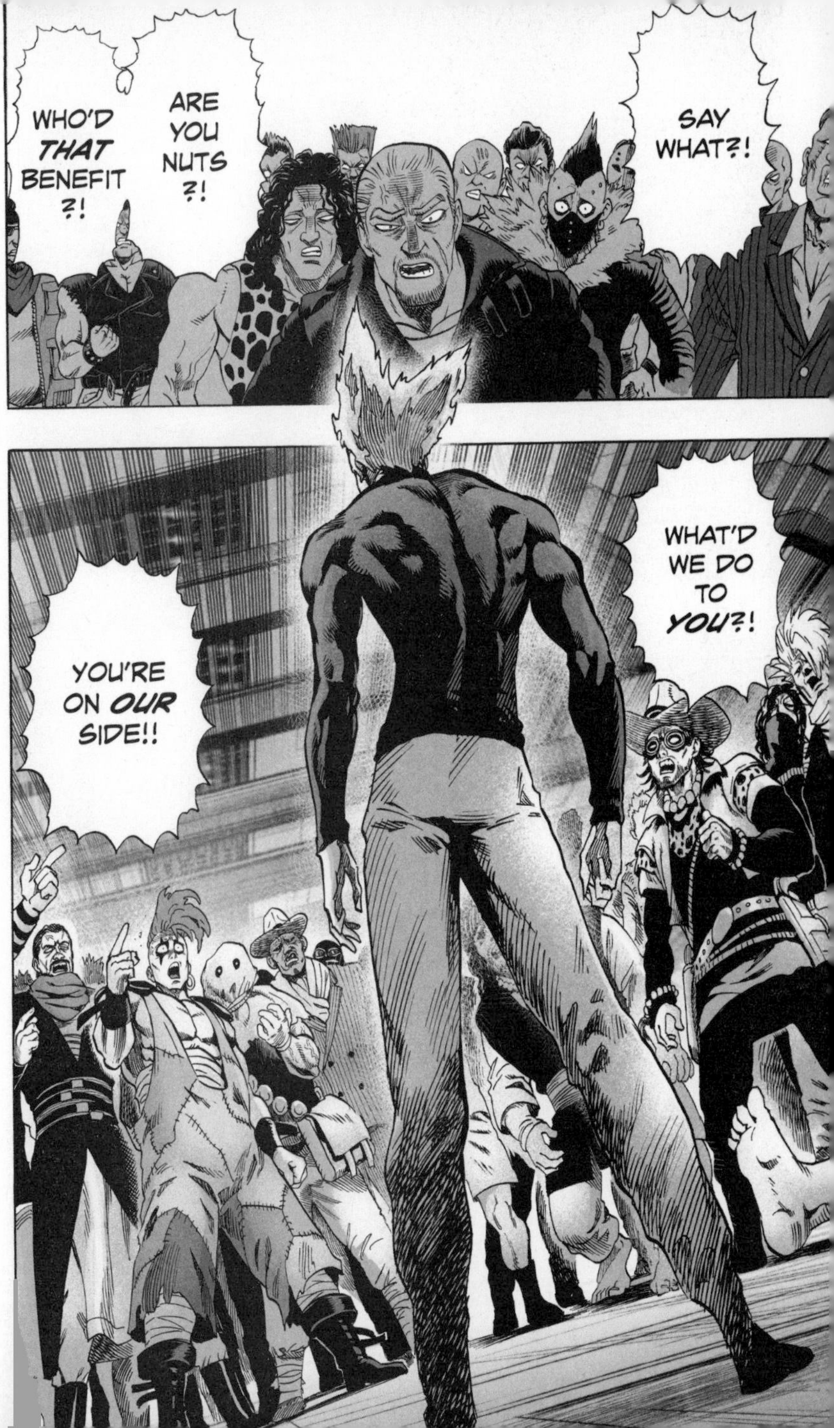
SAY WHAT?!
ARE YOU NUTS?!
WHO'D *THAT* BENEFIT?!
WHAT'D WE DO TO *YOU*?!
YOU'RE ON *OUR* SIDE!!

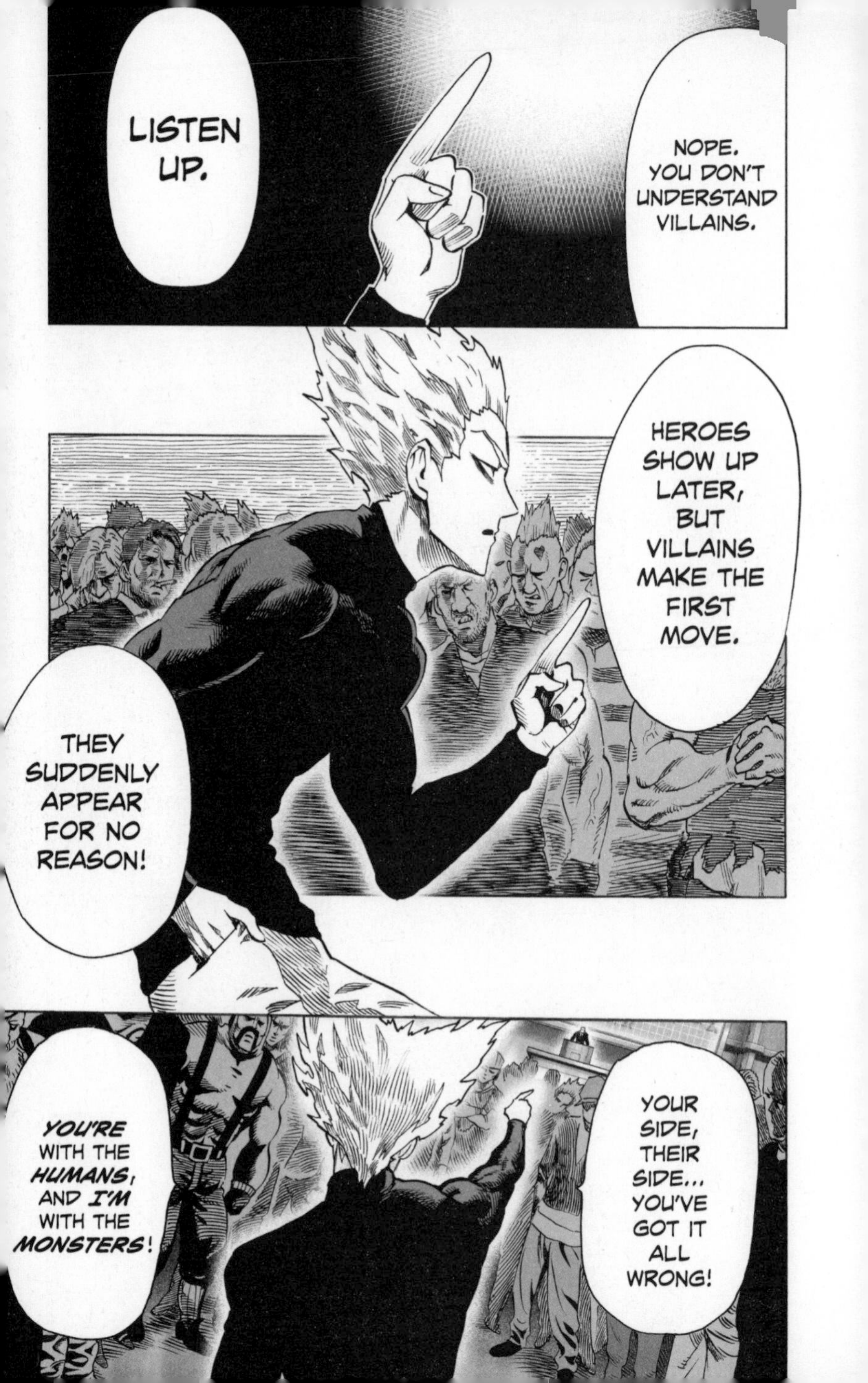
NOPE. YOU DON'T UNDERSTAND VILLAINS.
LISTEN UP.
HEROES SHOW UP LATER, BUT VILLAINS MAKE THE FIRST MOVE.
THEY SUDDENLY APPEAR FOR NO REASON!
YOUR SIDE, THEIR SIDE... YOU'VE GOT IT ALL WRONG!
YOU'RE WITH THE *HUMANS*, AND *I'M* WITH THE *MONSTERS*!

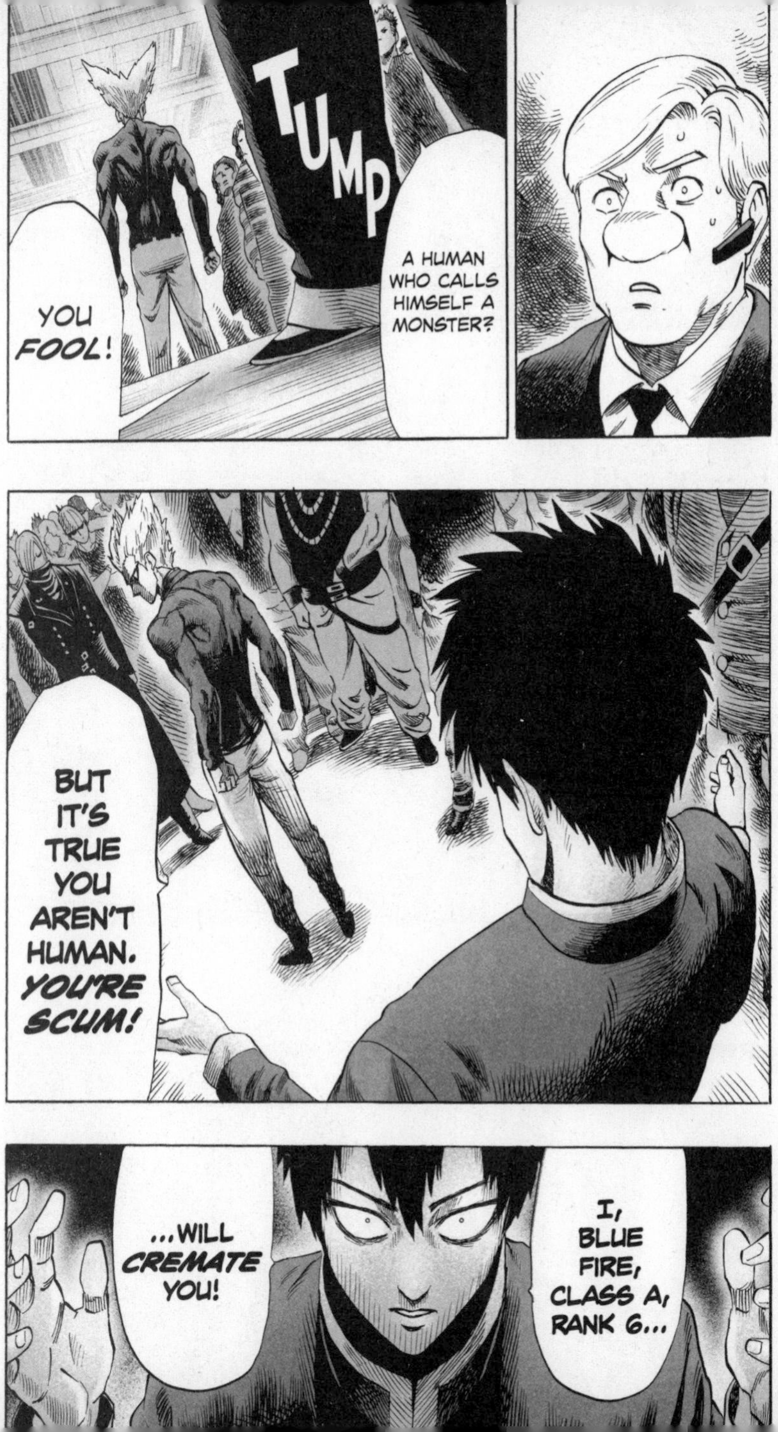
TUMP
A HUMAN WHO CALLS HIMSELF A MONSTER?
YOU FOOL!
BUT IT'S TRUE YOU AREN'T HUMAN. YOU'RE SCUM!
I, BLUE FIRE, CLASS A, RANK 6...
...WILL CREMATE YOU!

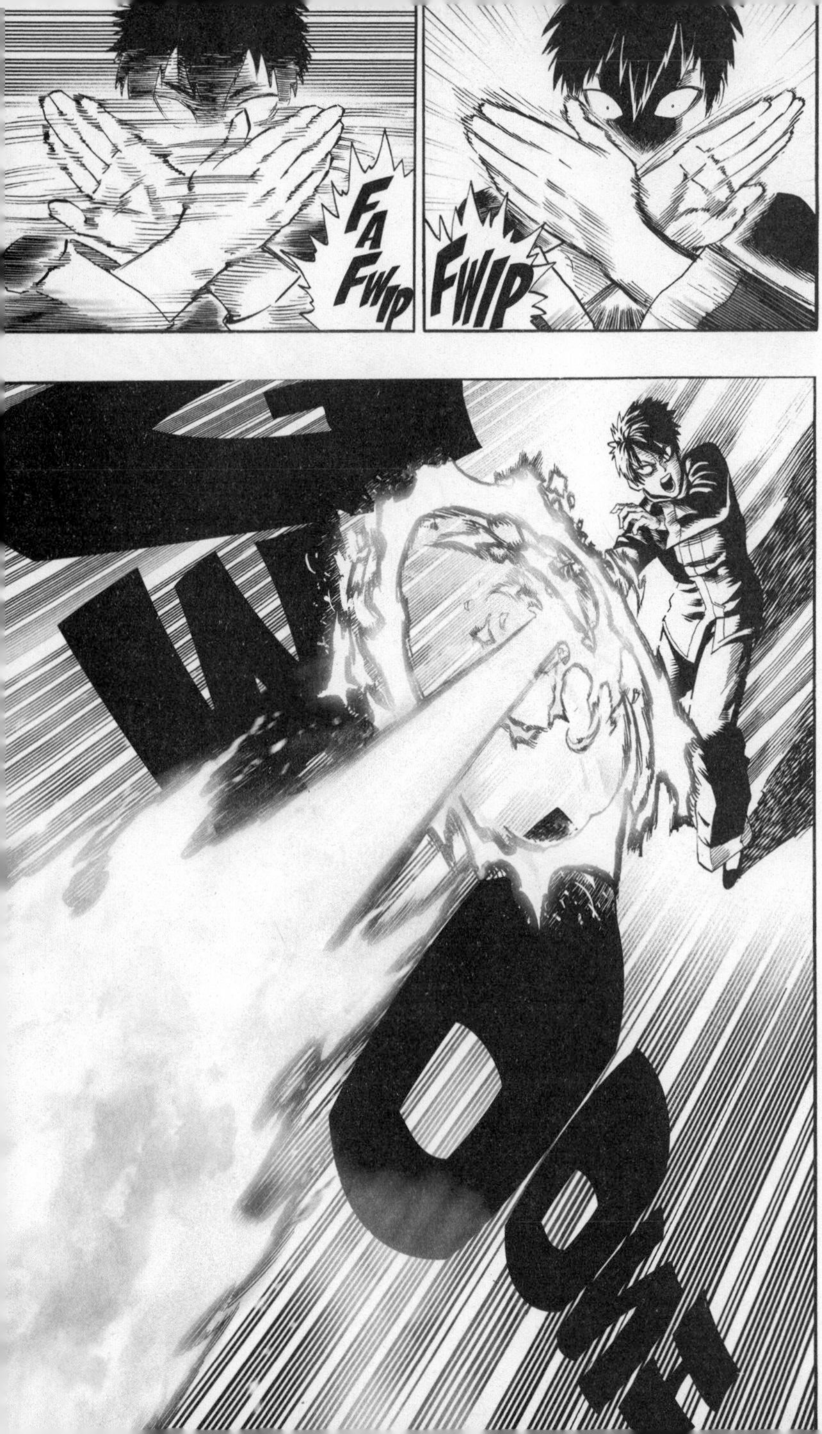
FWIP
FA FWIP

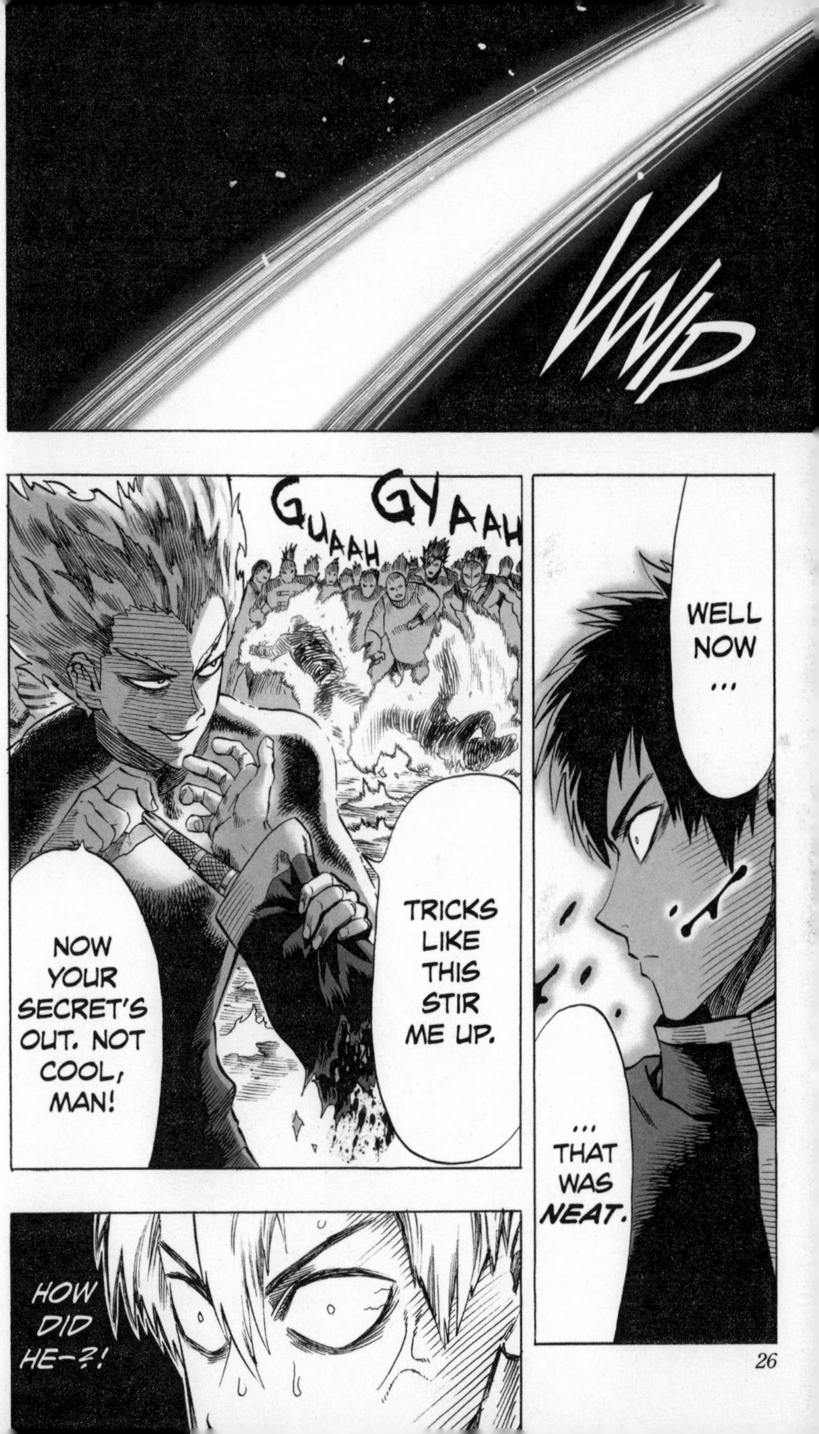
VWIP
WELL NOW ...
... THAT WAS NEAT.
GUAAH
GYAAH
TRICKS LIKE THIS STIR ME UP.
NOW YOUR SECRET'S OUT. NOT COOL, MAN!
HOW DID HE-?!

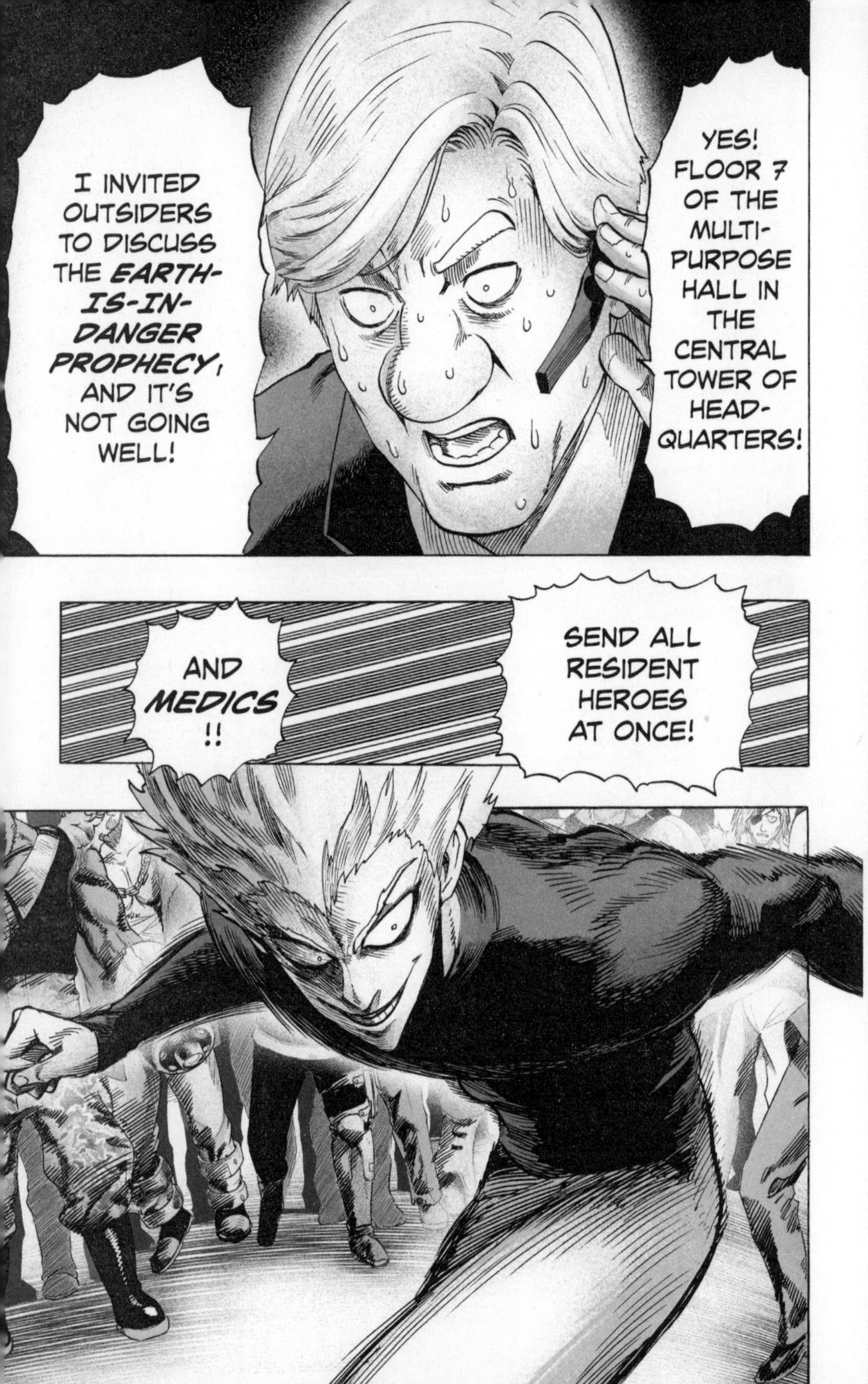
YES! FLOOR 7 OF THE MULTI-PURPOSE HALL IN THE CENTRAL TOWER OF HEAD-QUARTERS!
I INVITED OUTSIDERS TO DISCUSS THE *EARTH-IS-IN-DANGER PROPHECY*, AND IT'S NOT GOING WELL!
SEND ALL RESIDENT HEROES AT ONCE!
AND *MEDICS* !!

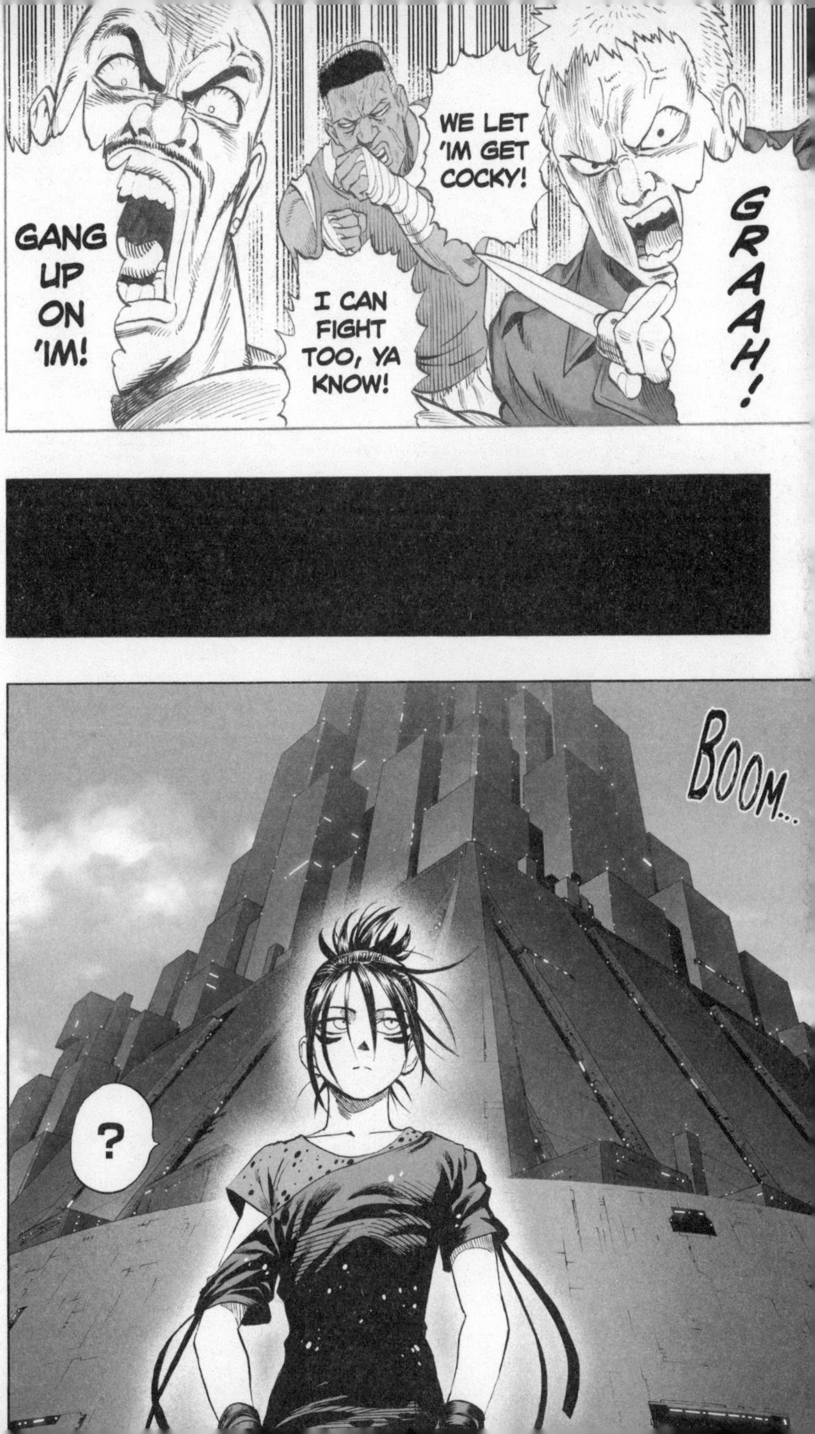
GRAAH!
WE LET 'IM GET COCKY!
I CAN FIGHT TOO, YA KNOW!
GANG UP ON 'IM!
BOOM...
?

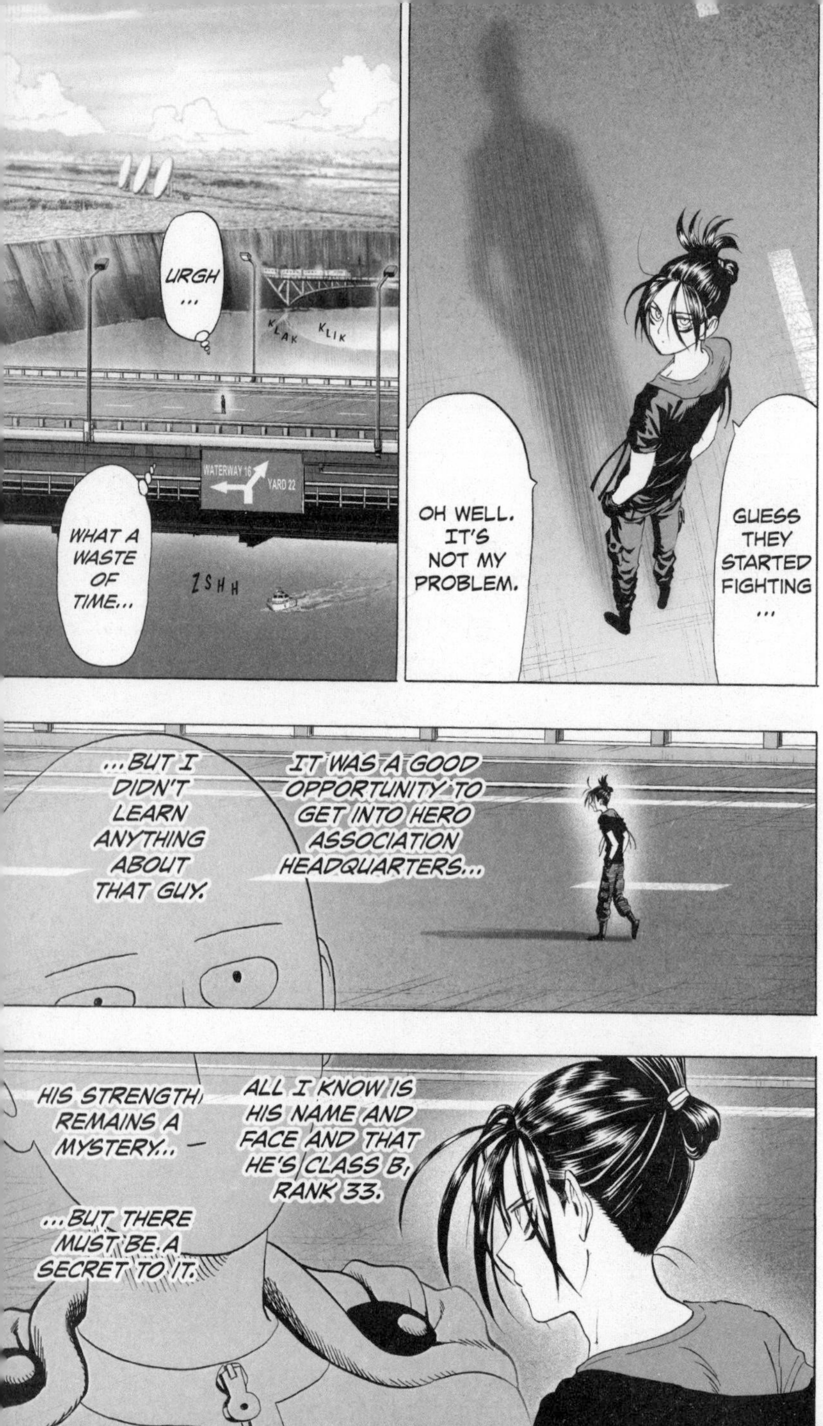
GUESS THEY STARTED FIGHTING ...
OH WELL. IT'S NOT MY PROBLEM.
URGH ...
KLAK
KLIK
WATERWAY 16
YARD 22
WHAT A WASTE OF TIME...
ZSHH
IT WAS A GOOD OPPORTUNITY TO GET INTO HERO ASSOCIATION HEADQUARTERS...
...BUT I DIDN'T LEARN ANYTHING ABOUT THAT GUY.
ALL I KNOW IS HIS NAME AND FACE AND THAT HE'S CLASS B, RANK 33.
HIS STRENGTH REMAINS A MYSTERY...
...BUT THERE MUST BE A SECRET TO IT.

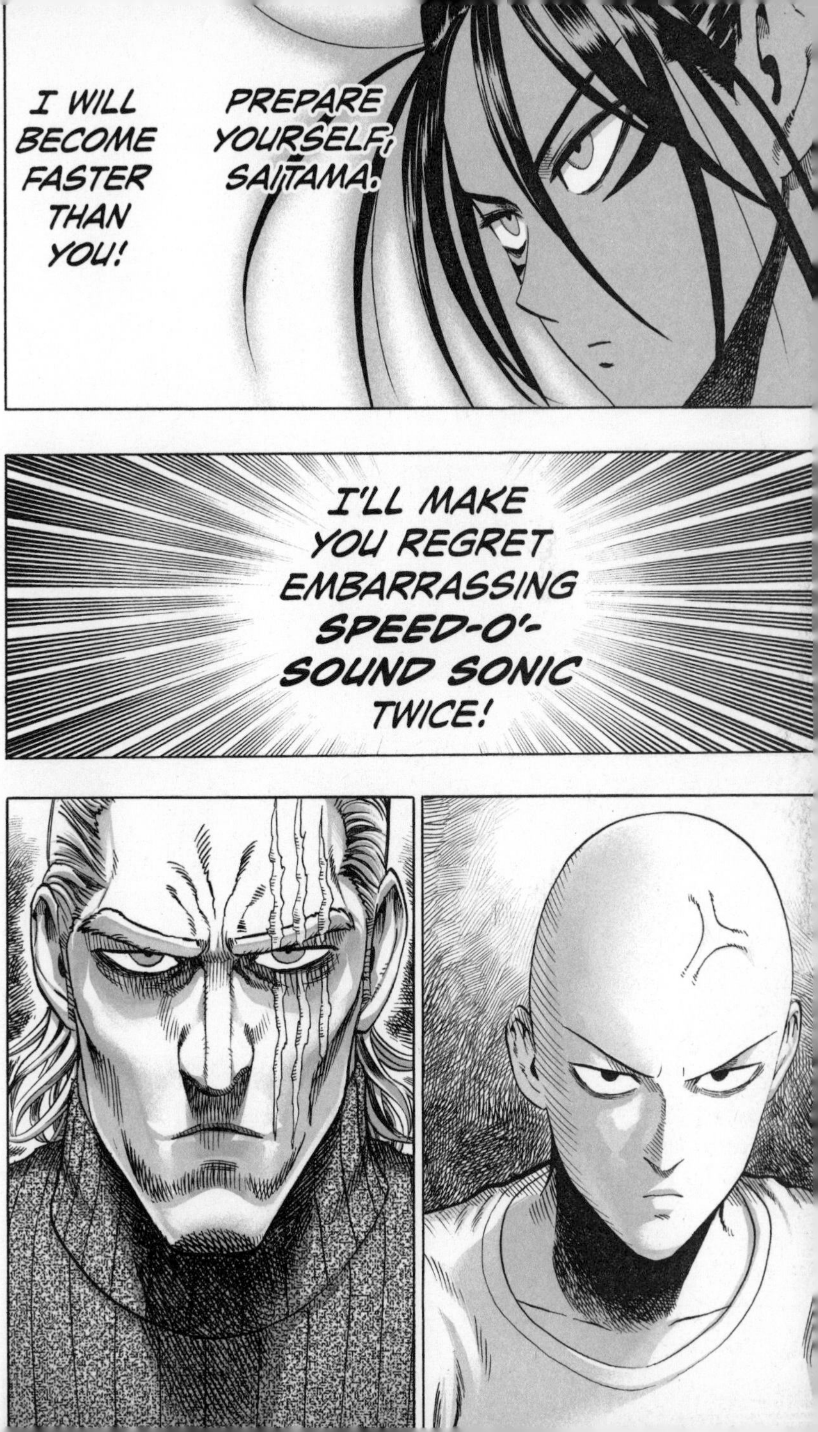
PREPARE YOURSELF, SAITAMA!
I WILL BECOME FASTER THAN YOU!
I'LL MAKE YOU REGRET EMBARRASSING SPEED-O'-SOUND SONIC TWICE!

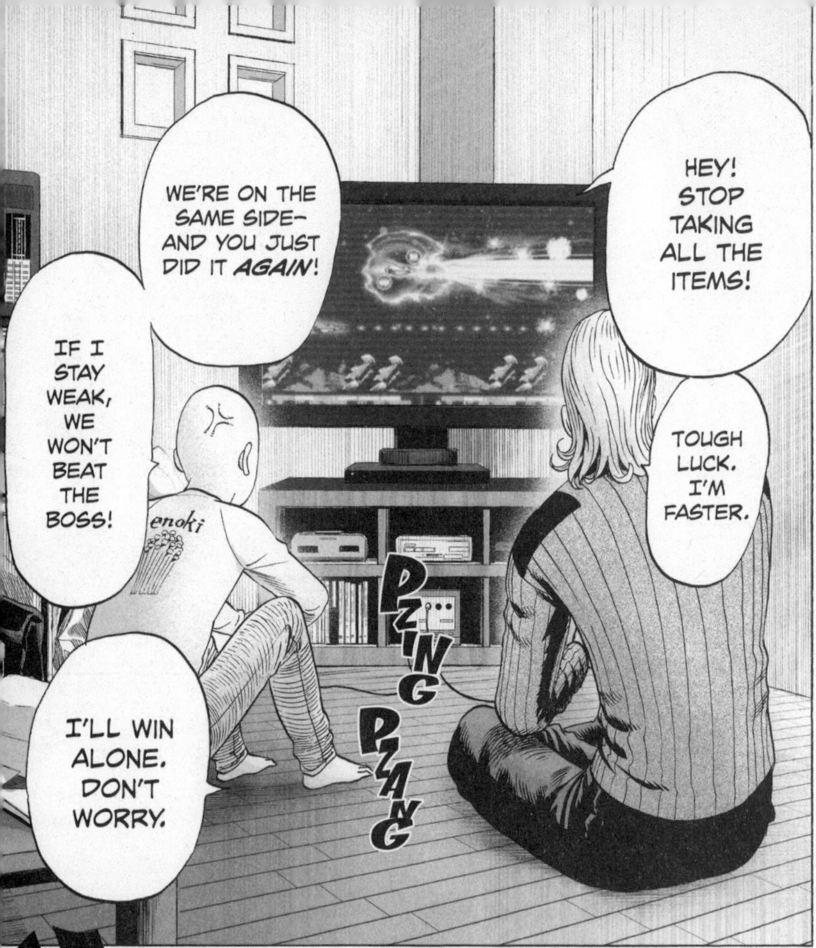
HEY! STOP TAKING ALL THE ITEMS!
WE'RE ON THE SAME SIDE—AND YOU JUST DID IT *AGAIN*!
TOUGH LUCK. I'M FASTER.
IF I STAY WEAK, WE WON'T BEAT THE BOSS!
enoki
PZING
PZANG
I'LL WIN ALONE. DON'T WORRY.
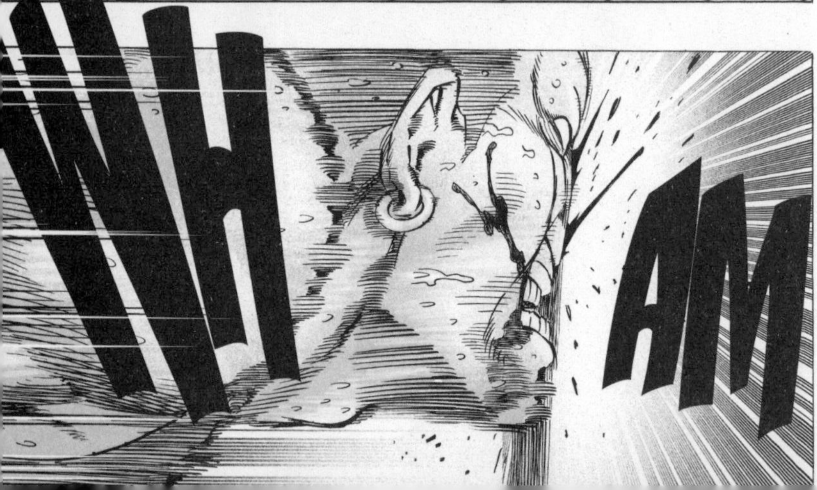
WHAM

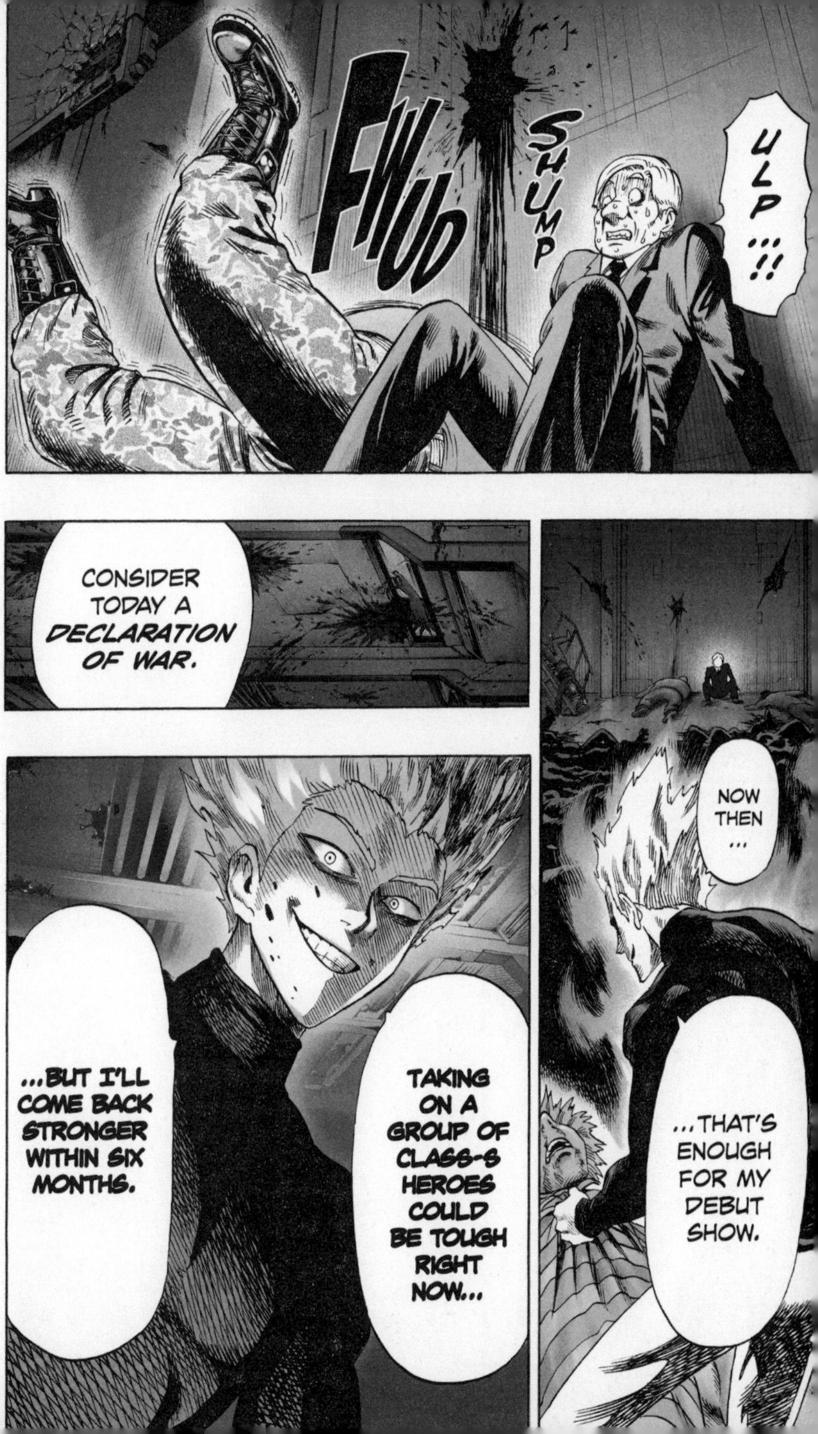
ULP...!!
SHUMP
FWUD
NOW THEN...
...THAT'S ENOUGH FOR MY DEBUT SHOW.
CONSIDER TODAY A *DECLARATION OF WAR.*
TAKING ON A GROUP OF CLASS-S HEROES COULD BE TOUGH RIGHT NOW...
...BUT I'LL COME BACK STRONGER WITHIN SIX MONTHS.

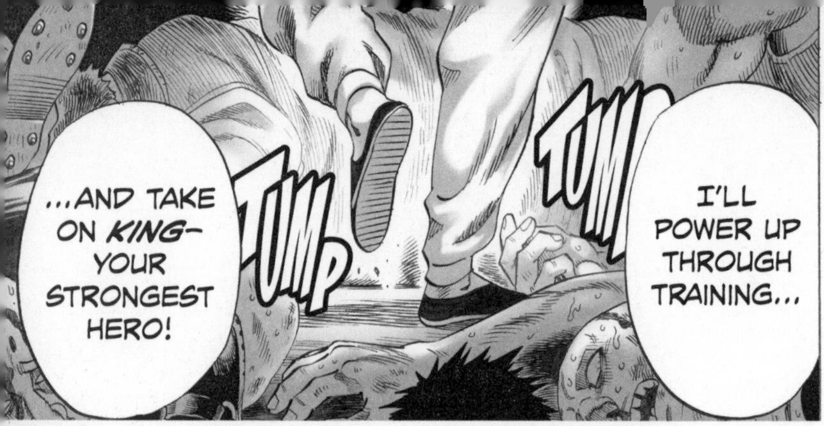
I'LL POWER UP THROUGH TRAINING...
TUM
TUMP
...AND TAKE ON *KING*—YOUR STRONGEST HERO!

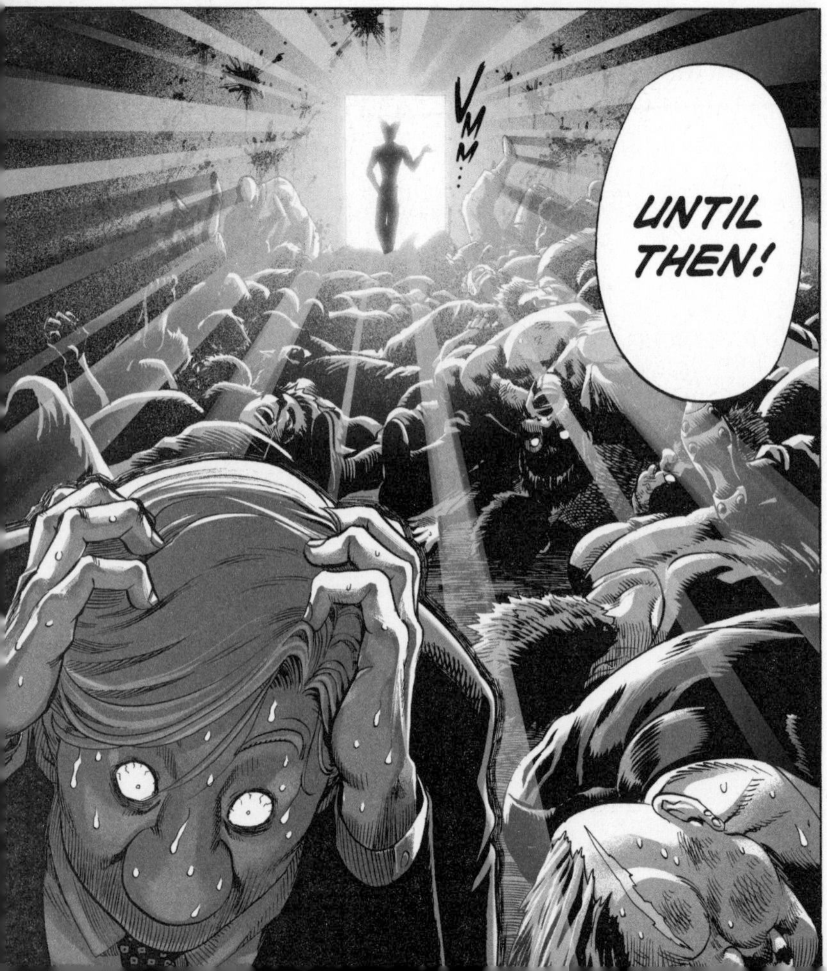
UNTIL THEN!
VMM...

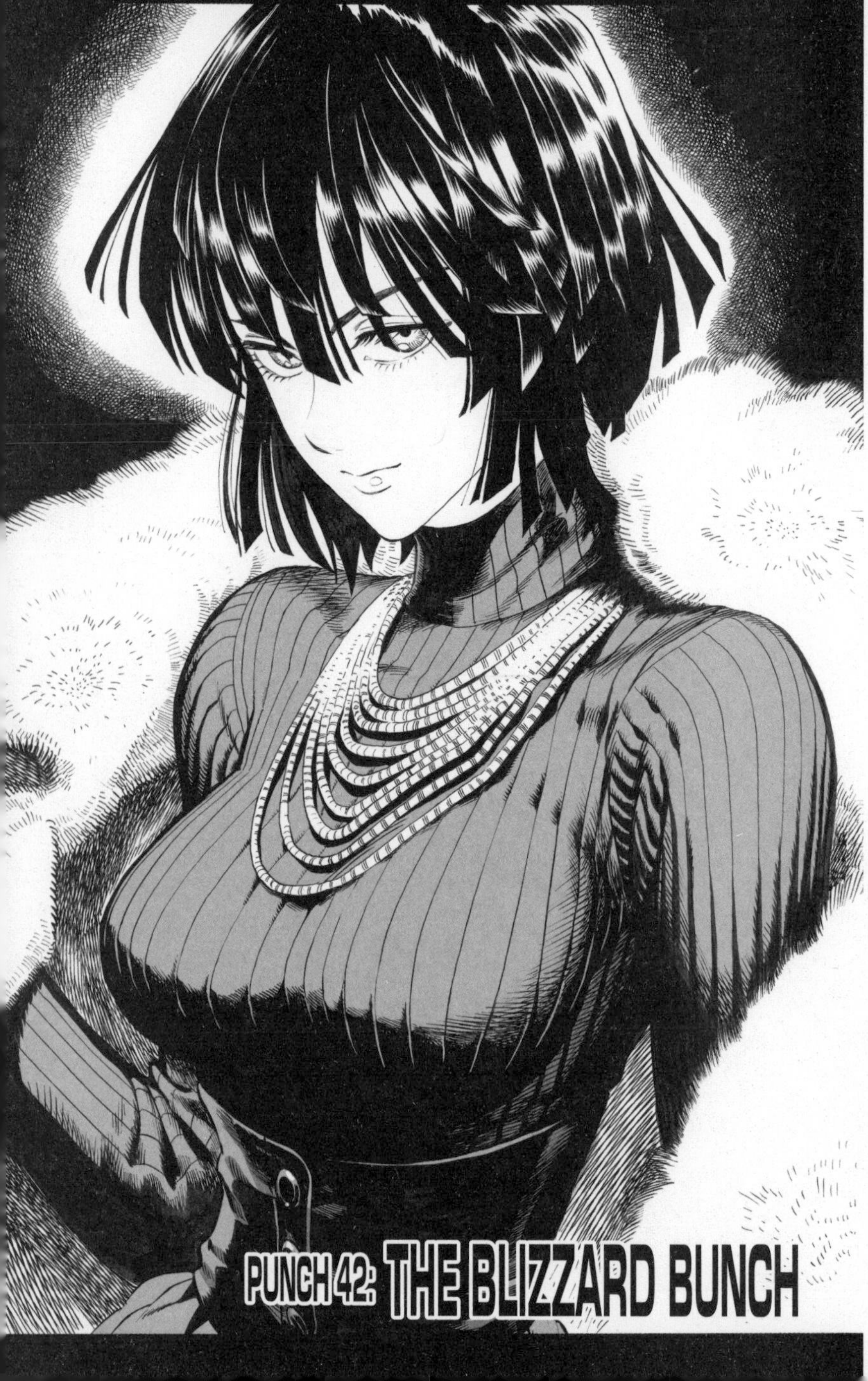
PUNCH 42: THE BLIZZARD BUNCH

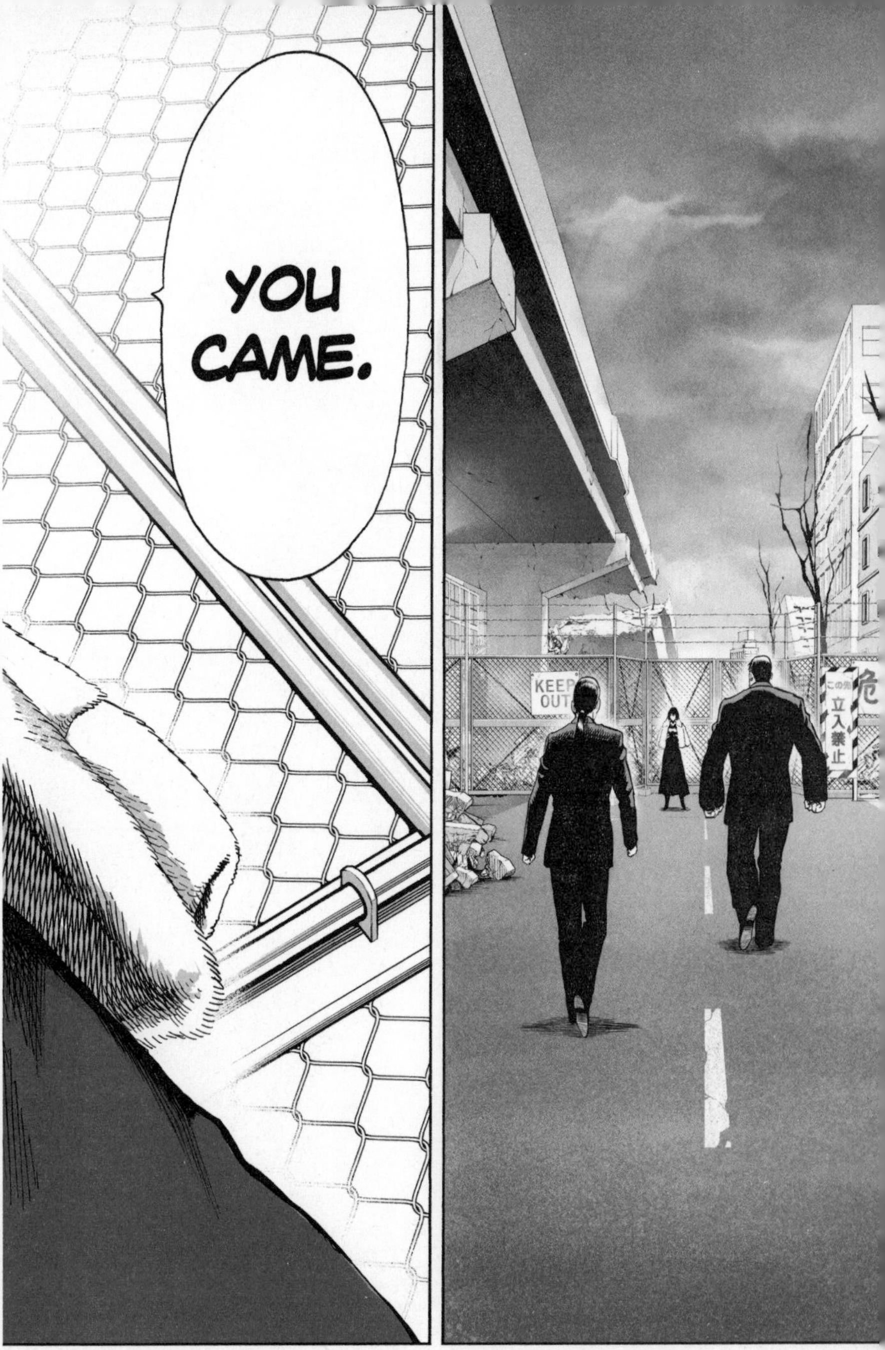
KEEP OUT
この先
立入禁止
危
YOU CAME.

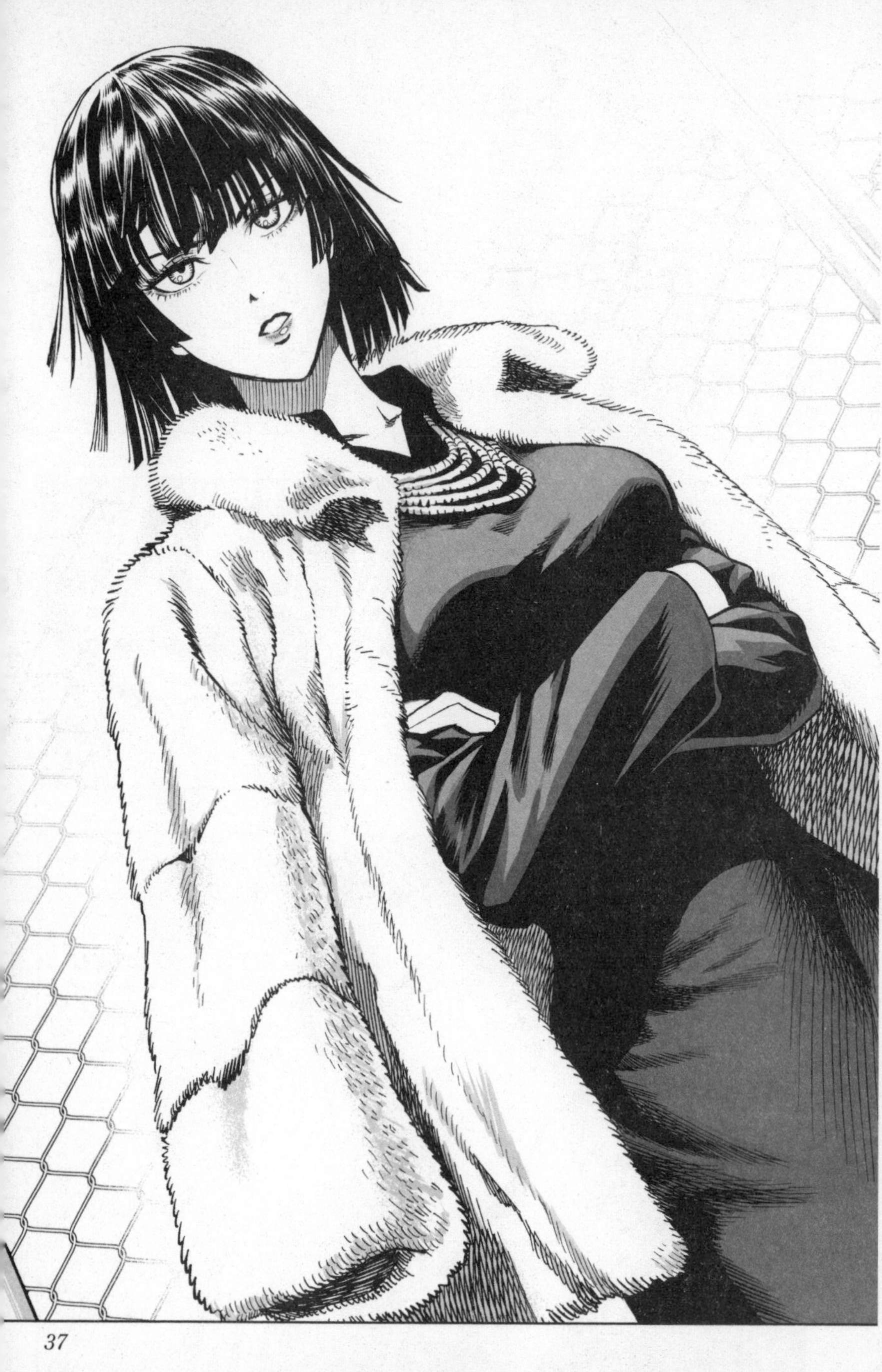

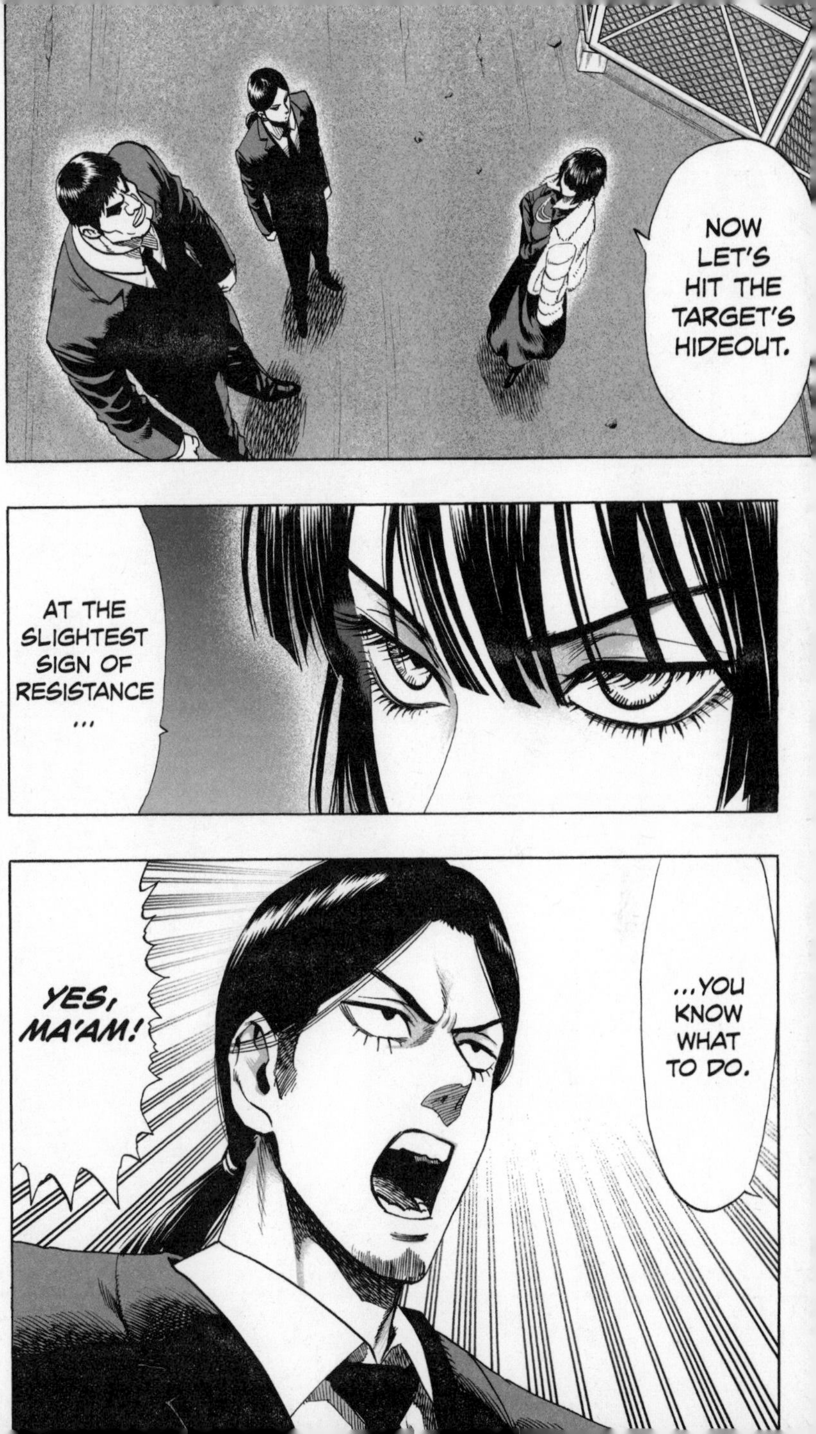
NOW LET'S HIT THE TARGET'S HIDEOUT.
AT THE SLIGHTEST SIGN OF RESISTANCE ...
...YOU KNOW WHAT TO DO.
YES, MA'AM!

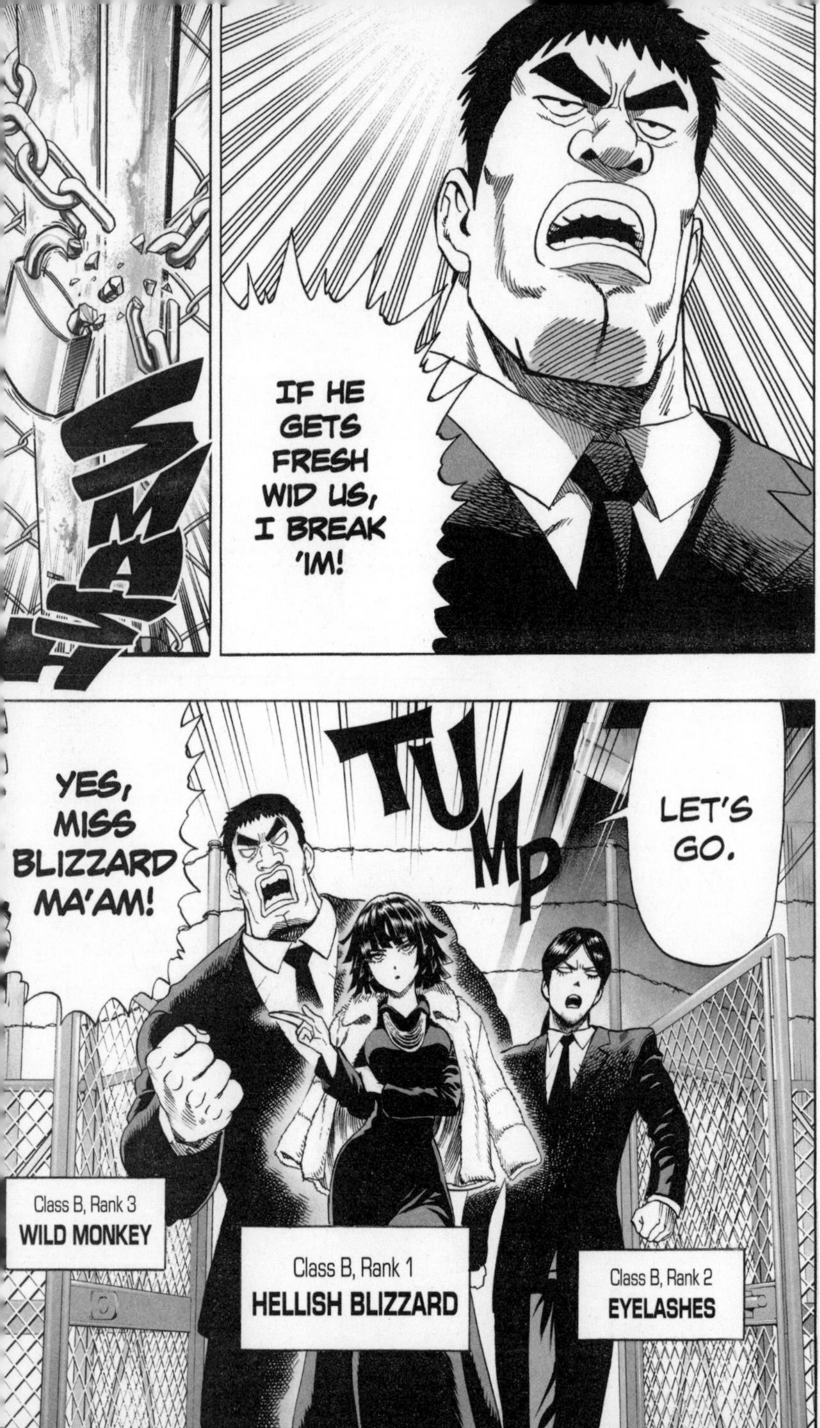
IF HE GETS FRESH WID US, I BREAK 'IM!
SMASH
LET'S GO.
TUMP
YES, MISS BLIZZARD MA'AM!
Class B, Rank 2
EYELASHES
Class B, Rank 1
HELLISH BLIZZARD
Class B, Rank 3
WILD MONKEY

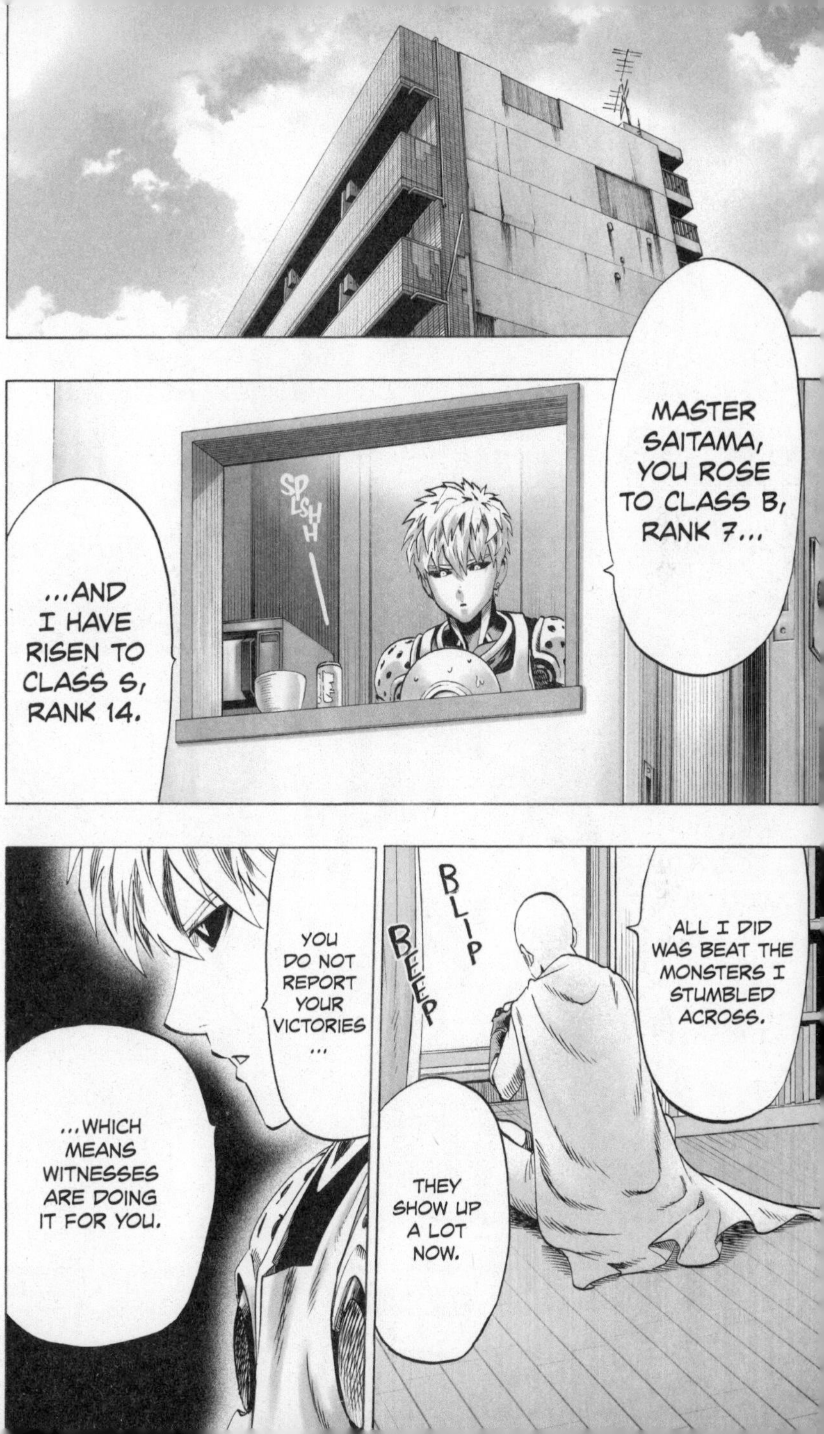
MASTER SAITAMA, YOU ROSE TO CLASS B, RANK 7...
SPLSHH
...AND I HAVE RISEN TO CLASS S, RANK 14.
ALL I DID WAS BEAT THE MONSTERS I STUMBLED ACROSS.
BLIP
BEEP
THEY SHOW UP A LOT NOW.
YOU DO NOT REPORT YOUR VICTORIES ...
...WHICH MEANS WITNESSES ARE DOING IT FOR YOU.

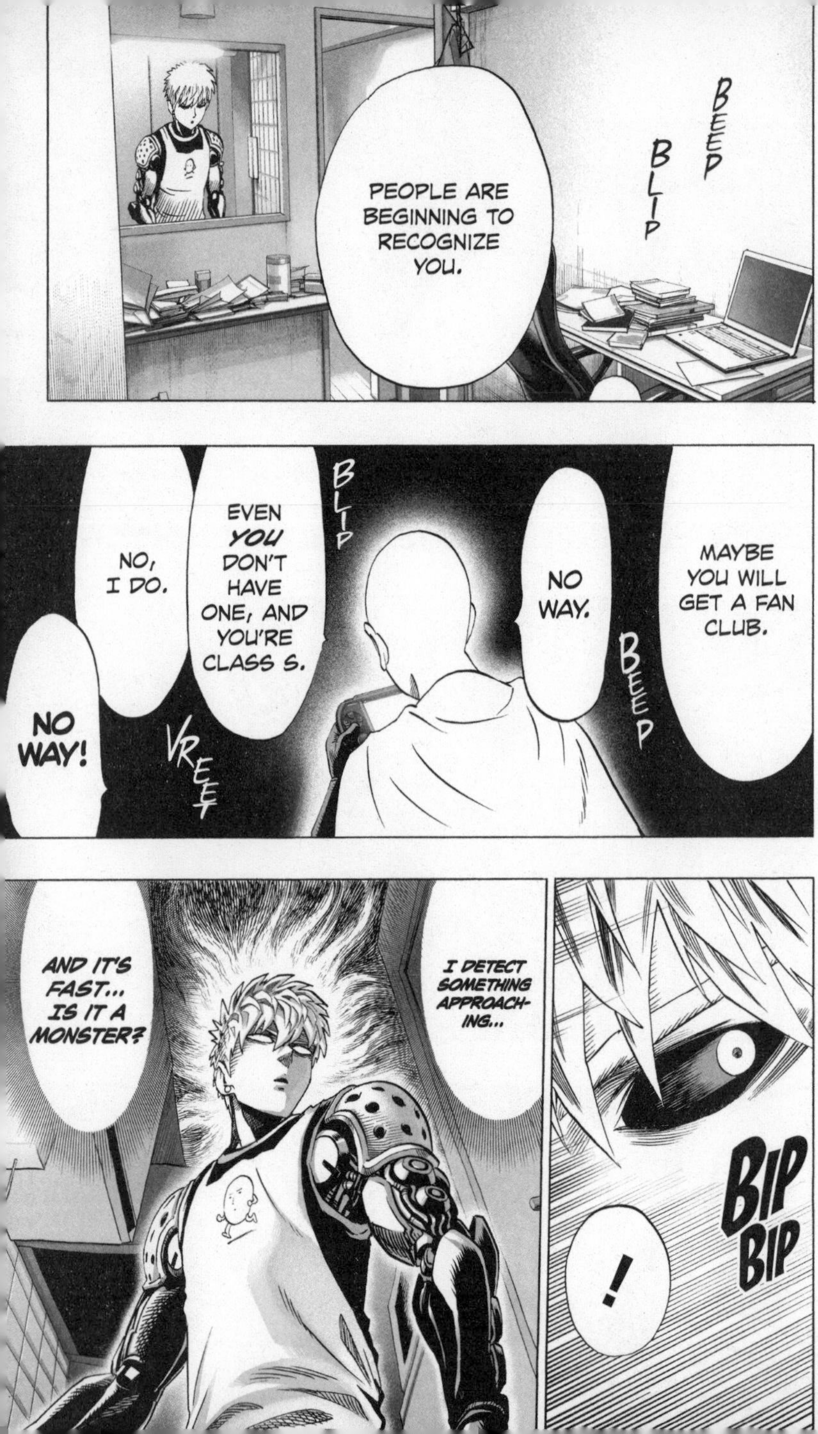
BEEP
BLIP
PEOPLE ARE BEGINNING TO RECOGNIZE YOU.
MAYBE YOU WILL GET A FAN CLUB.
NO WAY.
BEEP
BLIP
EVEN *YOU* DON'T HAVE ONE, AND YOU'RE CLASS S.
NO, I DO.
VREEET
NO WAY!
BIP BIP
!
I DETECT SOMETHING APPROACHING...
AND IT'S FAST... IS IT A MONSTER?

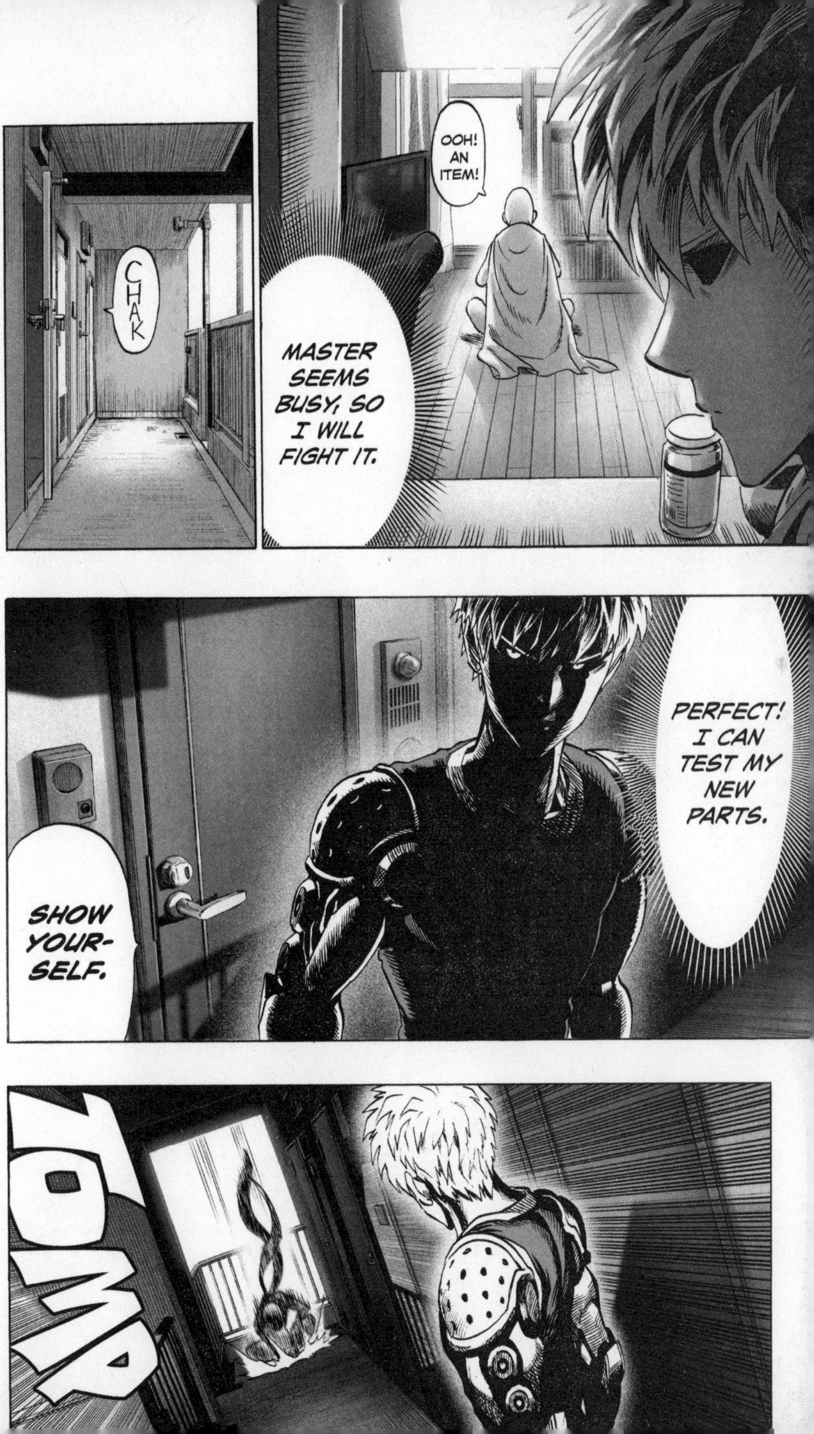
OOH! AN ITEM!
MASTER SEEMS BUSY, SO I WILL FIGHT IT.
CHAK
PERFECT! I CAN TEST MY NEW PARTS.
SHOW YOUR-SELF.
TOMP

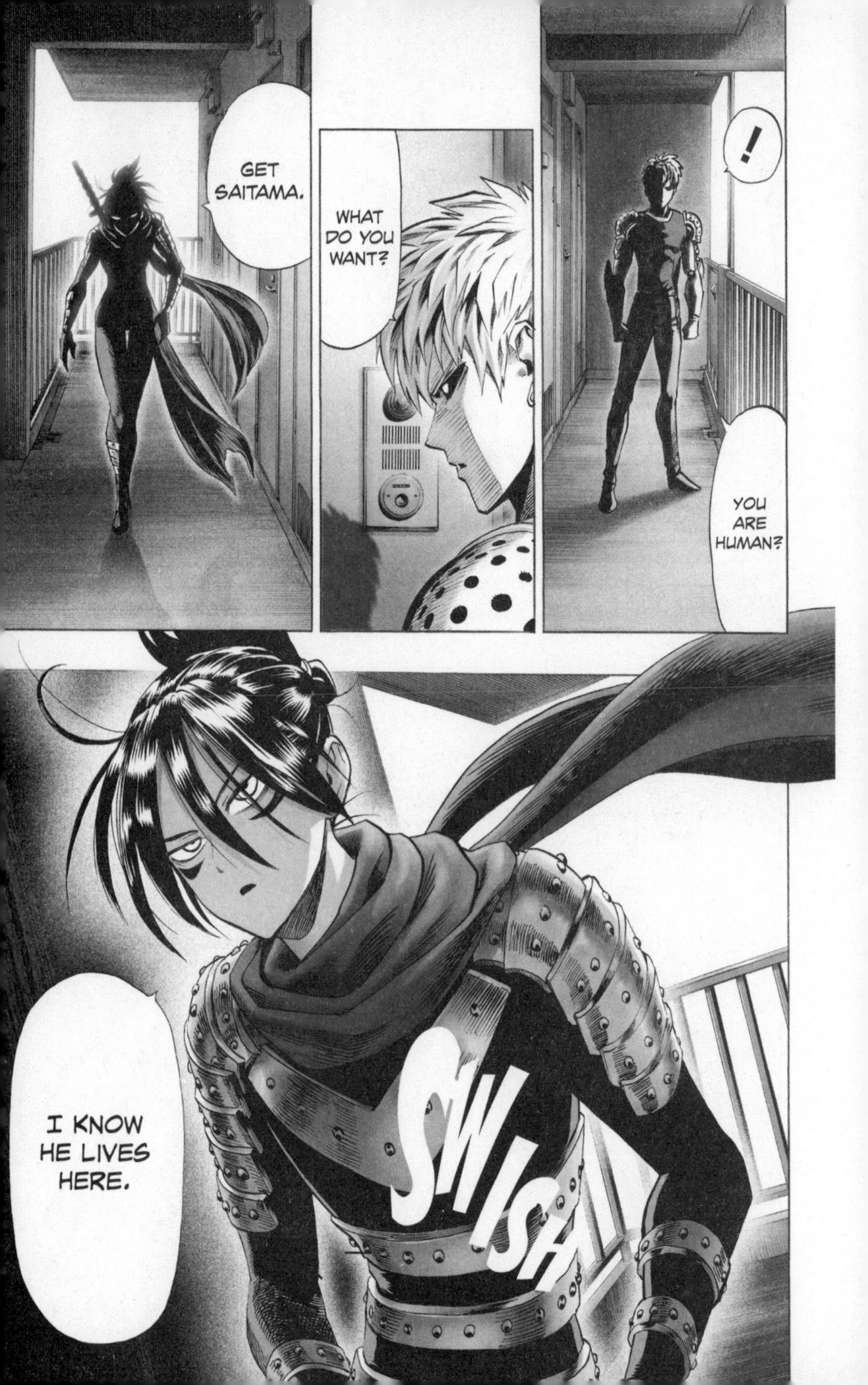
!
YOU ARE HUMAN?
WHAT DO YOU WANT?
GET SAITAMA.
I KNOW HE LIVES HERE.
SWISH

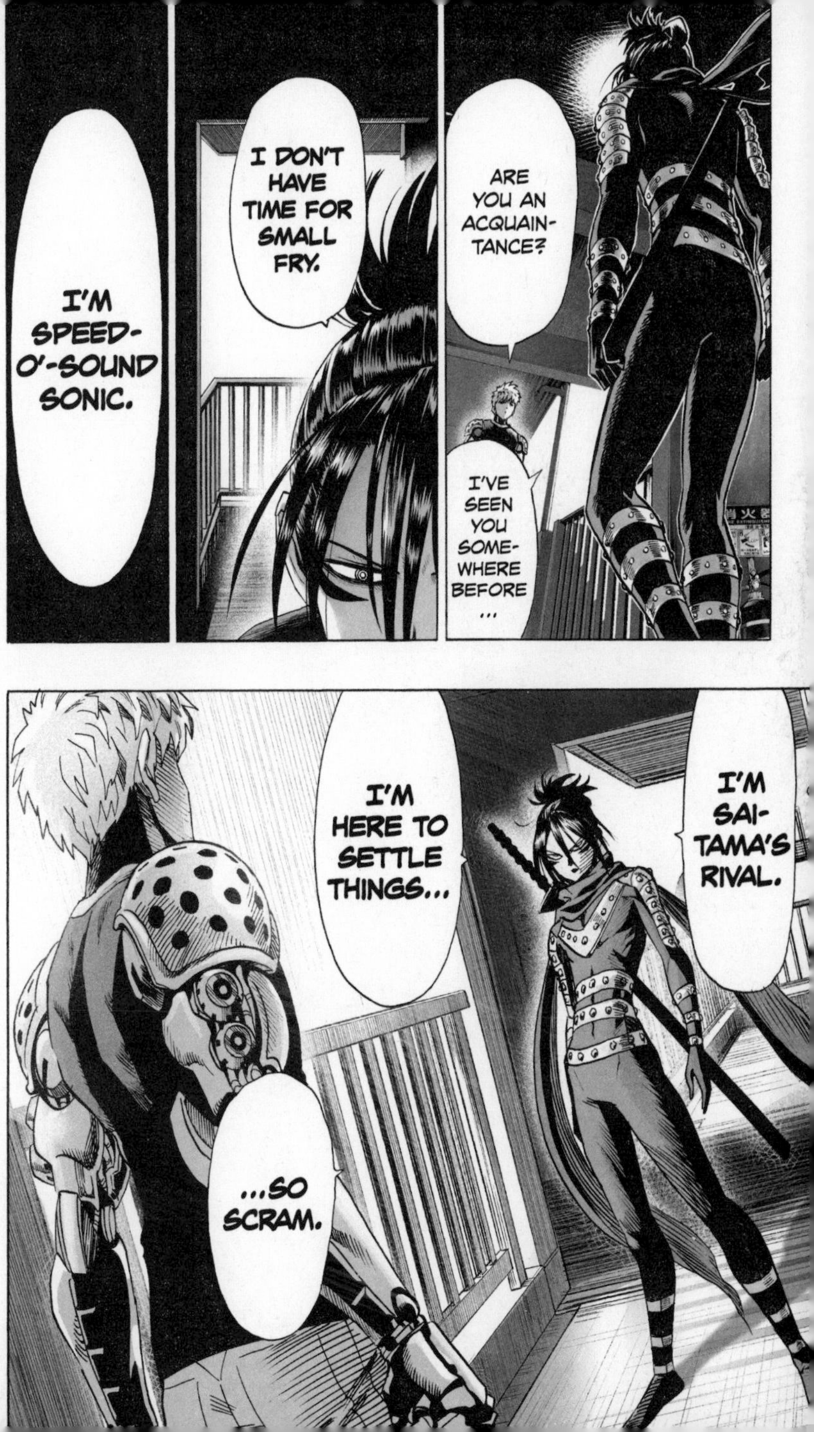
ARE YOU AN ACQUAINTANCE?
I'VE SEEN YOU SOMEWHERE BEFORE...
I DON'T HAVE TIME FOR SMALL FRY.
I'M SPEED-O'-SOUND SONIC.
I'M SAITAMA'S RIVAL.
I'M HERE TO SETTLE THINGS...
...SO SCRAM.

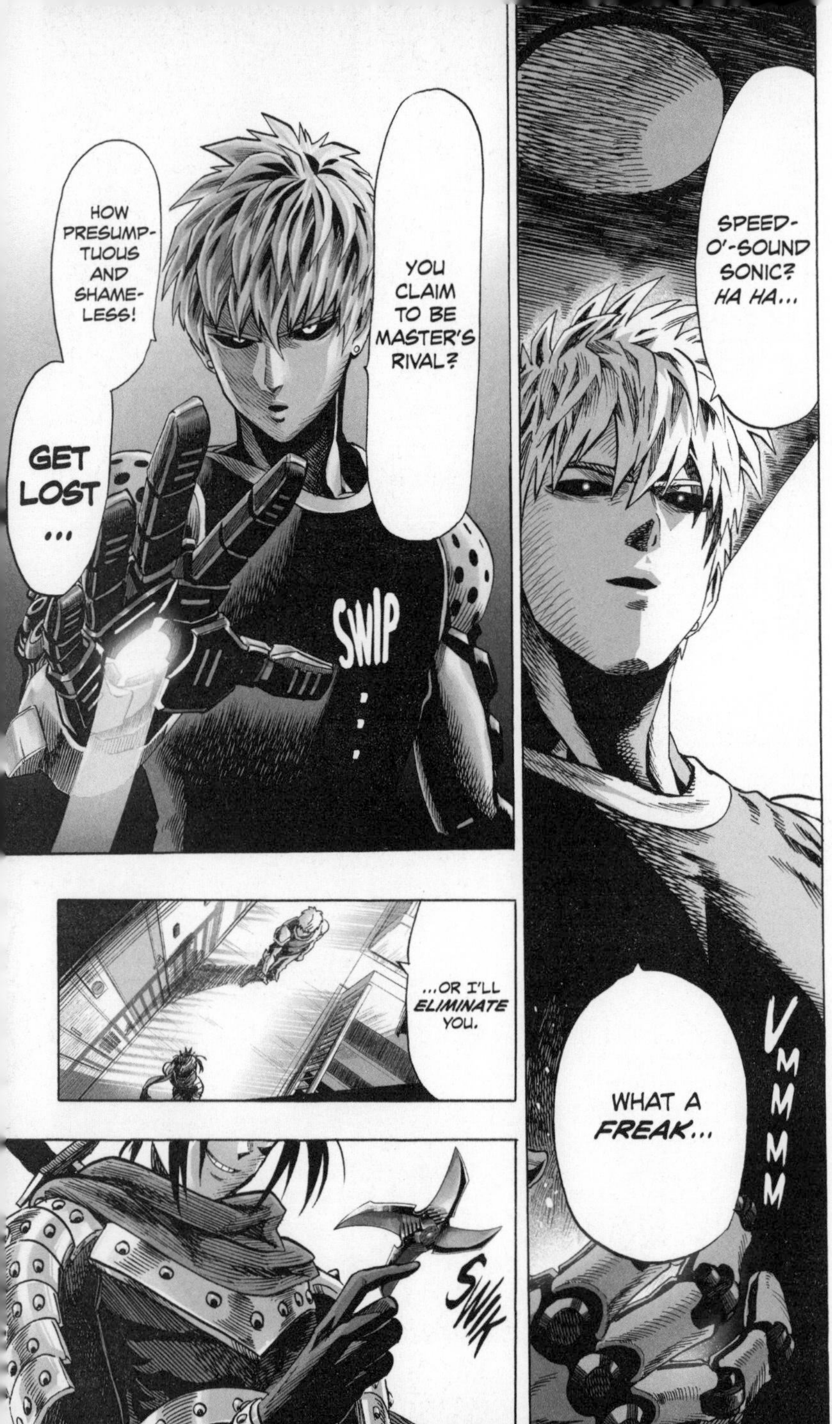
SPEED-O'-SOUND SONIC? HA HA...
WHAT A FREAK...
VMMMM
YOU CLAIM TO BE MASTER'S RIVAL?
HOW PRESUMPTUOUS AND SHAMELESS!
GET LOST...
SWIP
...OR I'LL ELIMINATE YOU.
SNIK

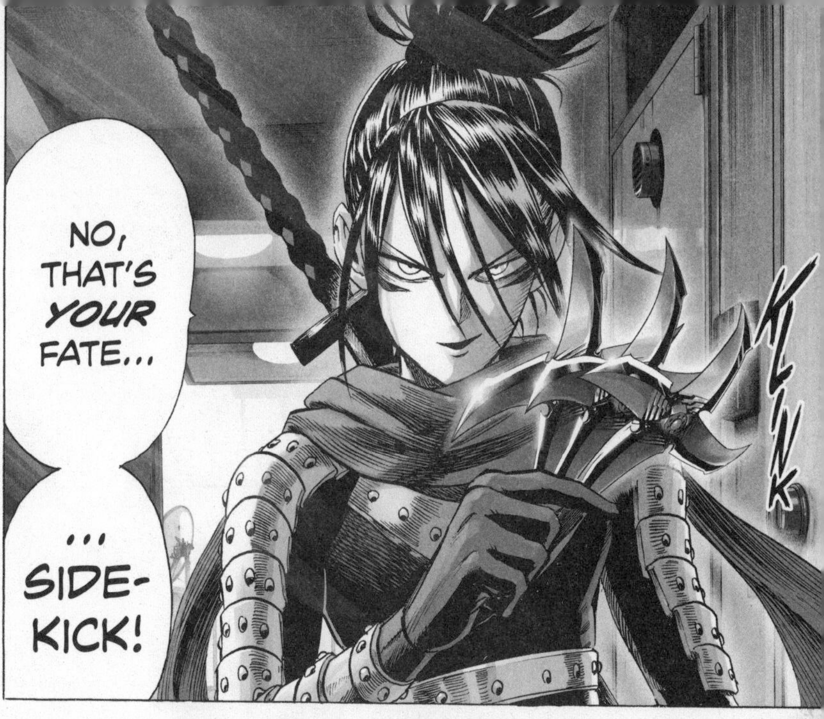
NO, THAT'S YOUR FATE...
...SIDE-KICK!
KLINK

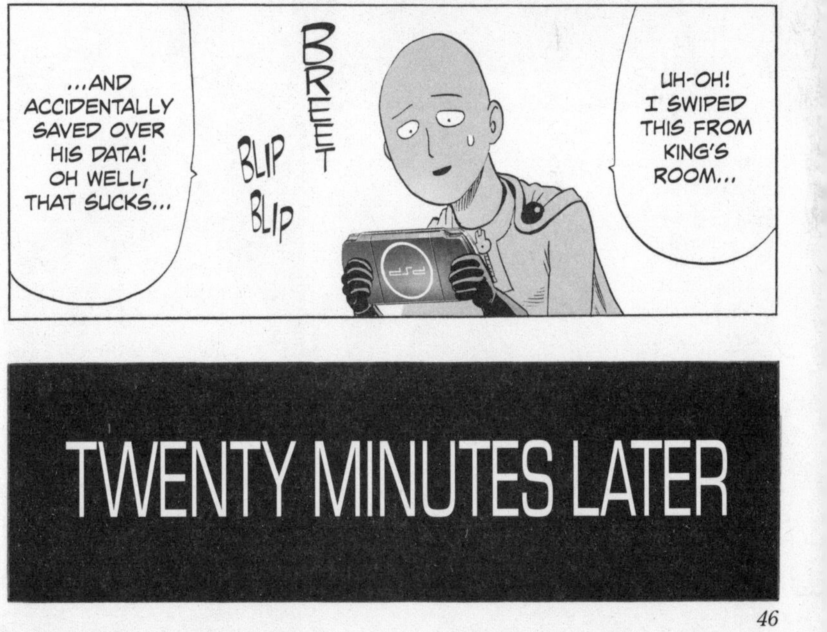
UH-OH! I SWIPED THIS FROM KING'S ROOM...
BREET
BLIP BLIP
...AND ACCIDENTALLY SAVED OVER HIS DATA! OH WELL, THAT SUCKS...

TWENTY MINUTES LATER

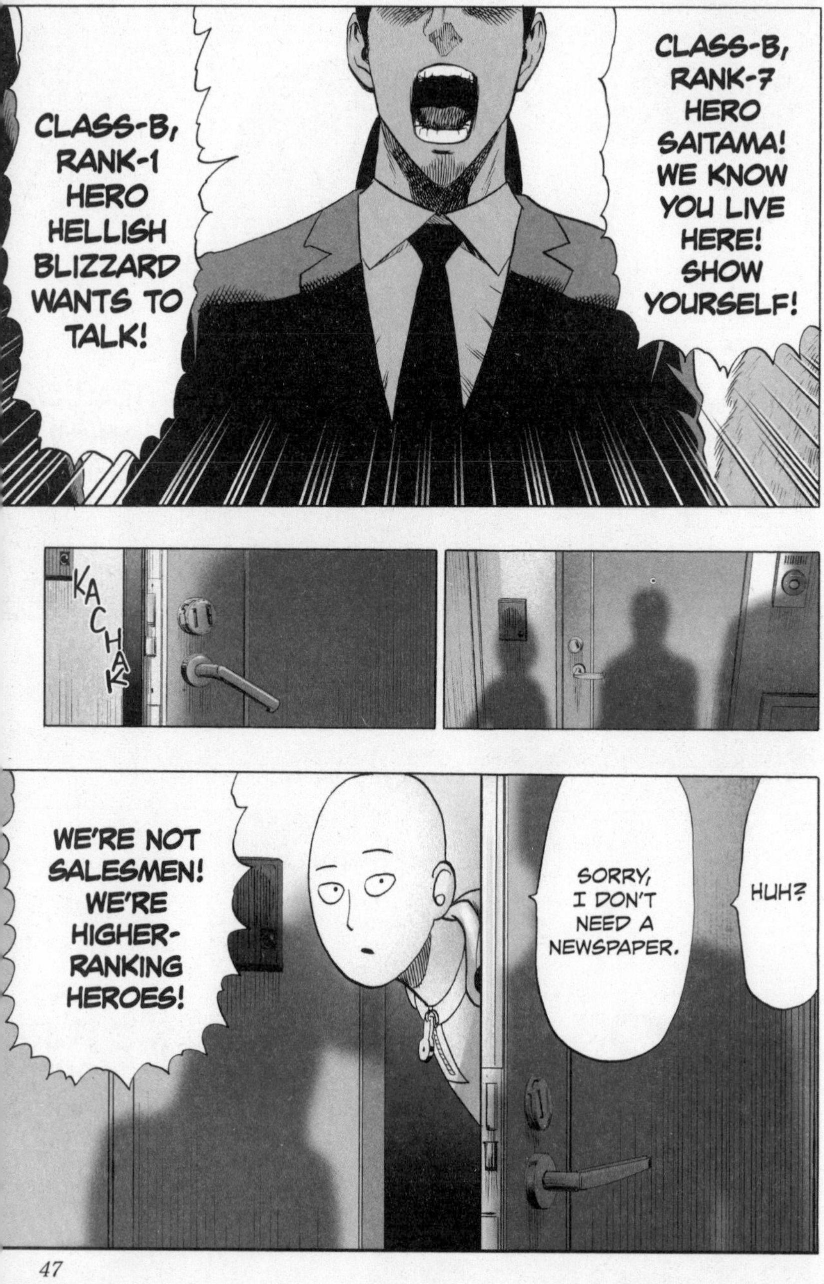
CLASS-B, RANK-7 HERO SAITAMA! WE KNOW YOU LIVE HERE! SHOW YOURSELF!
CLASS-B, RANK-1 HERO HELLISH BLIZZARD WANTS TO TALK!
KACHAK
HUH?
SORRY, I DON'T NEED A NEWSPAPER.
WE'RE NOT SALESMEN! WE'RE HIGHER-RANKING HEROES!

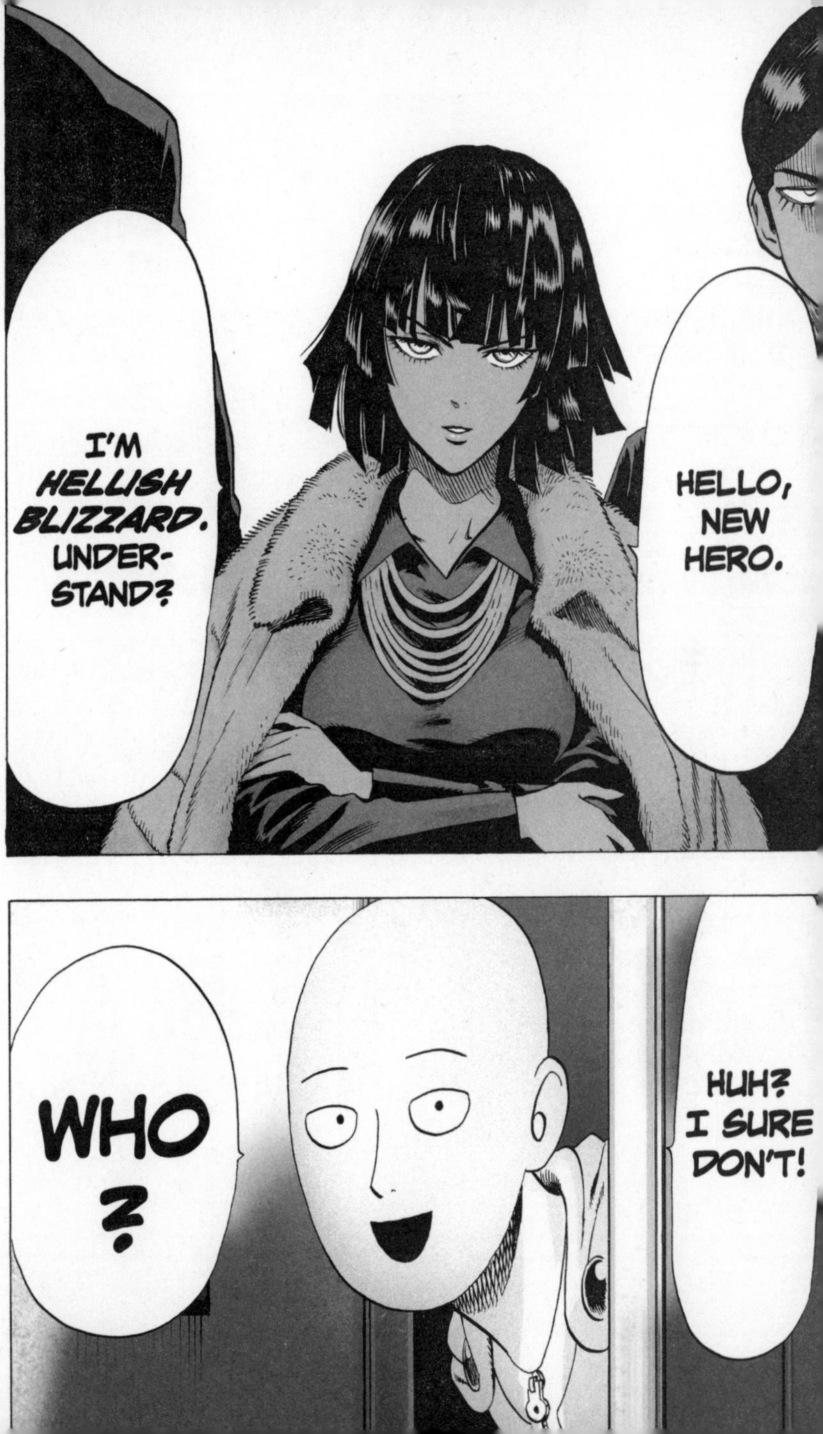
HELLO, NEW HERO.
I'M *HELLISH BLIZZARD*. UNDERSTAND?
HUH? I SURE DON'T!
WHO?

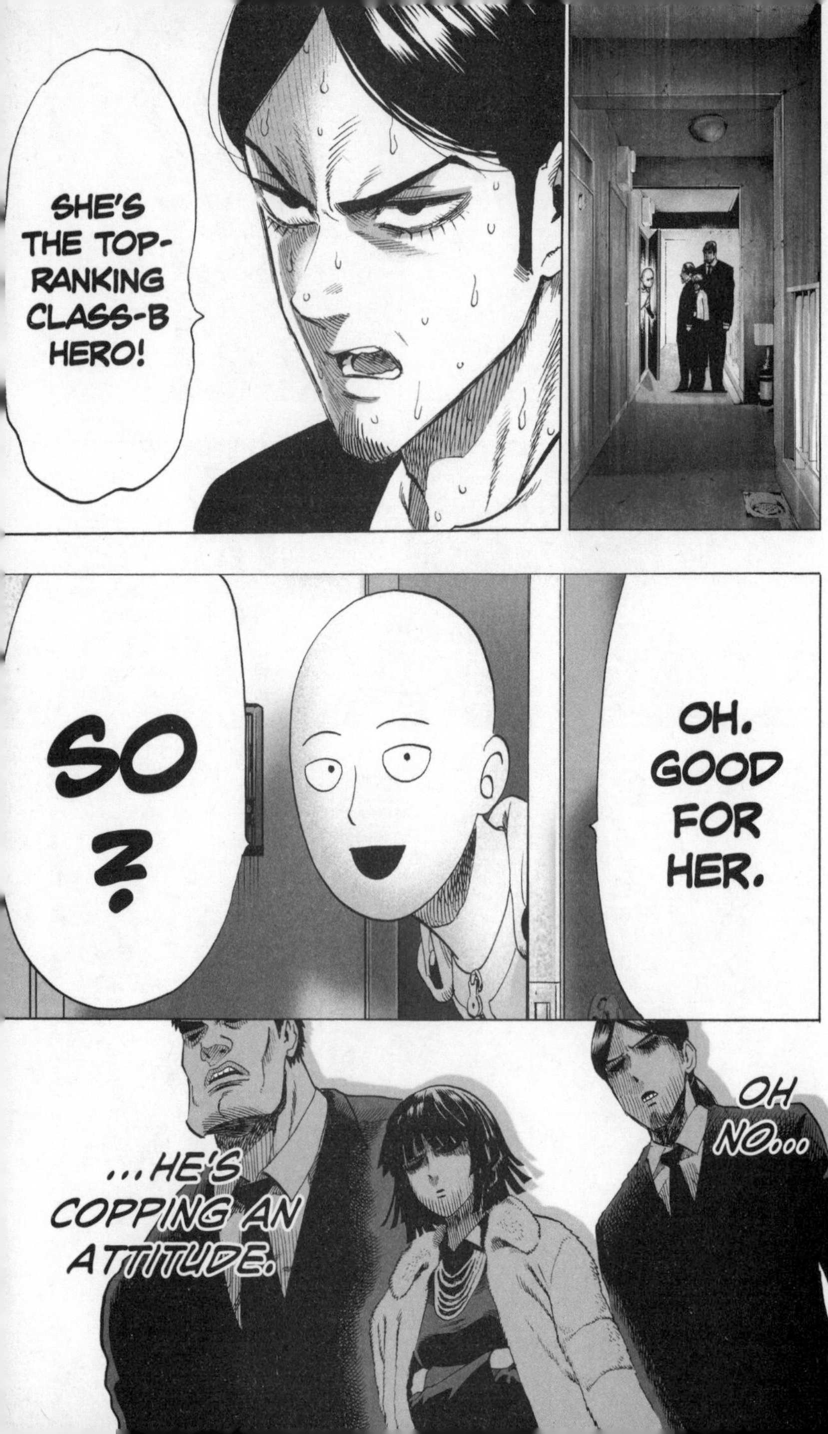
SHE'S THE TOP-RANKING CLASS-B HERO!
OH. GOOD FOR HER.
SO?
OH NO...
...HE'S COPPING AN ATTITUDE.

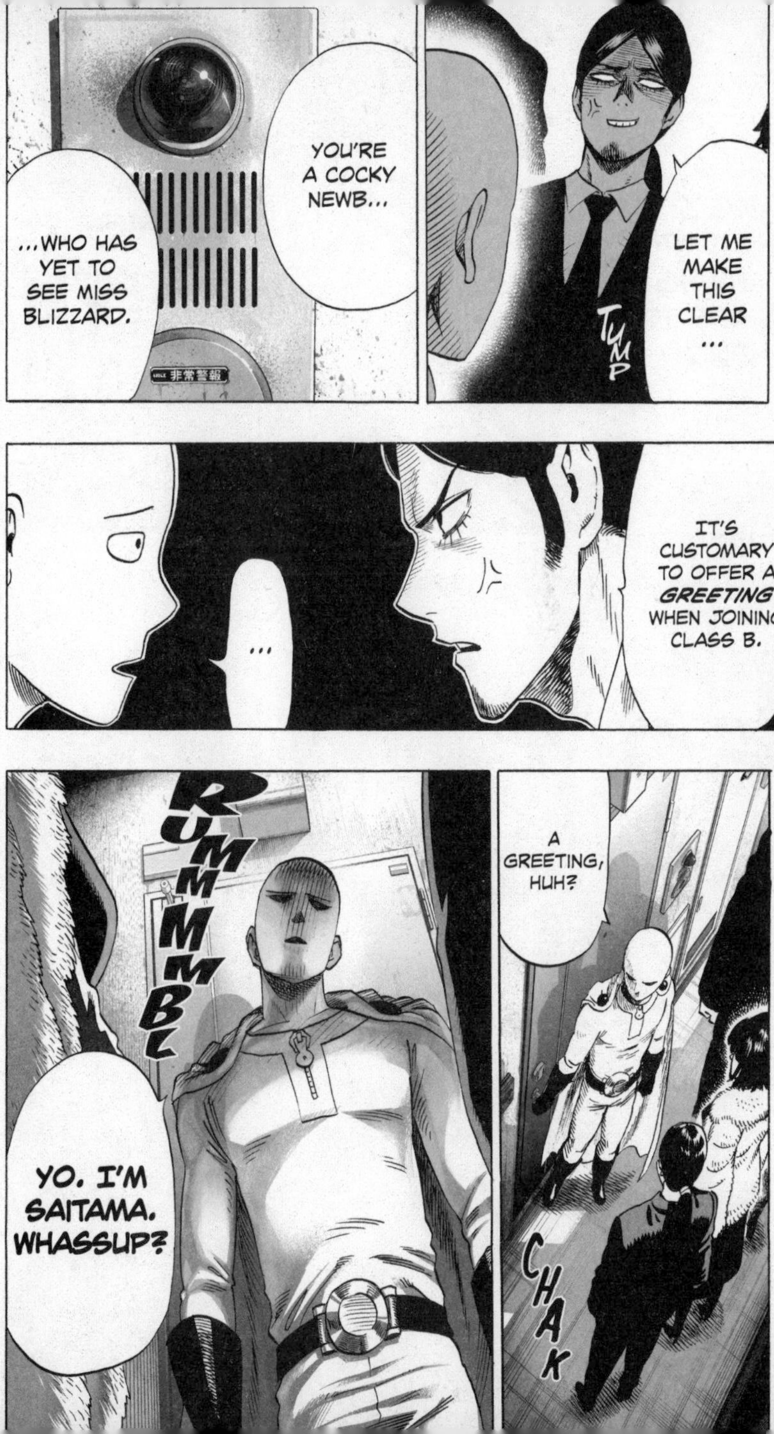
LET ME MAKE THIS CLEAR ...
TUMP
YOU'RE A COCKY NEWB...
...WHO HAS YET TO SEE MISS BLIZZARD.
非常警報
IT'S CUSTOMARY TO OFFER A *GREETING* WHEN JOINING CLASS B.
...
A GREETING, HUH?
CHAK
RUMMMMBL
YO. I'M SAITAMA. WHASSUP?

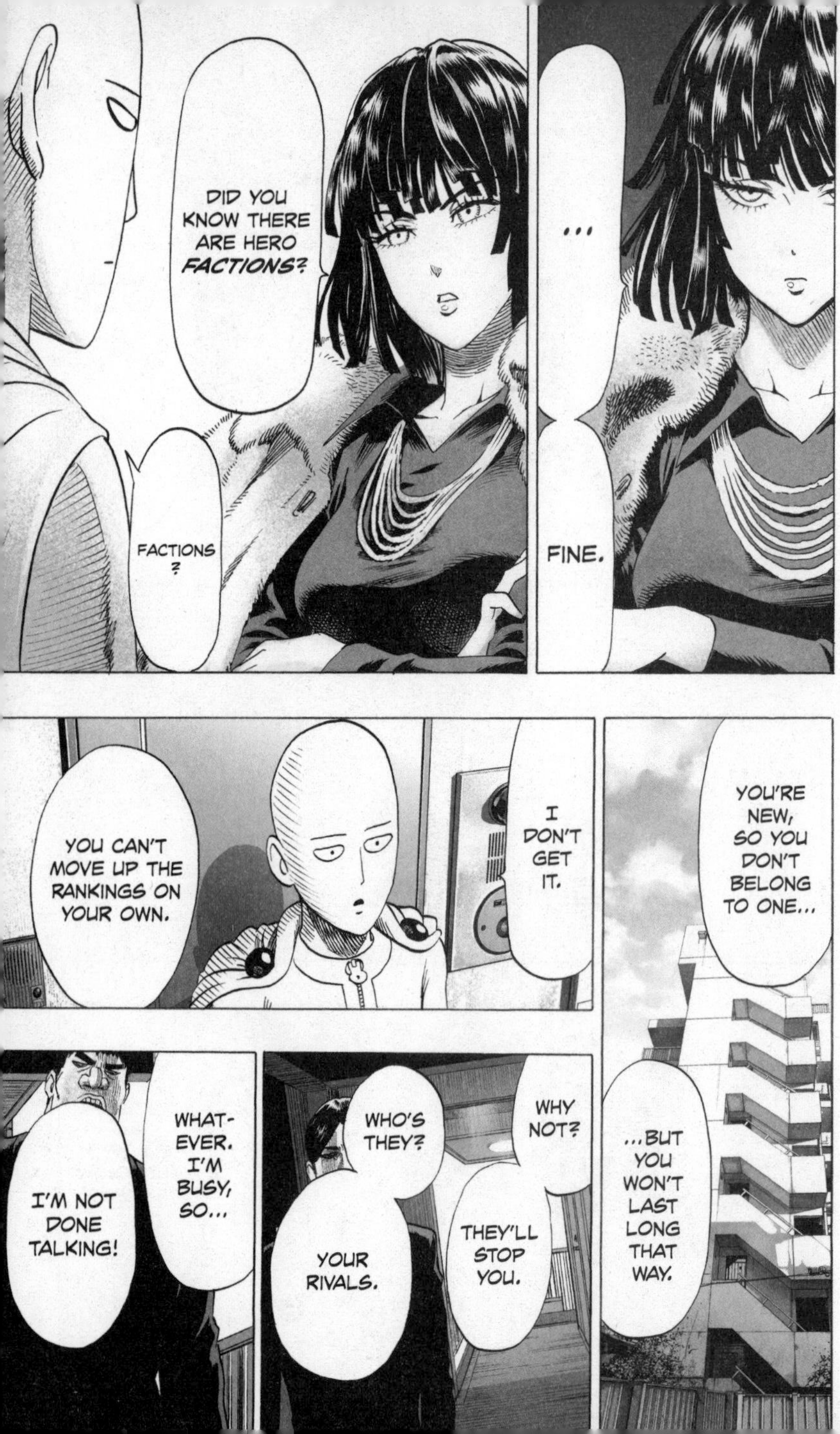
...
FINE.
DID YOU KNOW THERE ARE HERO *FACTIONS*?
FACTIONS?
YOU'RE NEW, SO YOU DON'T BELONG TO ONE...
...BUT YOU WON'T LAST LONG THAT WAY.
I DON'T GET IT.
YOU CAN'T MOVE UP THE RANKINGS ON YOUR OWN.
WHY NOT?
THEY'LL STOP YOU.
WHO'S THEY?
YOUR RIVALS.
WHAT-EVER. I'M BUSY, SO...
I'M NOT DONE TALKING!

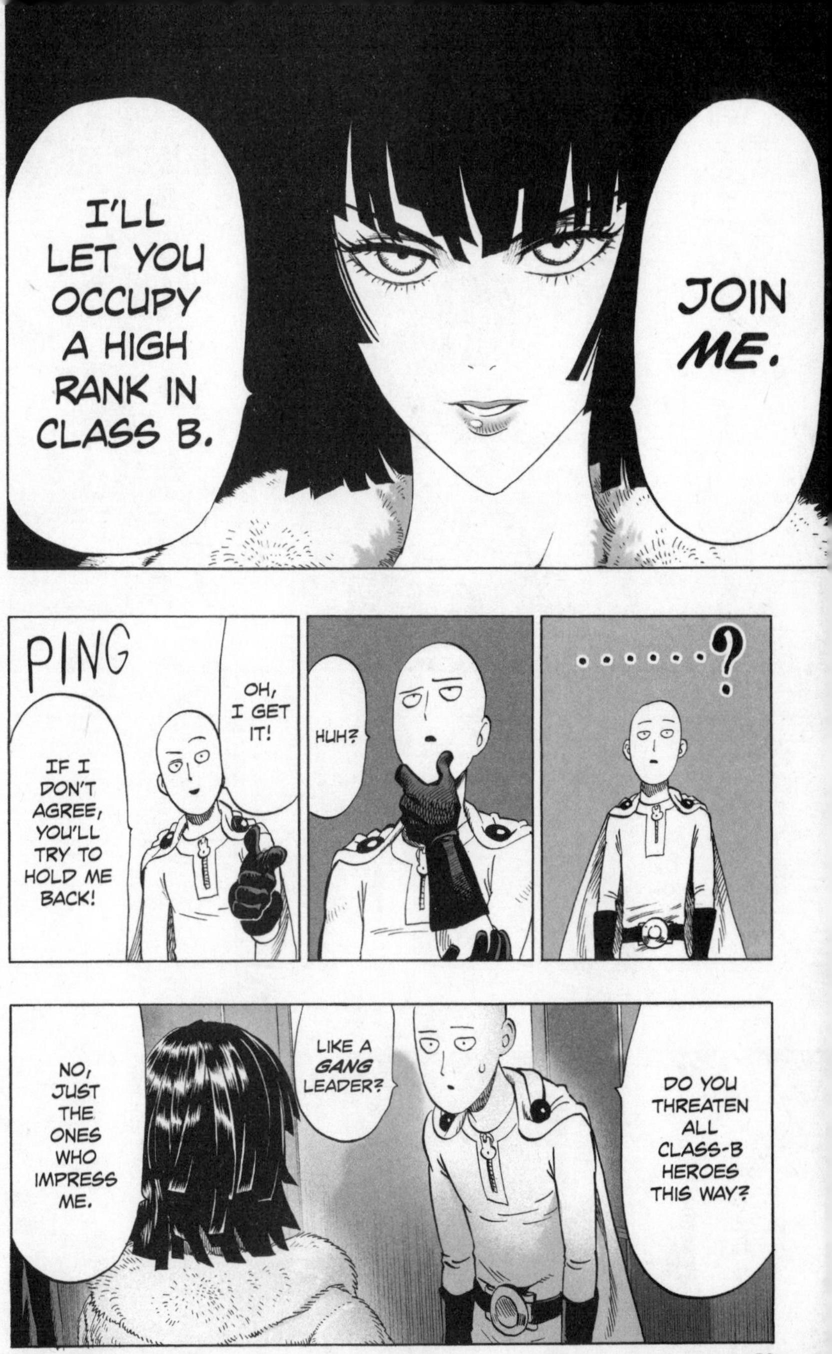
JOIN *ME.*
I'LL LET YOU OCCUPY A HIGH RANK IN CLASS B.
......?
HUH?
PING
OH, I GET IT!
IF I DON'T AGREE, YOU'LL TRY TO HOLD ME BACK!
DO YOU THREATEN ALL CLASS-B HEROES THIS WAY?
LIKE A *GANG* LEADER?
NO, JUST THE ONES WHO IMPRESS ME.

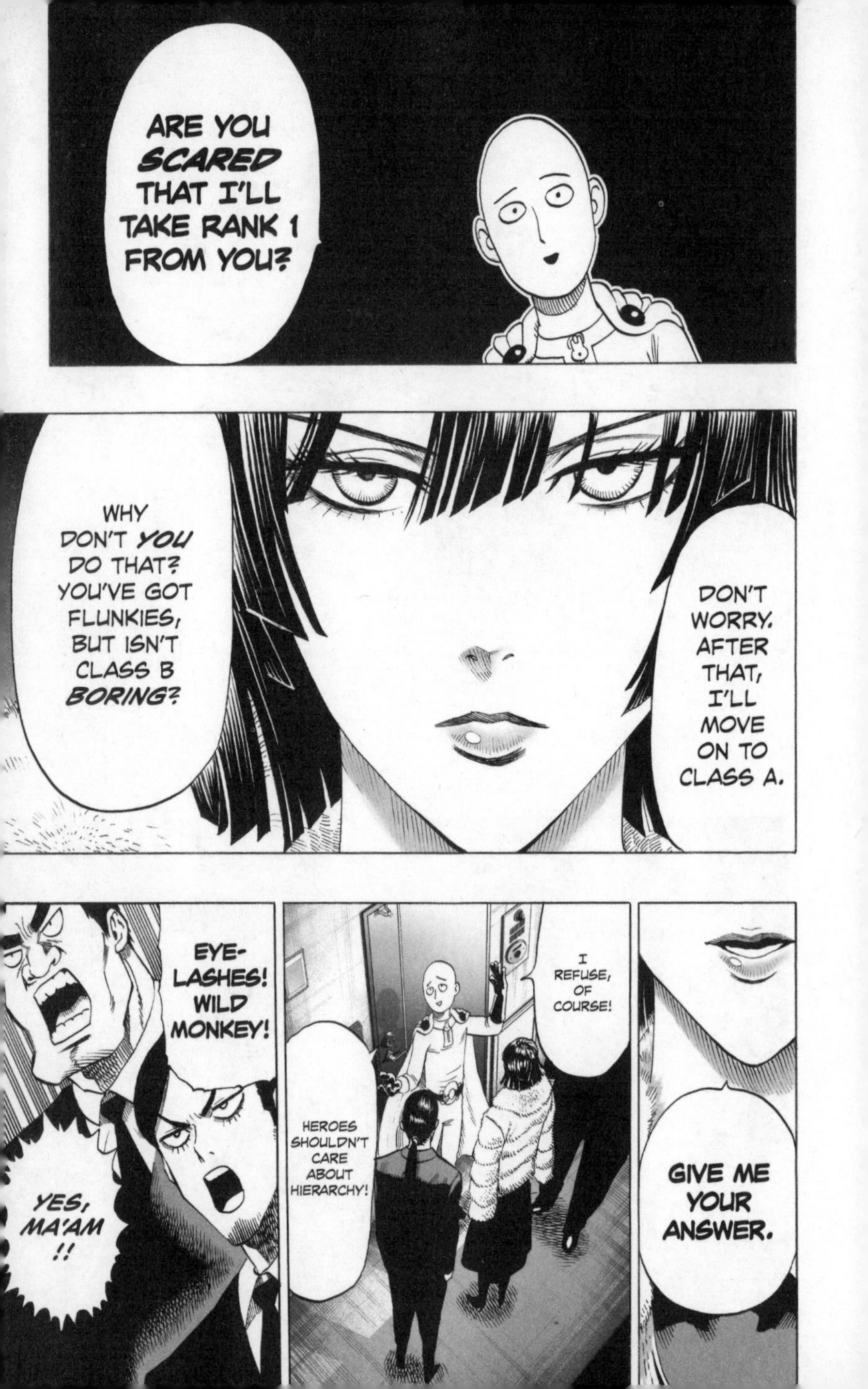
ARE YOU *SCARED* THAT I'LL TAKE RANK 1 FROM YOU?
DON'T WORRY. AFTER THAT, I'LL MOVE ON TO CLASS A.
WHY DON'T *YOU* DO THAT? YOU'VE GOT FLUNKIES, BUT ISN'T CLASS B *BORING*?
GIVE ME YOUR ANSWER.
I REFUSE, OF COURSE!
HEROES SHOULDN'T CARE ABOUT HIERARCHY!
EYE-LASHES! WILD MONKEY!
YES, MA'AM !!

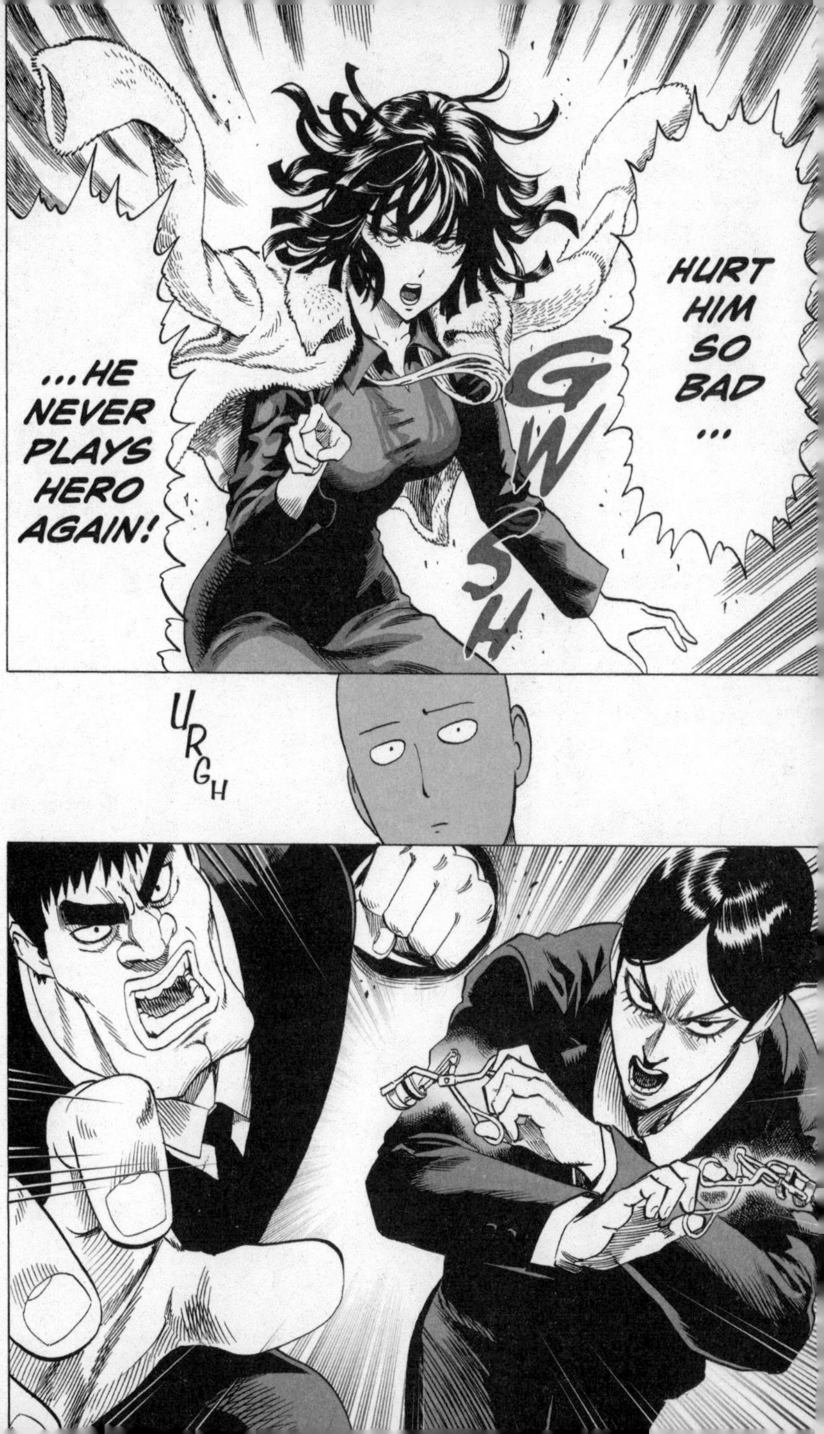
HURT HIM SO BAD ...
GWSH
...HE NEVER PLAYS HERO AGAIN!
URGH

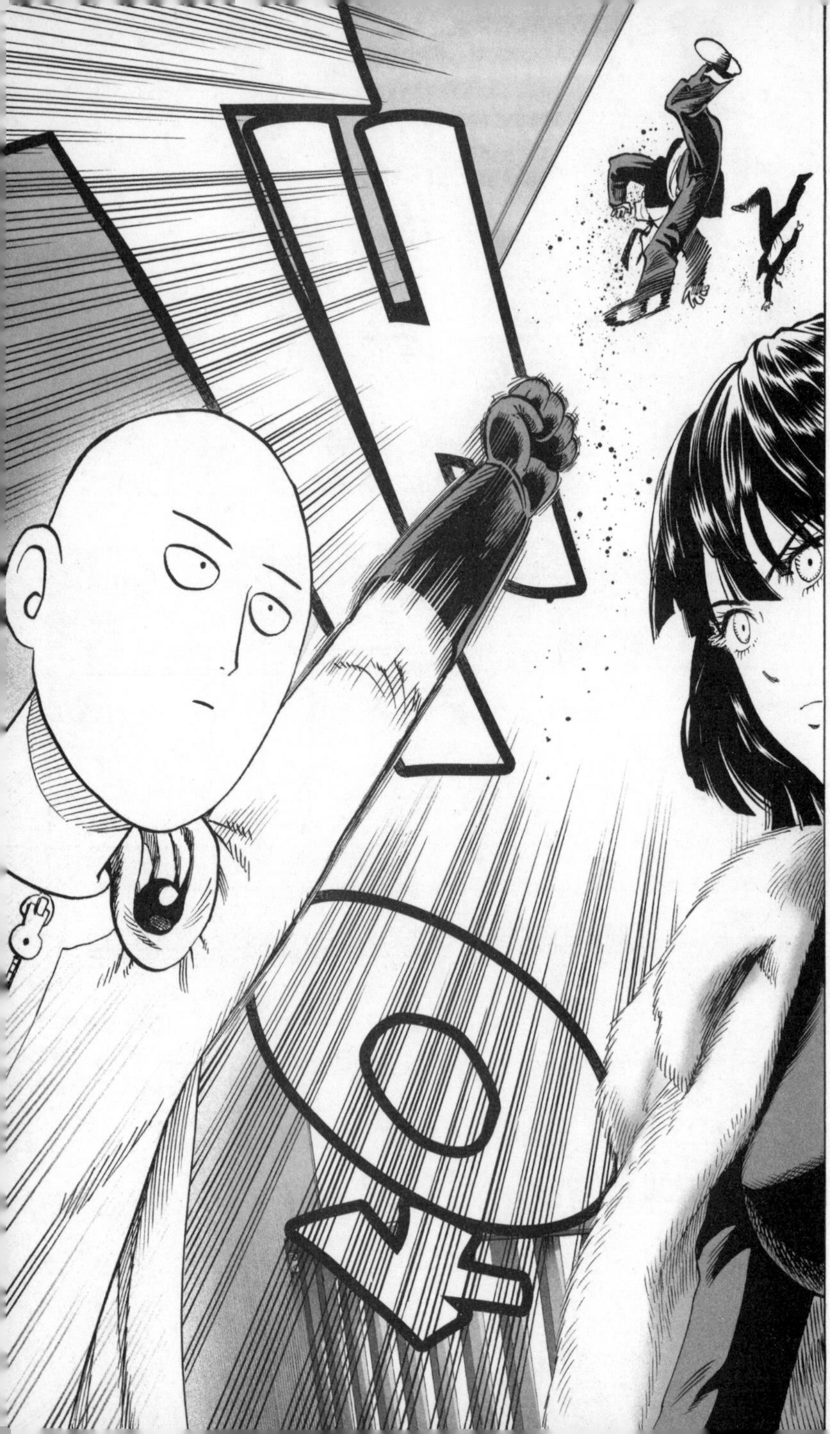

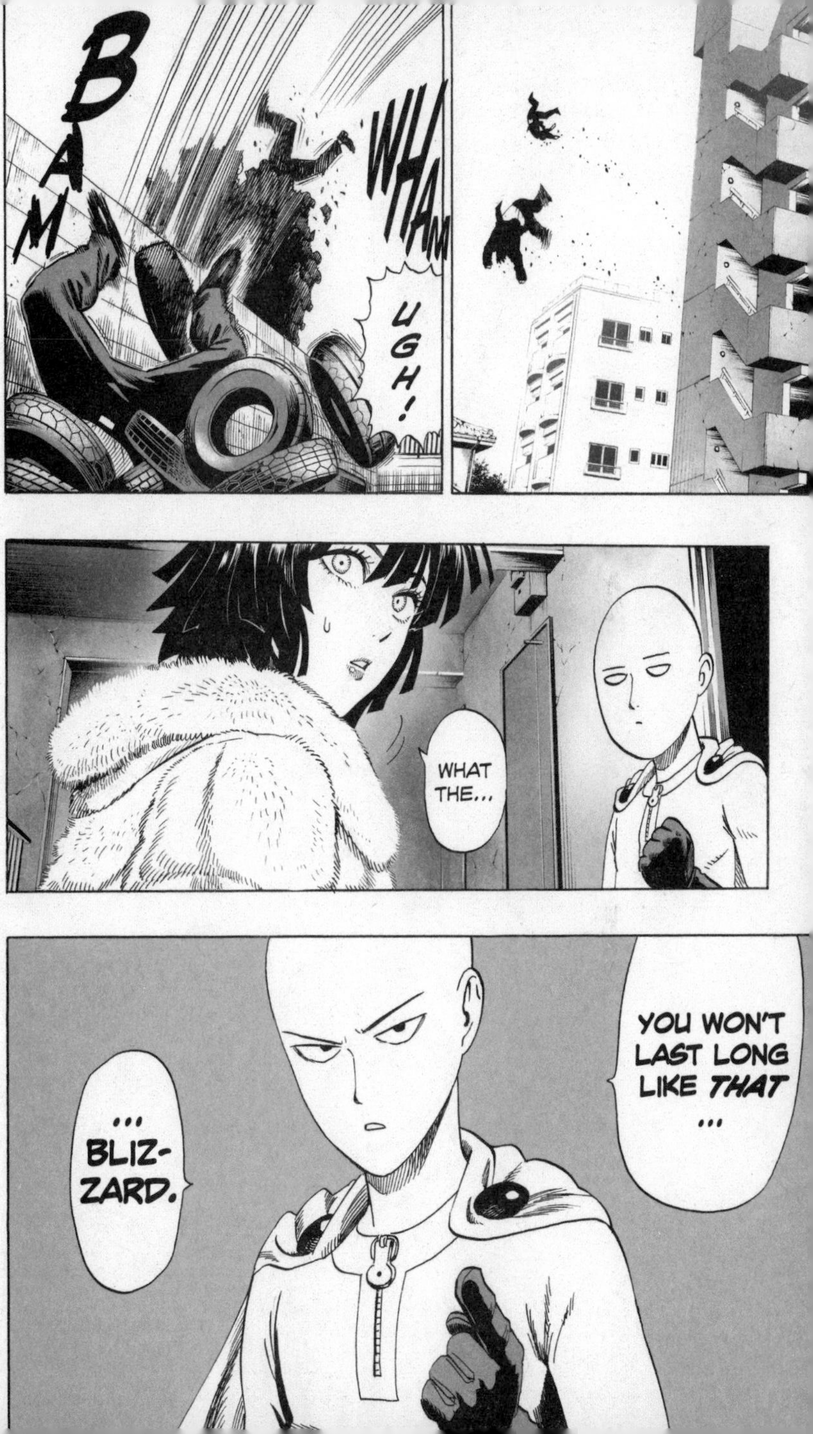
BAM
WHAM
UGH!
WHAT THE...
YOU WON'T LAST LONG LIKE *THAT* ...
... BLIZZARD.

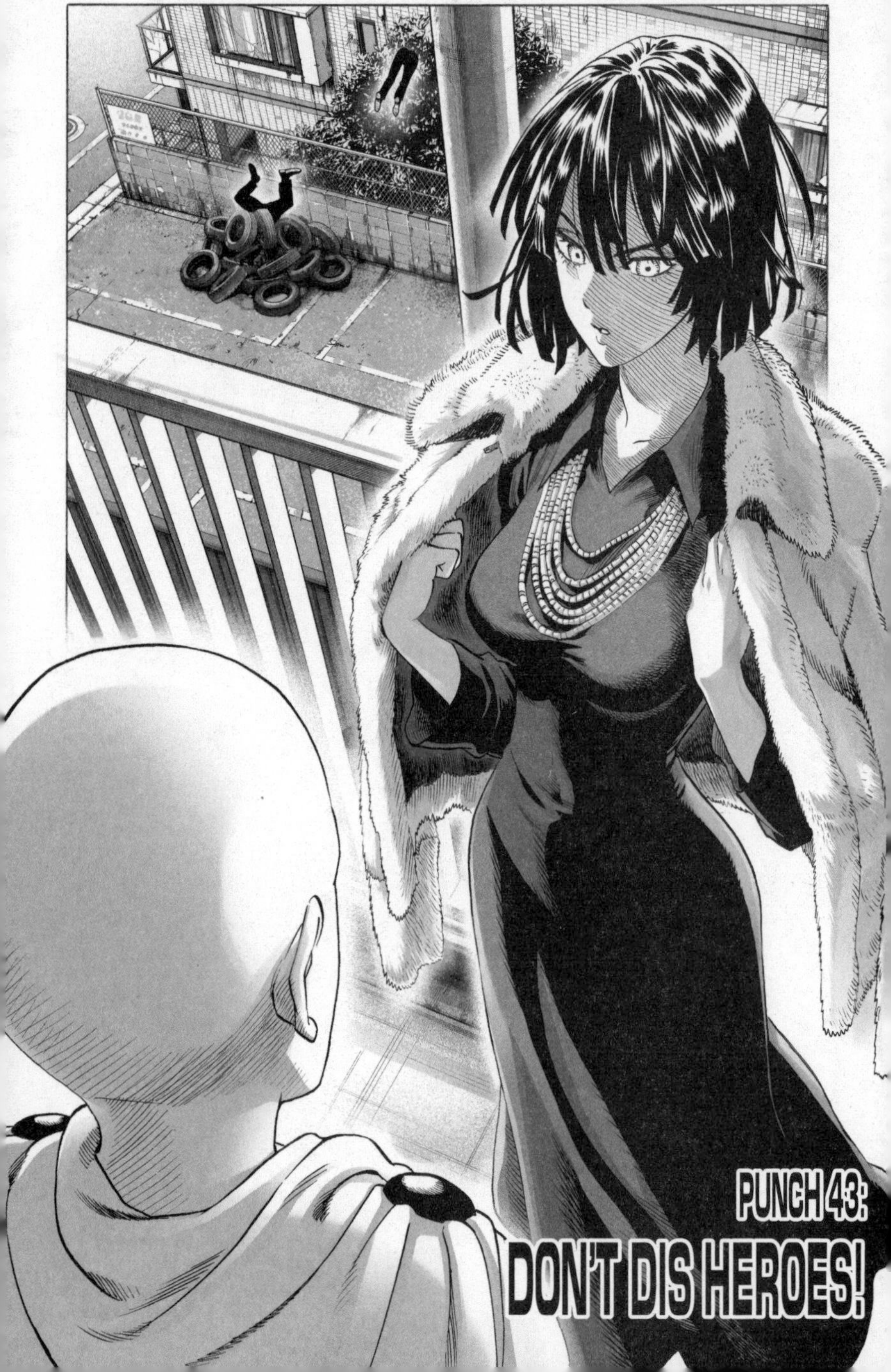
PUNCH 43:
DON'T DIS HEROES!

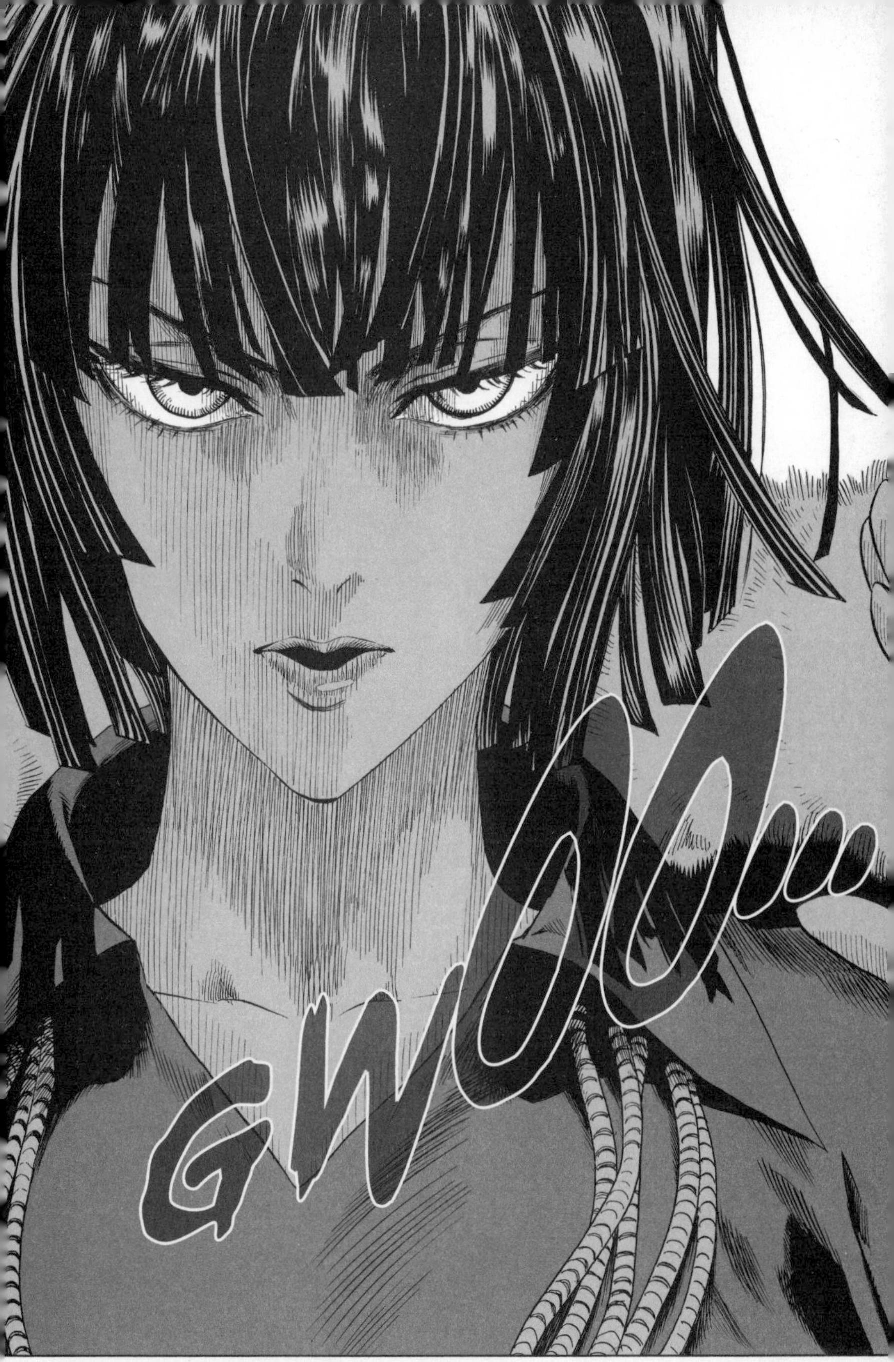
GWOOO...

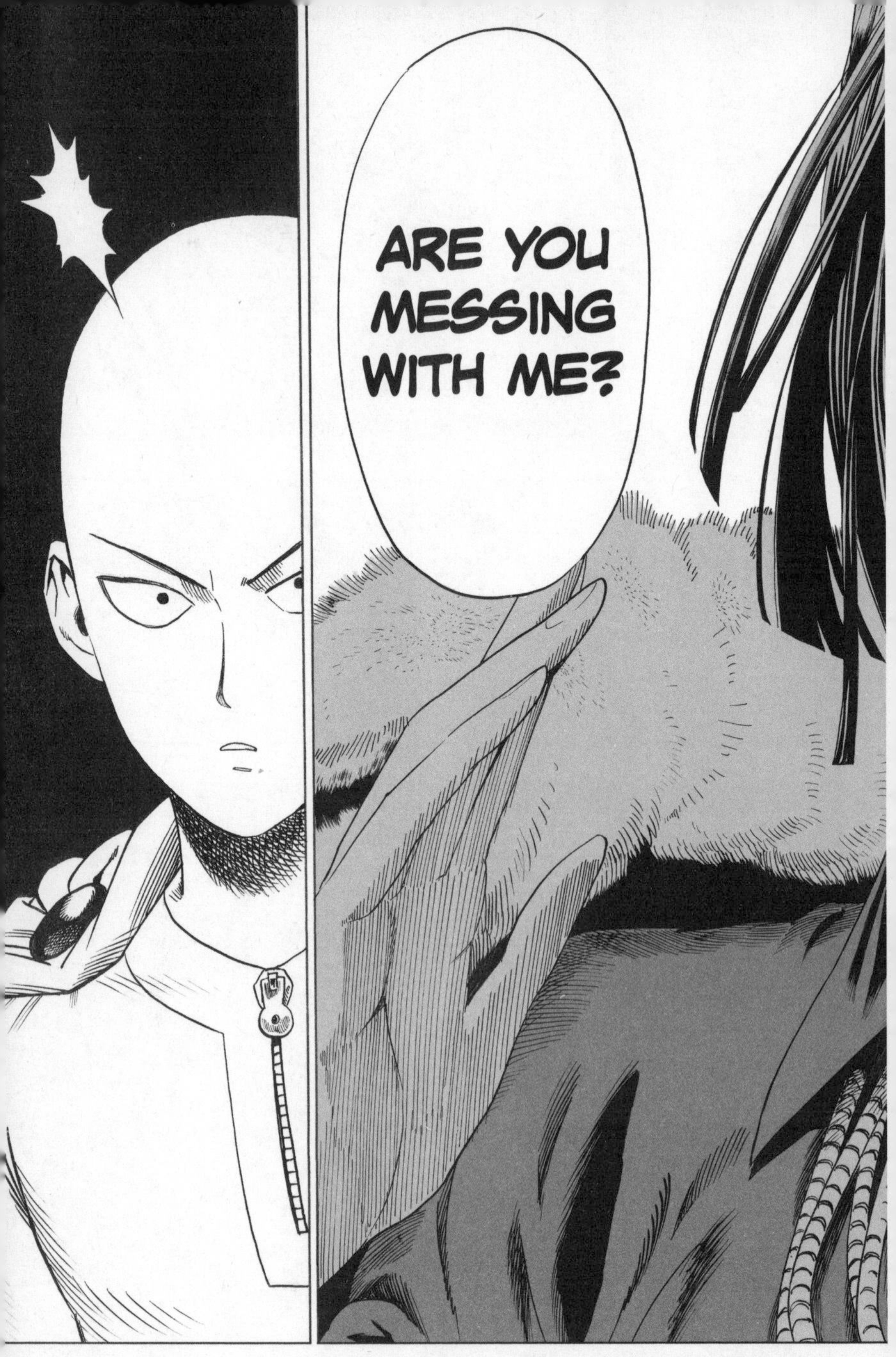
ARE YOU MESSING WITH ME?

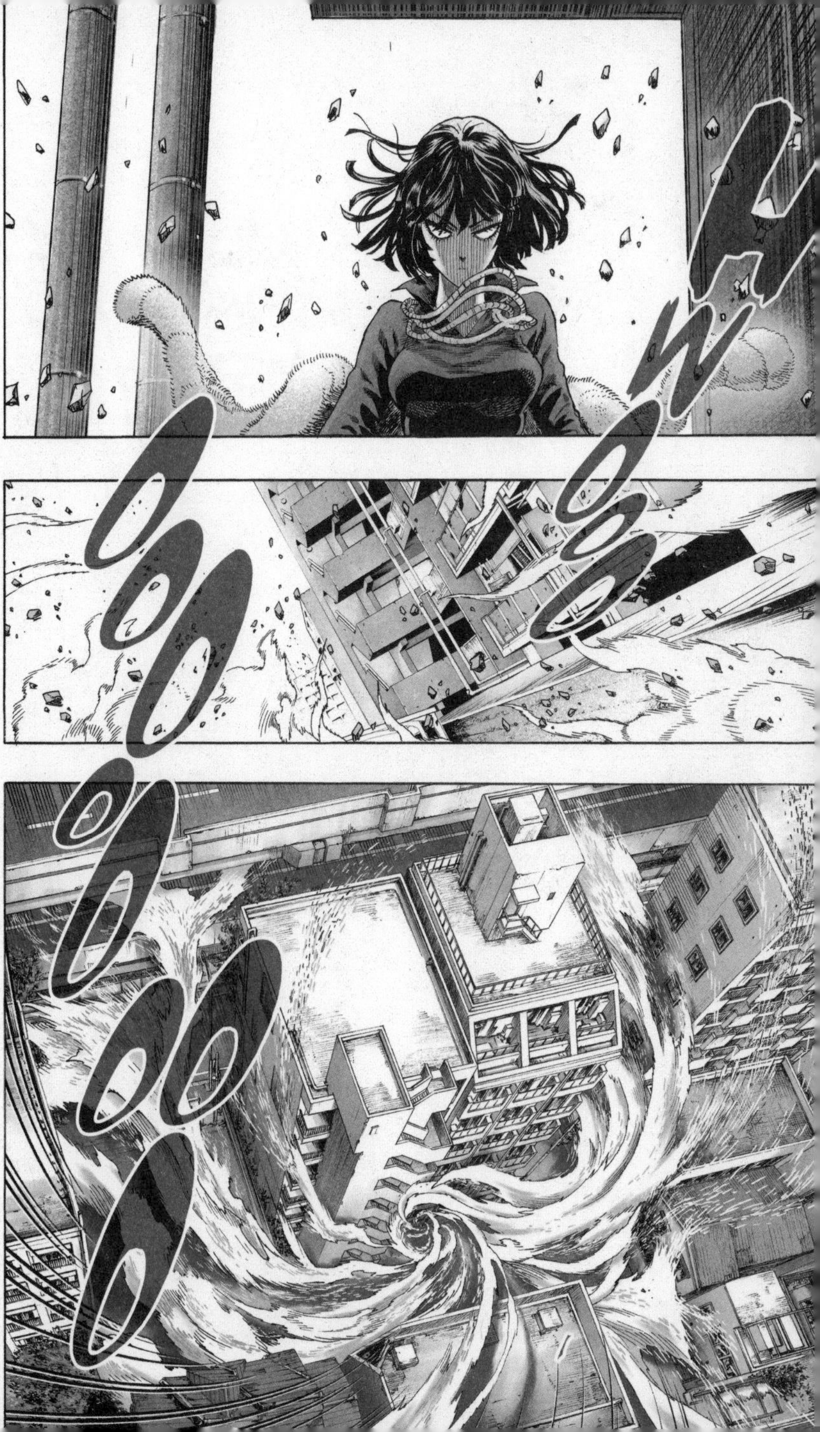

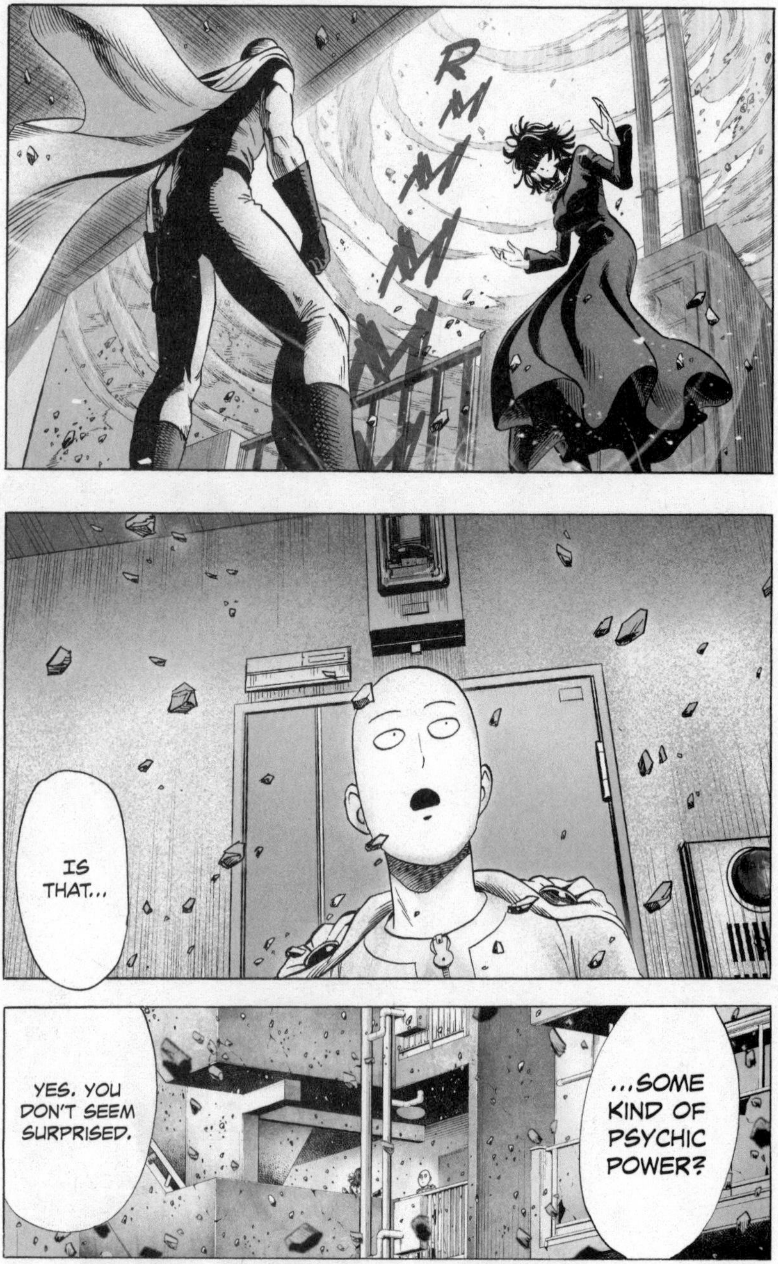
RMMMMM
IS THAT...
...SOME KIND OF PSYCHIC POWER?
YES. YOU DON'T SEEM SURPRISED.

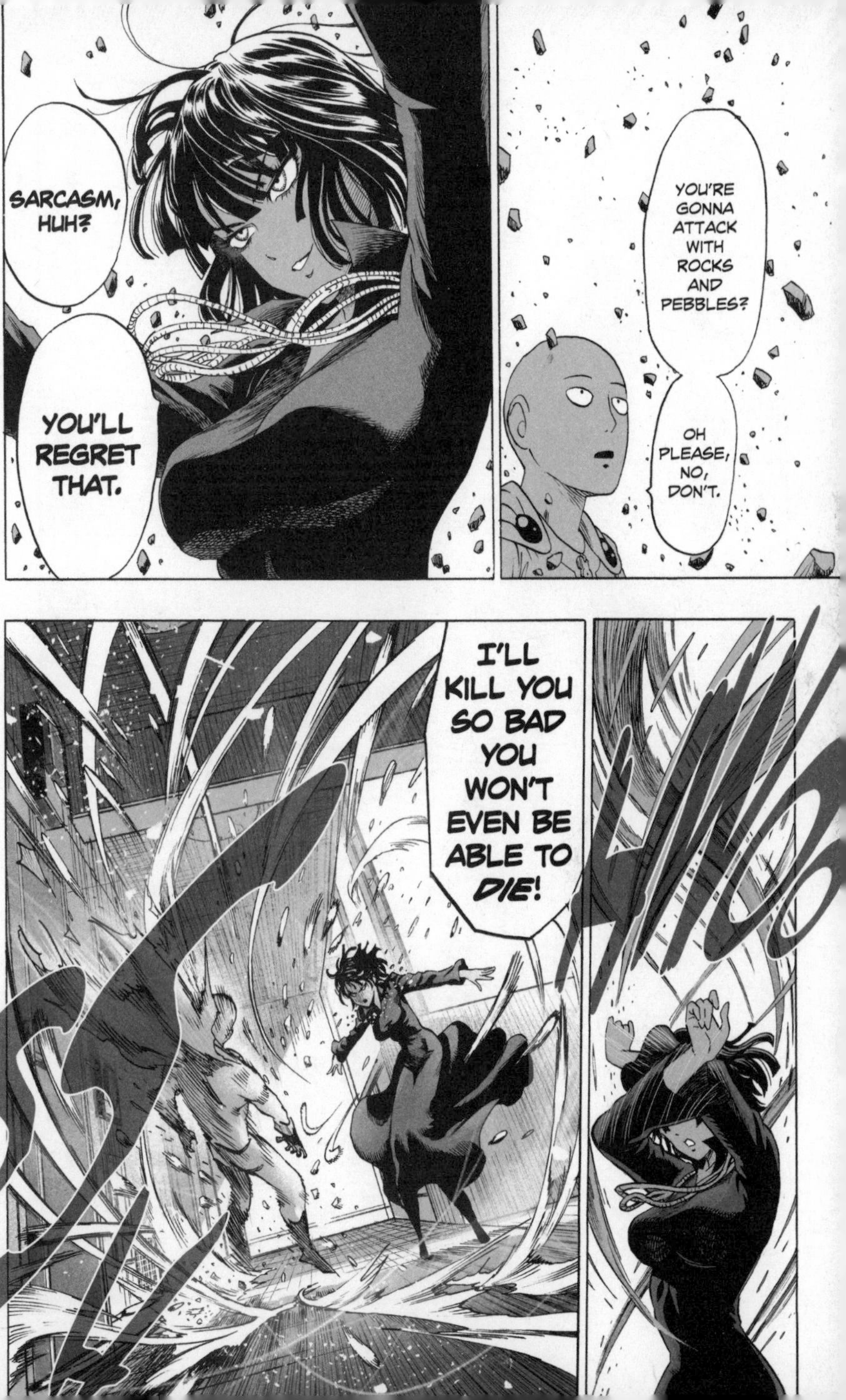
YOU'RE GONNA ATTACK WITH ROCKS AND PEBBLES?
OH PLEASE, NO, DON'T.
SARCASM, HUH?
YOU'LL REGRET THAT.
I'LL KILL YOU SO BAD YOU WON'T EVEN BE ABLE TO *DIE*!

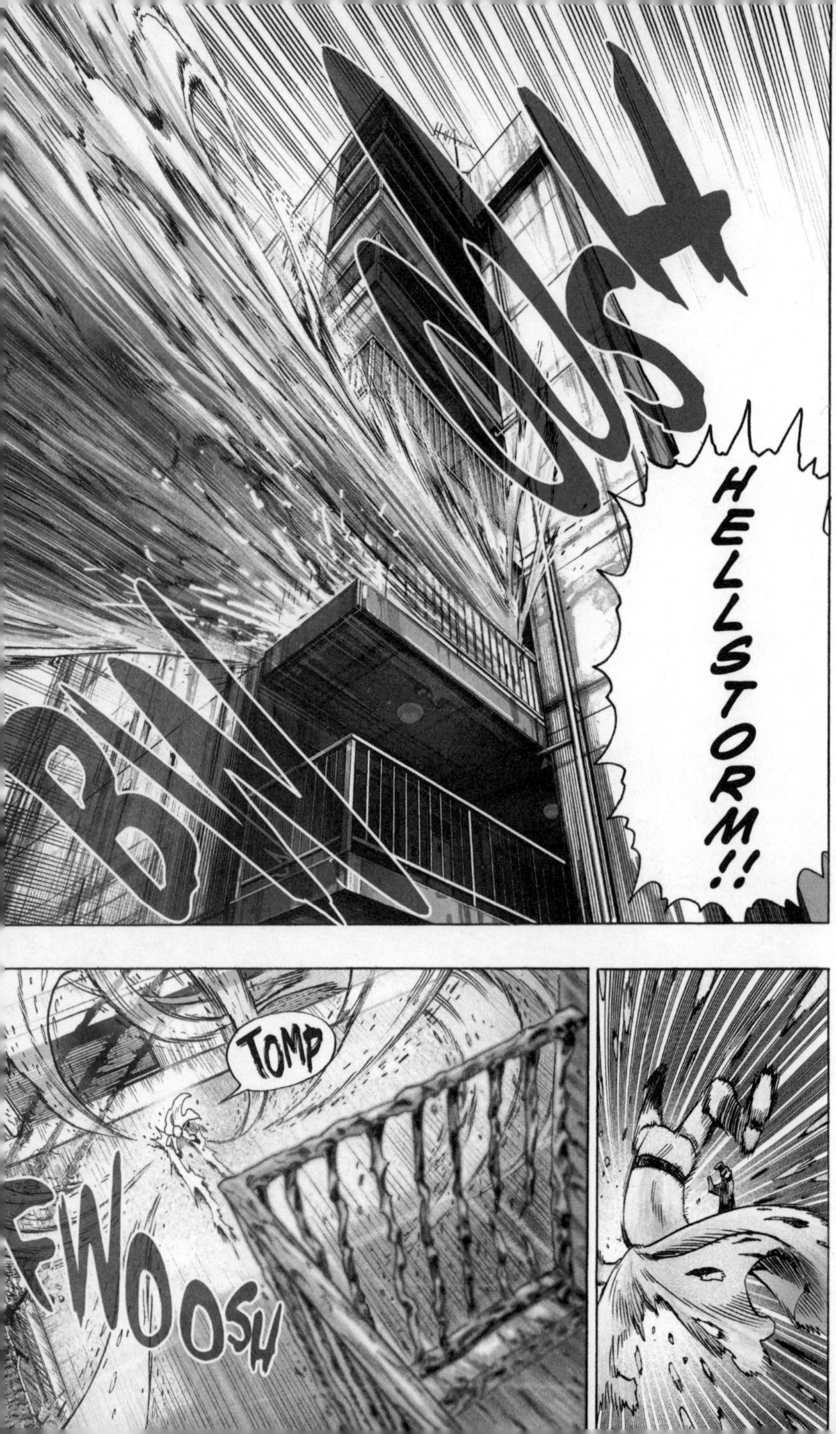
HELLSTORM!!
TOMP
FWOOSH

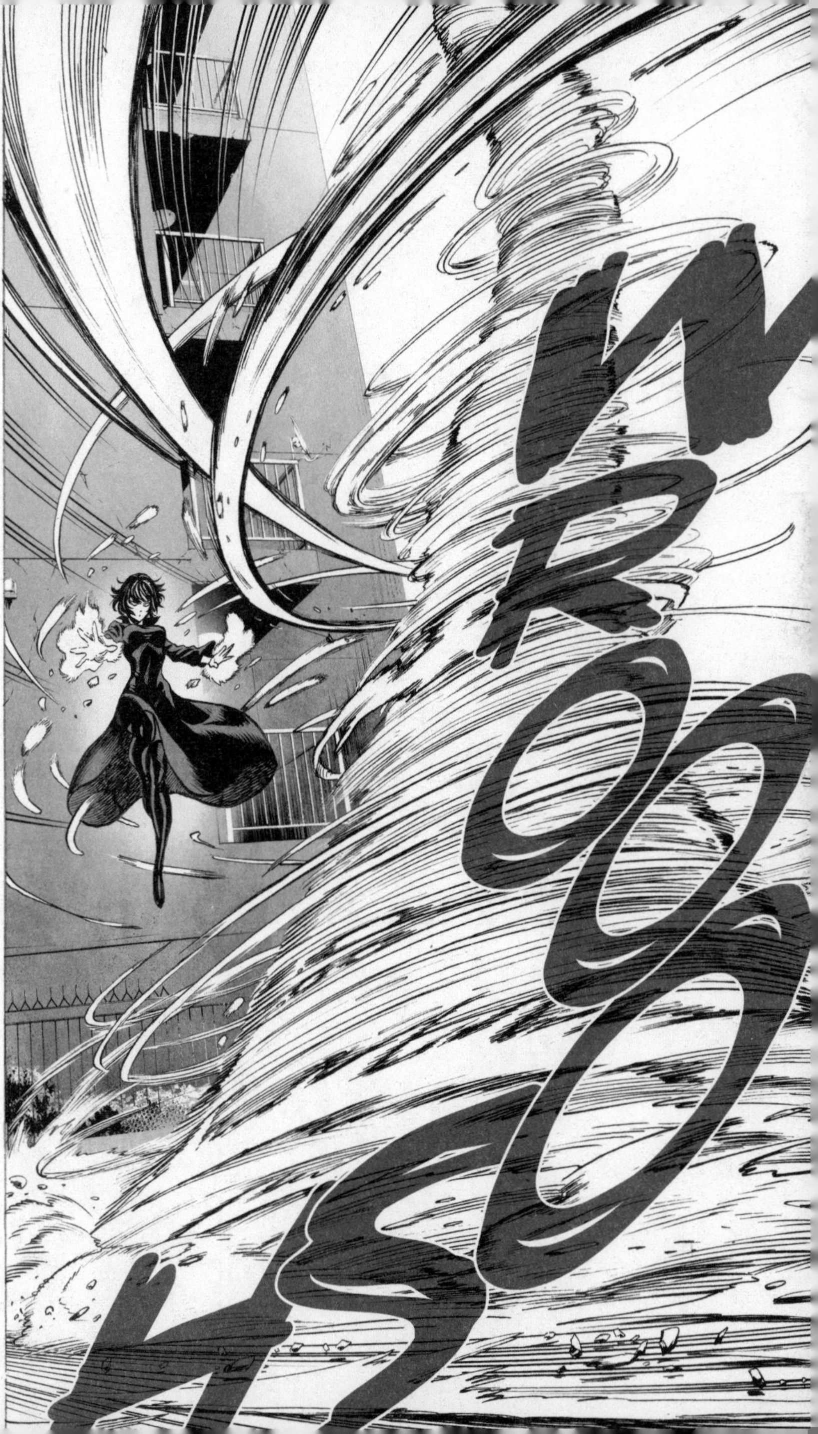
WHOOOSH

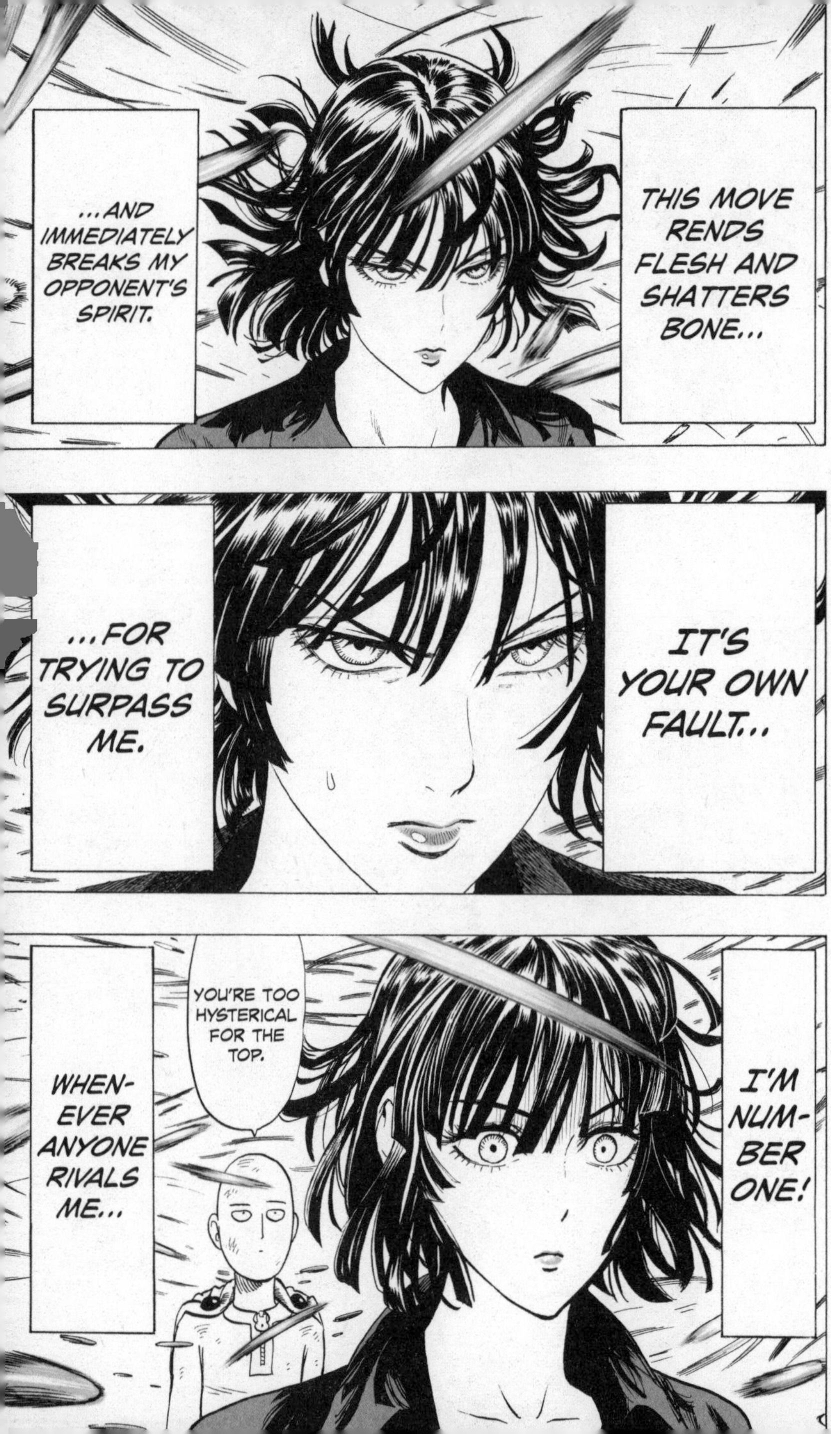
THIS MOVE RENDS FLESH AND SHATTERS BONE...
...AND IMMEDIATELY BREAKS MY OPPONENT'S SPIRIT.
IT'S YOUR OWN FAULT...
...FOR TRYING TO SURPASS ME.
I'M NUMBER ONE!
WHENEVER ANYONE RIVALS ME...
YOU'RE TOO HYSTERICAL FOR THE TOP.

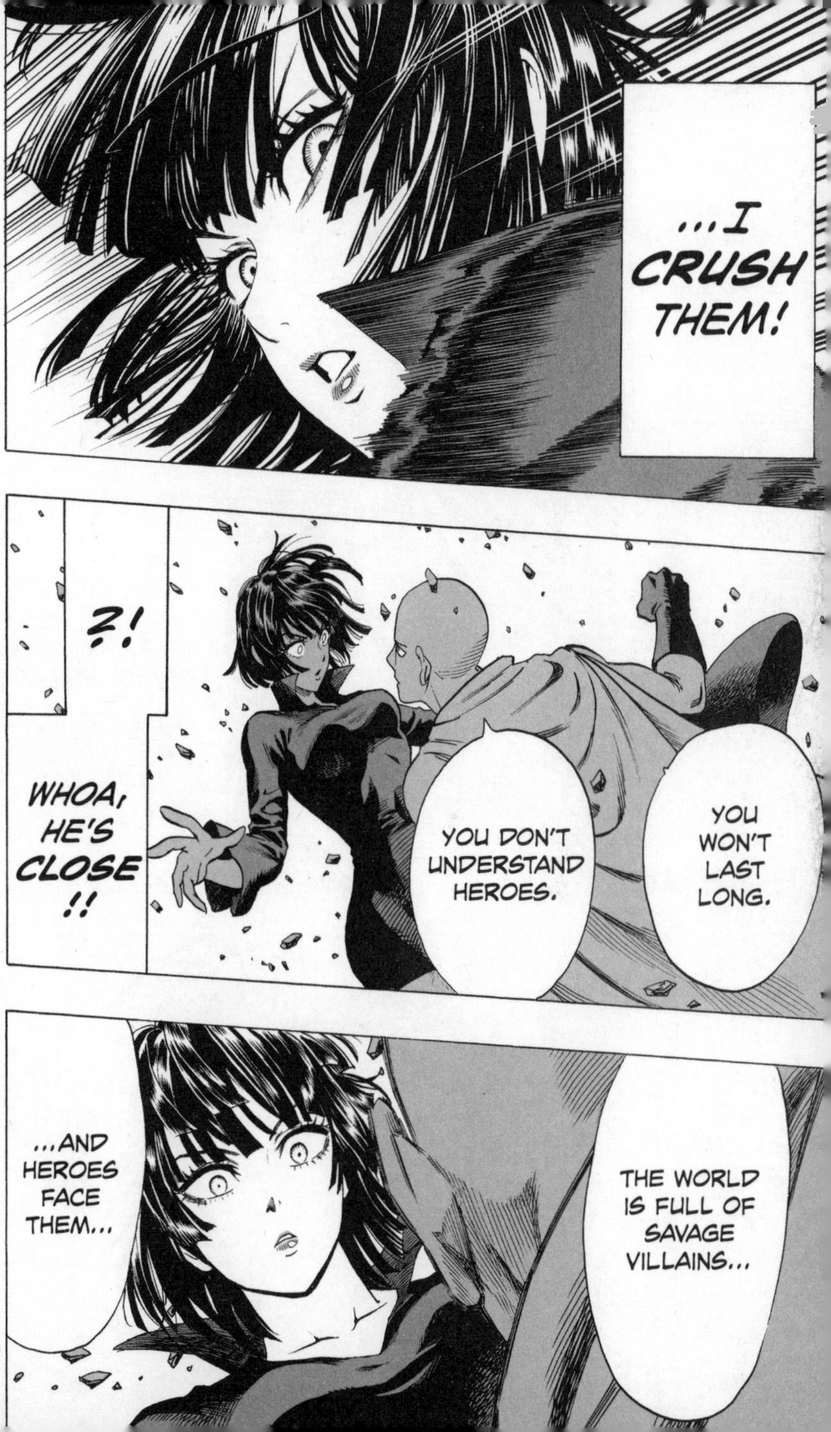
...I CRUSH THEM!
YOU WON'T LAST LONG.
YOU DON'T UNDERSTAND HEROES.
?!
WHOA, HE'S CLOSE !!
THE WORLD IS FULL OF SAVAGE VILLAINS...
...AND HEROES FACE THEM...

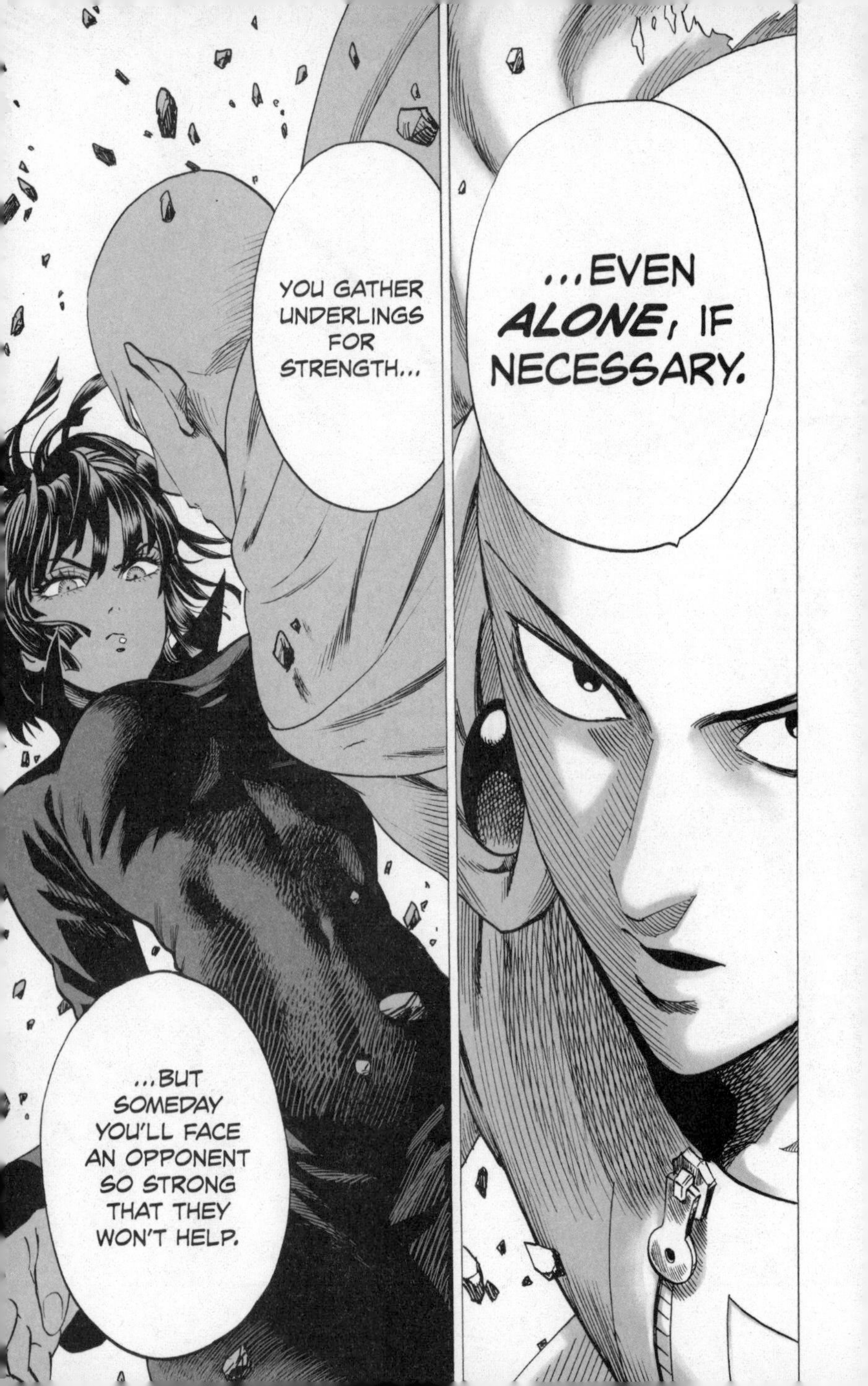
...EVEN *ALONE*, IF NECESSARY.
YOU GATHER UNDERLINGS FOR STRENGTH...
...BUT SOMEDAY YOU'LL FACE AN OPPONENT SO STRONG THAT THEY WON'T HELP.

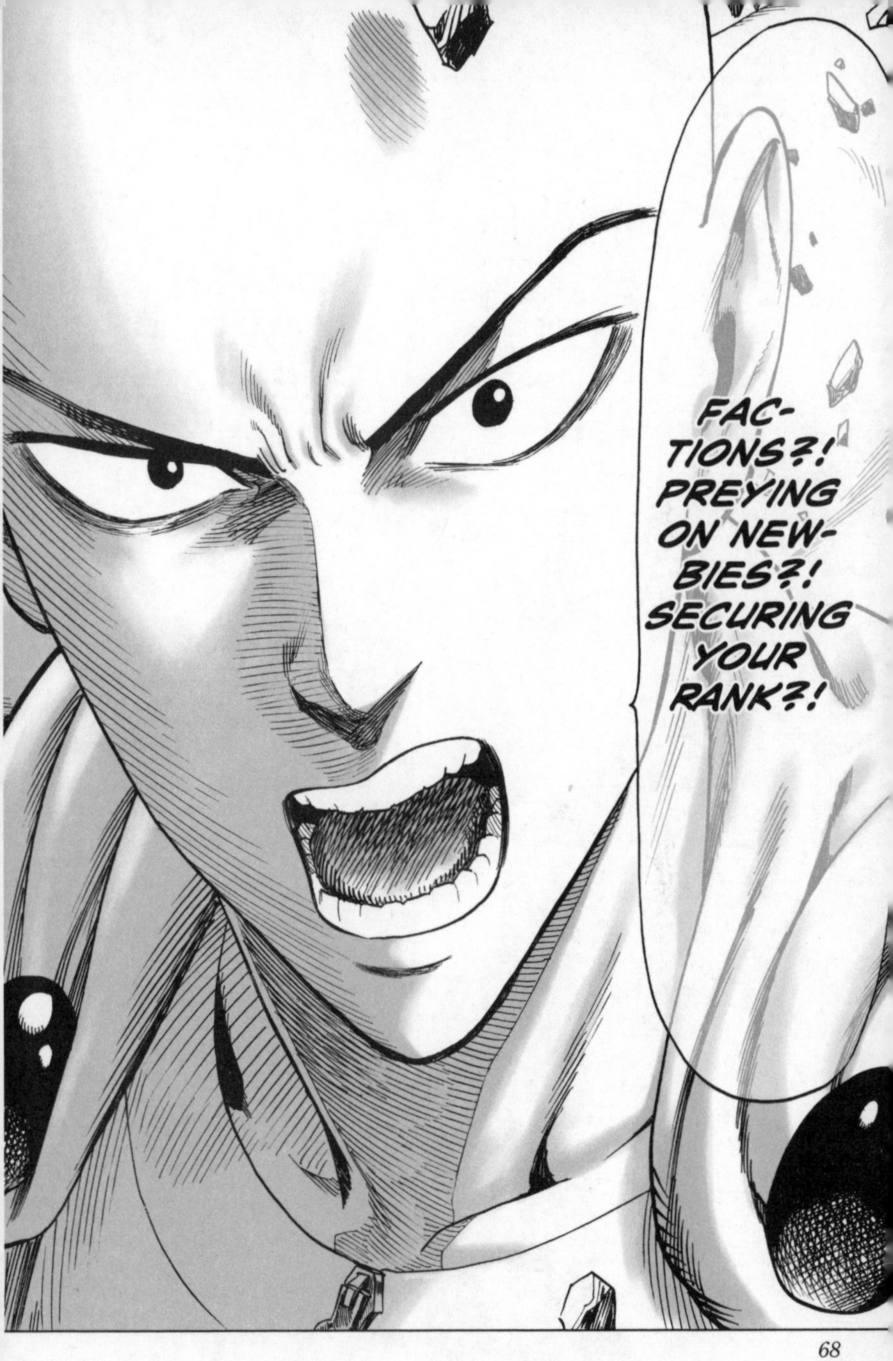
FAC-
TIONS?! PREYING ON NEW-BIES?! SECURING YOUR RANK?!

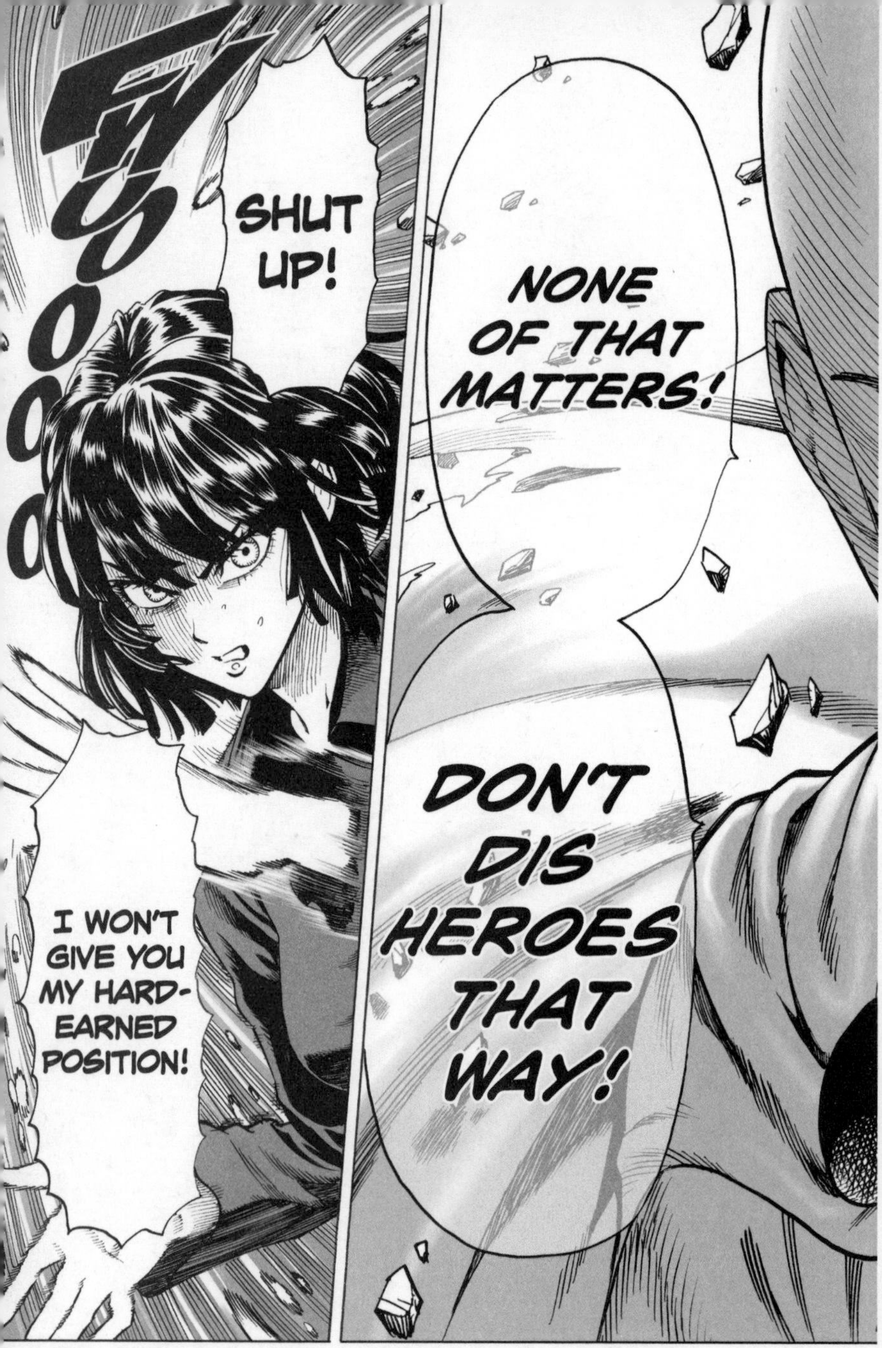
NONE OF THAT MATTERS!
DON'T DIS HEROES THAT WAY!
SHUT UP!
I WON'T GIVE YOU MY HARD-EARNED POSITION!

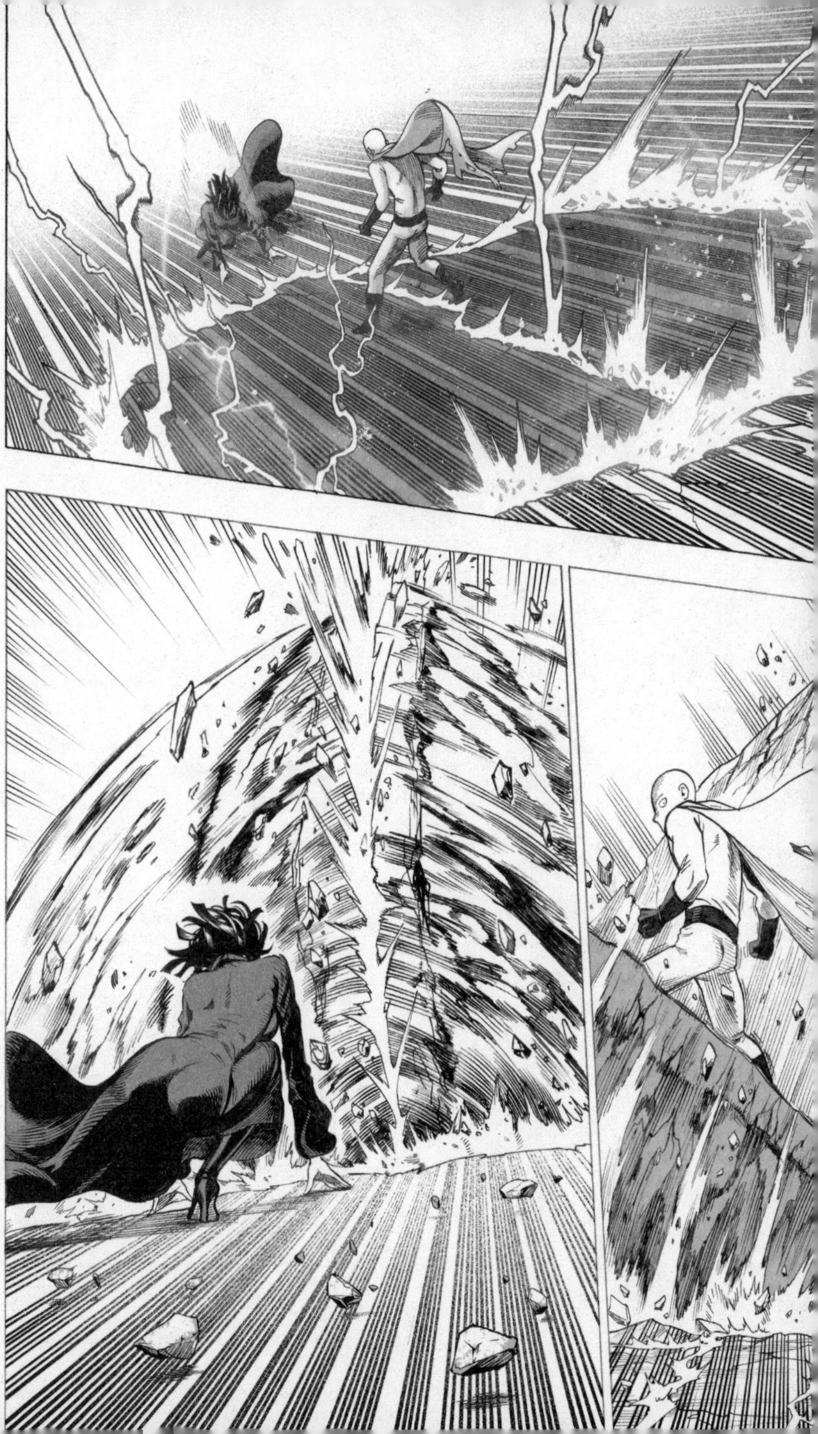

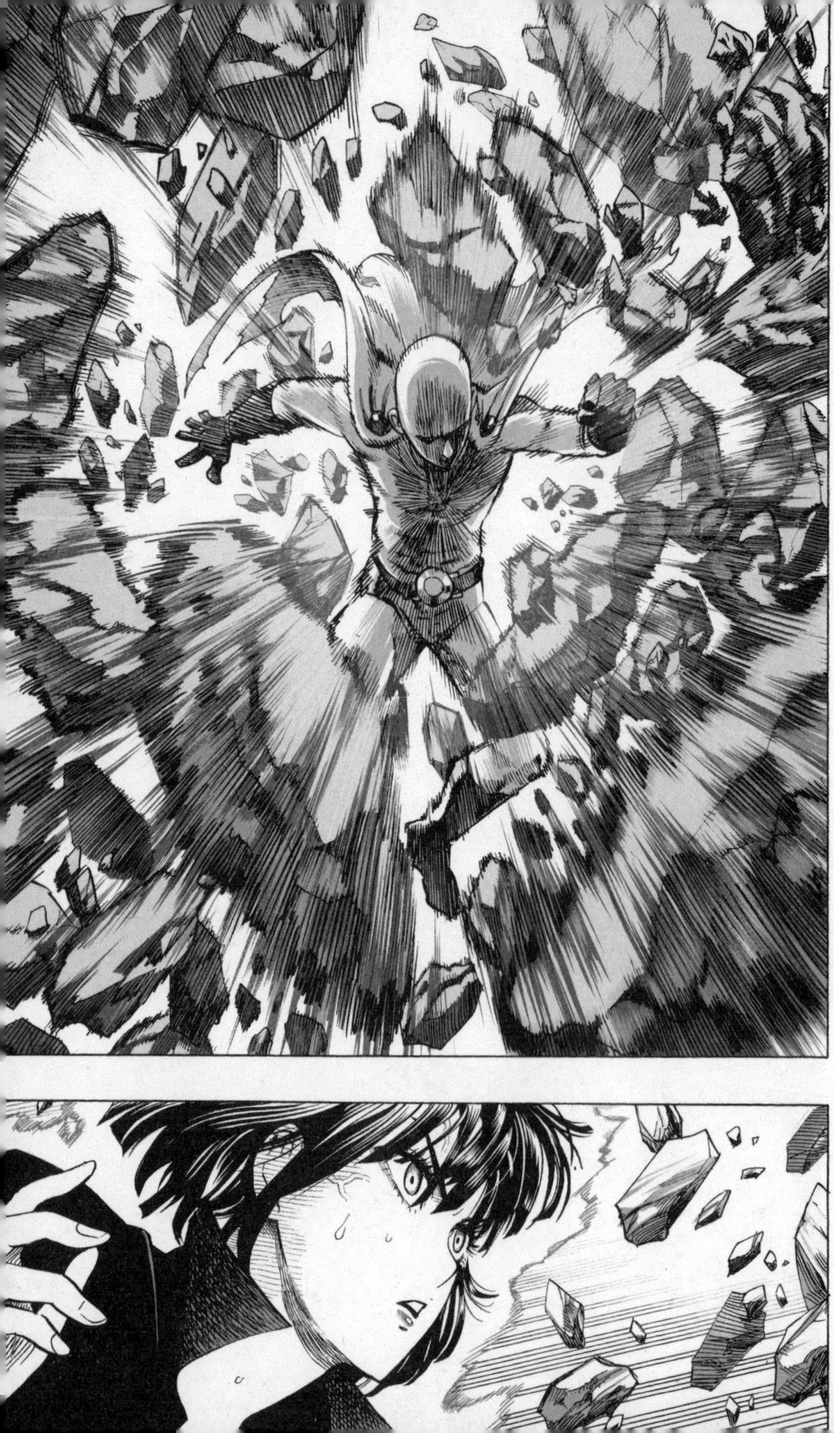

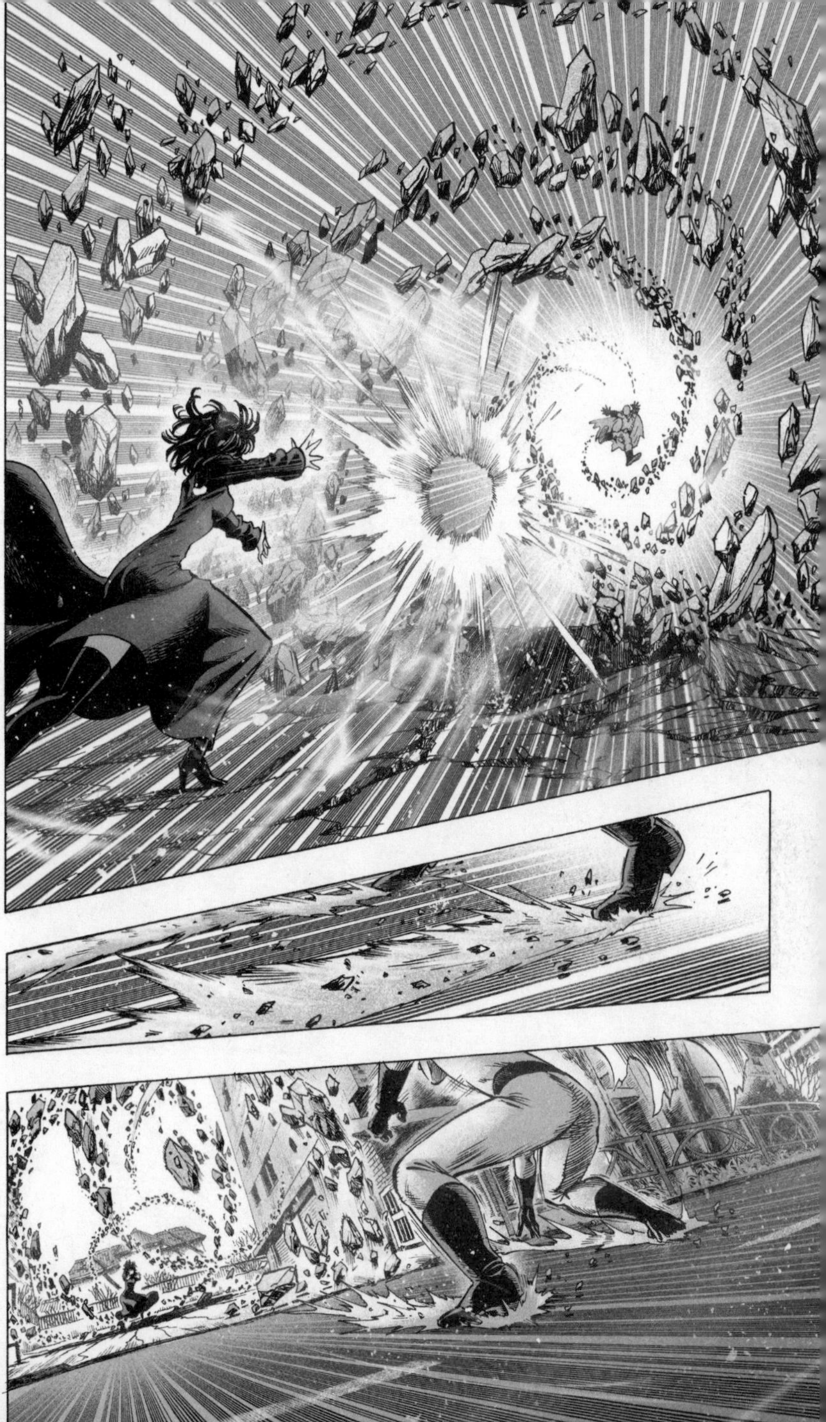

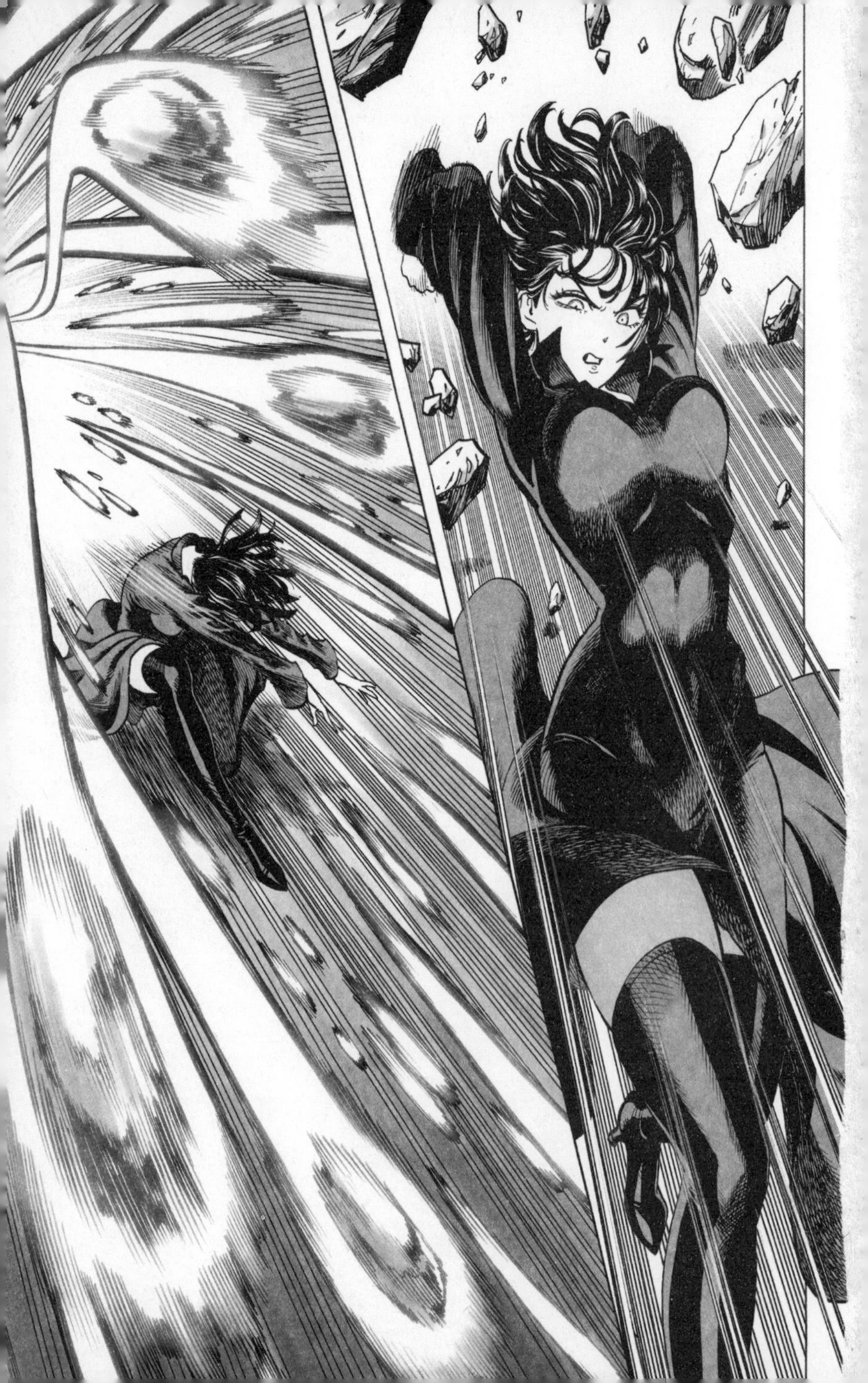

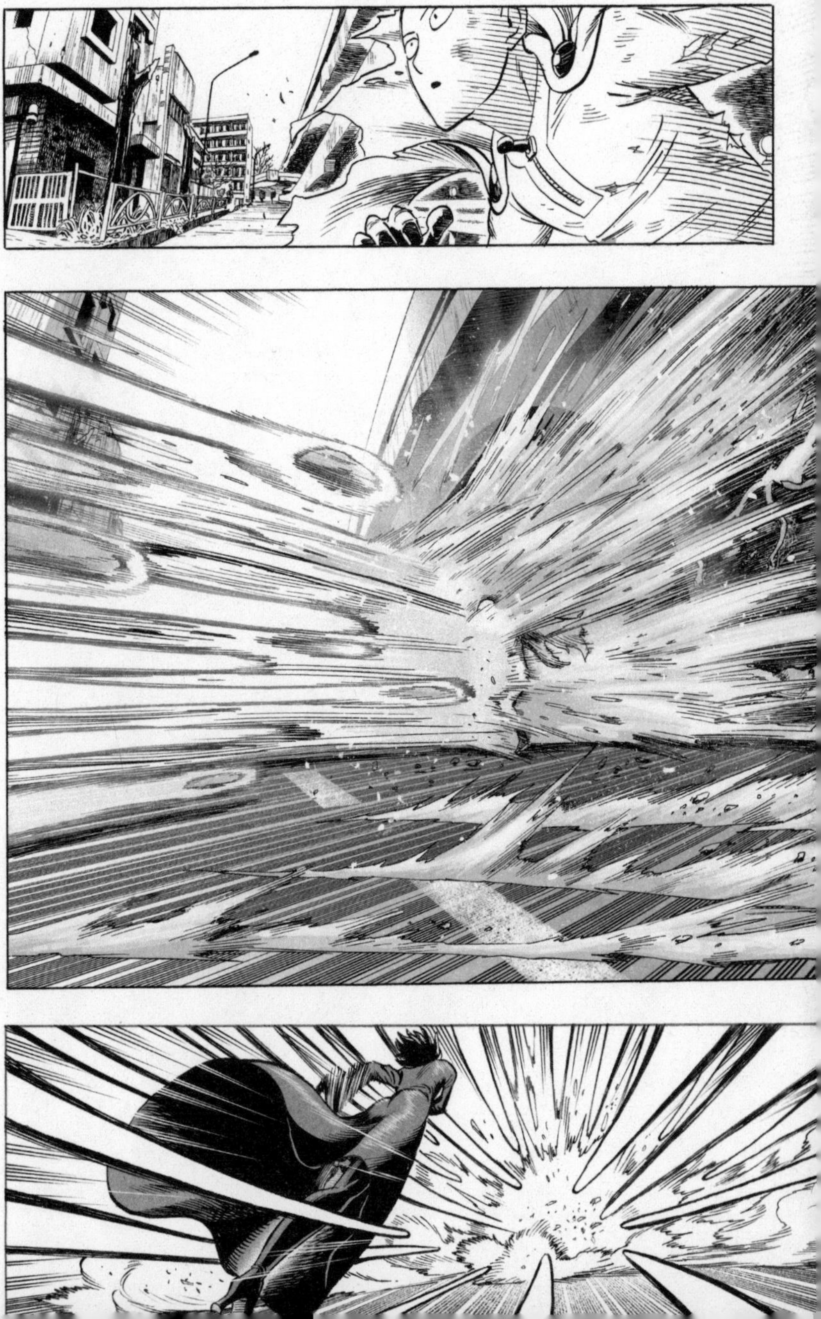

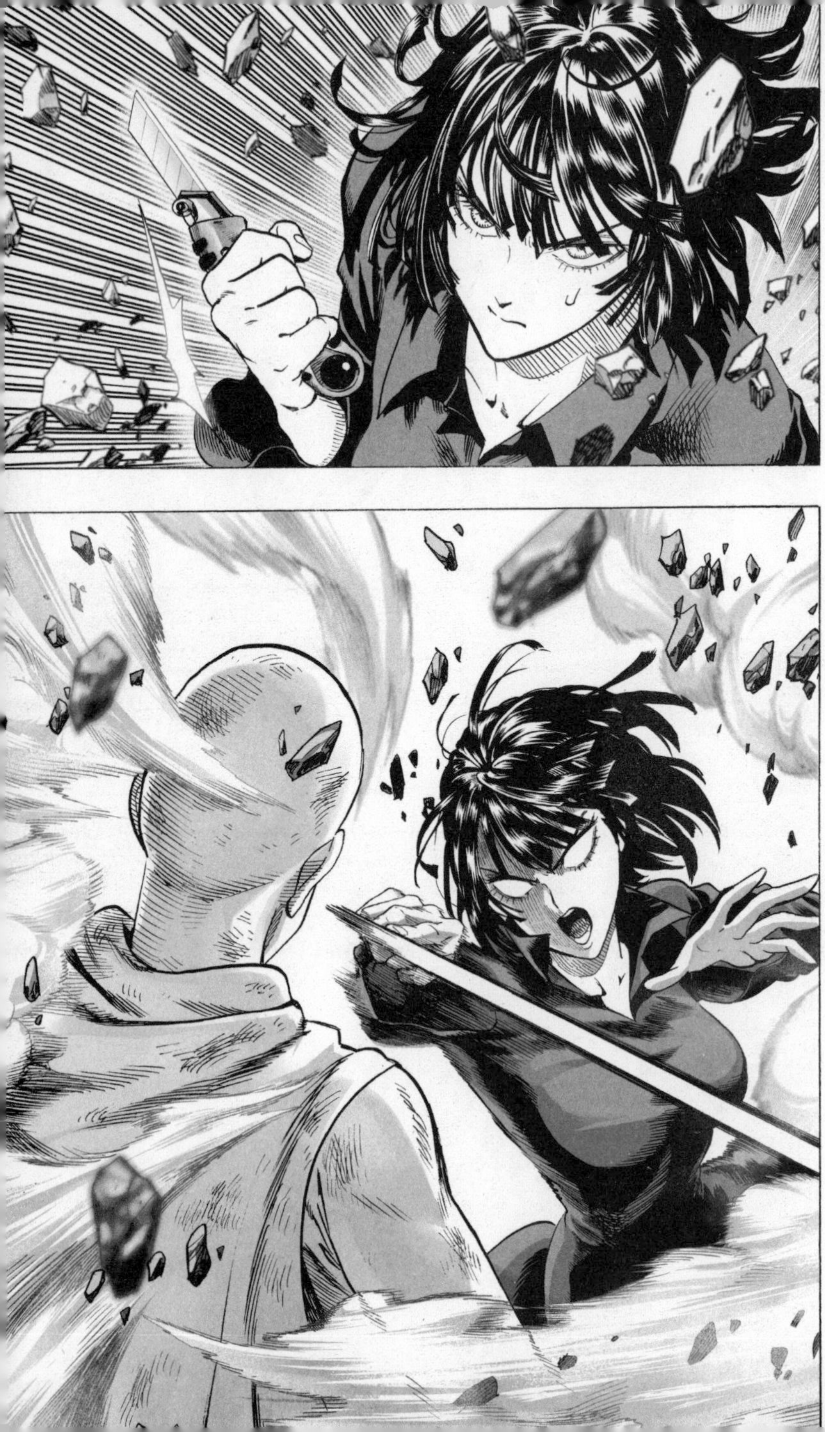

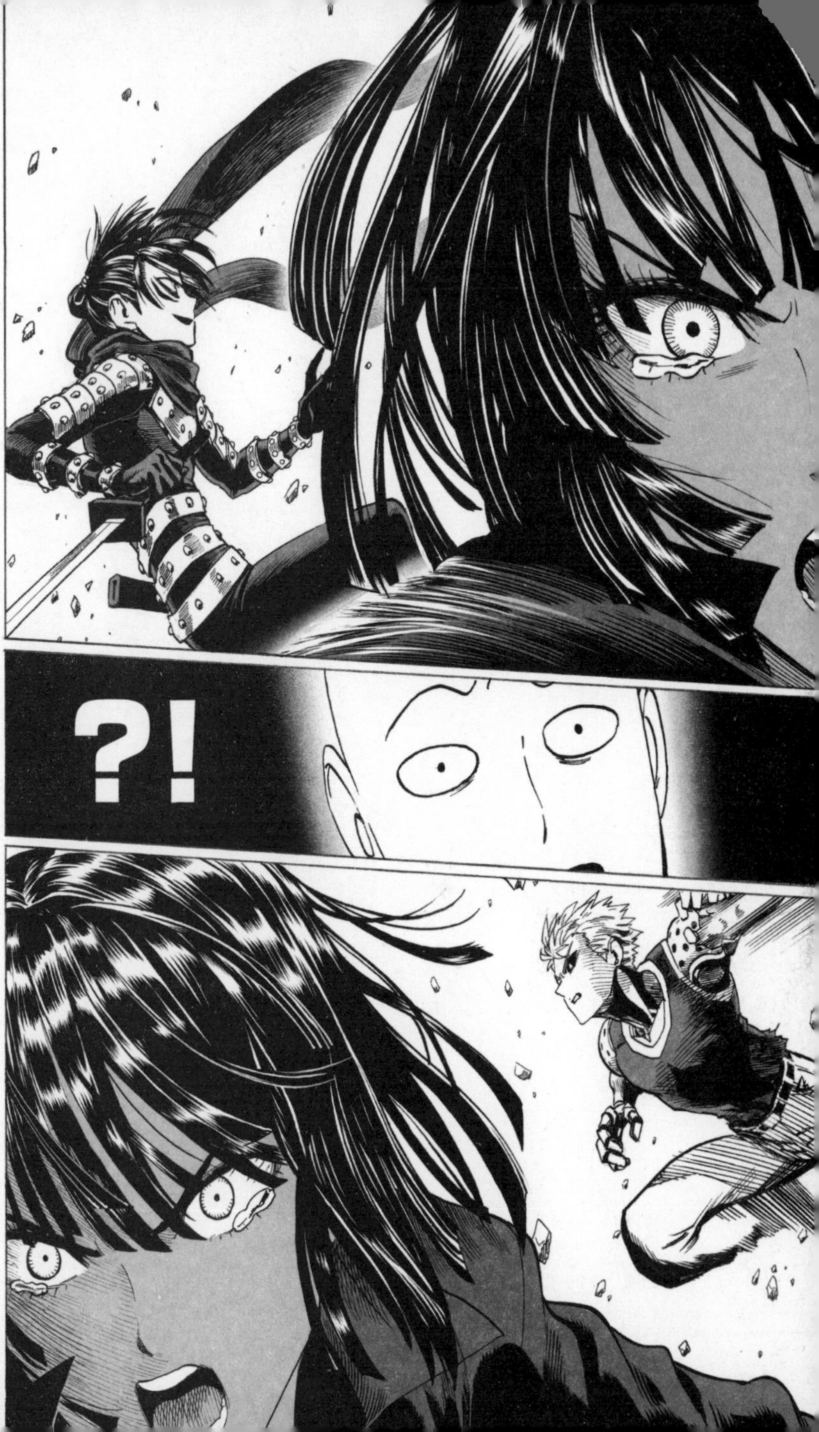
?!

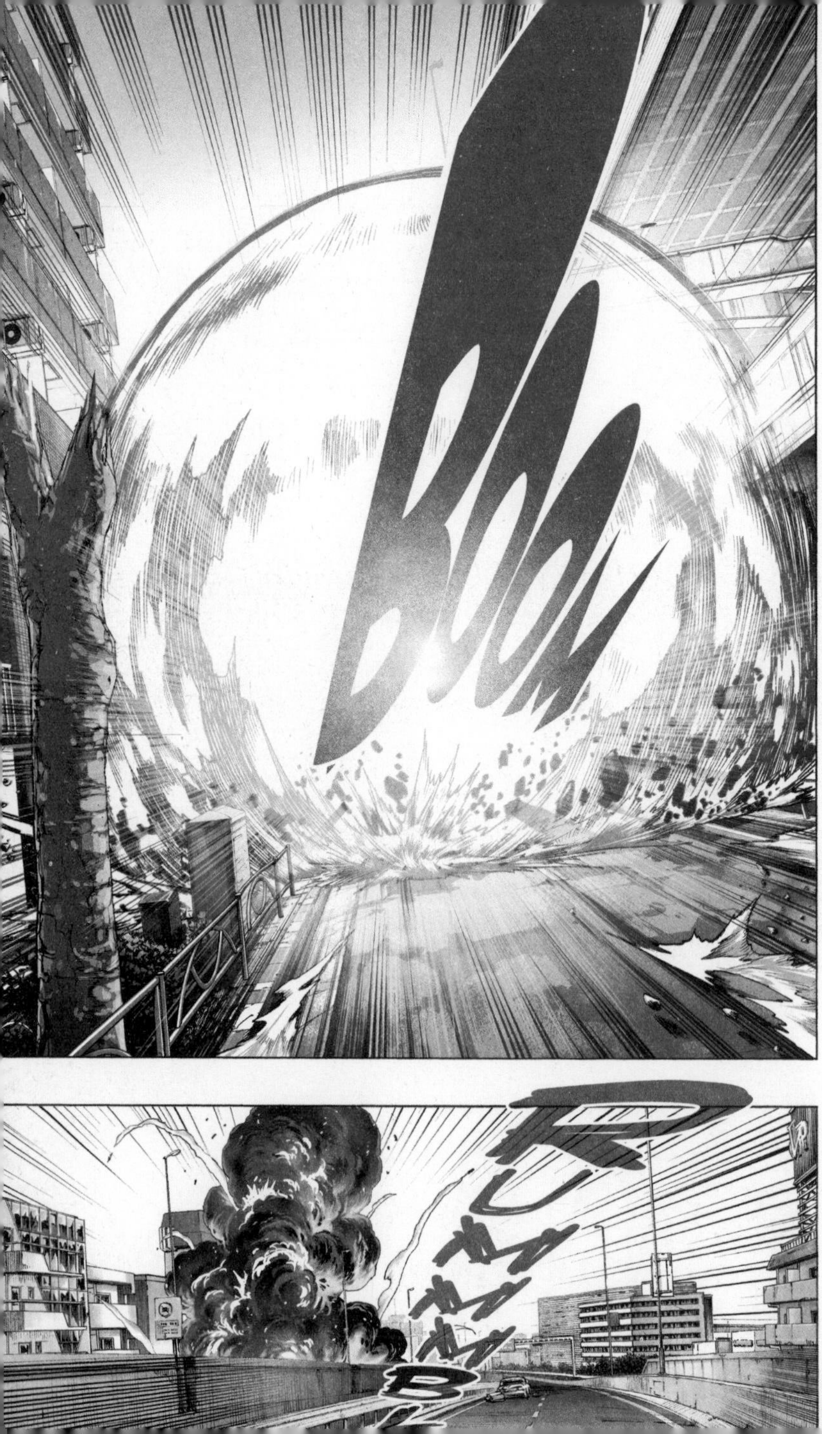

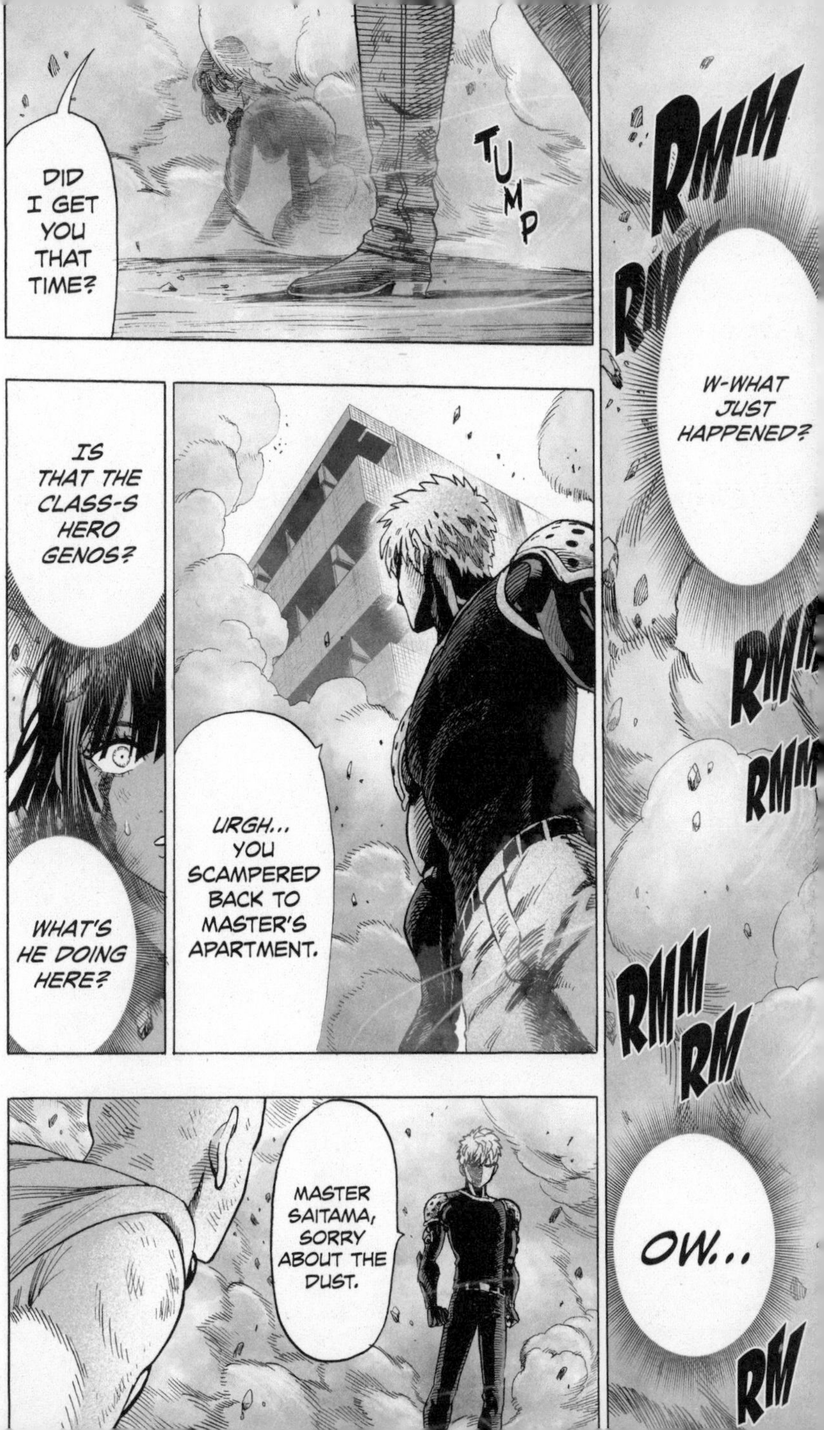
RMM
RMM
W-WHAT JUST HAPPENED?
RMM
RMM
RMM
RM
OW...
RM
TUMP
DID I GET YOU THAT TIME?
URGH... YOU SCAMPERED BACK TO MASTER'S APARTMENT.
IS THAT THE CLASS-S HERO GENOS?
WHAT'S HE DOING HERE?
MASTER SAITAMA, SORRY ABOUT THE DUST.

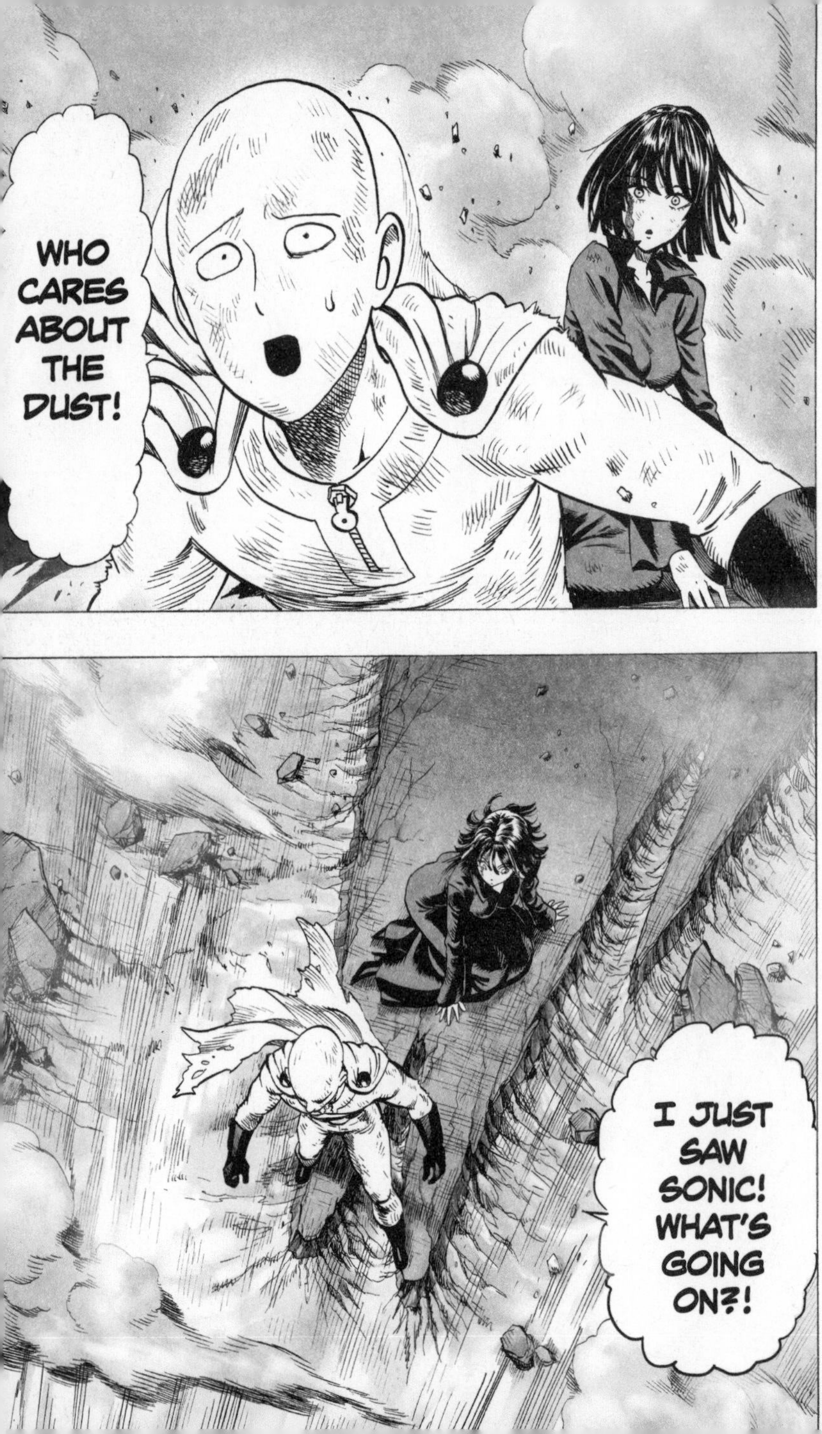
WHO CARES ABOUT THE DUST!
I JUST SAW SONIC! WHAT'S GOING ON?!

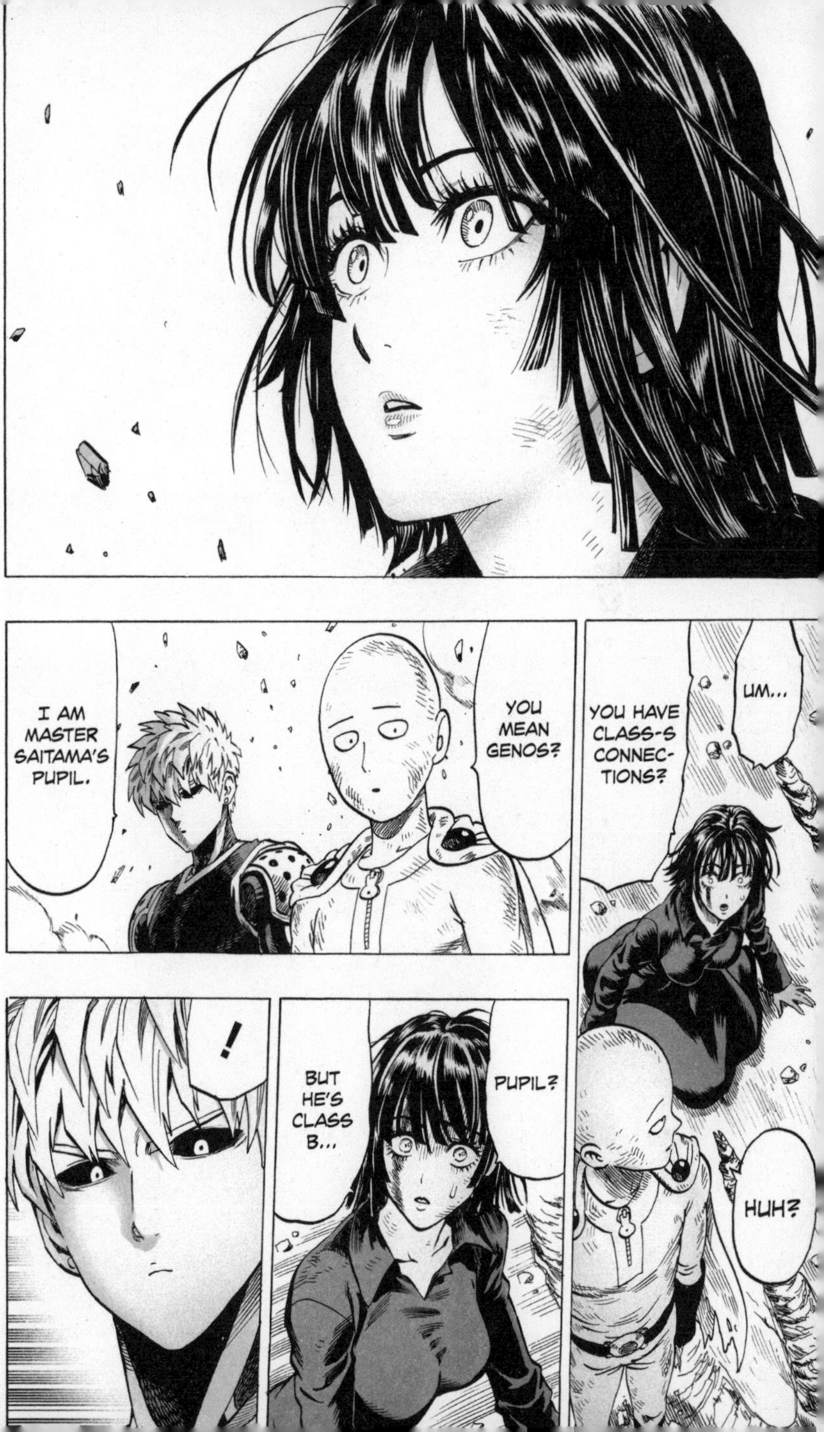
UM...
YOU HAVE CLASS-S CONNECTIONS?
HUH?
YOU MEAN GENOS?
I AM MASTER SAITAMA'S PUPIL.
PUPIL?
BUT HE'S CLASS B...
!

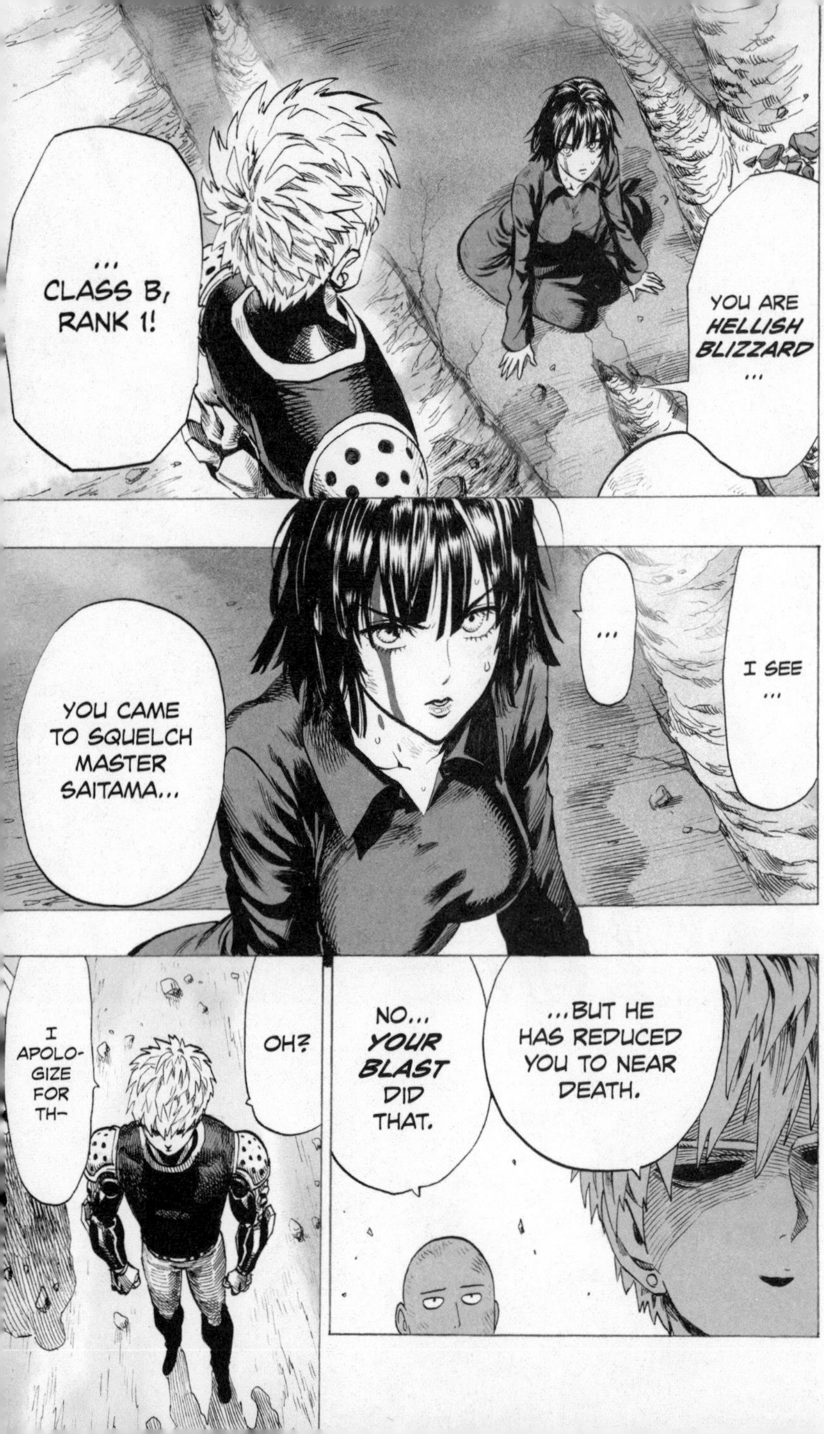
YOU ARE HELLISH BLIZZARD ...
... CLASS B, RANK 1!
...
I SEE ...
YOU CAME TO SQUELCH MASTER SAITAMA...
...BUT HE HAS REDUCED YOU TO NEAR DEATH.
NO... YOUR BLAST DID THAT.
OH?
I APOLOGIZE FOR TH-

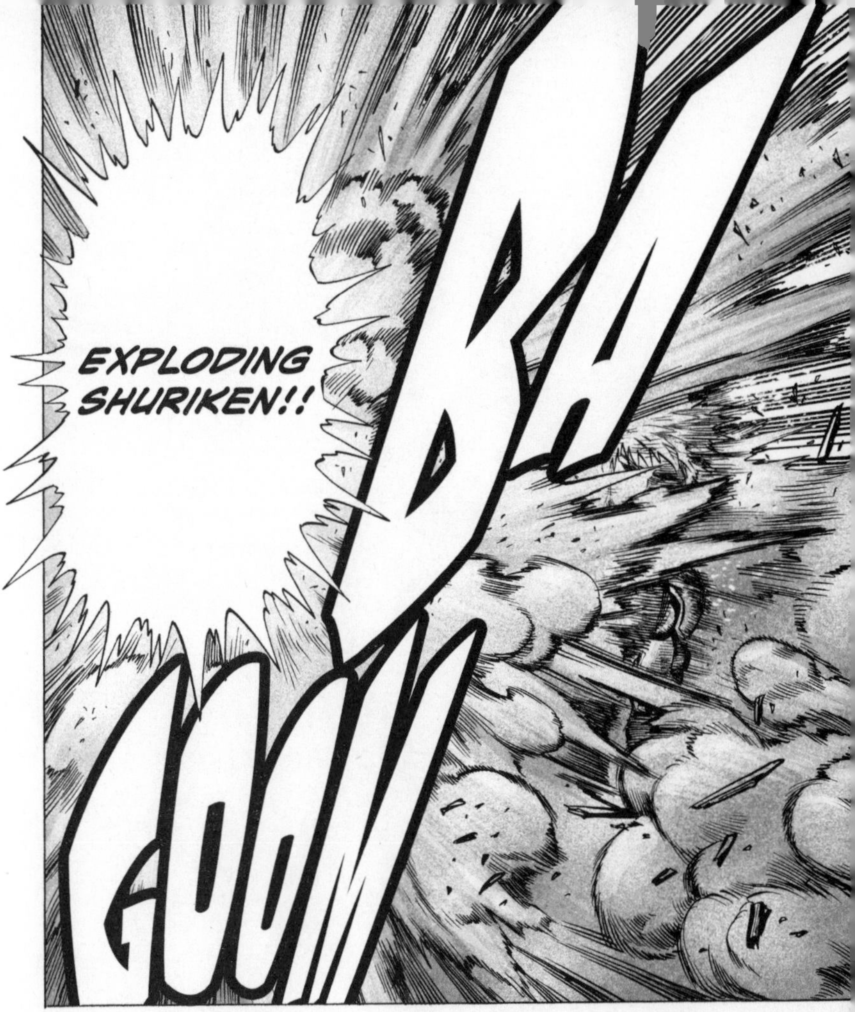
EXPLODING SHURIKEN!!
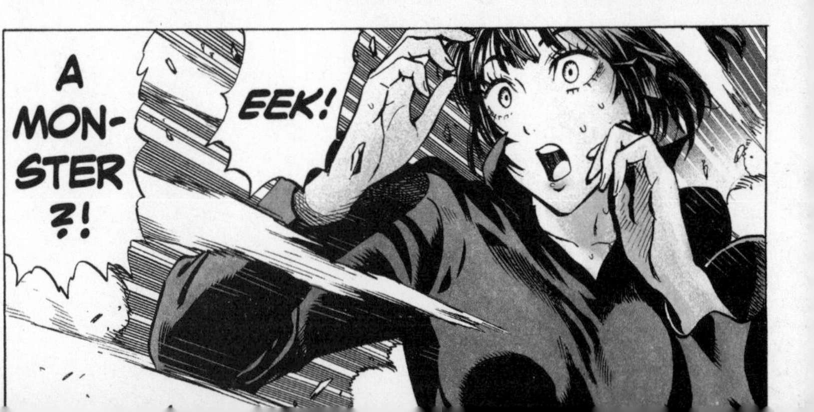
EEK!
A MON-STER?!

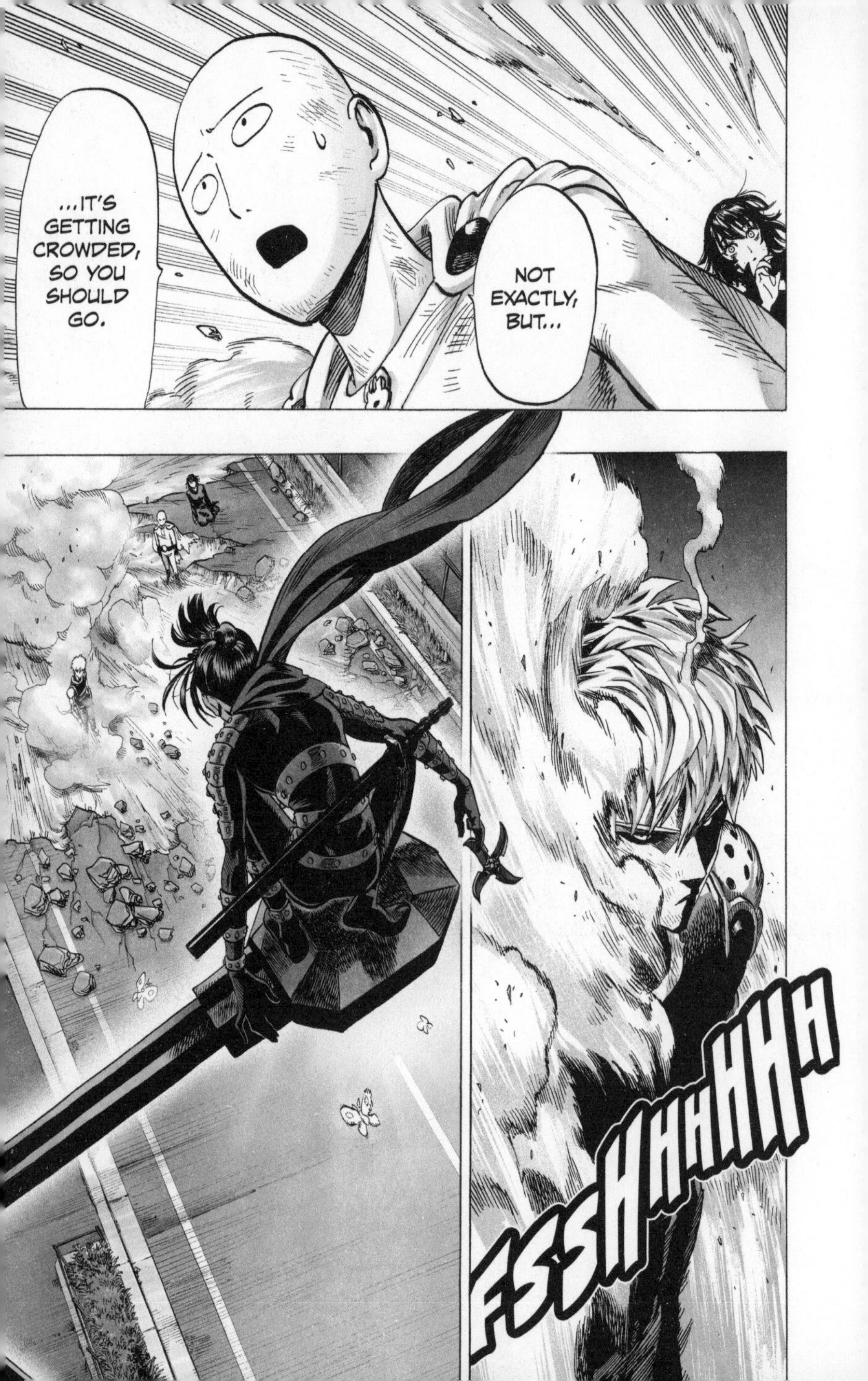
NOT EXACTLY, BUT...
...IT'S GETTING CROWDED, SO YOU SHOULD GO.
FSSHHHHHHH

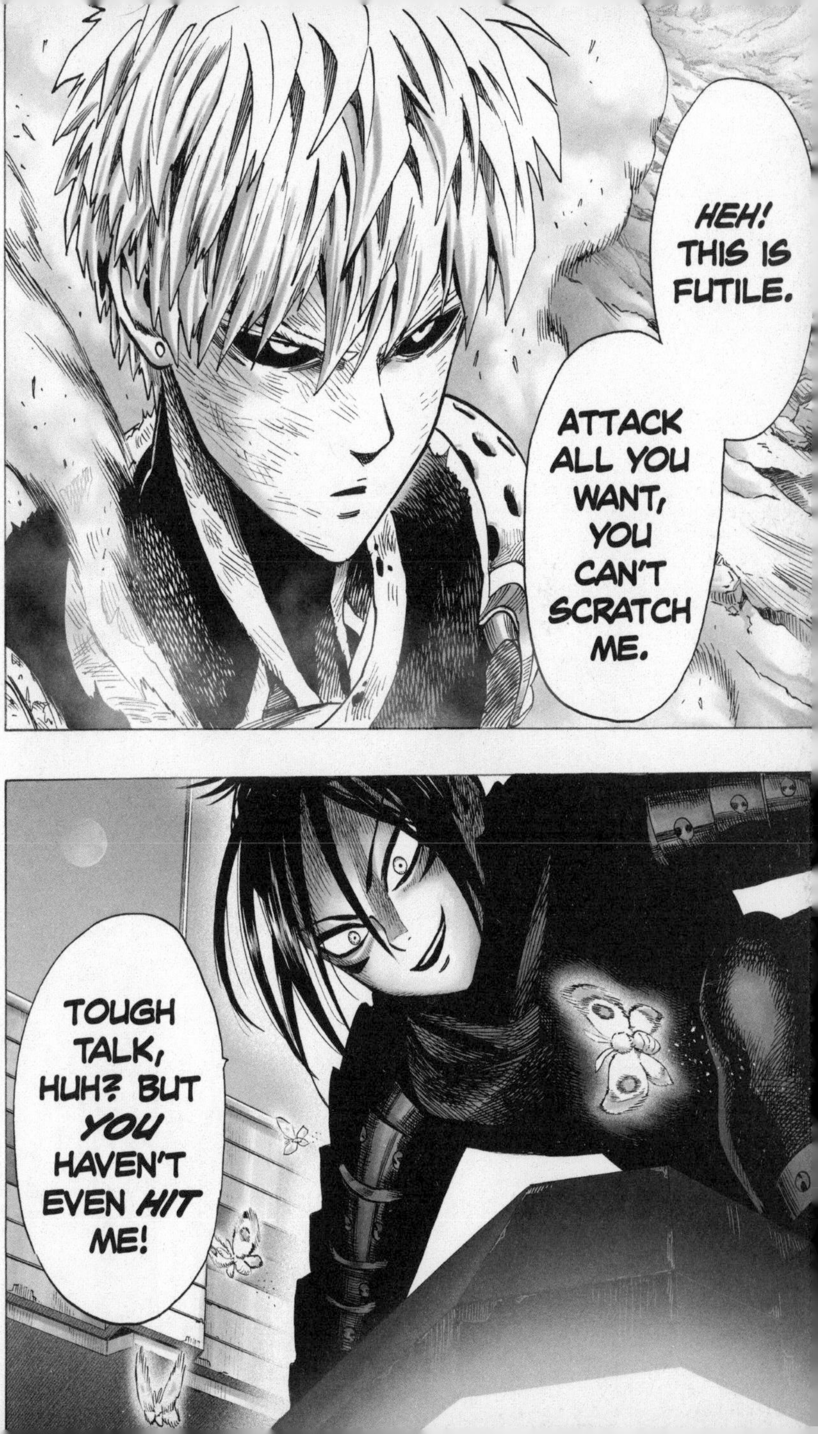
HEH! THIS IS FUTILE.
ATTACK ALL YOU WANT, YOU CAN'T SCRATCH ME.
TOUGH TALK, HUH? BUT YOU HAVEN'T EVEN HIT ME!

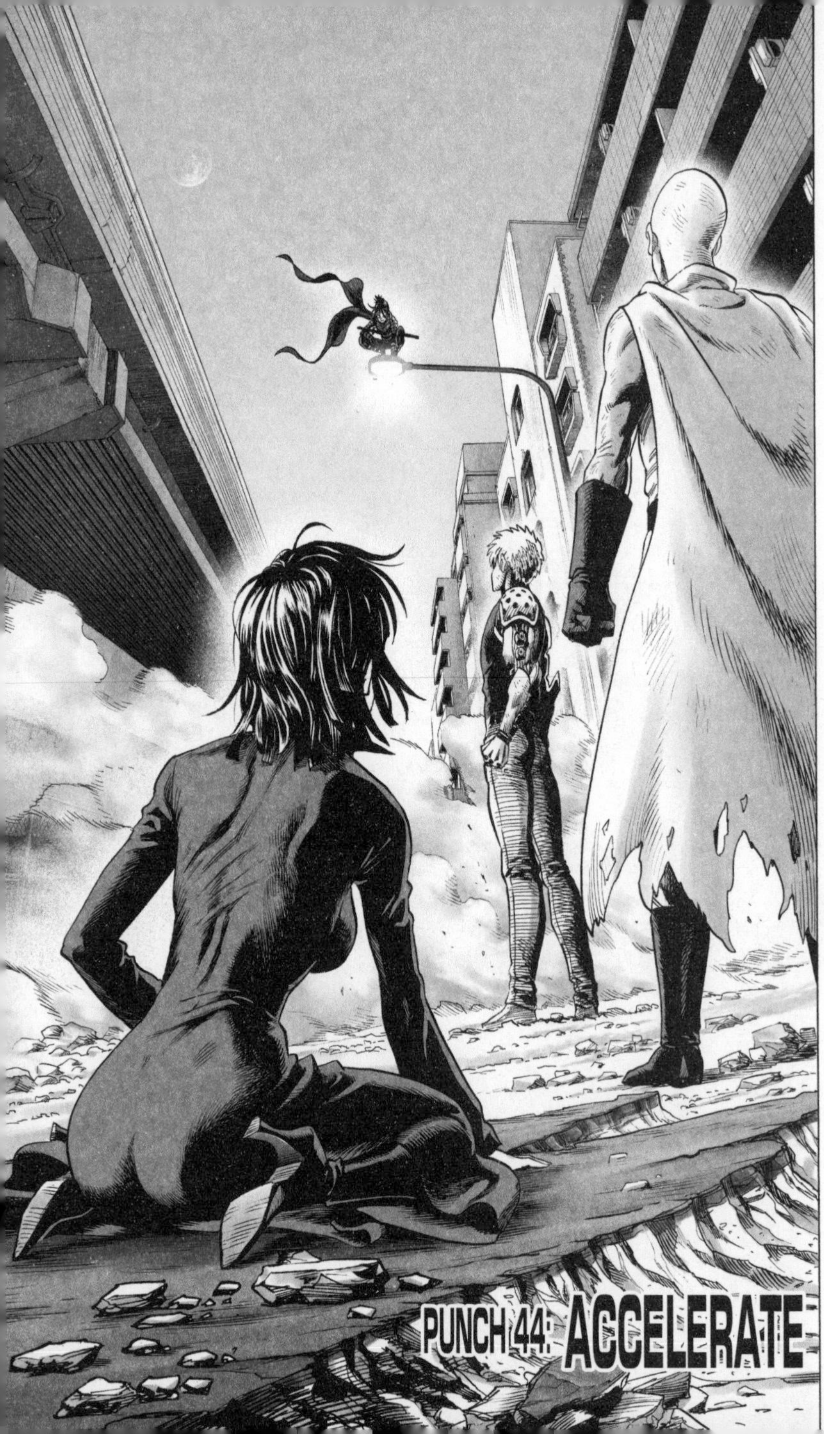
PUNCH 44: ACCELERATE

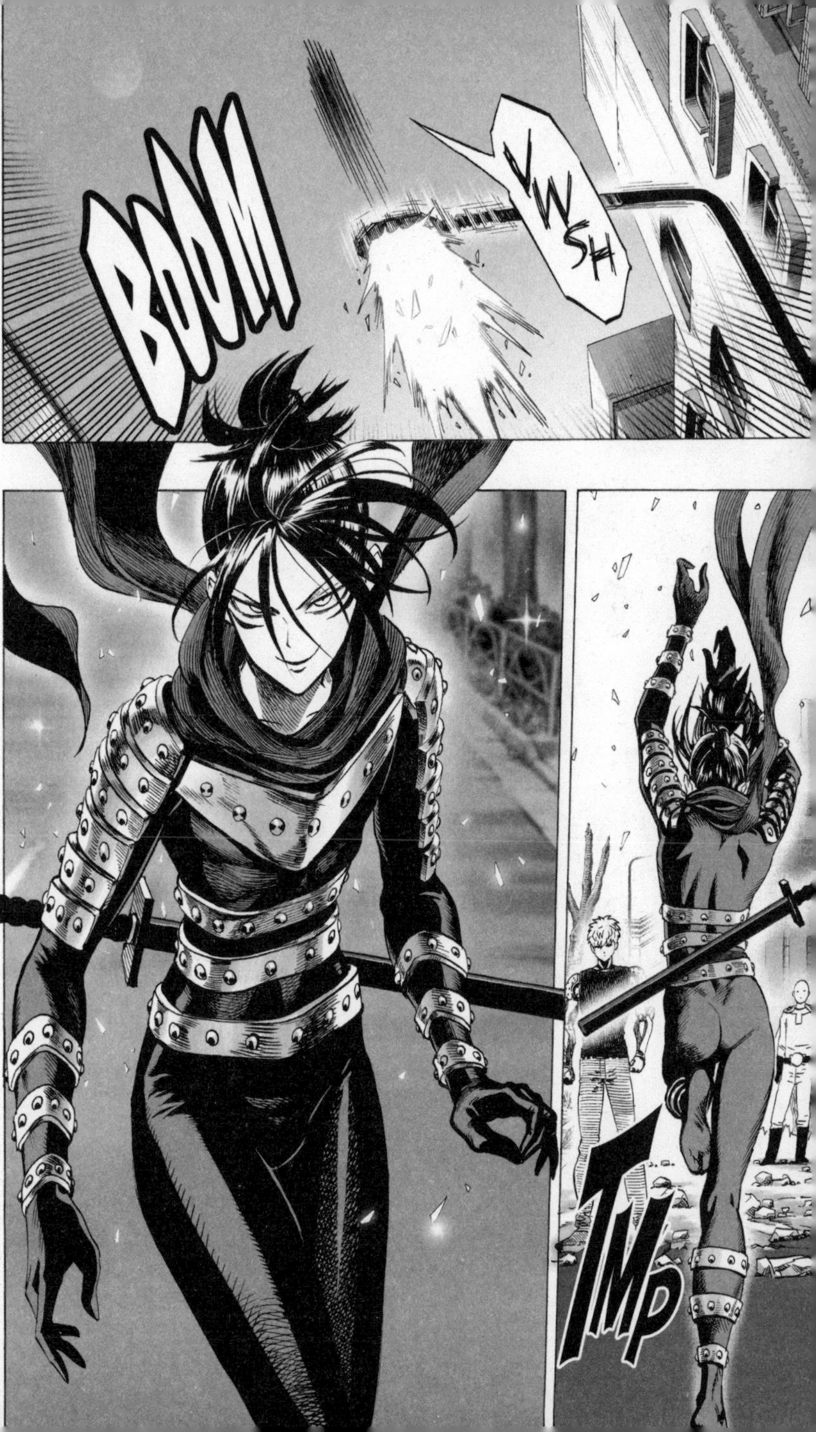
VWSH
BOOM
TMP

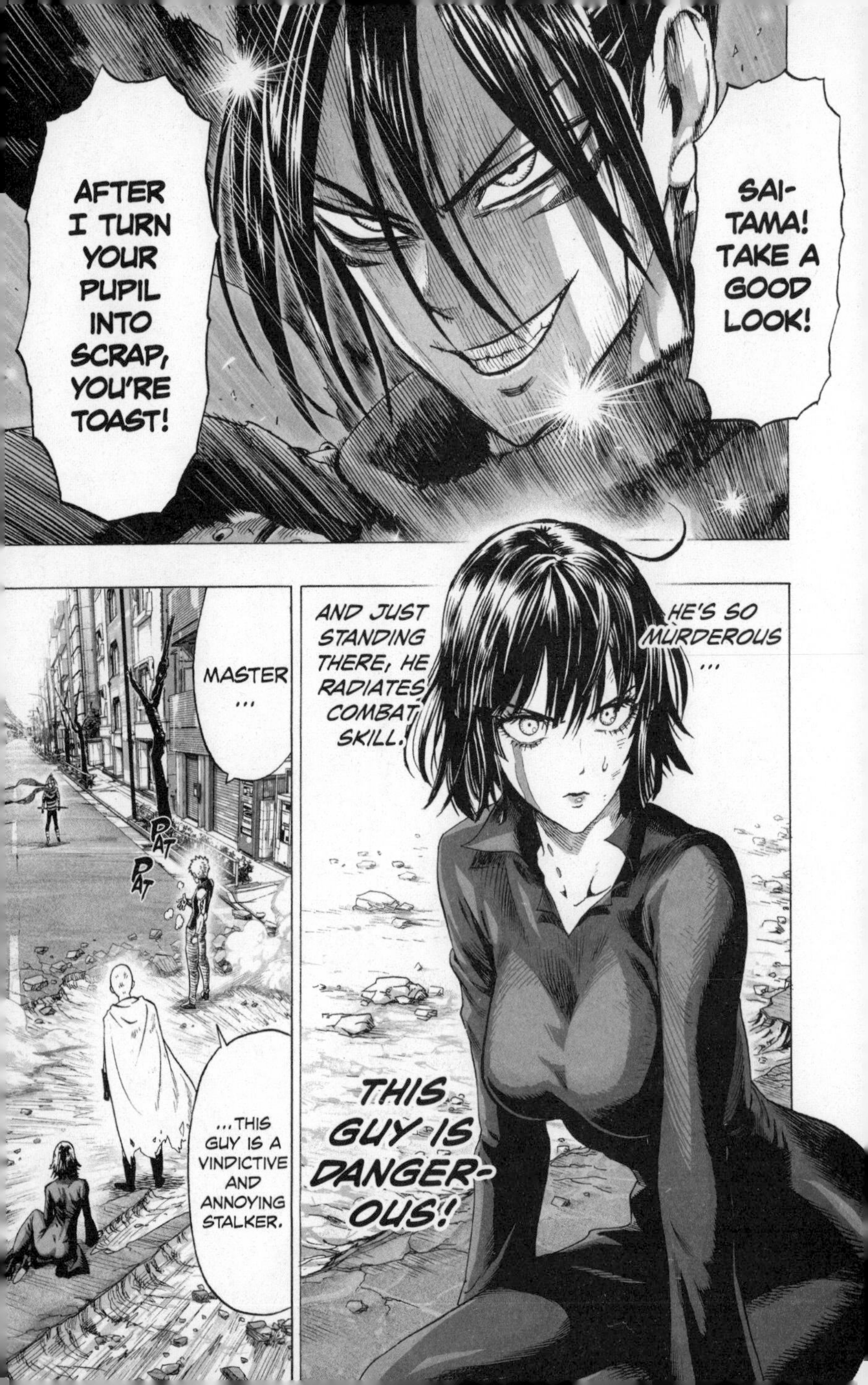
SAI-TAMA! TAKE A GOOD LOOK!
AFTER I TURN YOUR PUPIL INTO SCRAP, YOU'RE TOAST!
HE'S SO MURDEROUS...
AND JUST STANDING THERE, HE RADIATES COMBAT SKILL.
THIS GUY IS DANGER-OUS!
MASTER...
PAT
PAT
...THIS GUY IS A VINDICTIVE AND ANNOYING STALKER.

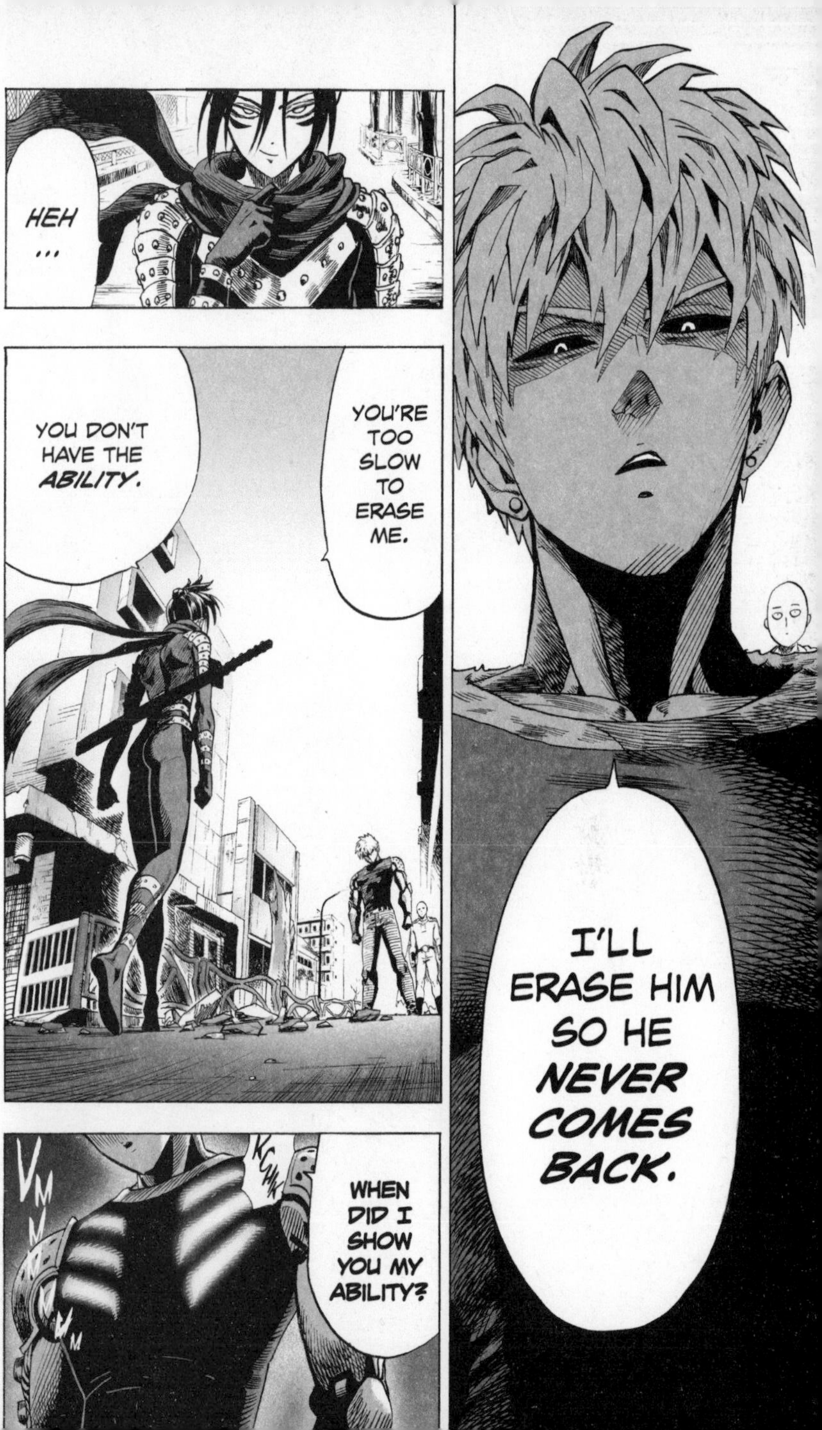
I'LL ERASE HIM SO HE *NEVER COMES BACK.*
HEH ...
YOU'RE TOO SLOW TO ERASE ME.
YOU DON'T HAVE THE *ABILITY.*
KCHAK
WHEN DID I SHOW YOU MY ABILITY?

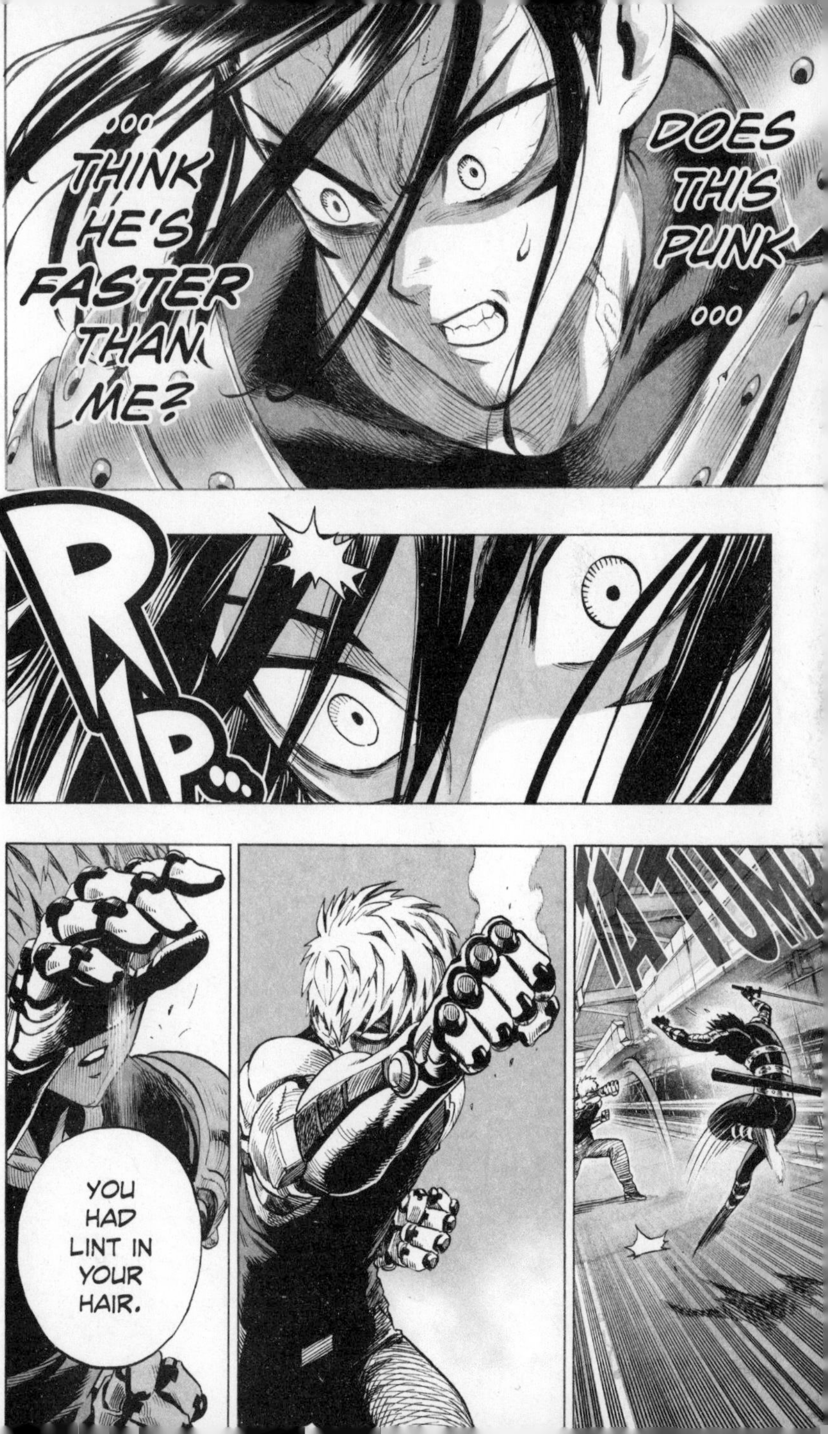
DOES THIS PUNK...
...THINK HE'S FASTER THAN ME?
RIP...
YOU HAD LINT IN YOUR HAIR.

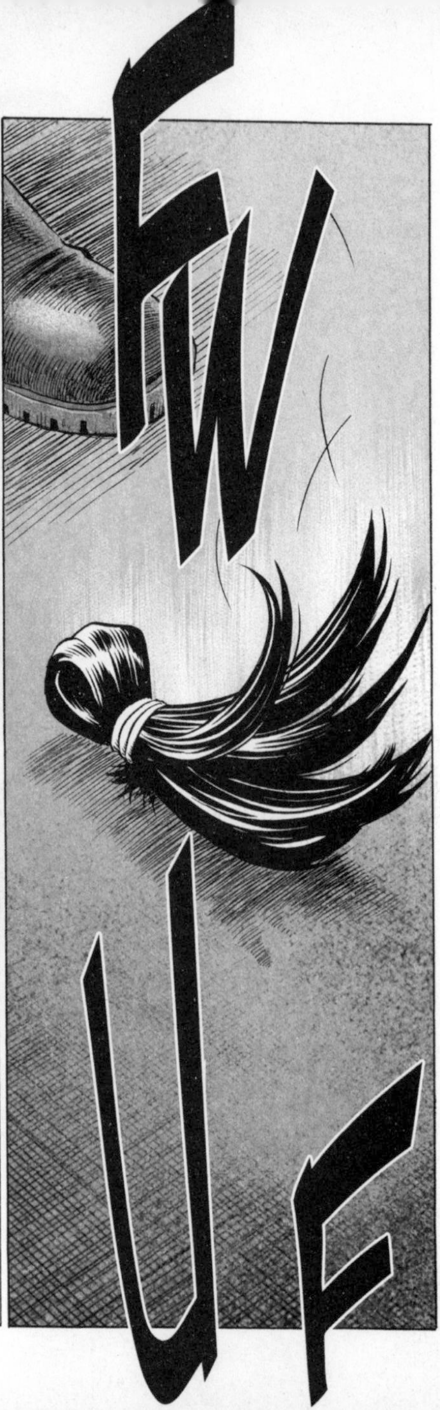

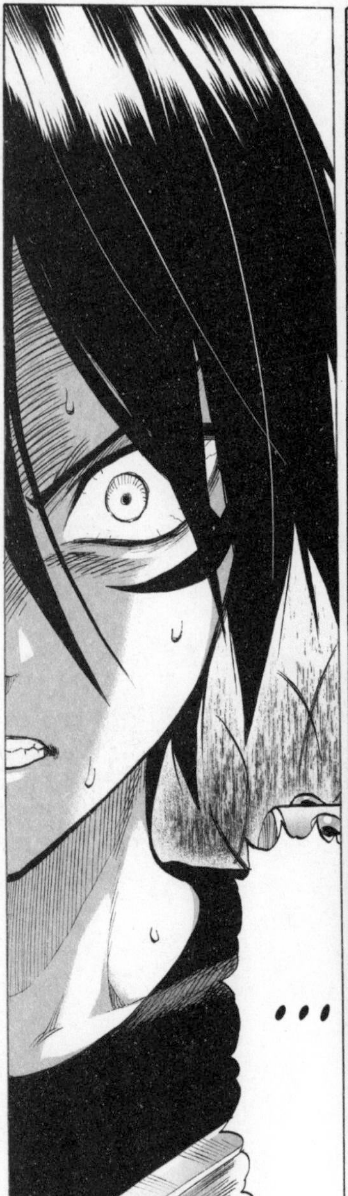
...

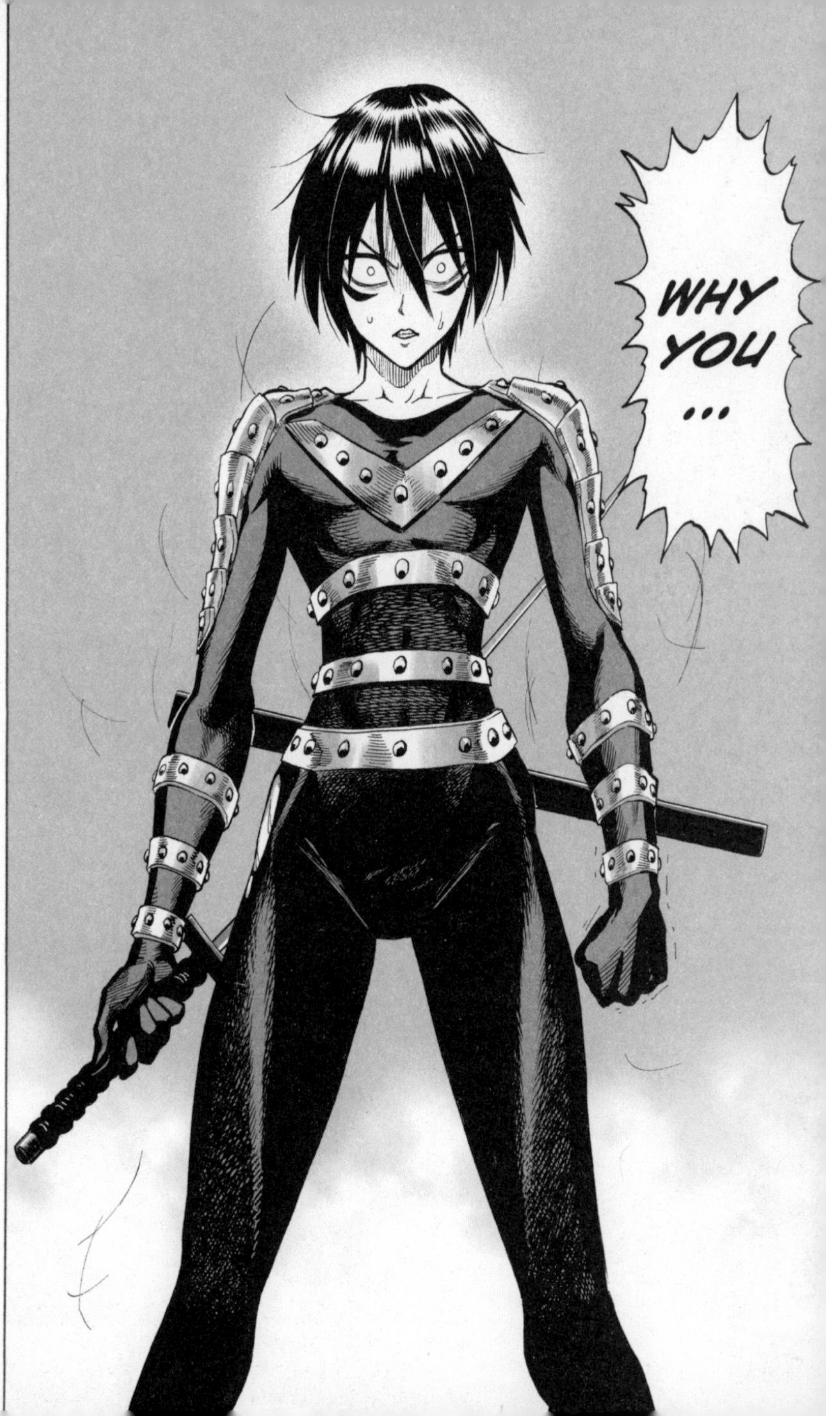
WHY YOU ...

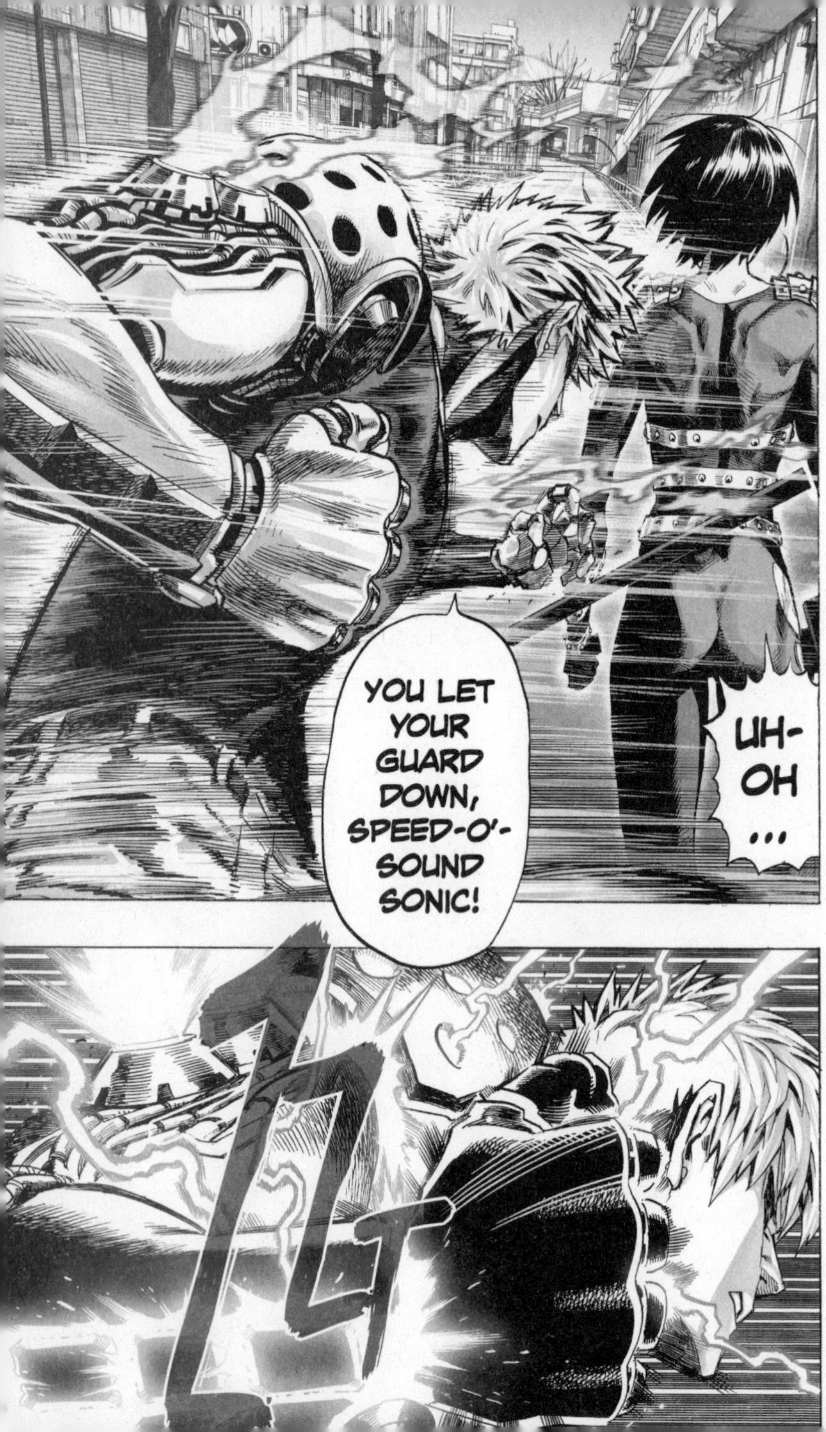
UH-OH ...
YOU LET YOUR GUARD DOWN, SPEED-O'-SOUND SONIC!

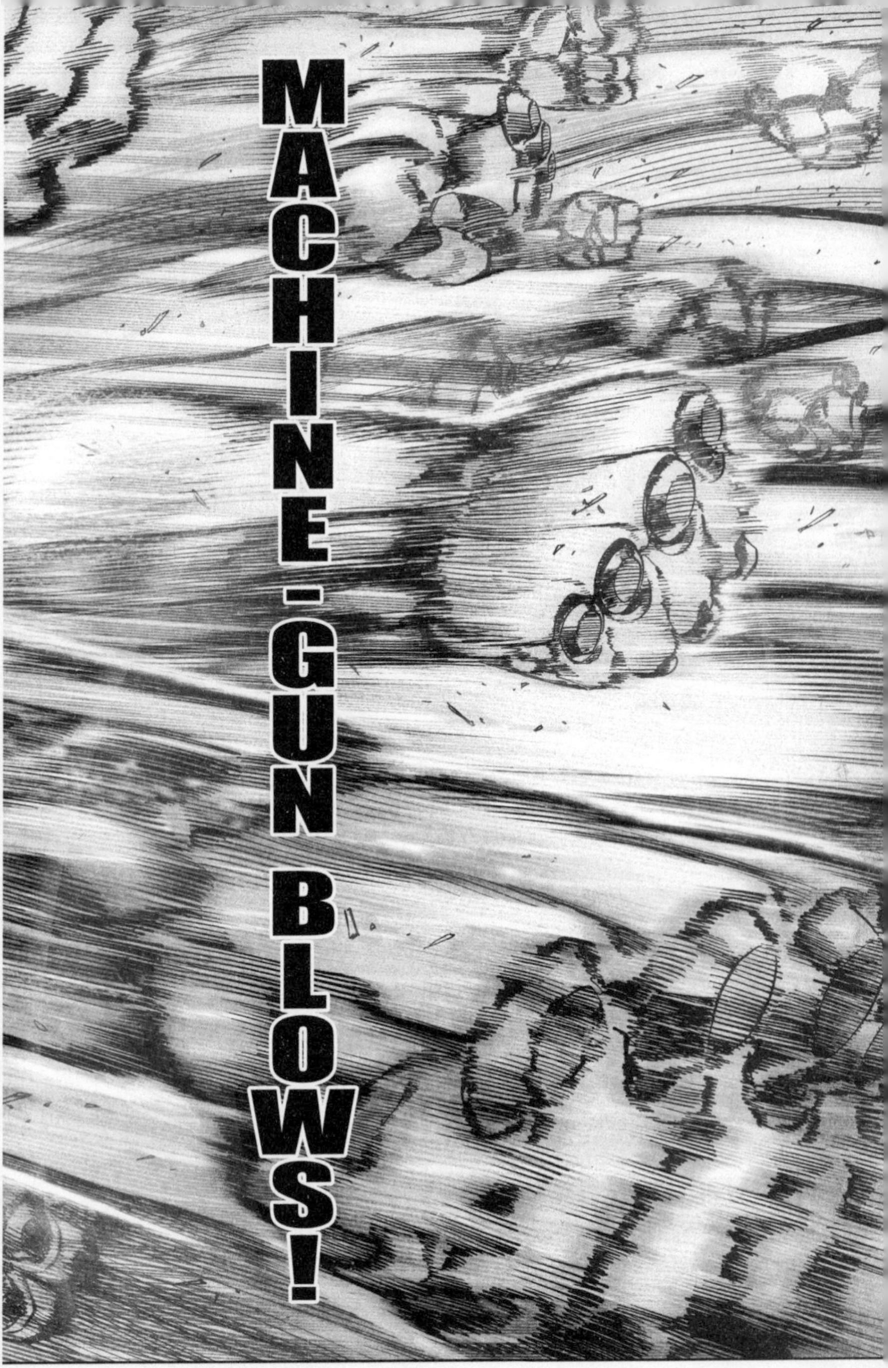
MACHINE-GUN BLOWS!

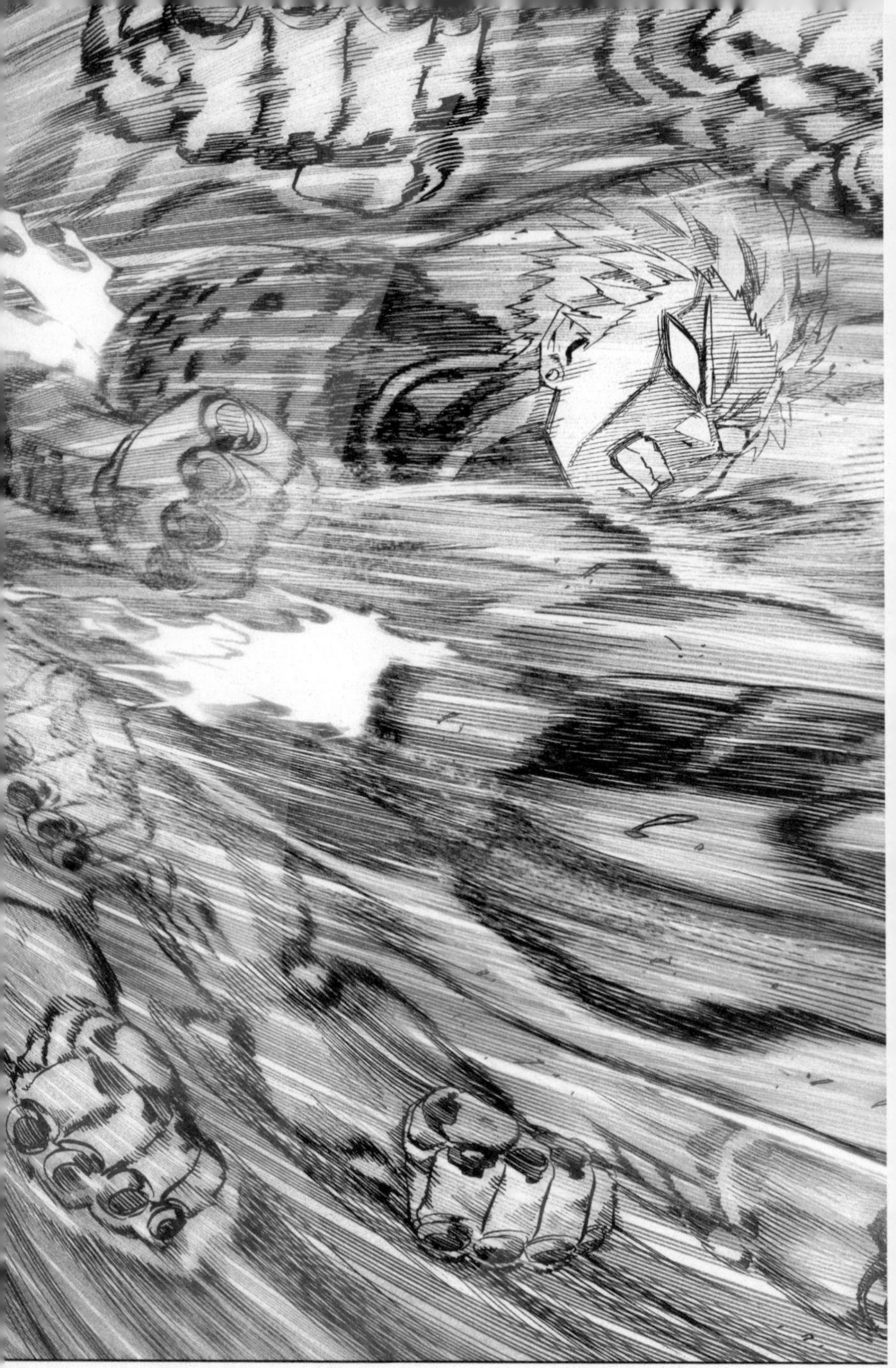

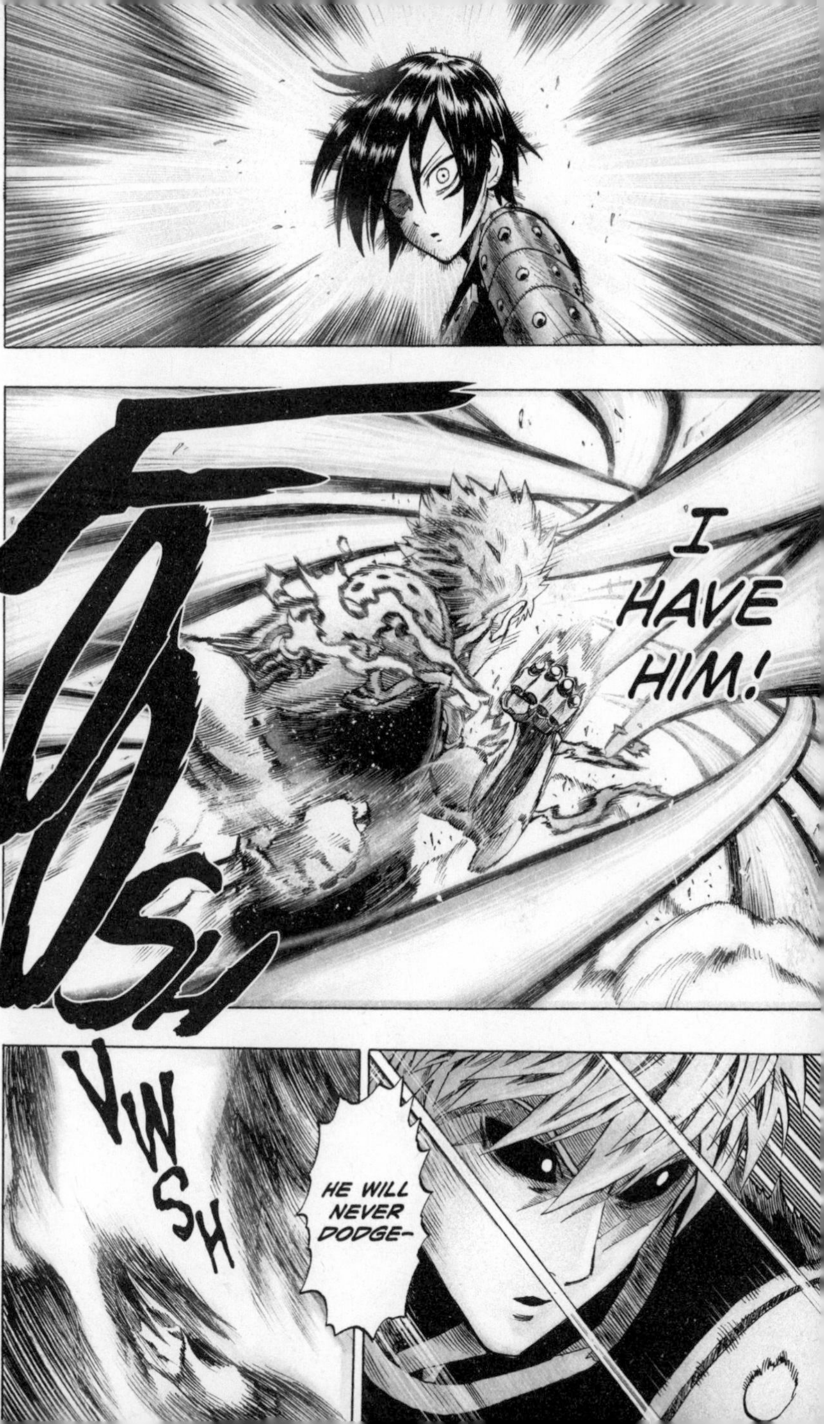
I HAVE HIM!
SHUSH
HE WILL NEVER DODGE-
VWSH

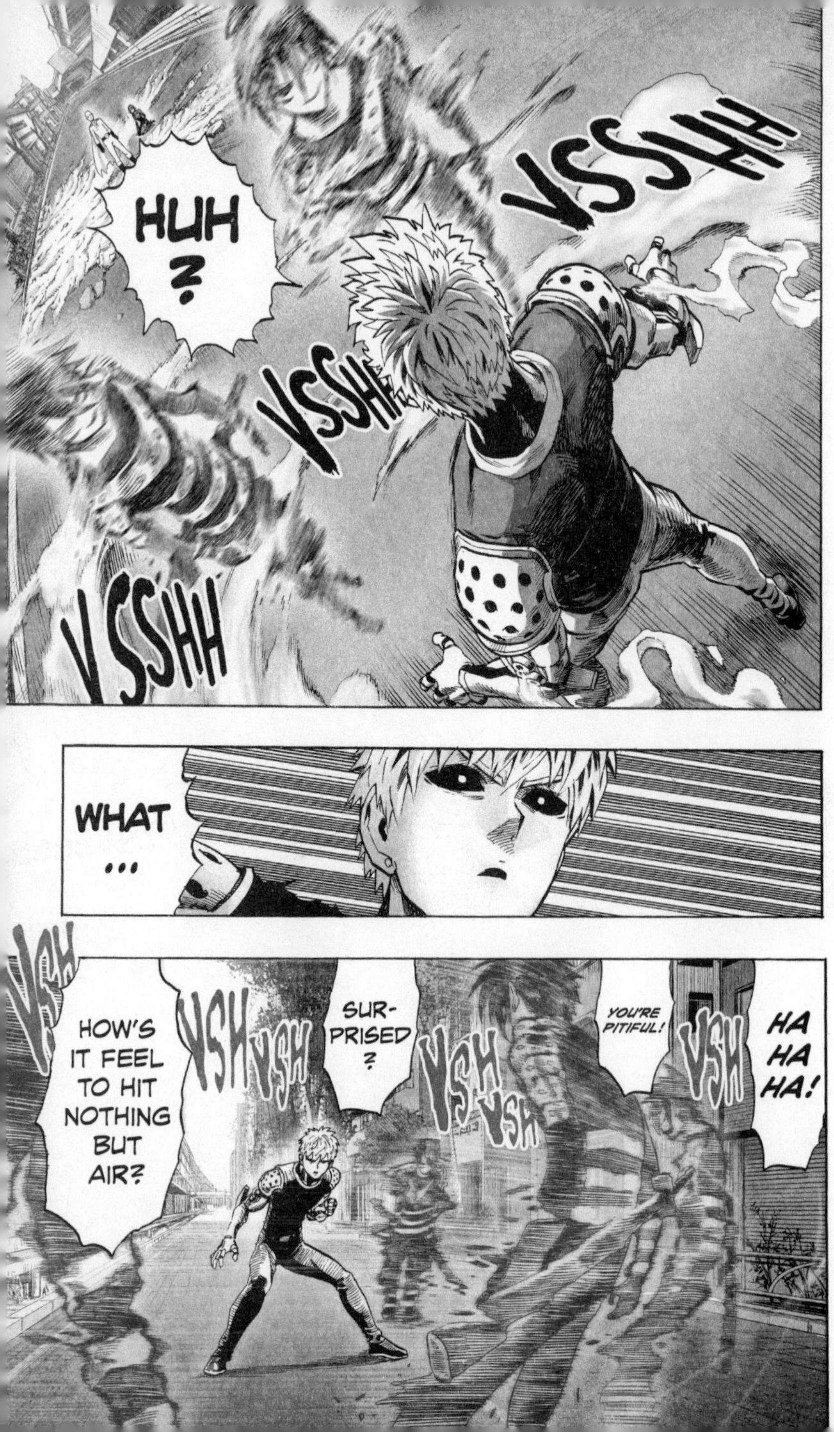
VSSHH
HUH?
VSSHH
VSSHH
WHAT...
HA HA HA!
VSH
YOU'RE PITIFUL!
VSH
VSH
SUR-PRISED?
VSH
VSH
HOW'S IT FEEL TO HIT NOTHING BUT AIR?
VSH

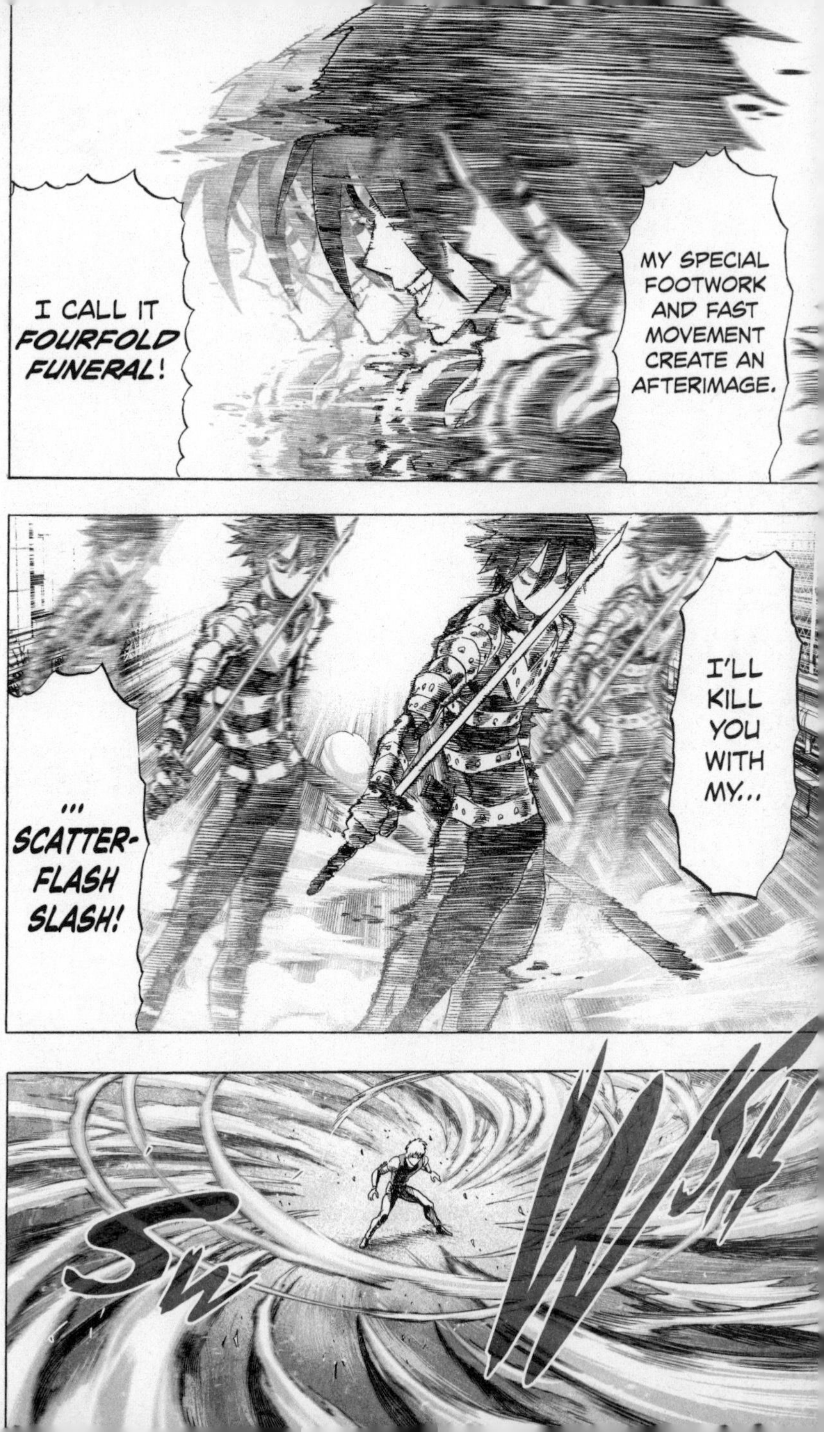
MY SPECIAL FOOTWORK AND FAST MOVEMENT CREATE AN AFTERIMAGE.
I CALL IT *FOURFOLD FUNERAL*!
I'LL KILL YOU WITH MY...
...SCATTER-FLASH SLASH!

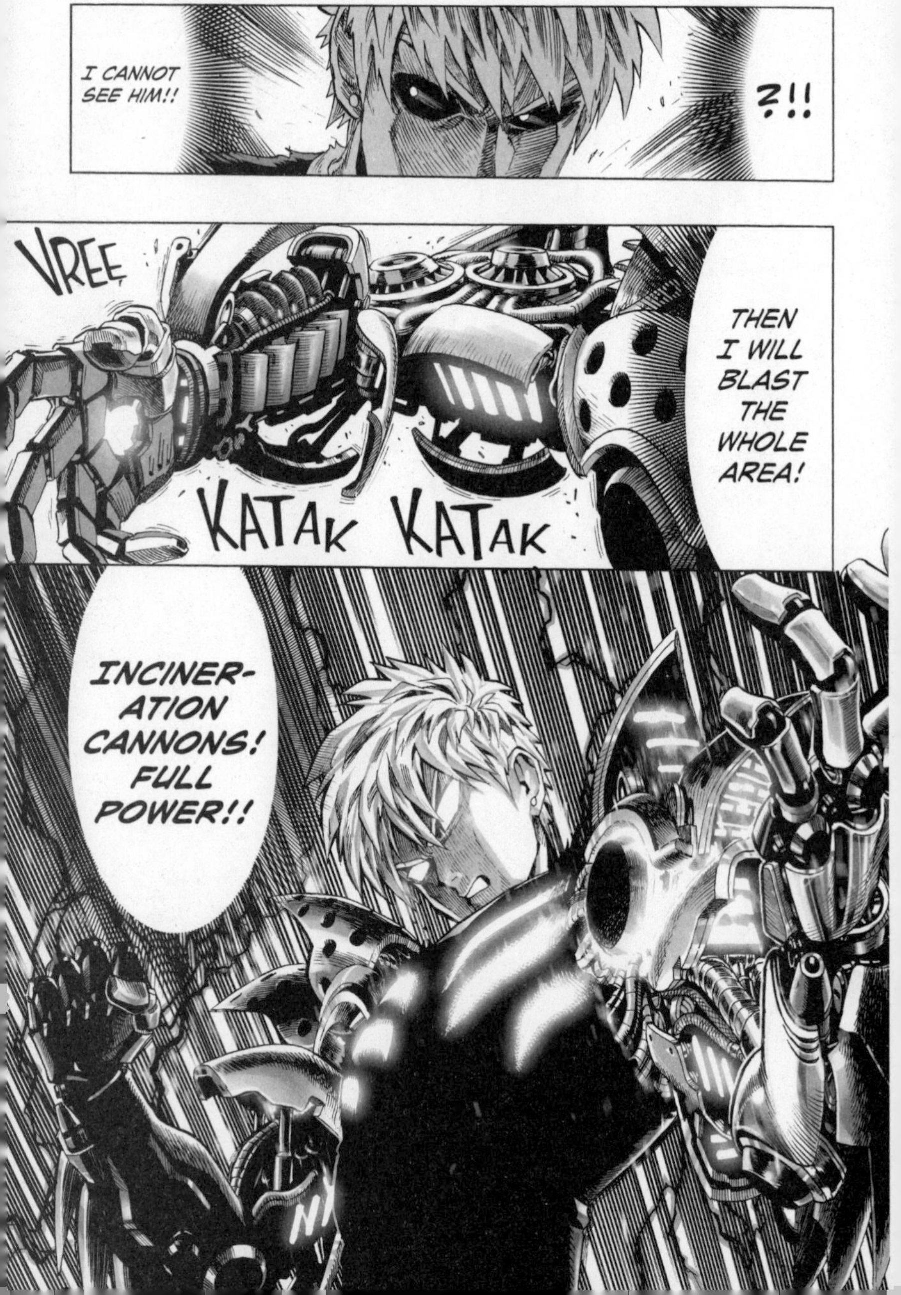
?!!
I CANNOT SEE HIM!!
THEN I WILL BLAST THE WHOLE AREA!
VREE
KATAK KATAK
INCINER-ATION CANNONS! FULL POWER!!

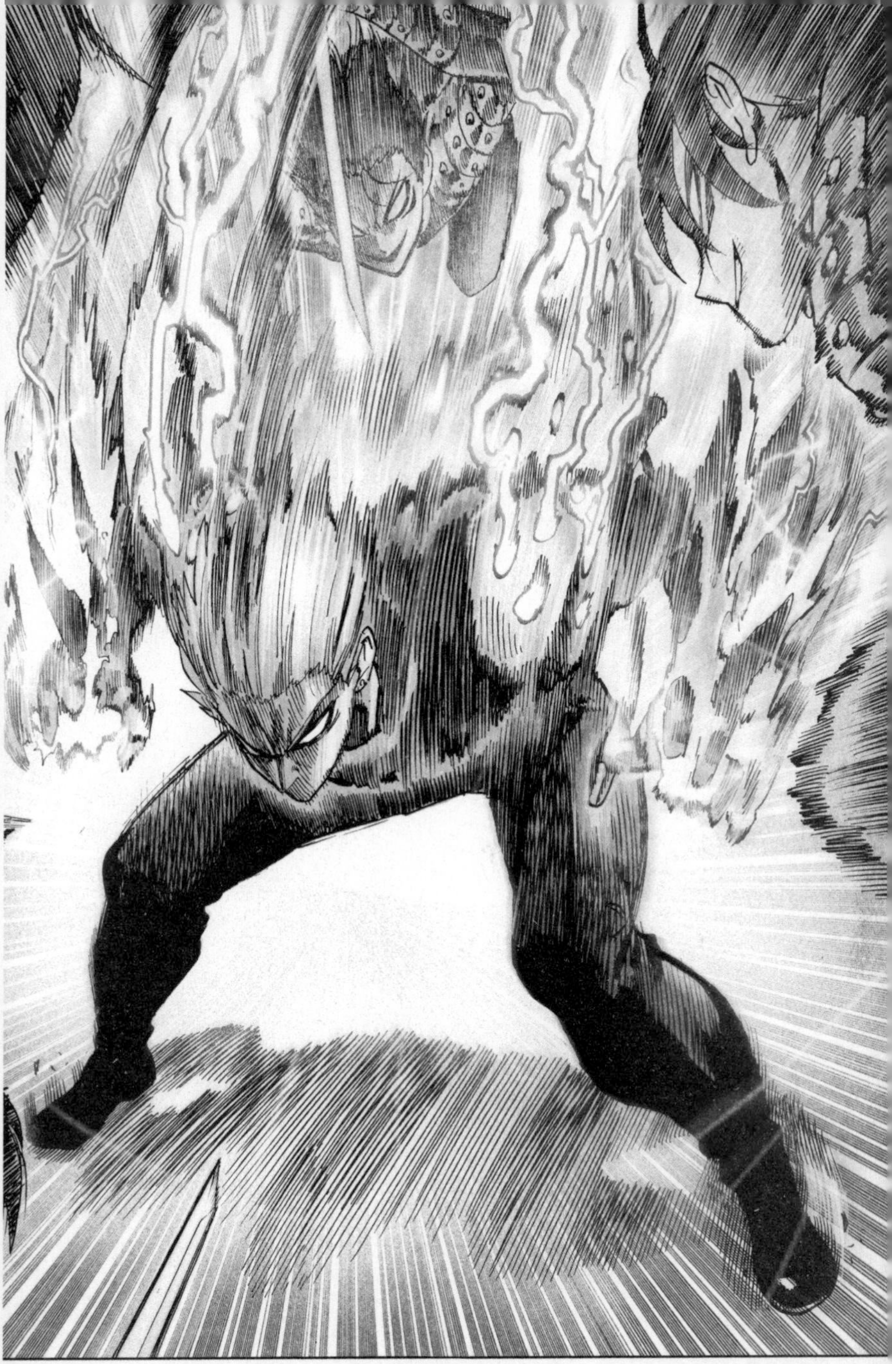

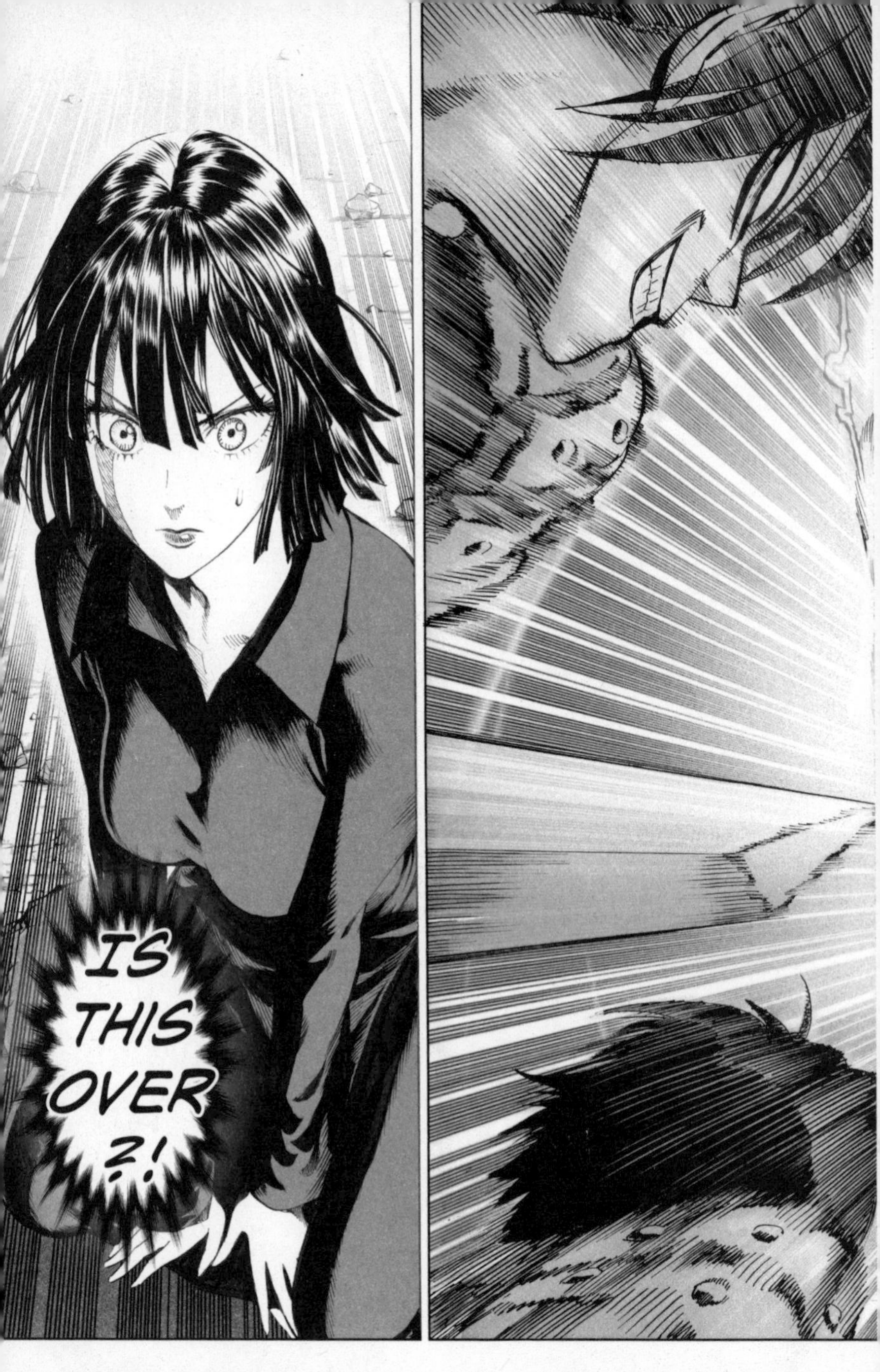
IS THIS OVER ?!

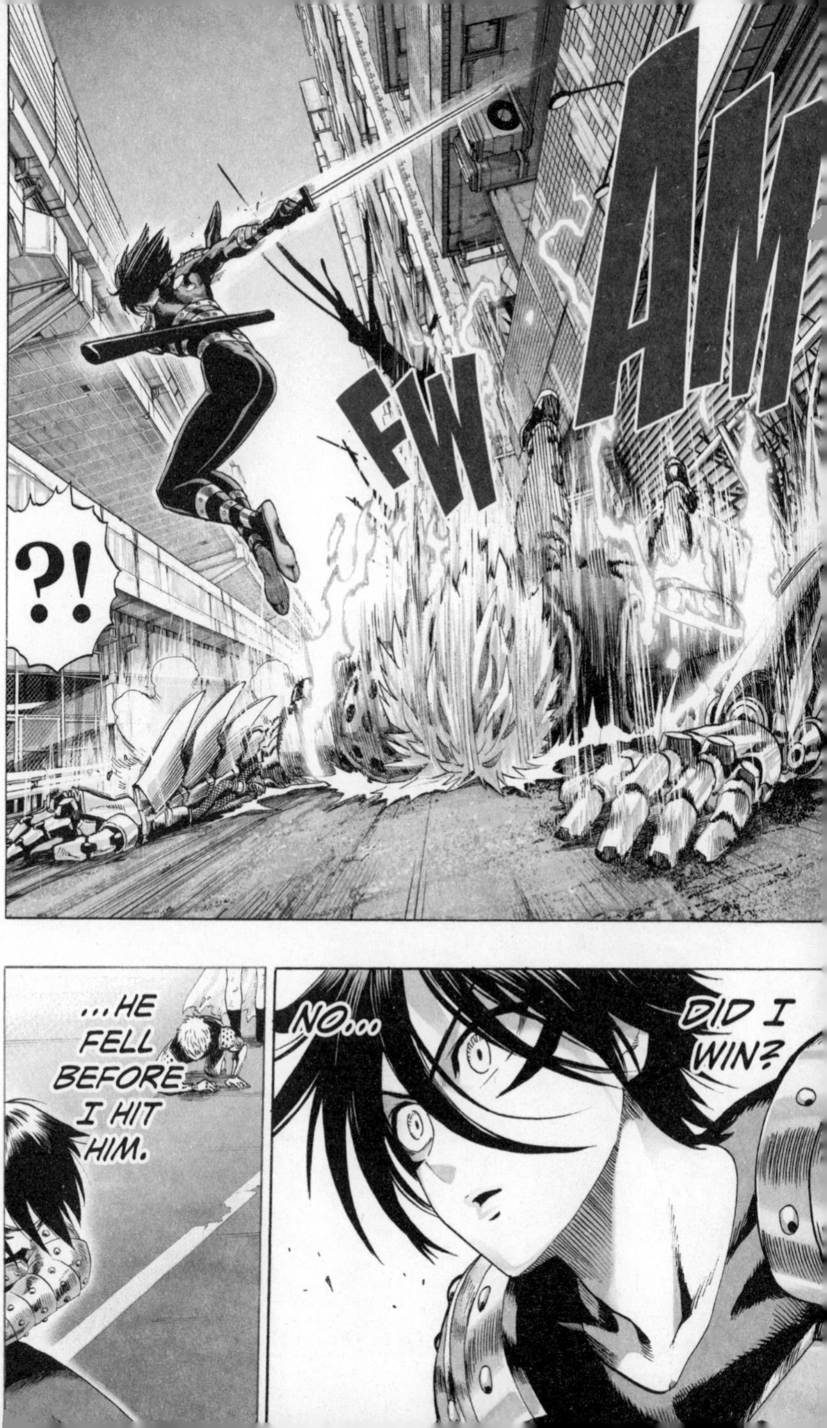
FWAM
?!
DID I WIN?
NO...
...HE FELL BEFORE I HIT HIM.

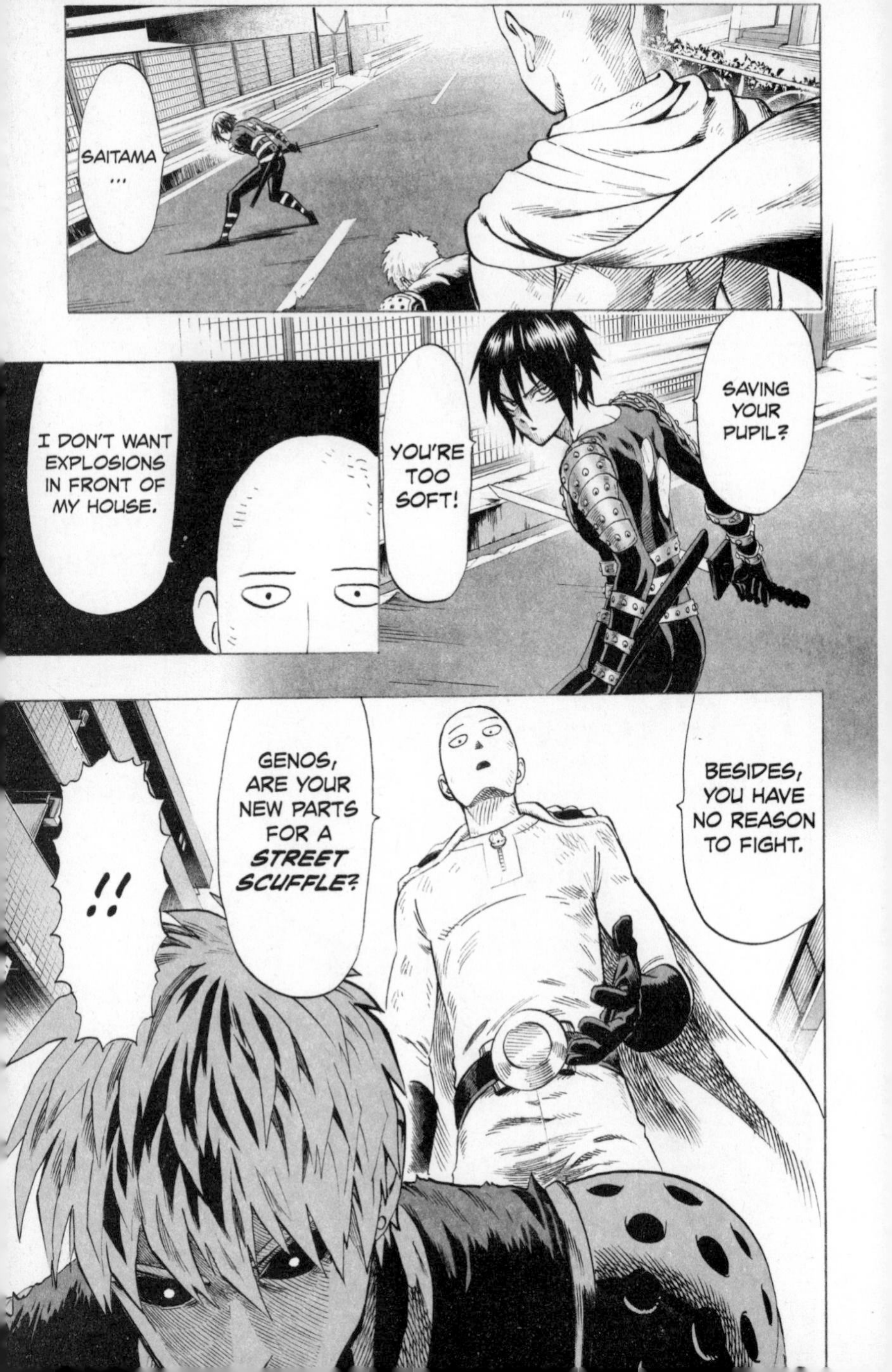
SAITAMA ...
SAVING YOUR PUPIL?
YOU'RE TOO SOFT!
I DON'T WANT EXPLOSIONS IN FRONT OF MY HOUSE.
BESIDES, YOU HAVE NO REASON TO FIGHT.
GENOS, ARE YOUR NEW PARTS FOR A *STREET SCUFFLE*?
!!

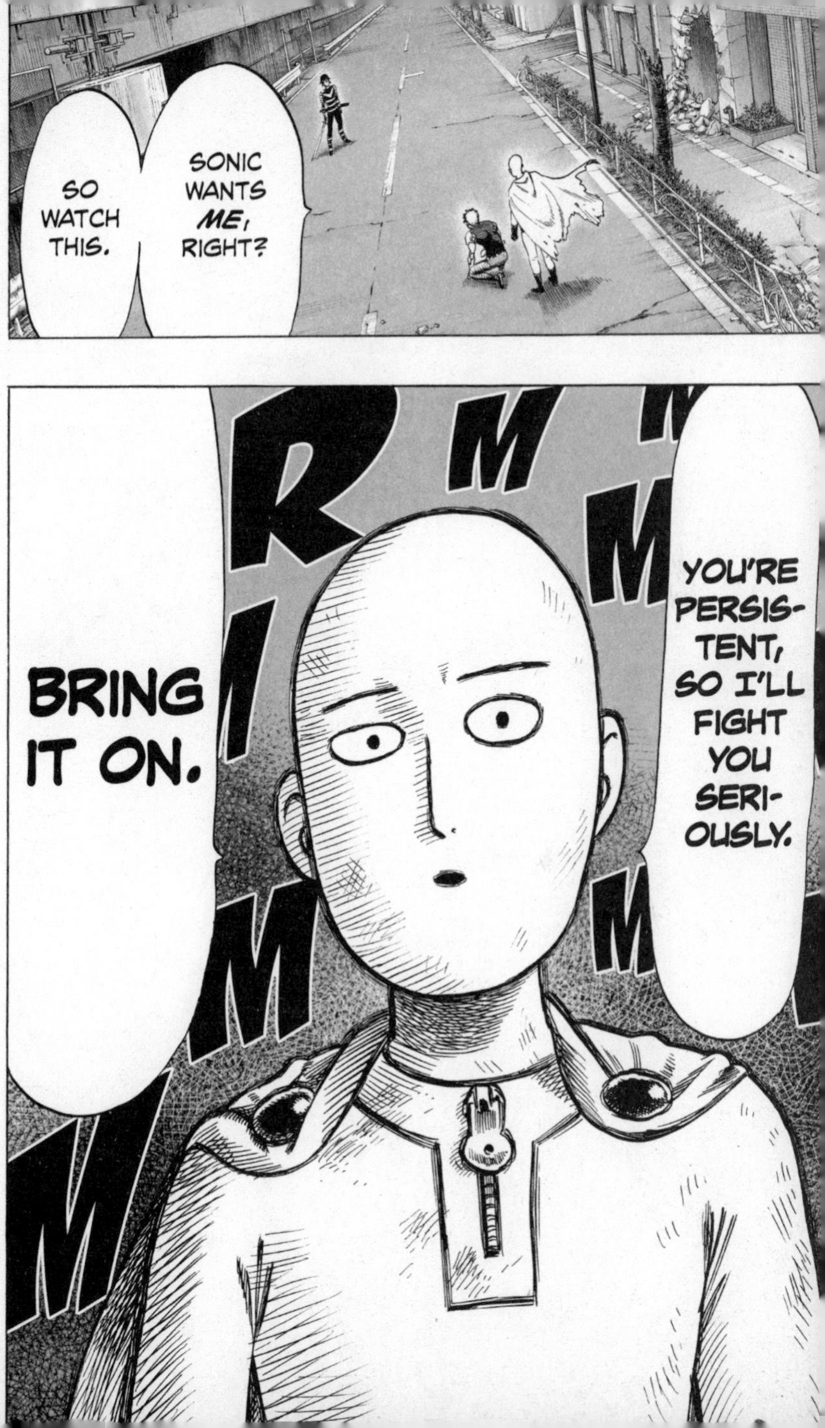
SONIC WANTS *ME*, RIGHT?
SO WATCH THIS.
YOU'RE PERSISTENT, SO I'LL FIGHT YOU SERIOUSLY.
BRING IT ON.

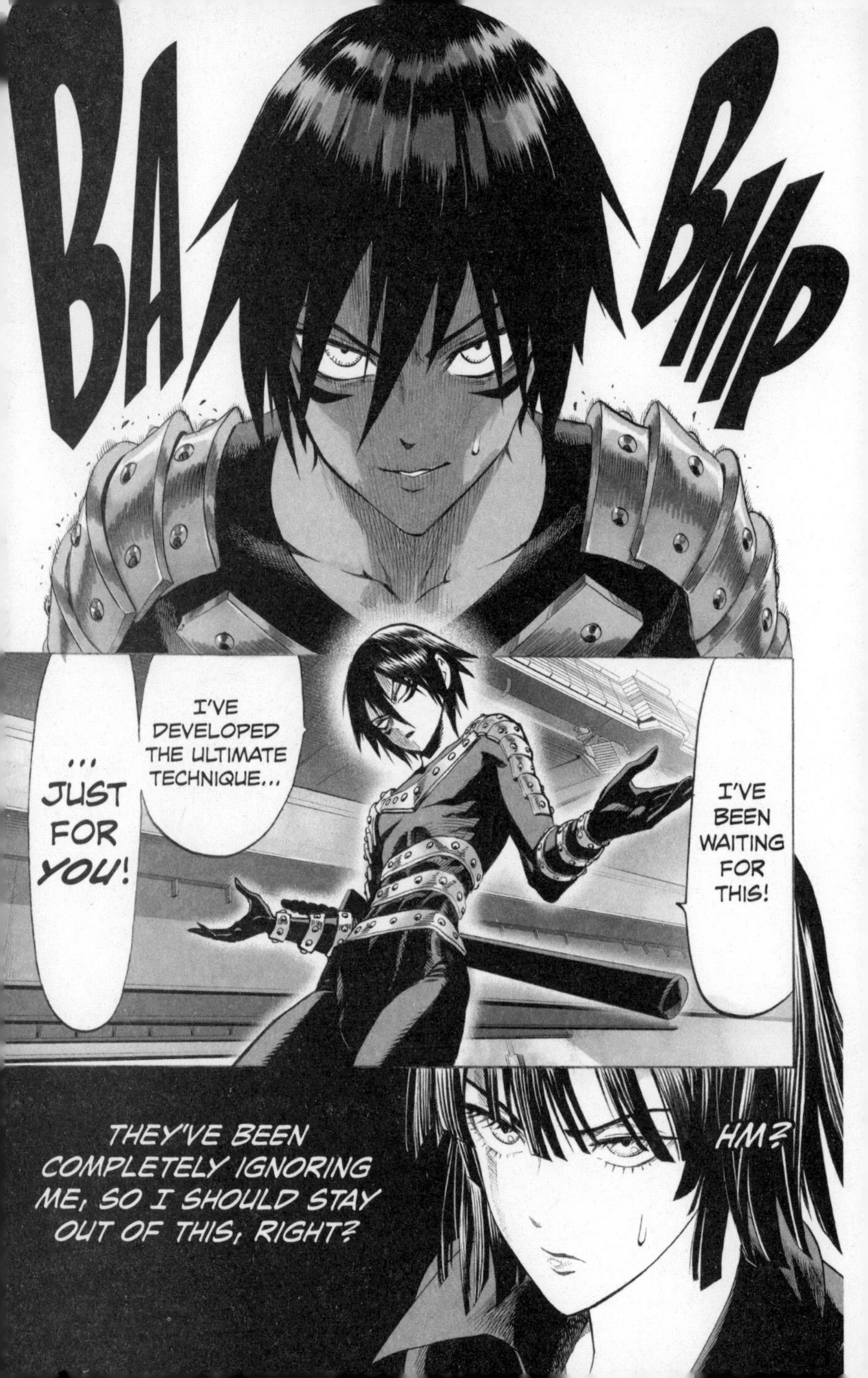
BA
BMP
I'VE BEEN WAITING FOR THIS!
I'VE DEVELOPED THE ULTIMATE TECHNIQUE...
... JUST FOR YOU!
HM?
THEY'VE BEEN COMPLETELY IGNORING ME, SO I SHOULD STAY OUT OF THIS, RIGHT?

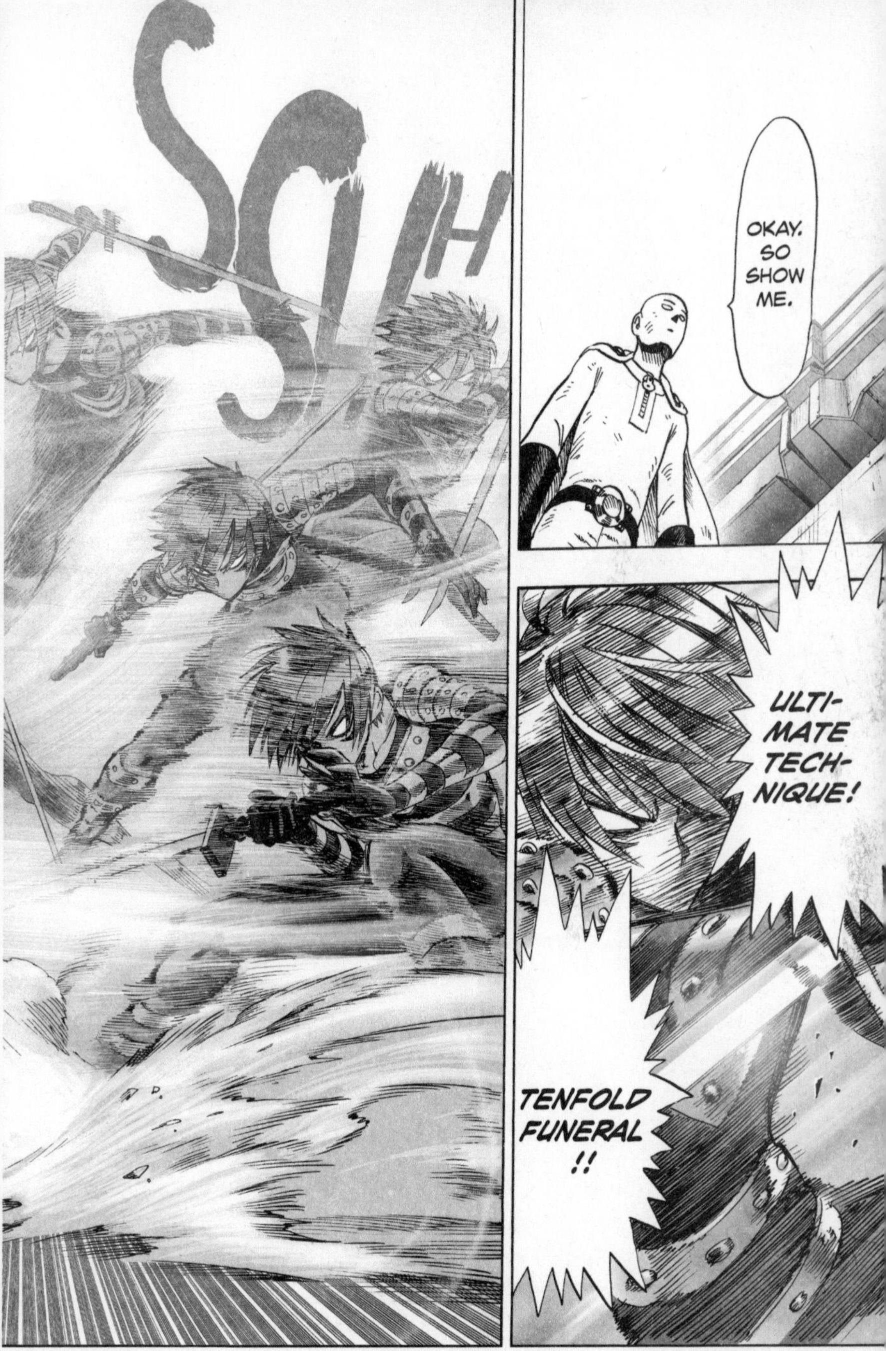
OKAY. SO SHOW ME.
ULTI-MATE TECH-NIQUE!
TENFOLD FUNERAL !!
SCH

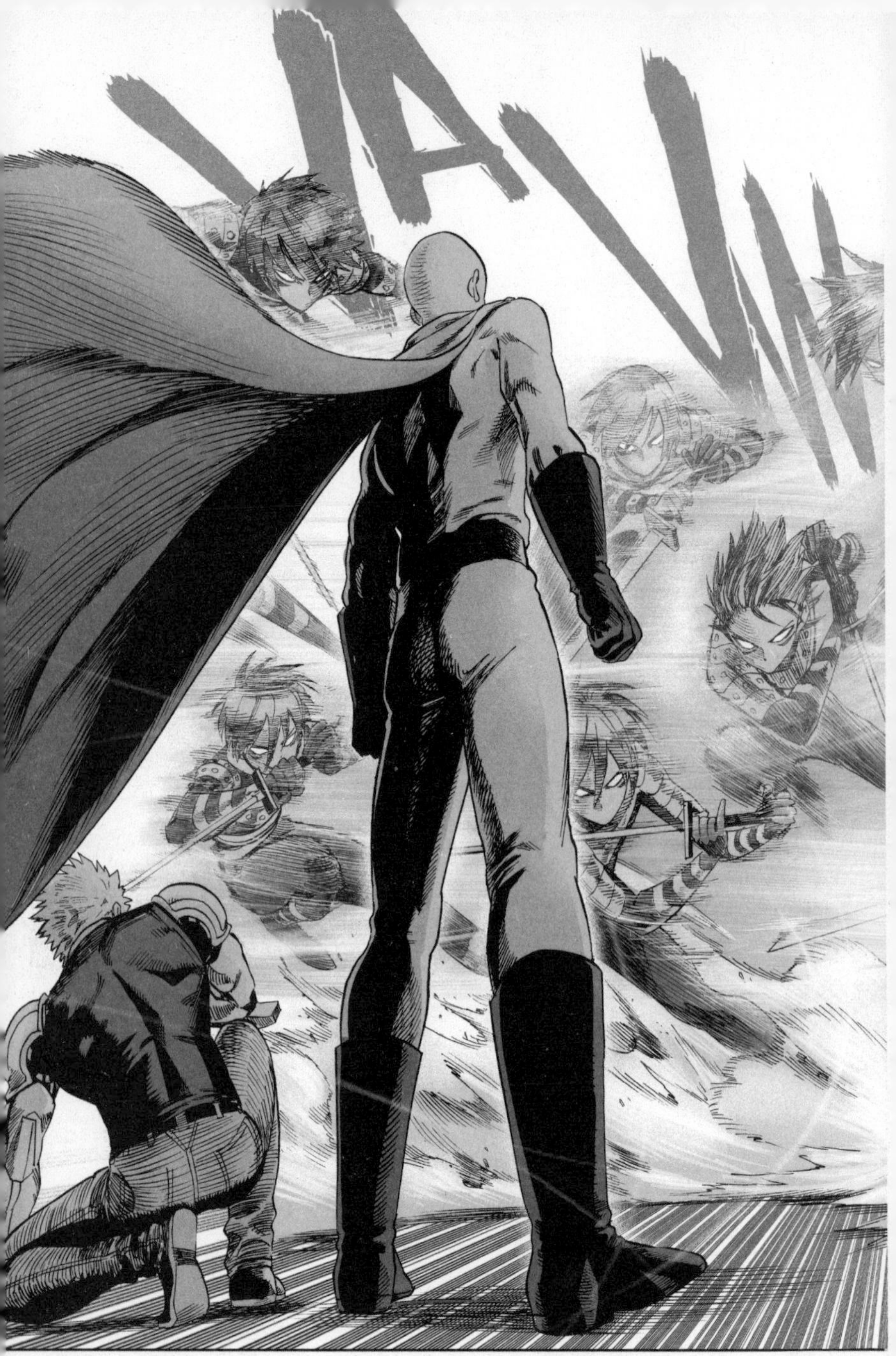

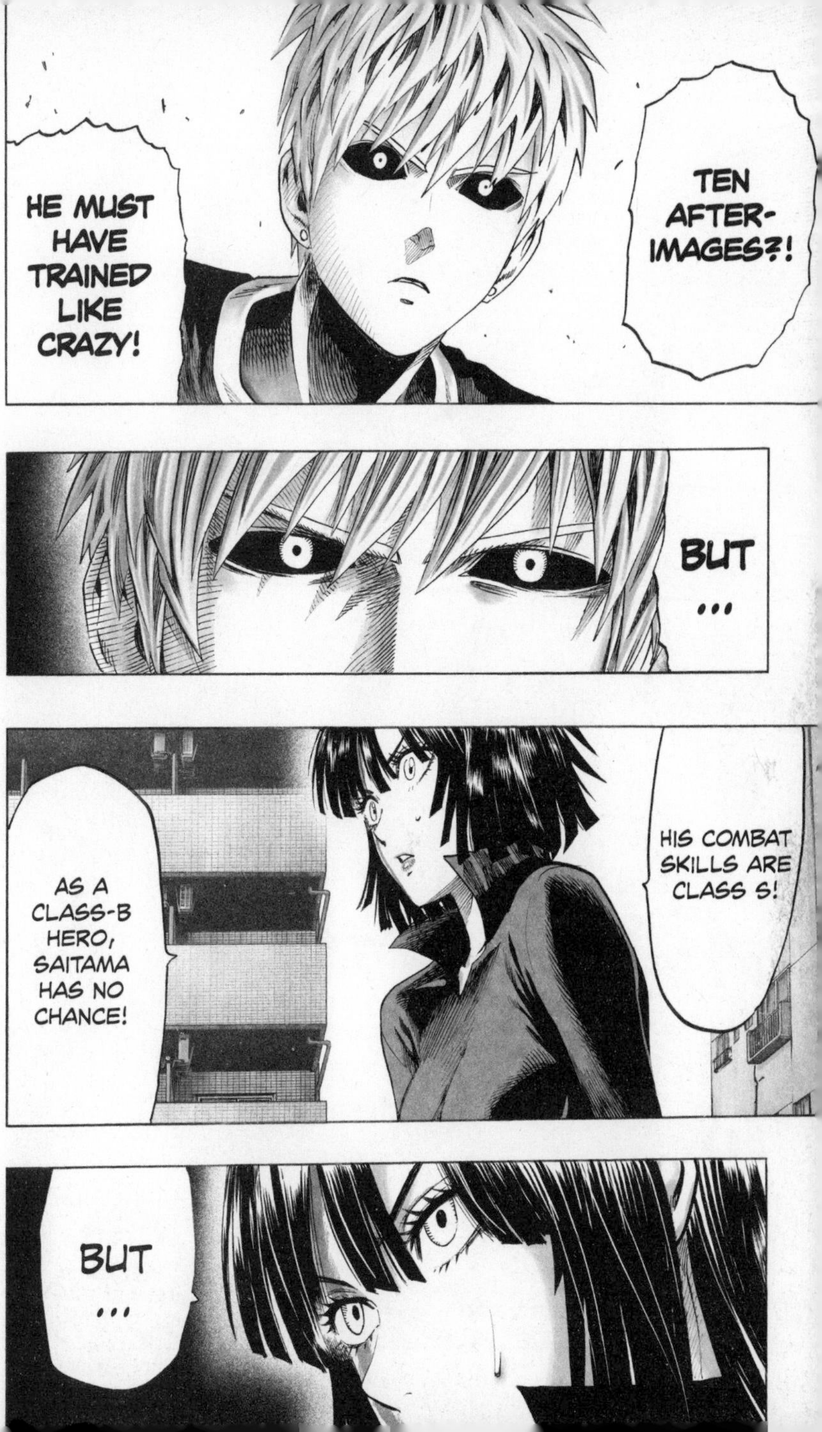
TEN AFTER-IMAGES?!
HE MUST HAVE TRAINED LIKE CRAZY!
BUT ...
HIS COMBAT SKILLS ARE CLASS S!
AS A CLASS-B HERO, SAITAMA HAS NO CHANCE!
BUT ...

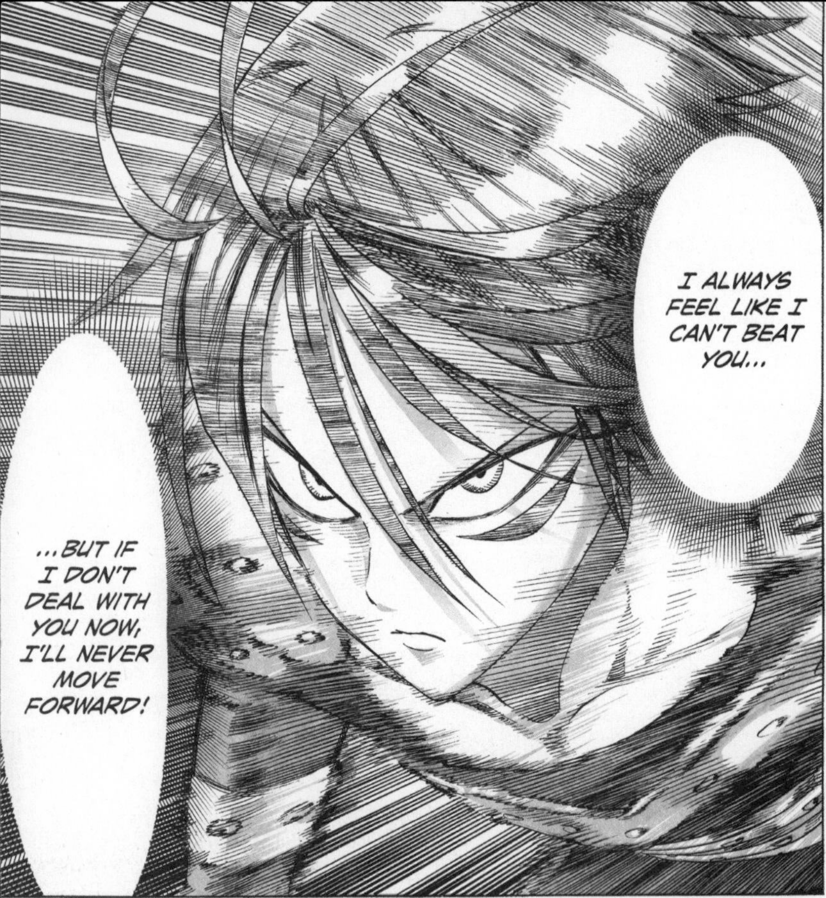
I ALWAYS FEEL LIKE I CAN'T BEAT YOU...
...BUT IF I DON'T DEAL WITH YOU NOW, I'LL NEVER MOVE FORWARD!
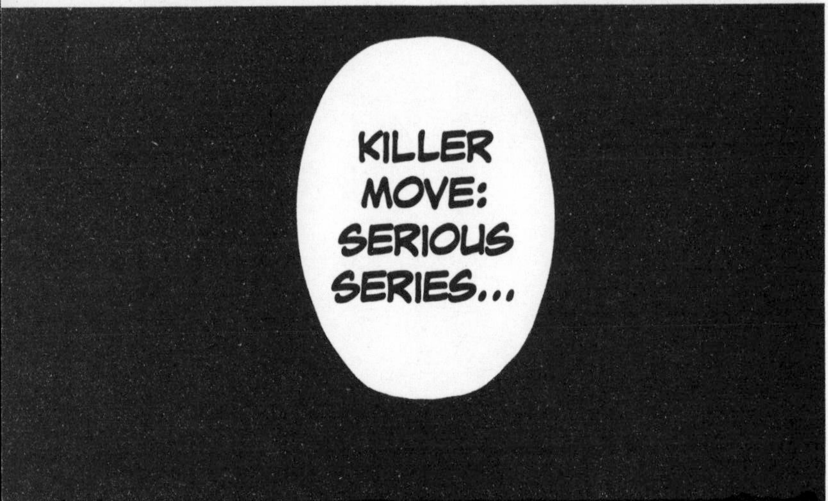
KILLER MOVE: SERIOUS SERIES...

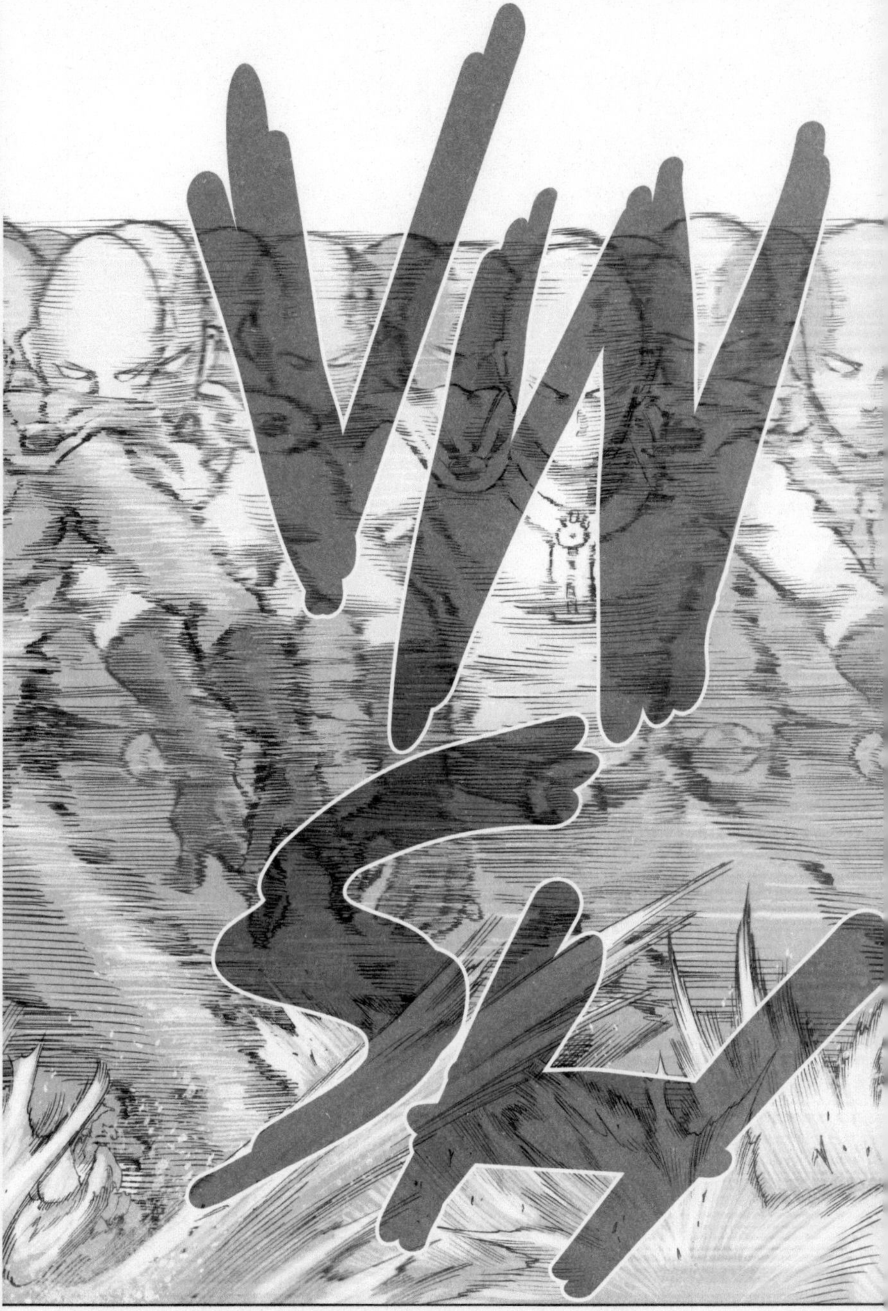

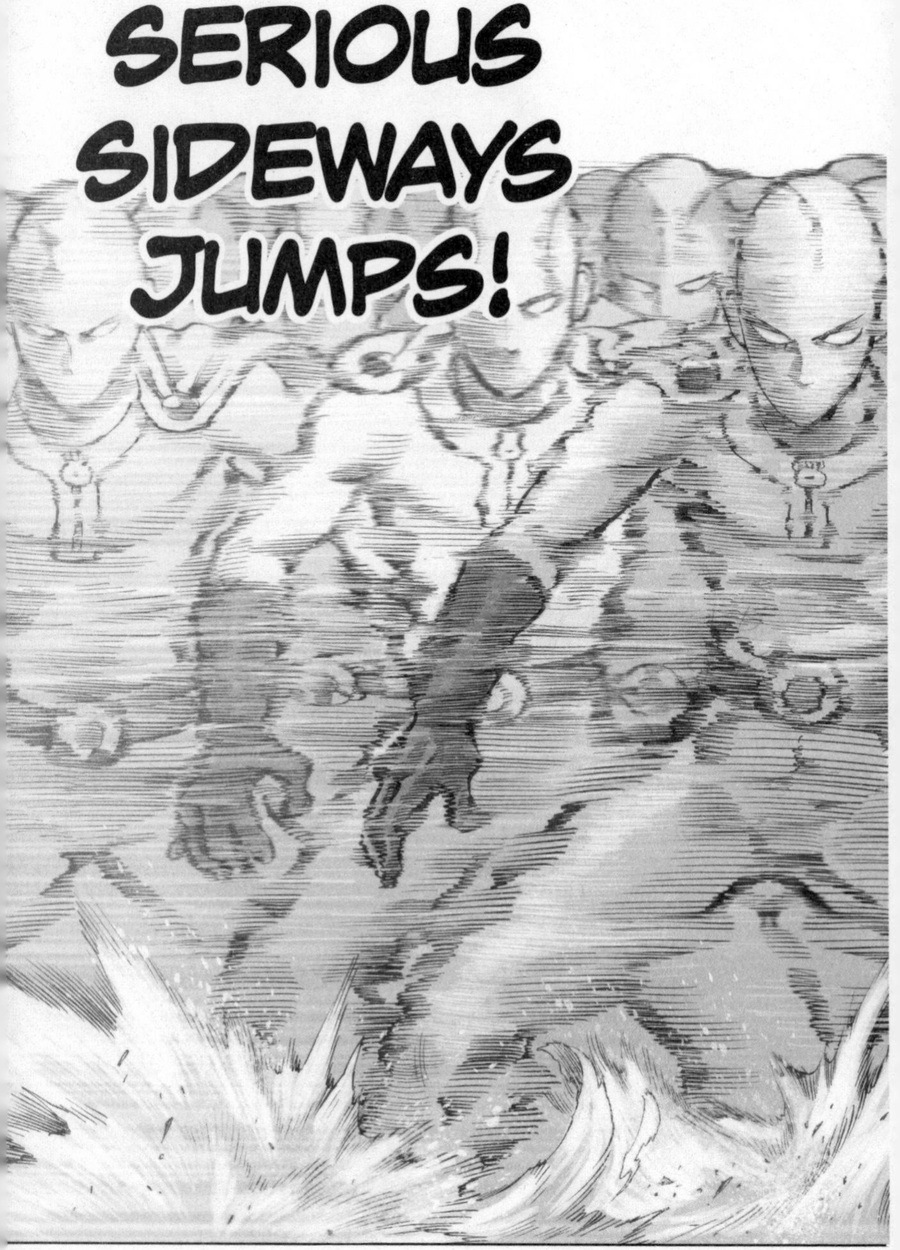
SERIOUS SIDEWAYS JUMPS!

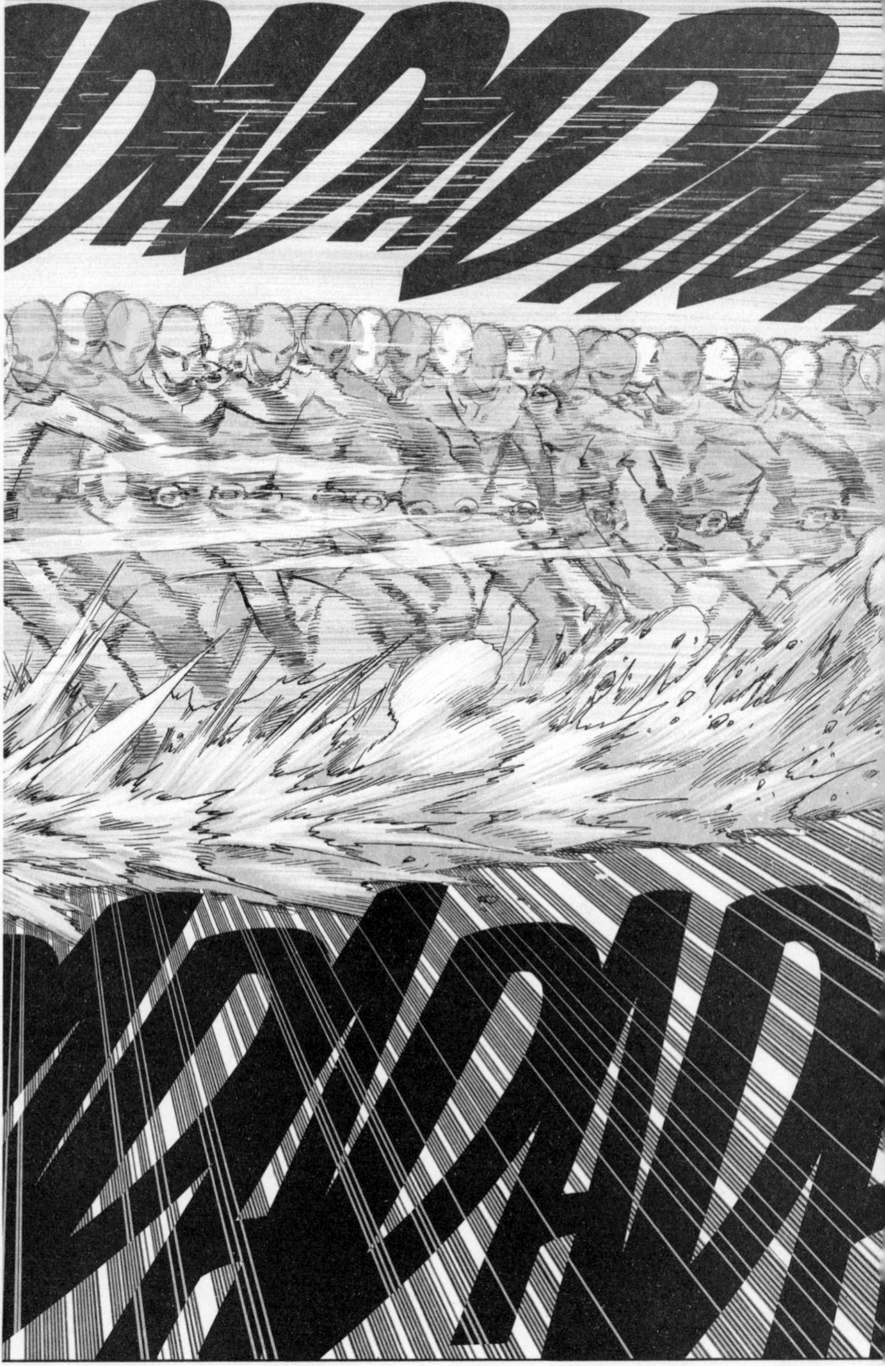

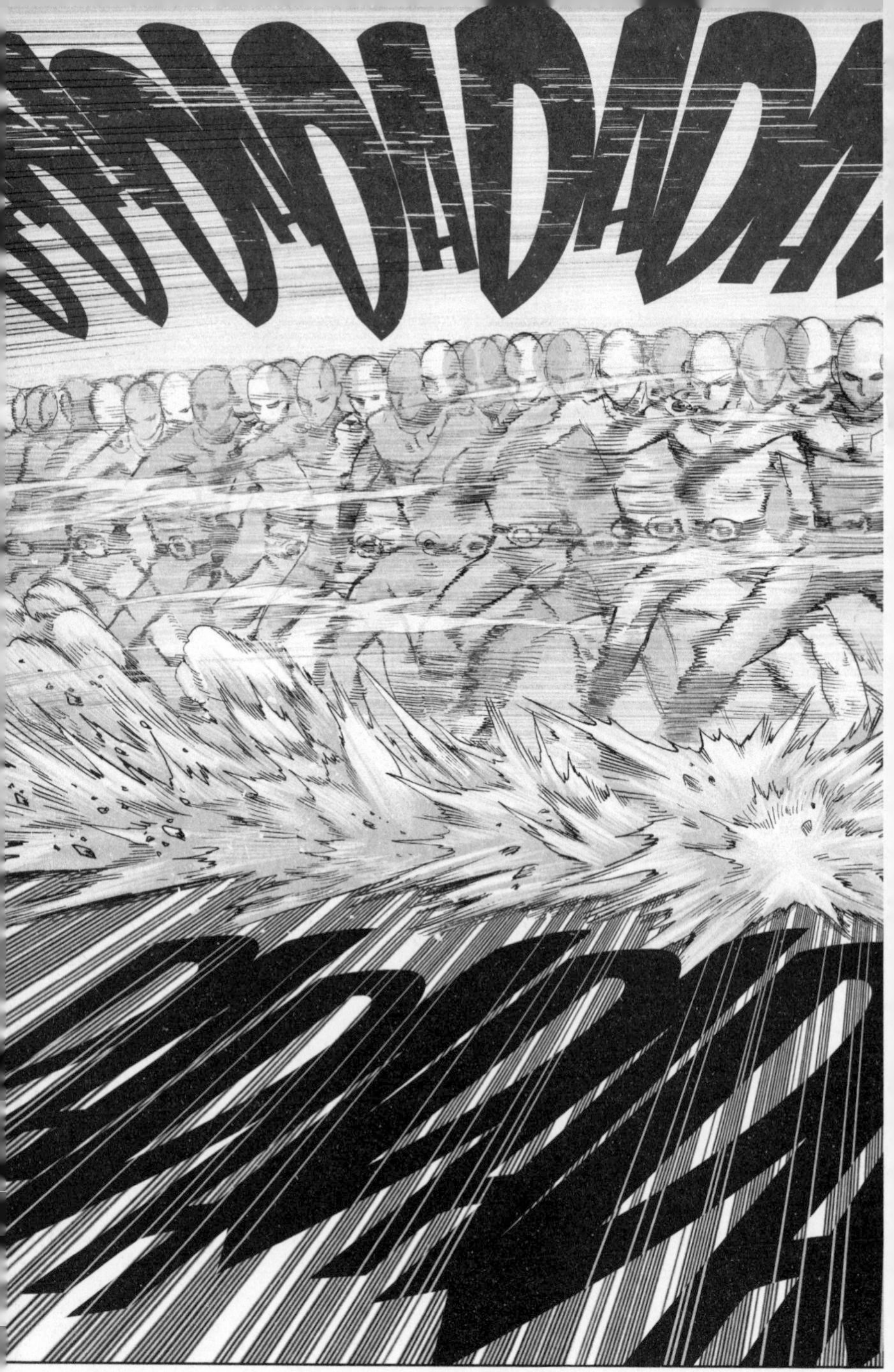
DADADADA
DADADADA

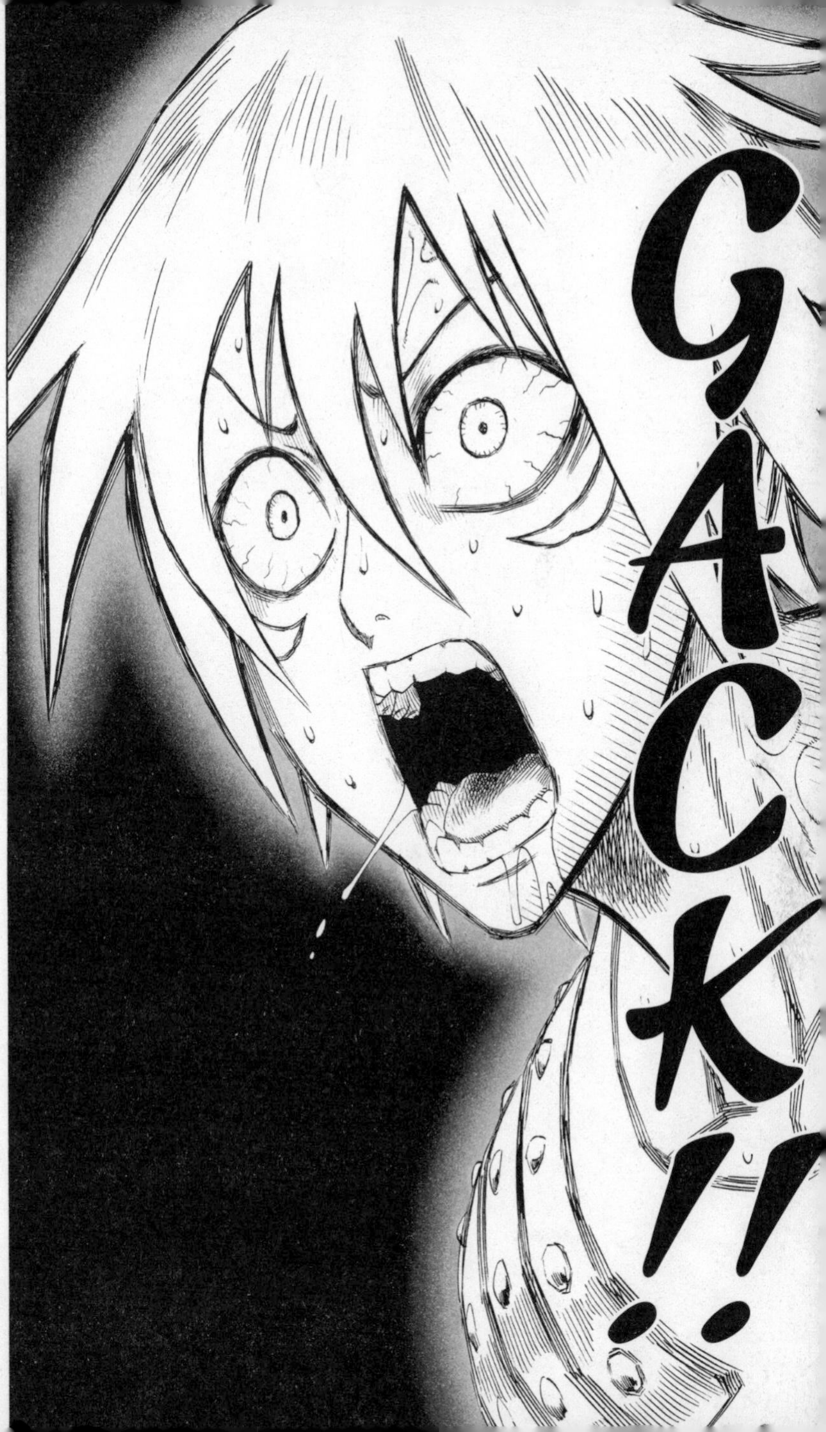
GACK!!

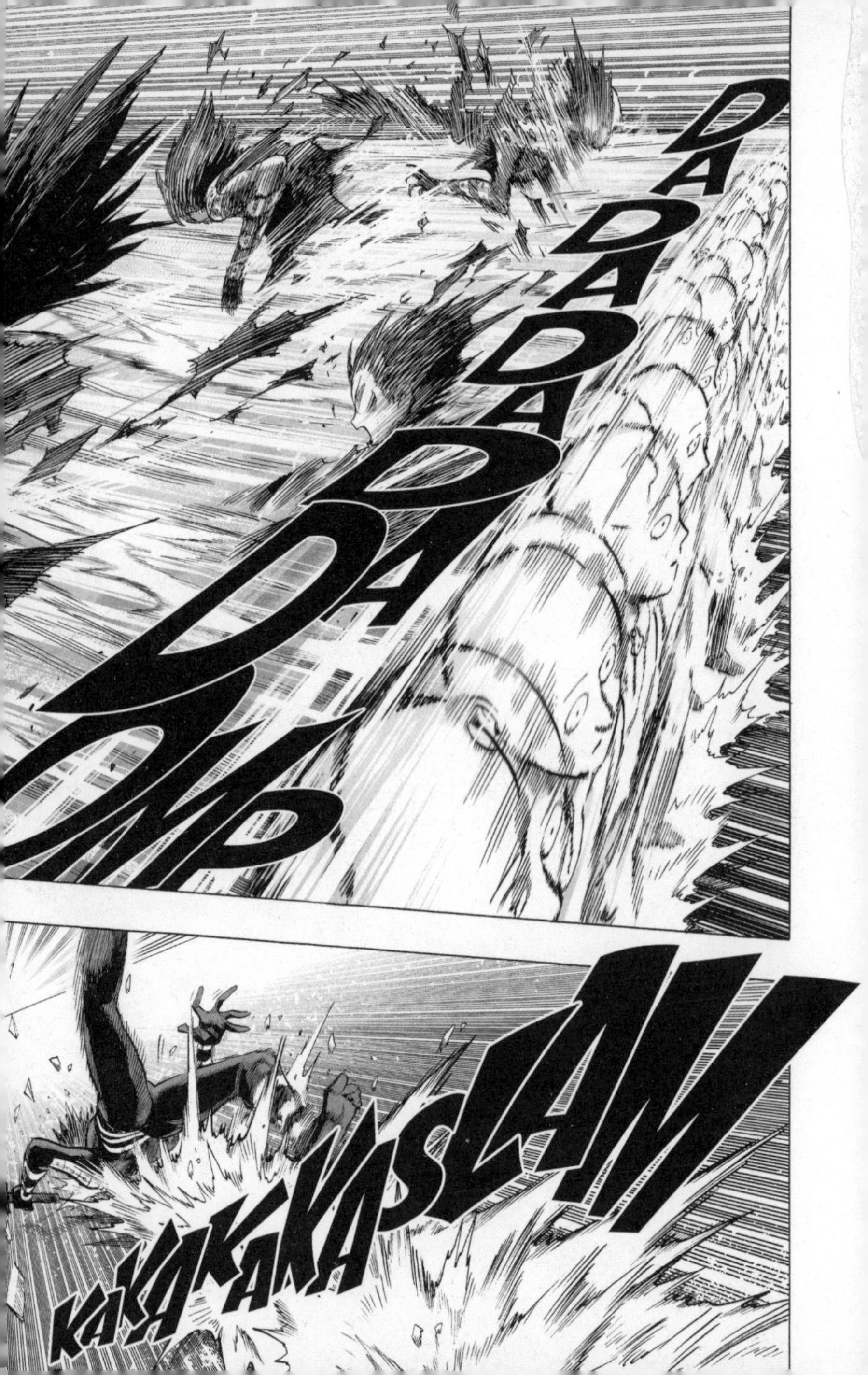

DADADADADADADOMP
KAKAKAKAKASLAM

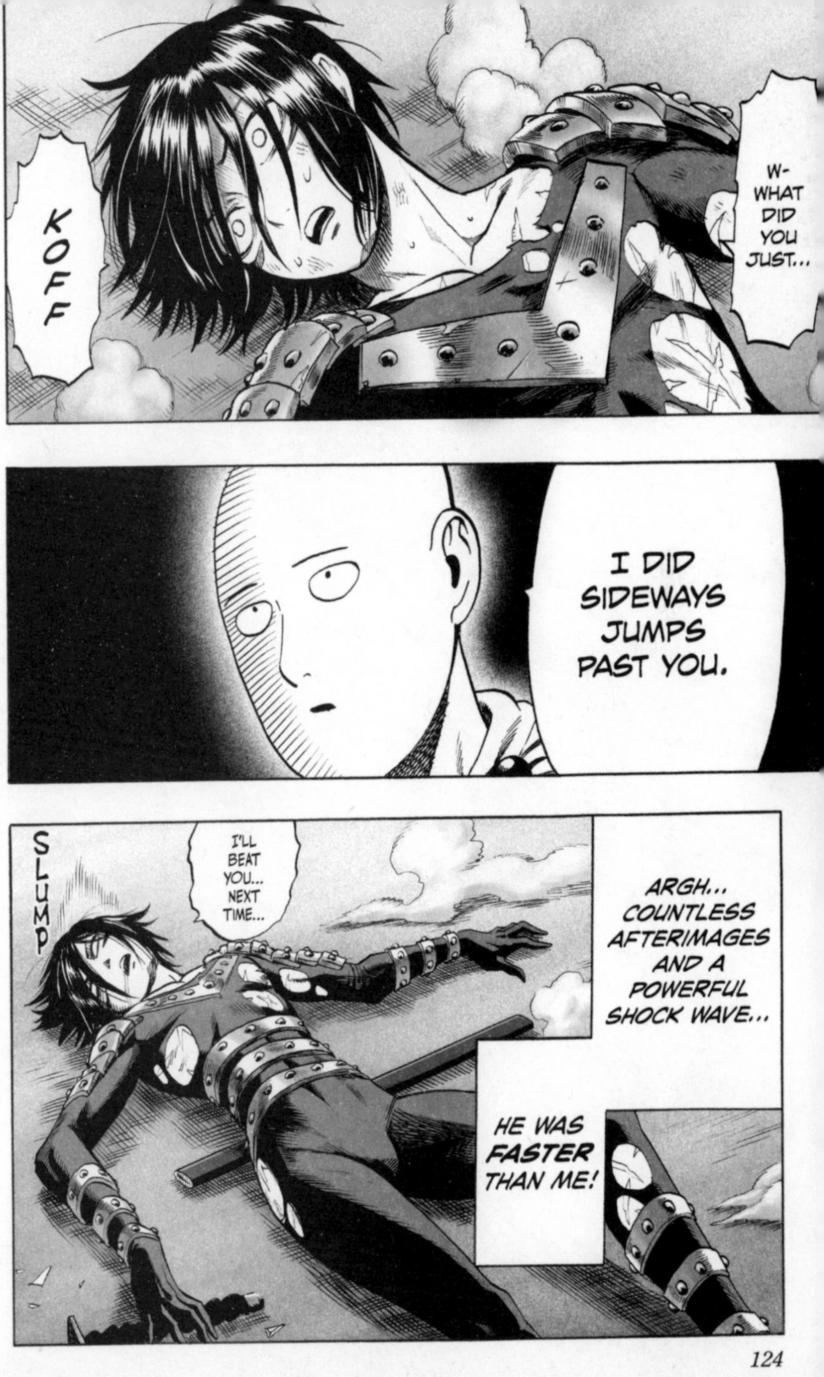
W-WHAT DID YOU JUST...
KOFF
I DID SIDEWAYS JUMPS PAST YOU.
ARGH... COUNTLESS AFTERIMAGES AND A POWERFUL SHOCK WAVE...
I'LL BEAT YOU... NEXT TIME...
SLUMP
HE WAS FASTER THAN ME!

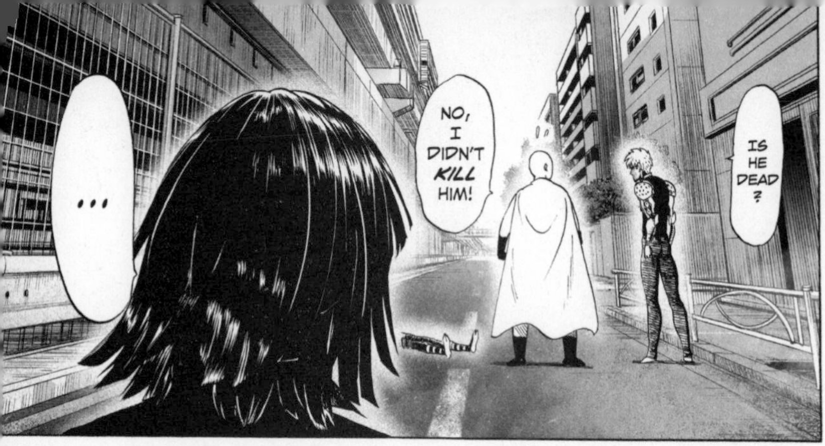
IS HE DEAD?
NO, I DIDN'T KILL HIM!
...

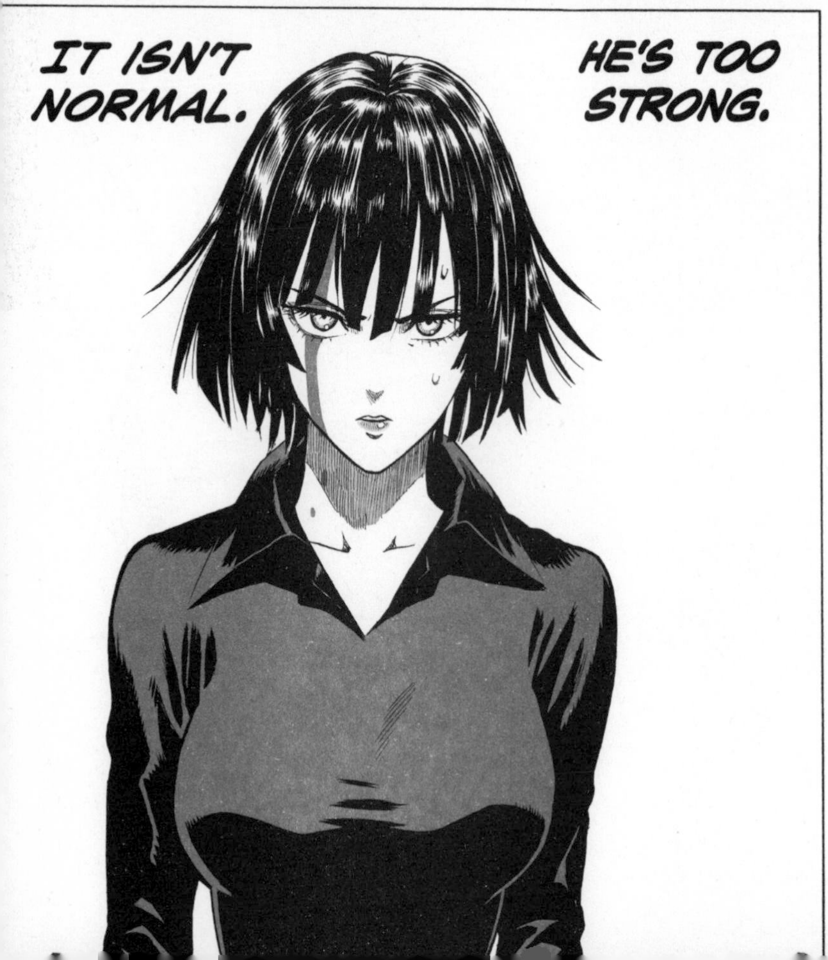
HE'S TOO STRONG.
IT ISN'T NORMAL.

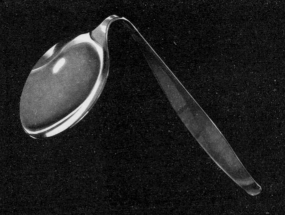

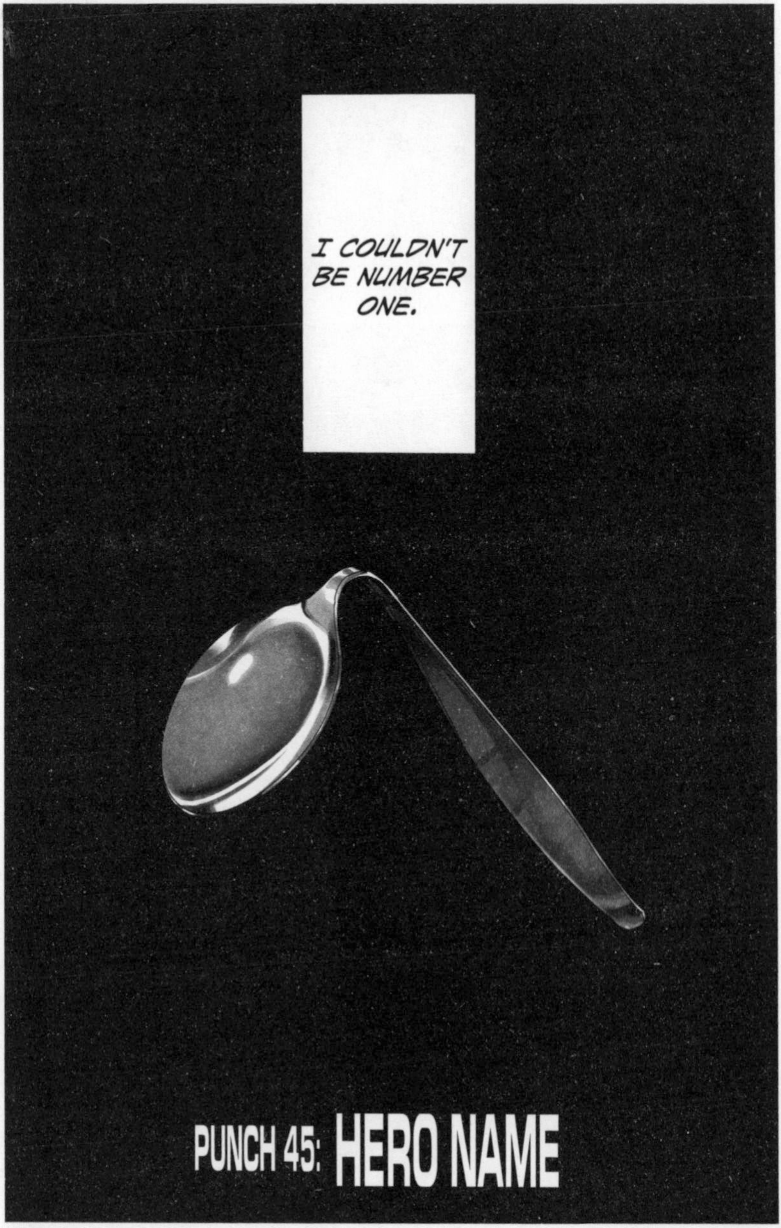

I COULDN'T BE NUMBER ONE.

PUNCH 45: **HERO NAME**

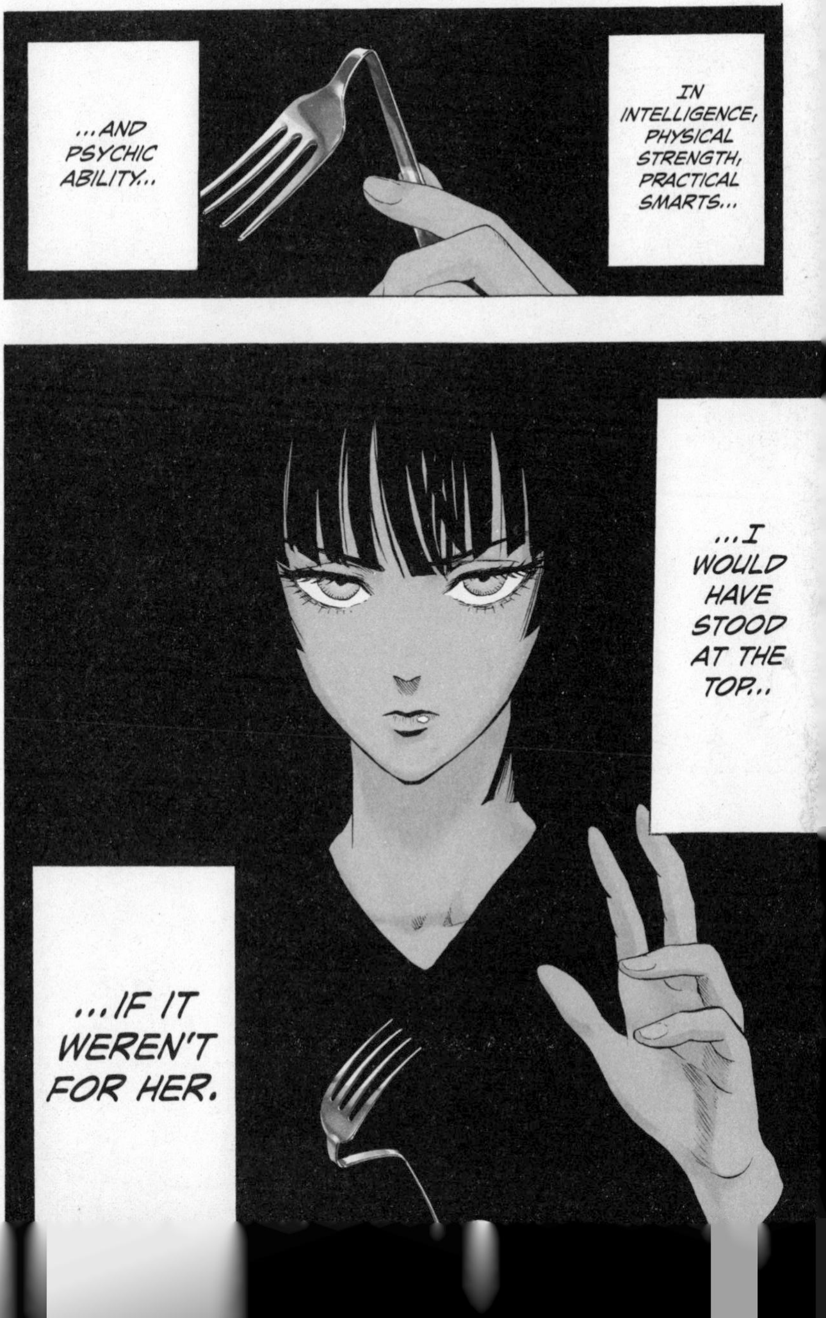
IN INTELLIGENCE, PHYSICAL STRENGTH, PRACTICAL SMARTS...
...AND PSYCHIC ABILITY...
...I WOULD HAVE STOOD AT THE TOP...
...IF IT WEREN'T FOR HER.

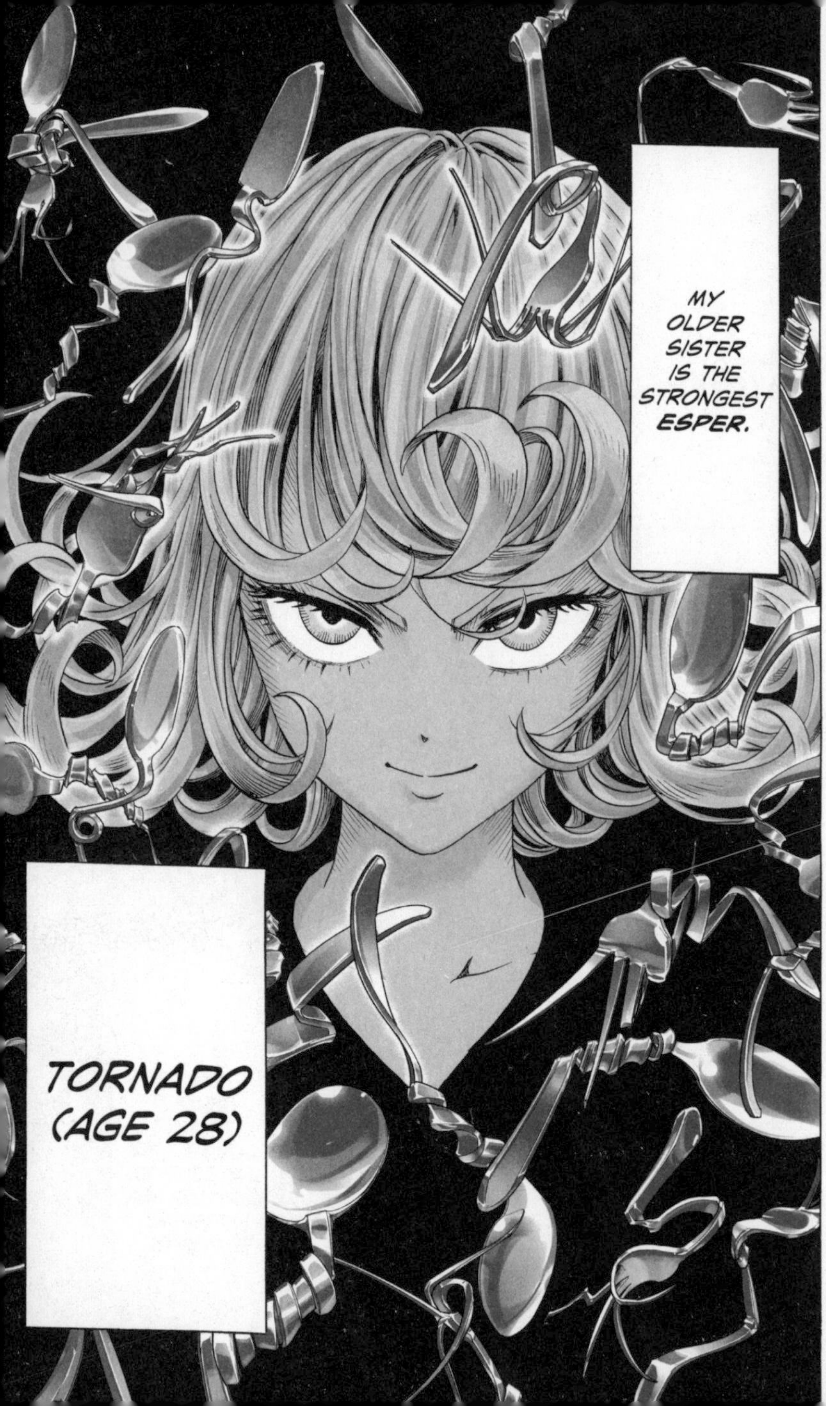
MY OLDER SISTER IS THE STRONGEST ESPER.
TORNADO (AGE 28)

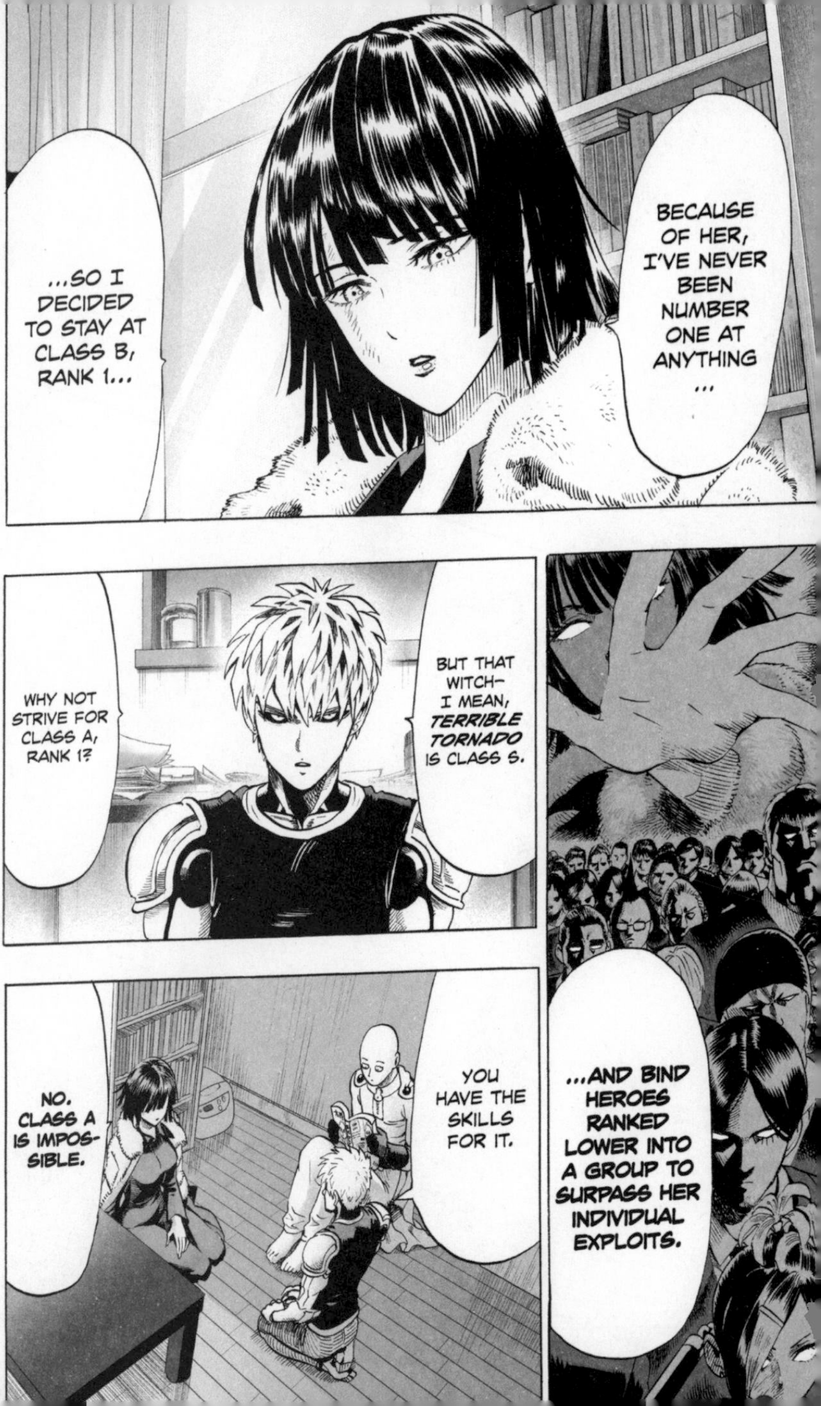
BECAUSE OF HER, I'VE NEVER BEEN NUMBER ONE AT ANYTHING...
...SO I DECIDED TO STAY AT CLASS B, RANK 1...
...AND BIND HEROES RANKED LOWER INTO A GROUP TO SURPASS HER INDIVIDUAL EXPLOITS.
BUT THAT WITCH— I MEAN, *TERRIBLE TORNADO* IS CLASS S.
WHY NOT STRIVE FOR CLASS A, RANK 1?
YOU HAVE THE SKILLS FOR IT.
NO. CLASS A IS IMPOSSIBLE.

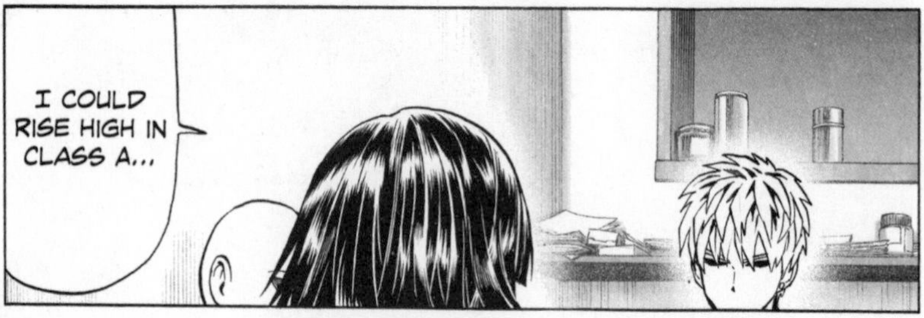
I COULD RISE HIGH IN CLASS A...
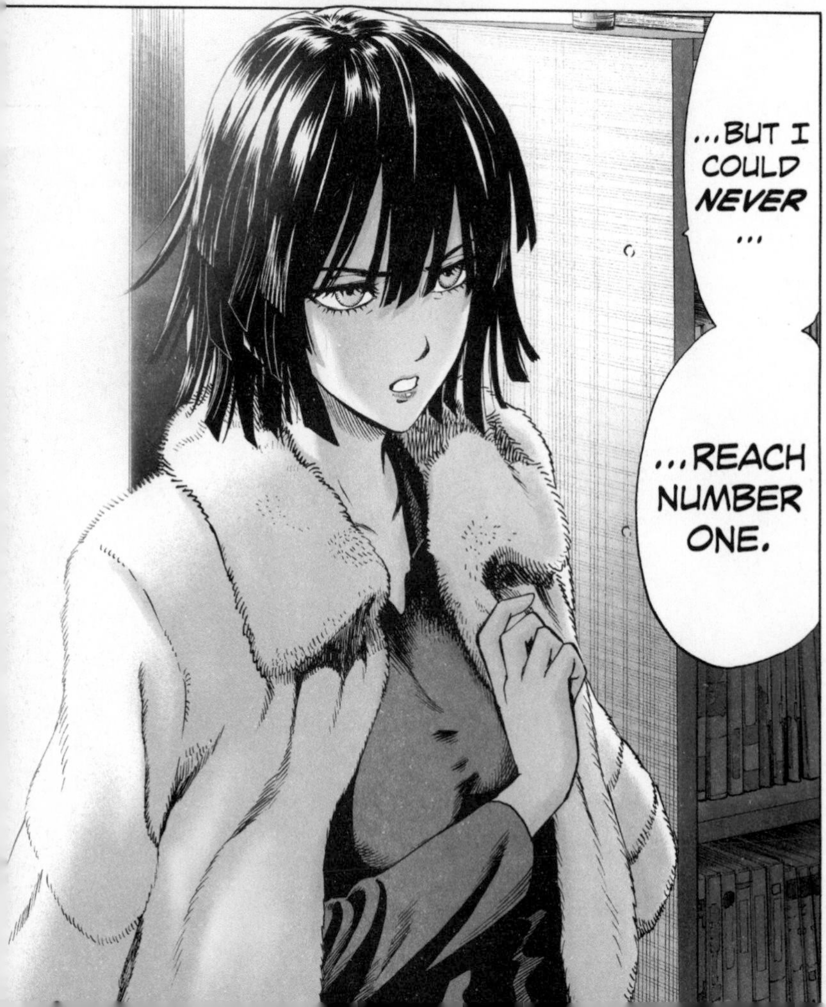
...BUT I COULD NEVER ...
...REACH NUMBER ONE.

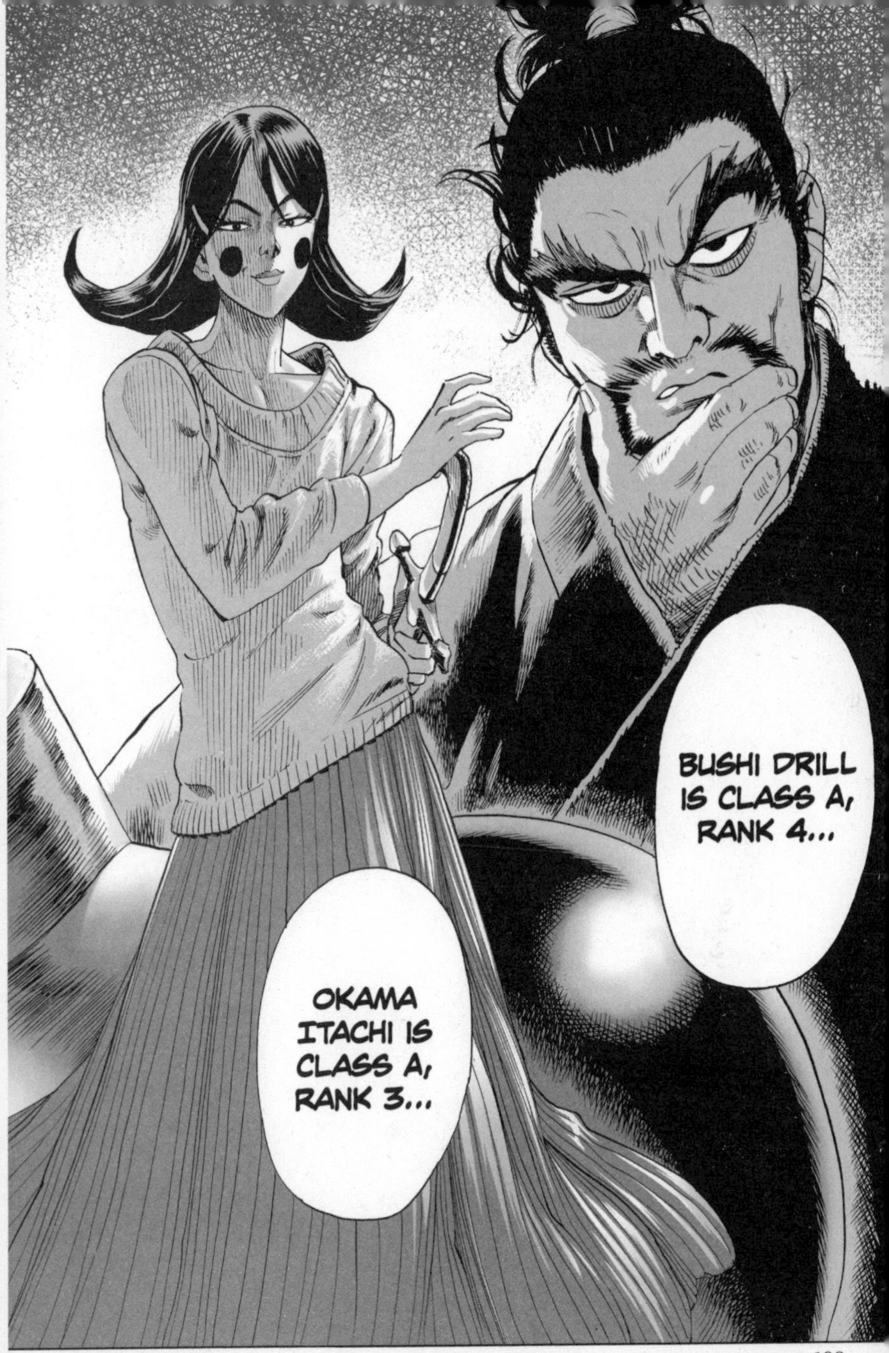
BUSHI DRILL IS CLASS A, RANK 4...
OKAMA ITACHI IS CLASS A, RANK 3...

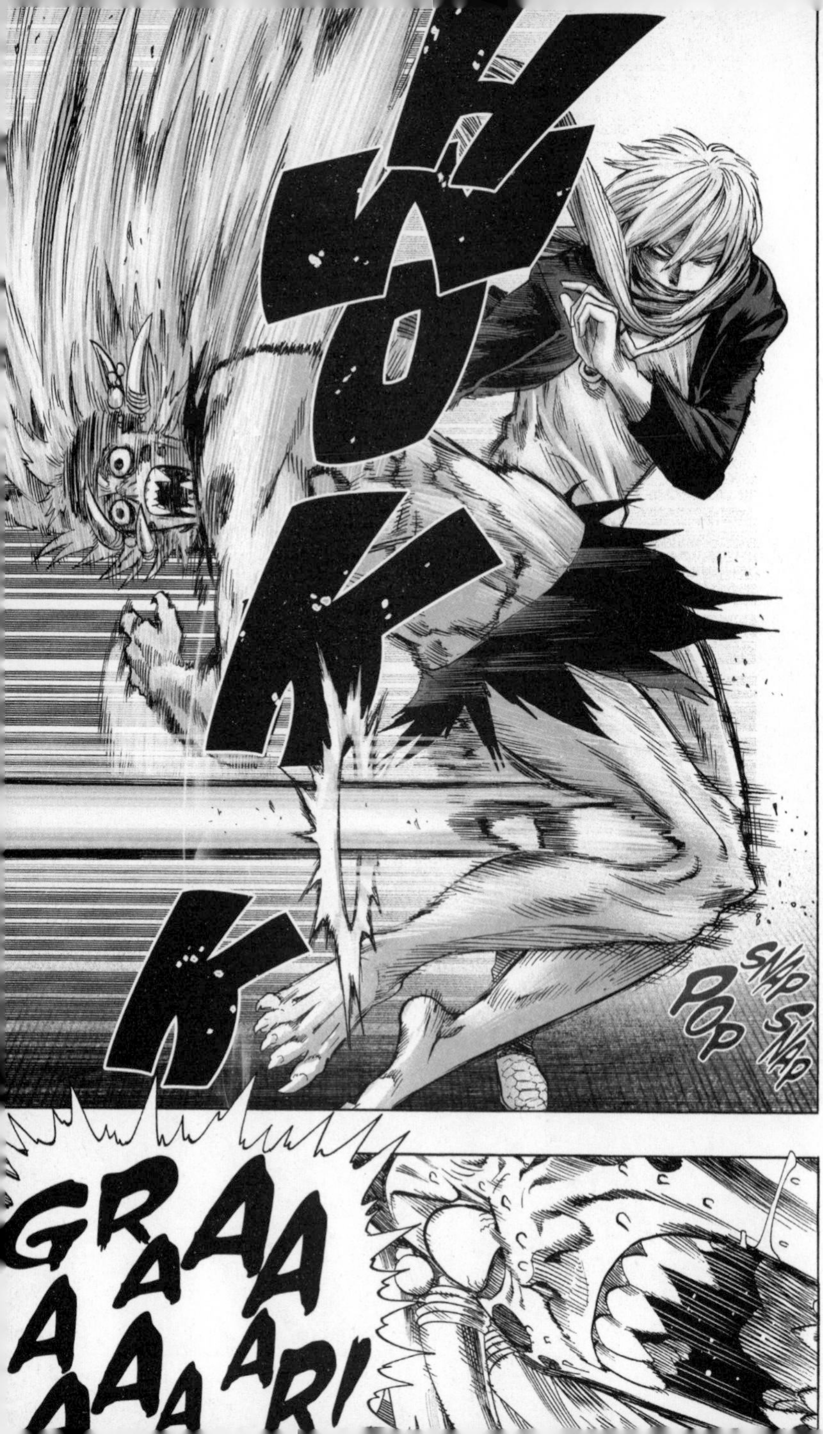
SNAP SNAP
POP
GRAAAAAAAARI

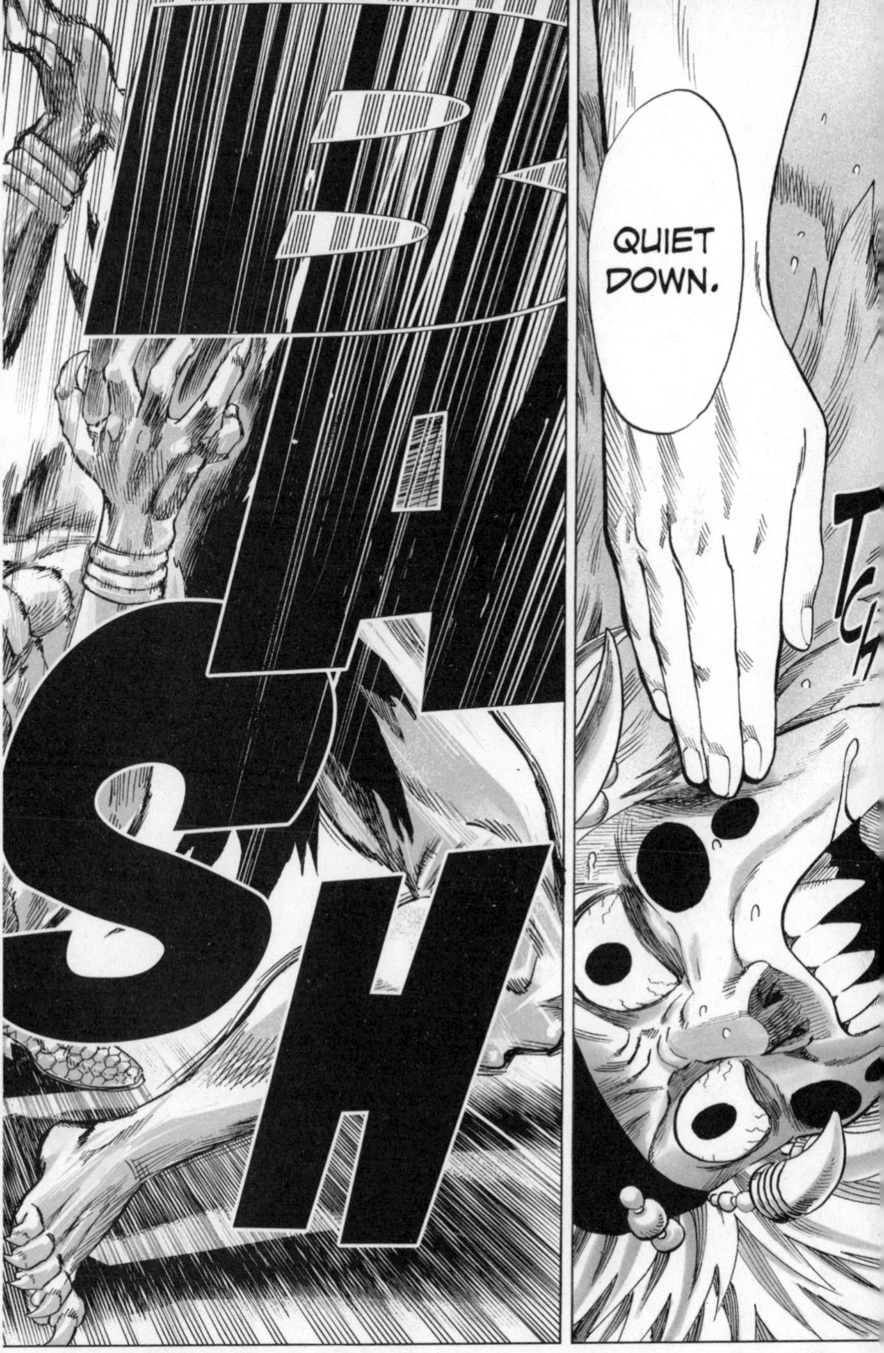
QUIET DOWN.
TCH
SH

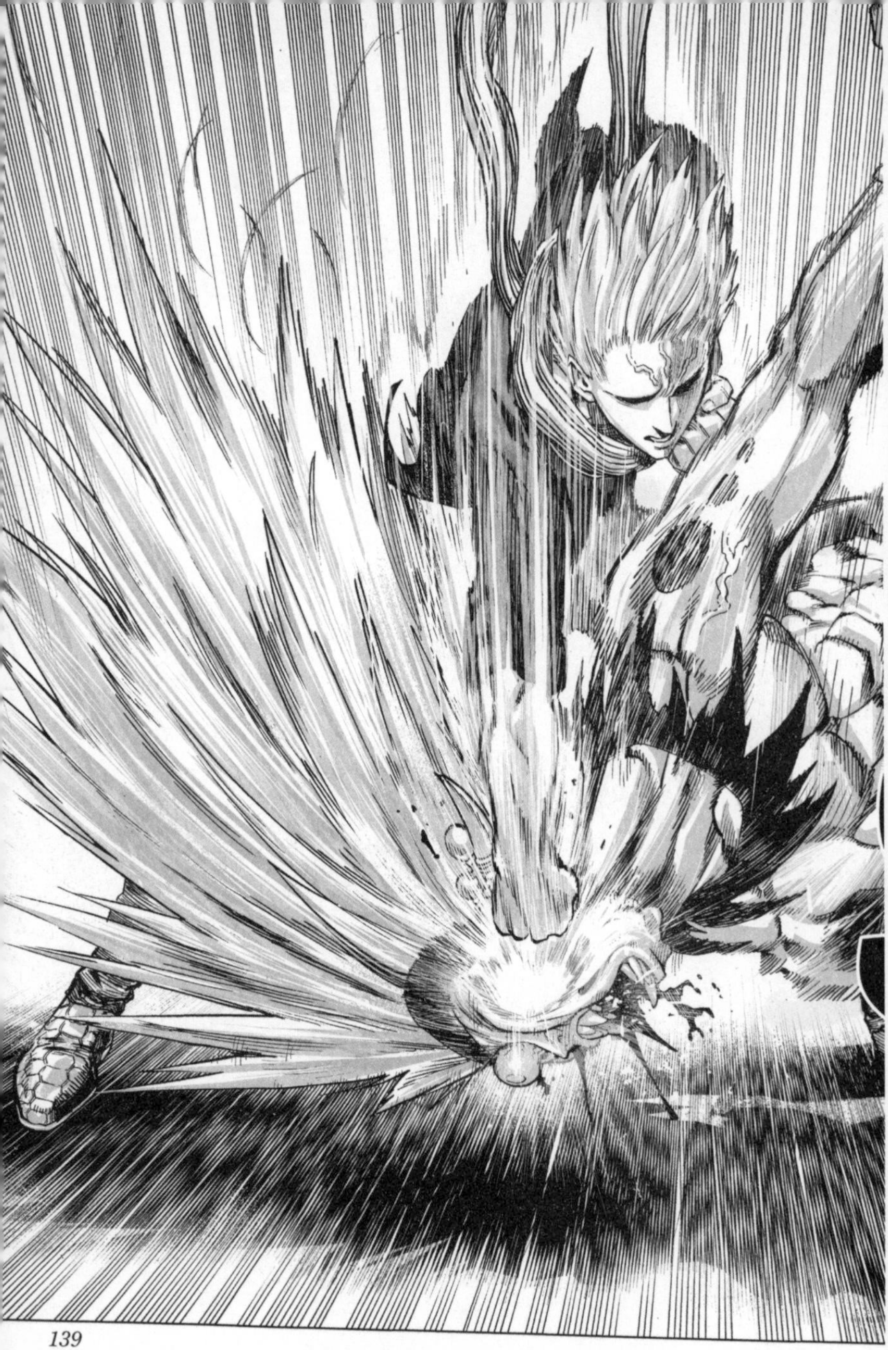

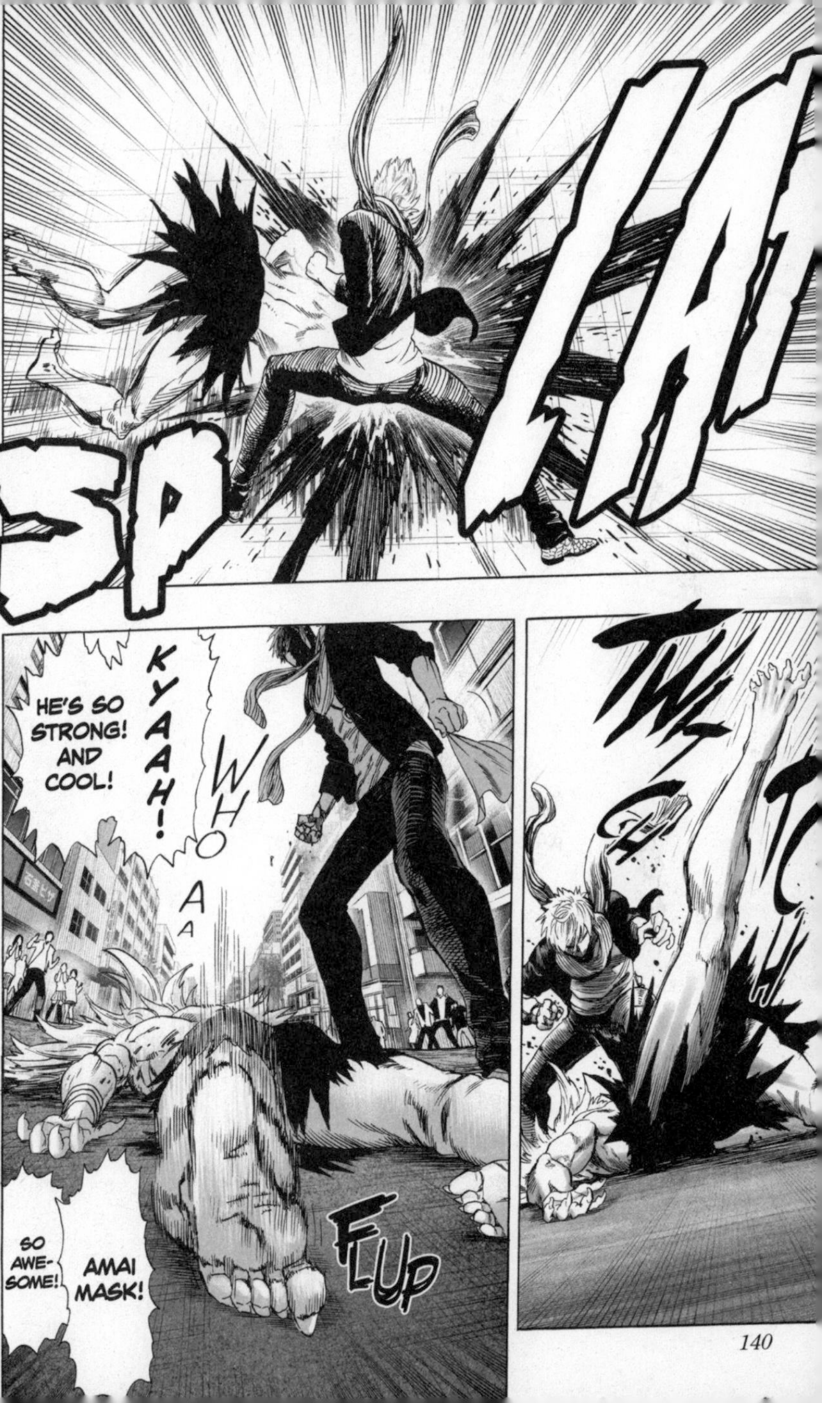
SP
WHOAAA
KYAAAH!
HE'S SO STRONG! AND COOL!
FLUP
AMAI MASK!
SO AWE-SOME!

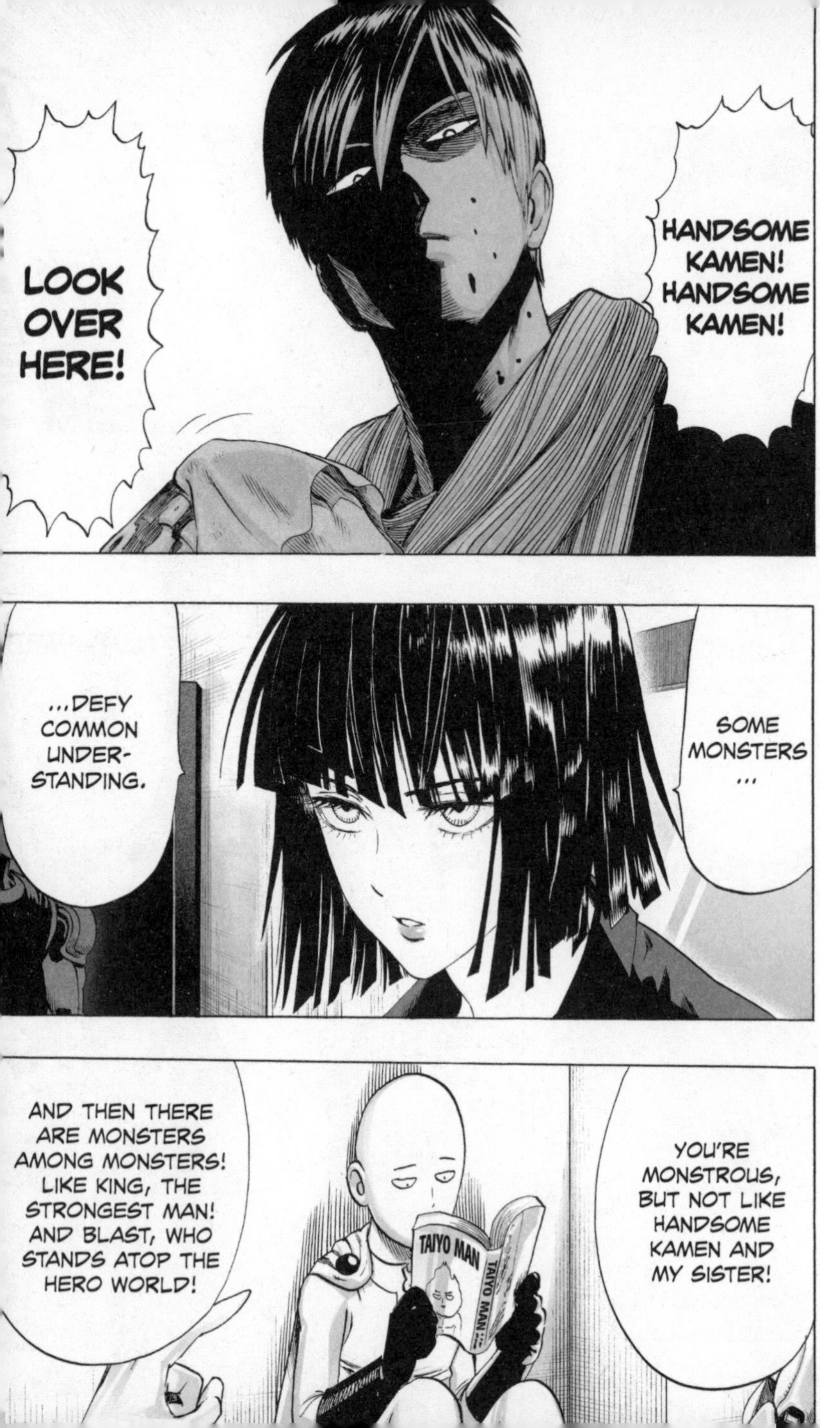
HANDSOME KAMEN! HANDSOME KAMEN!
LOOK OVER HERE!
SOME MONSTERS ...
...DEFY COMMON UNDER-STANDING.
YOU'RE MONSTROUS, BUT NOT LIKE HANDSOME KAMEN AND MY SISTER!
AND THEN THERE ARE MONSTERS AMONG MONSTERS! LIKE KING, THE STRONGEST MAN! AND BLAST, WHO STANDS ATOP THE HERO WORLD!
TAIYO MAN
TAIYO MAN

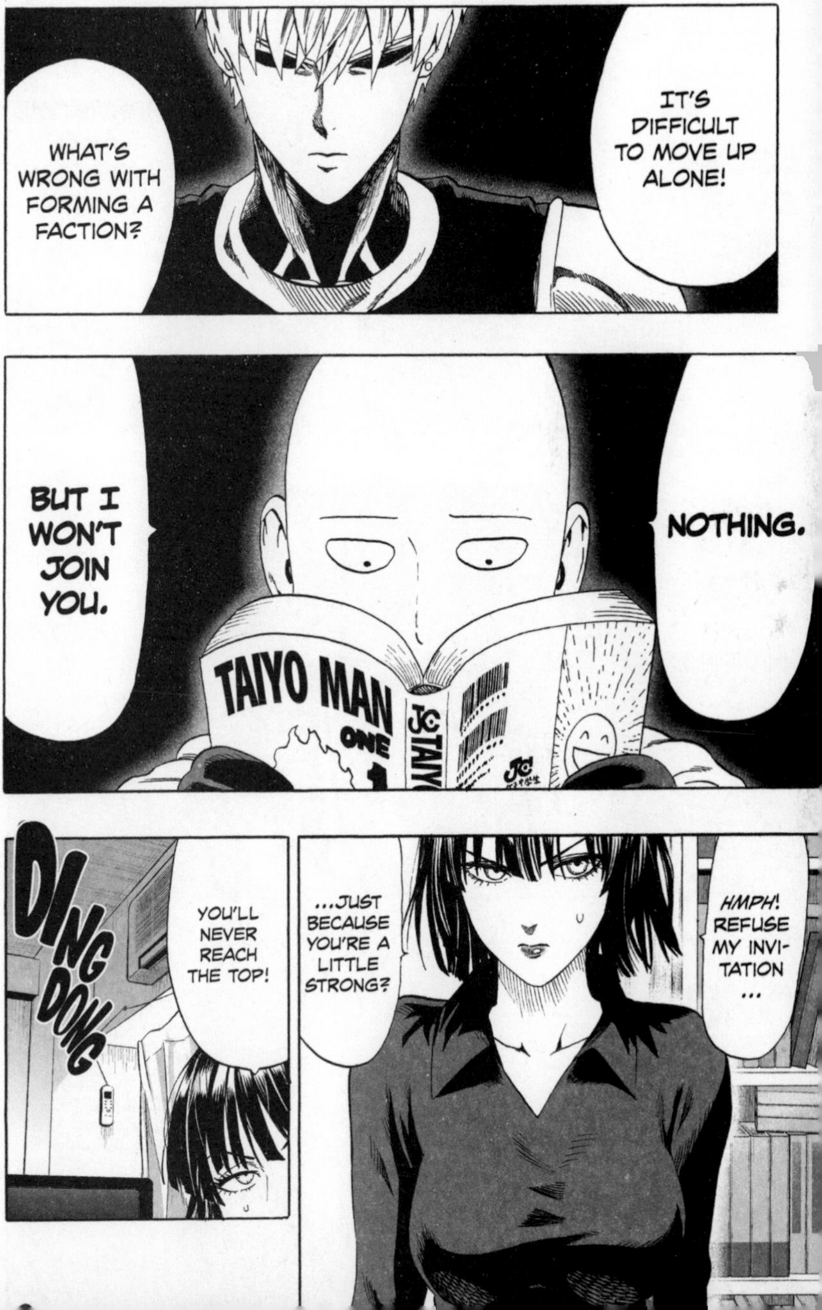
IT'S DIFFICULT TO MOVE UP ALONE!
WHAT'S WRONG WITH FORMING A FACTION?
NOTHING.
BUT I WON'T JOIN YOU.
TAIYO MAN
ONE
HMPH! REFUSE MY INVITATION ...
...JUST BECAUSE YOU'RE A LITTLE STRONG?
YOU'LL NEVER REACH THE TOP!
DING DONG

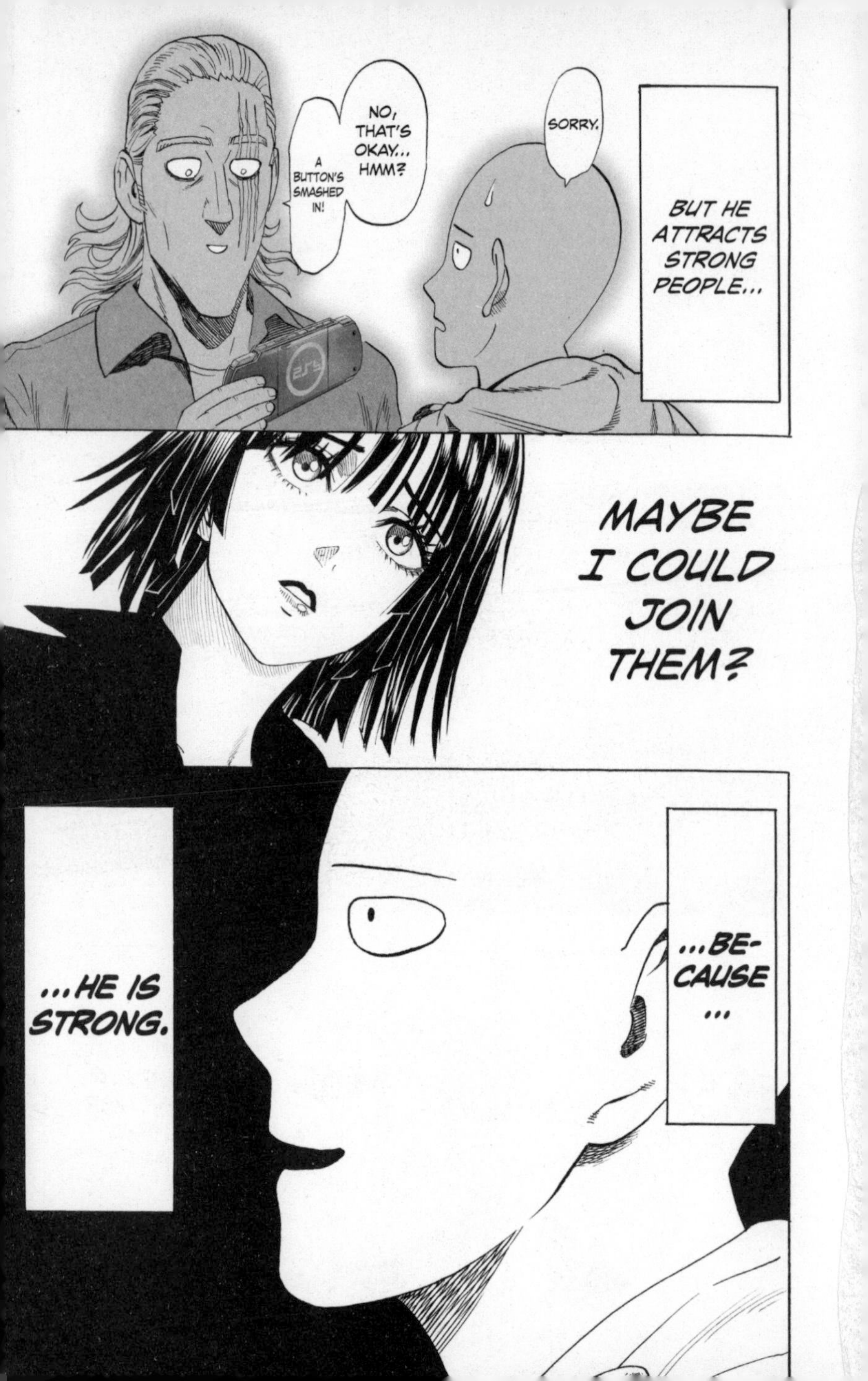
BUT HE ATTRACTS STRONG PEOPLE...
SORRY.
NO, THAT'S OKAY... HMM?
A BUTTON'S SMASHED IN!
MAYBE I COULD JOIN THEM?
...BE-CAUSE ...
...HE IS STRONG.

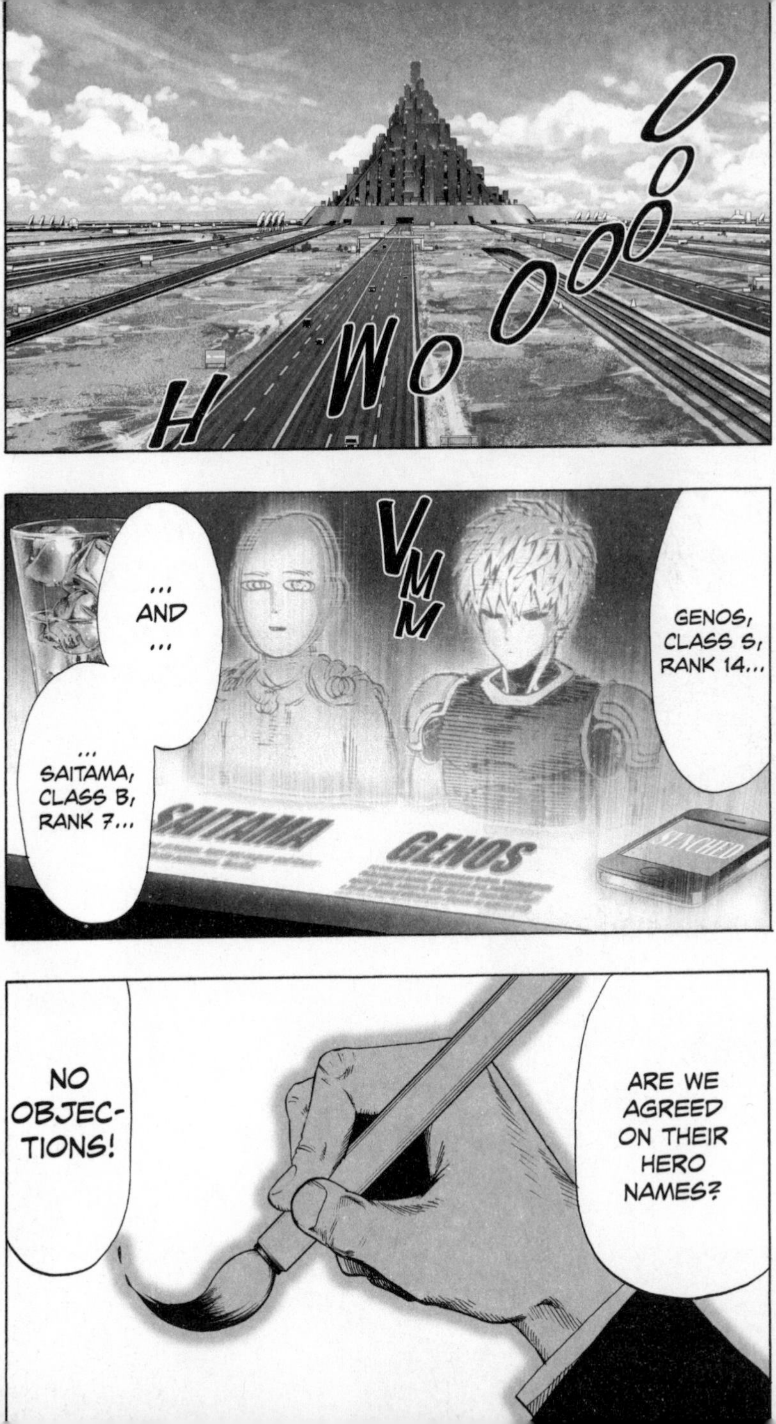
HWOOOOOO
GENOS, CLASS S, RANK 14...
VMM
... AND ...
... SAITAMA, CLASS B, RANK 7...
SAITAMA
GENOS
ARE WE AGREED ON THEIR HERO NAMES?
NO OBJECTIONS!

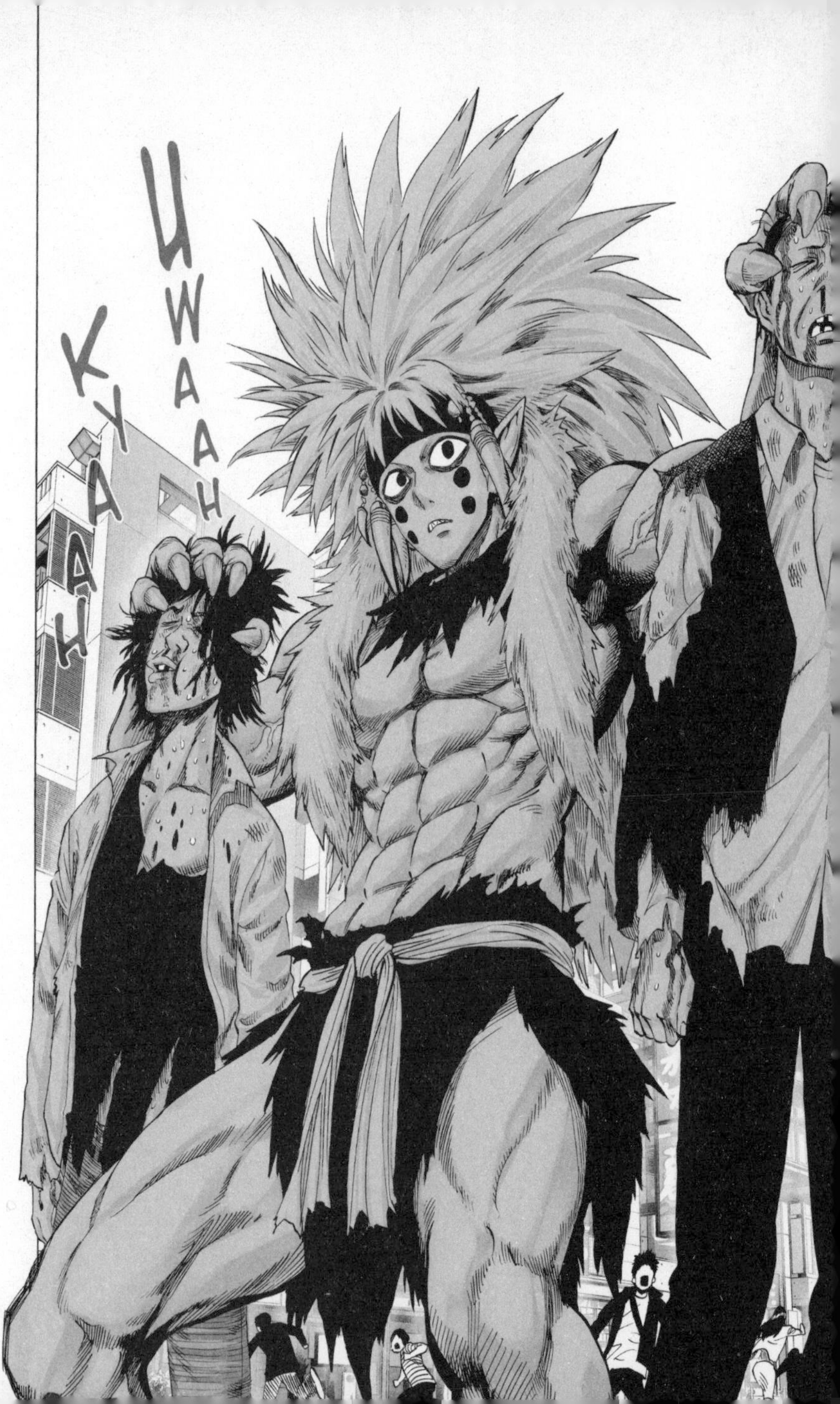
UWAAH
KYAAH

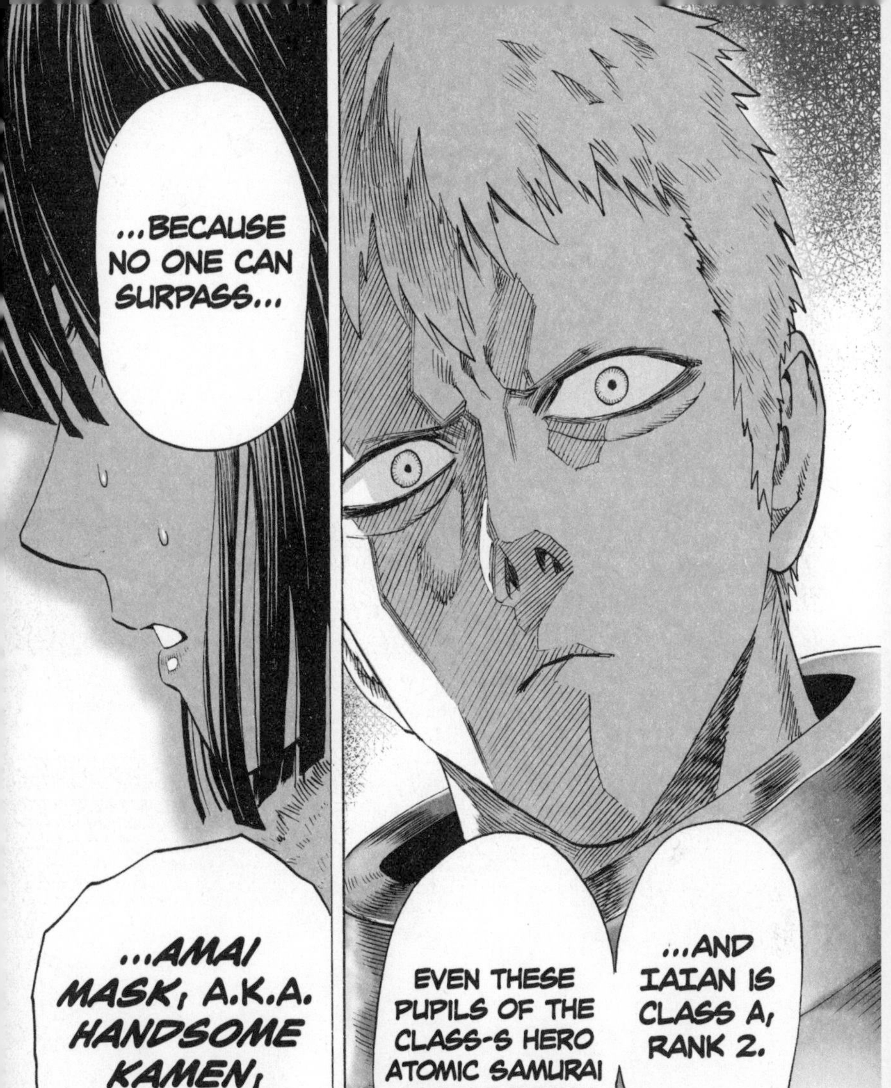
...AND IAIAN IS CLASS A, RANK 2.
EVEN THESE PUPILS OF THE CLASS-S HERO ATOMIC SAMURAI CANNOT REACH CLASS S...
...BECAUSE NO ONE CAN SURPASS...
...AMAI MASK, A.K.A. HANDSOME KAMEN, WHO HOLDS CLASS A, RANK 1.

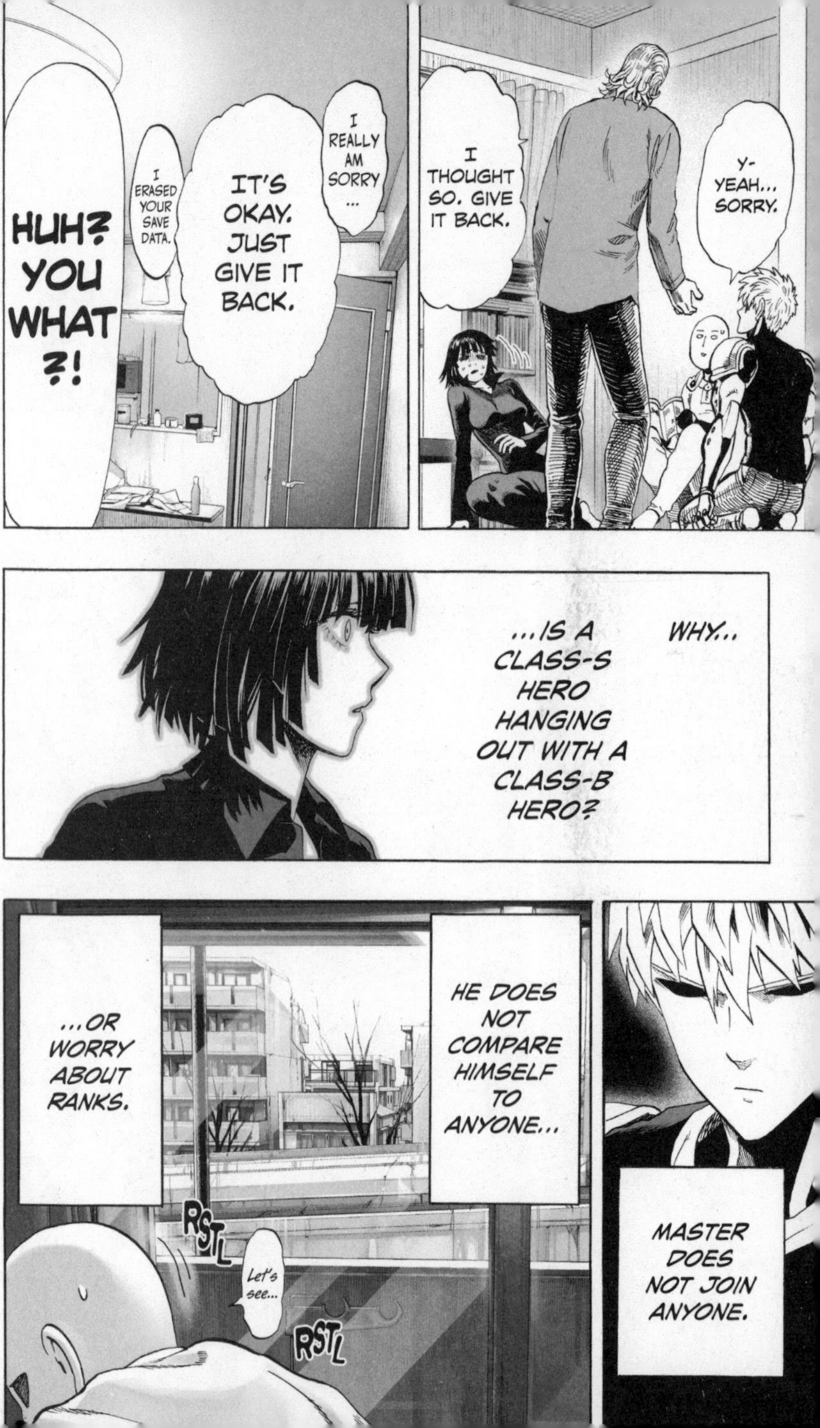
Y- YEAH... SORRY.
I THOUGHT SO. GIVE IT BACK.
I REALLY AM SORRY ...
IT'S OKAY. JUST GIVE IT BACK.
I ERASED YOUR SAVE DATA.
HUH? YOU WHAT?!
WHY...
...IS A CLASS-S HERO HANGING OUT WITH A CLASS-B HERO?
MASTER DOES NOT JOIN ANYONE.
HE DOES NOT COMPARE HIMSELF TO ANYONE...
...OR WORRY ABOUT RANKS.
RSTL
Let's see...
RSTL

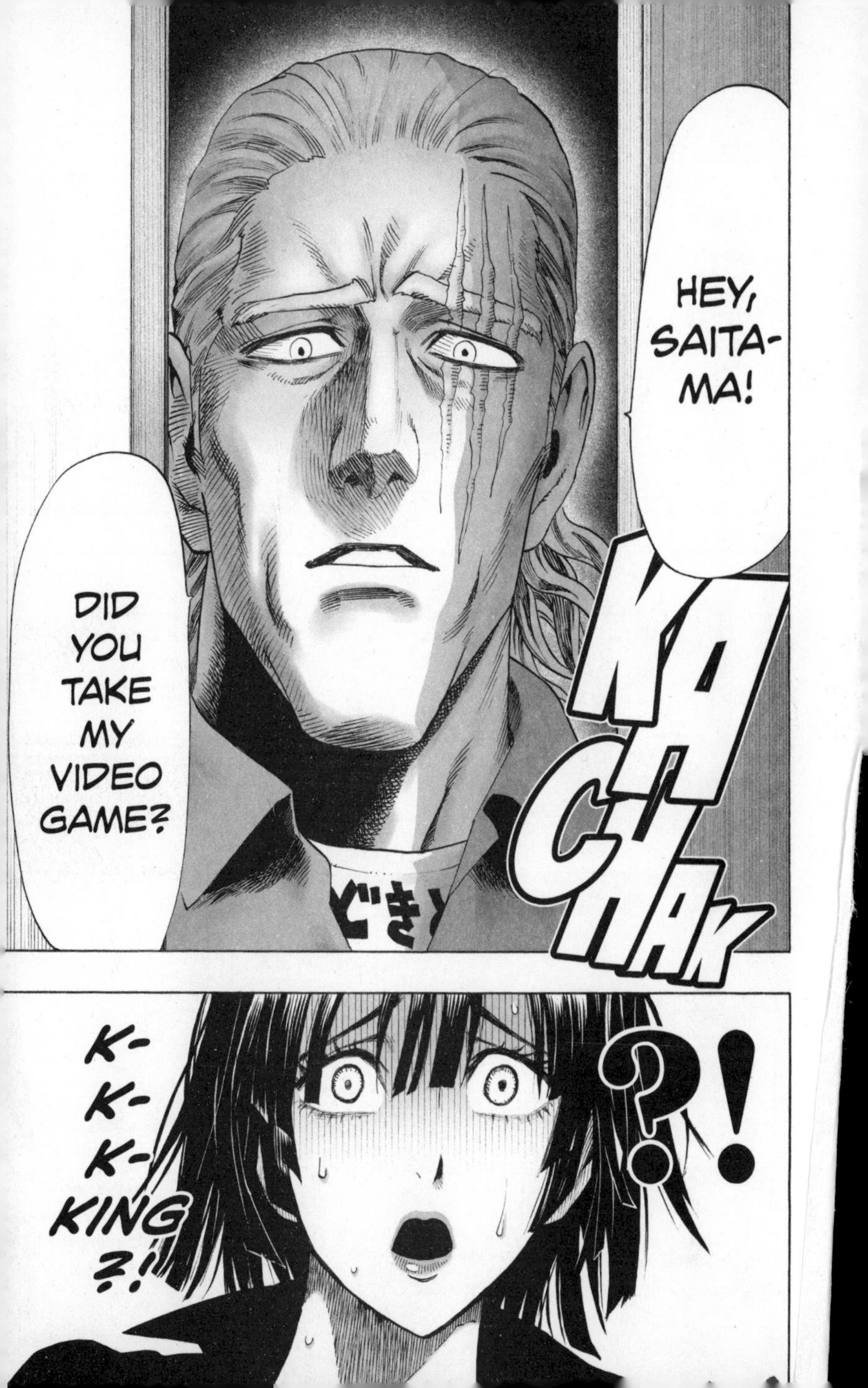
HEY, SAITAMA!
KACHAK
DID YOU TAKE MY VIDEO GAME?
?!
K-K-K-KING?!

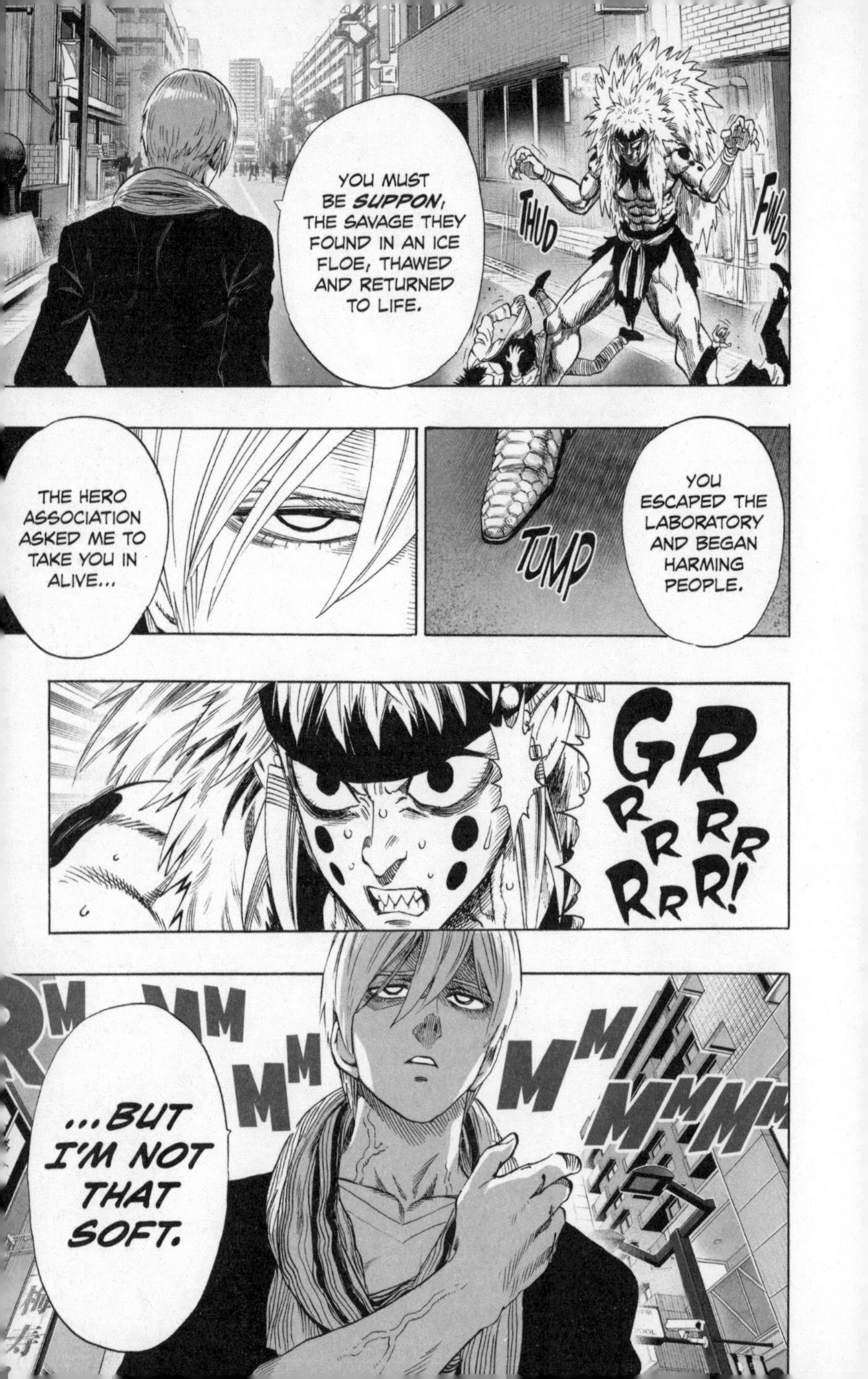
FWUD
YOU MUST BE *SUPPON*, THE SAVAGE THEY FOUND IN AN ICE FLOE, THAWED AND RETURNED TO LIFE.
THUD
YOU ESCAPED THE LABORATORY AND BEGAN HARMING PEOPLE.
TUMP
THE HERO ASSOCIATION ASKED ME TO TAKE YOU IN ALIVE...
GRRRRRRRRRR!
...BUT I'M NOT THAT SOFT.

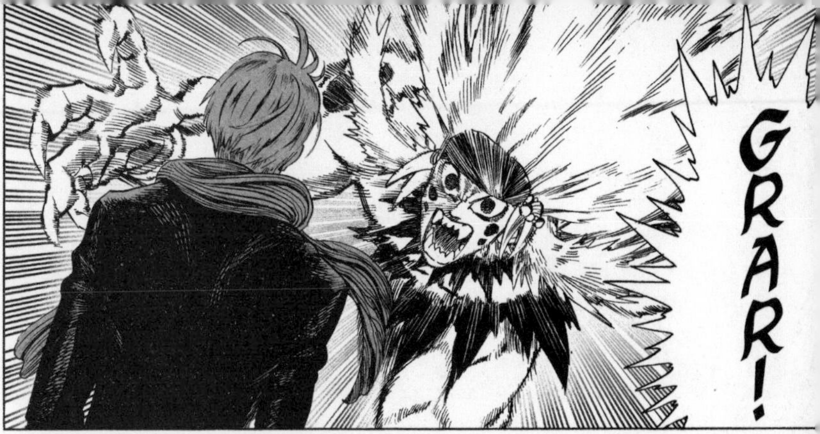
GRAR!
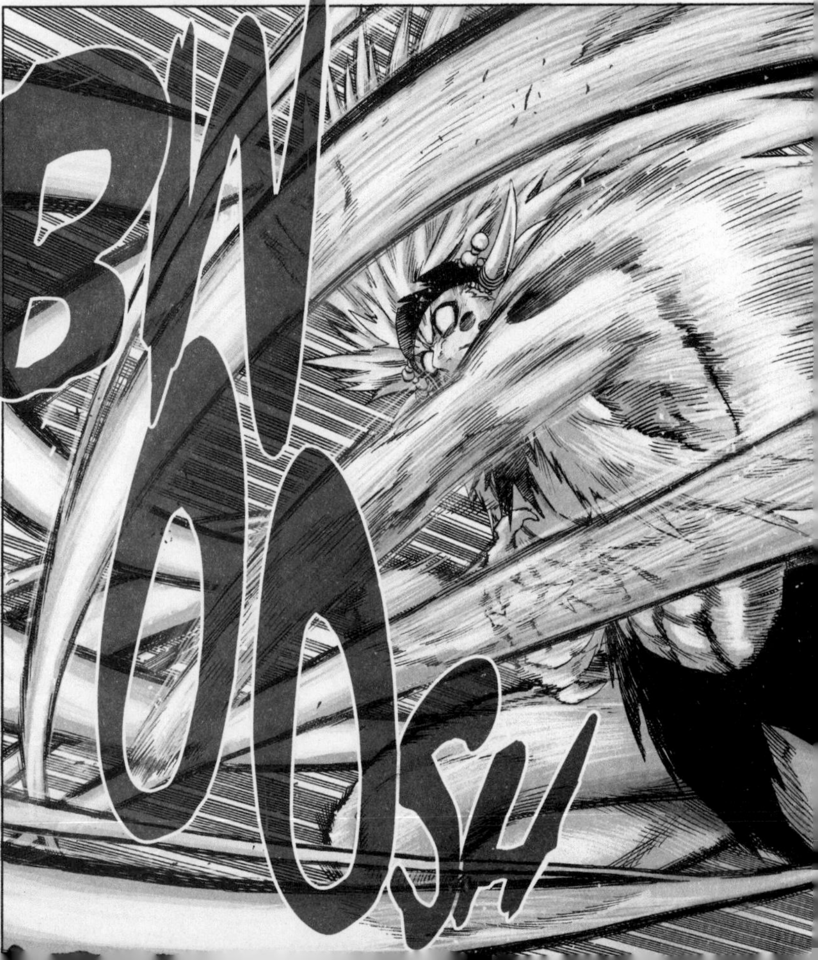
BWOOSH!

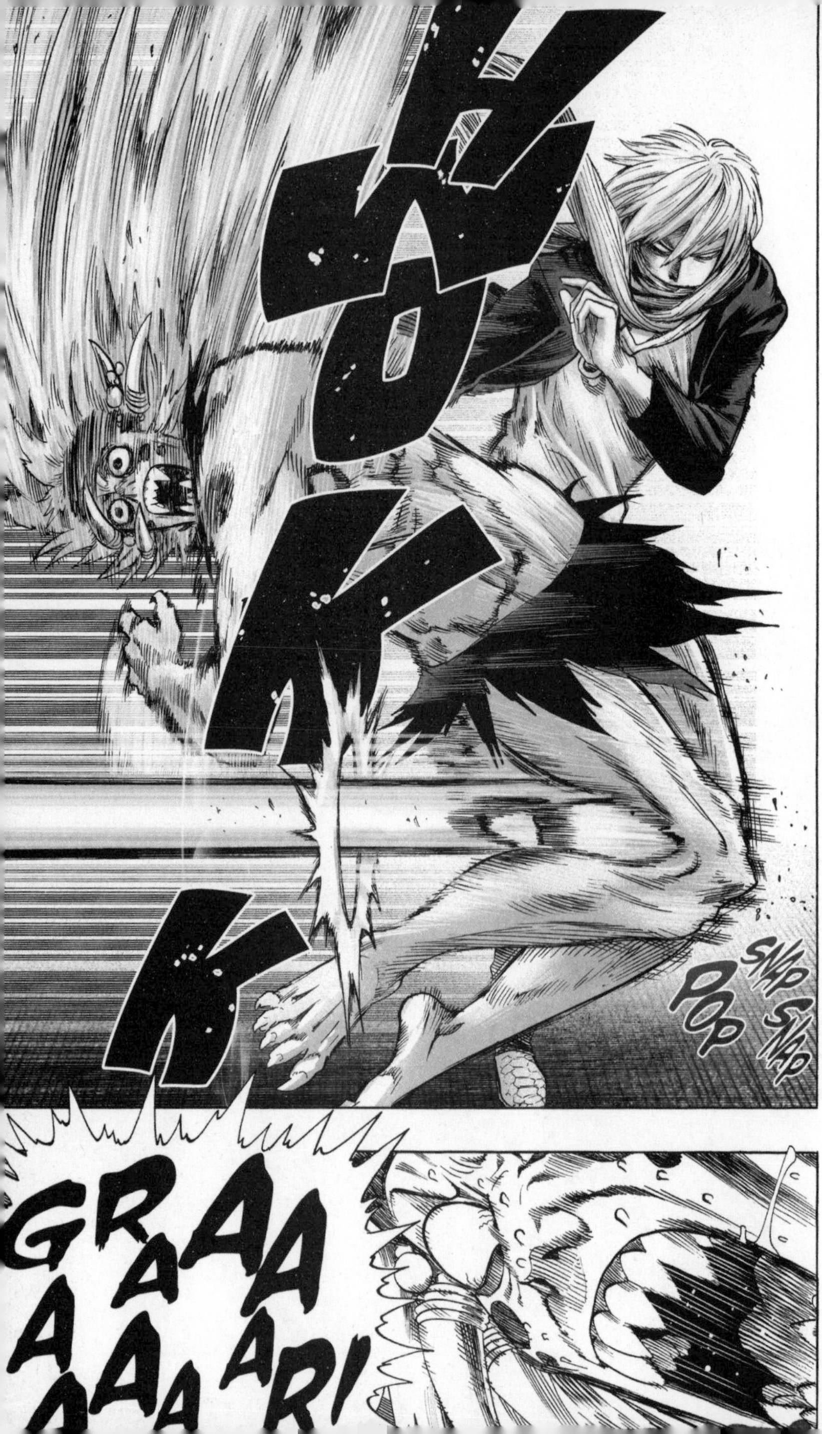
SNAP SNAP
POP
GRAAAAAAAAAARI

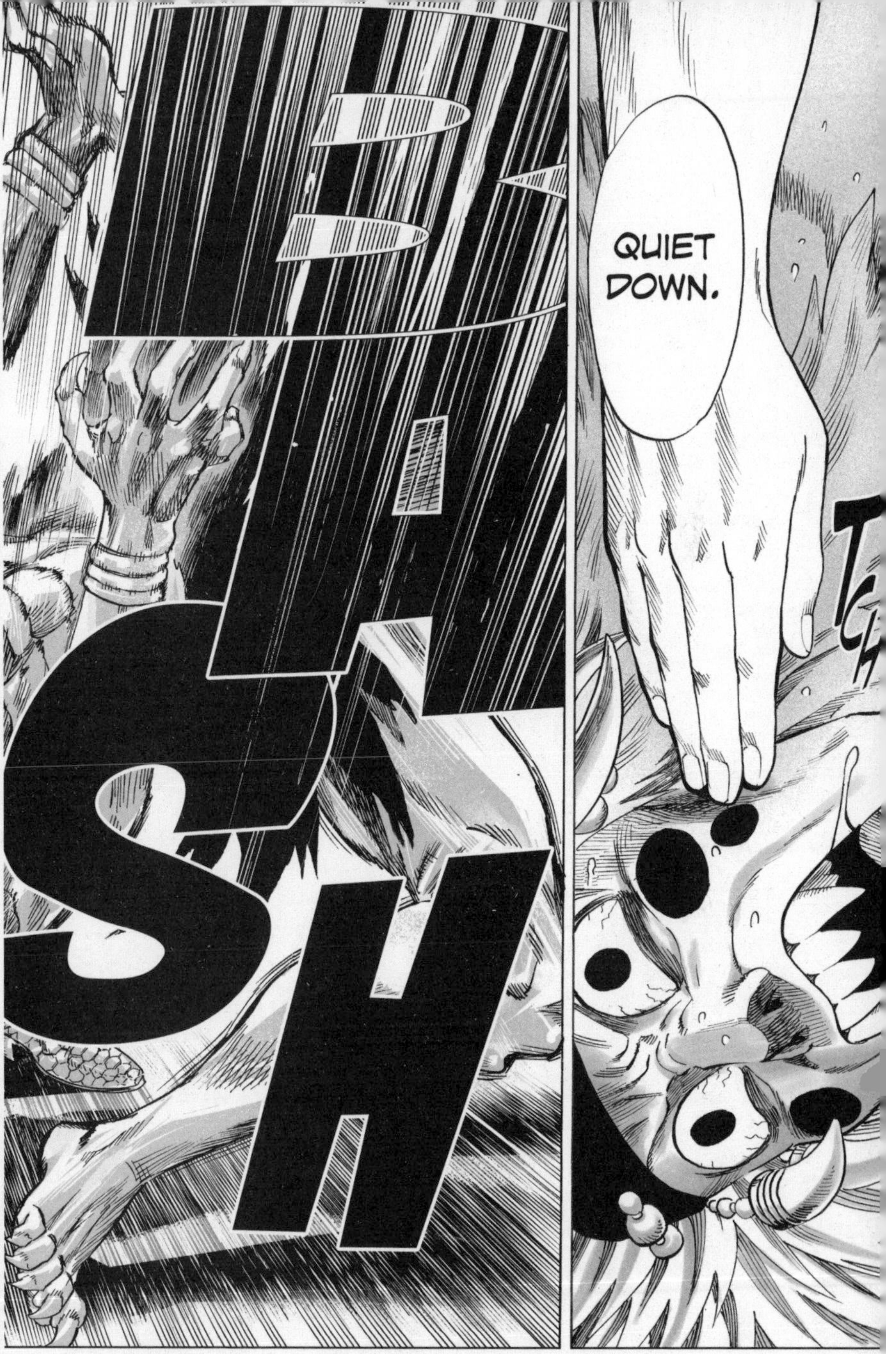
QUIET DOWN.
TCH
SH

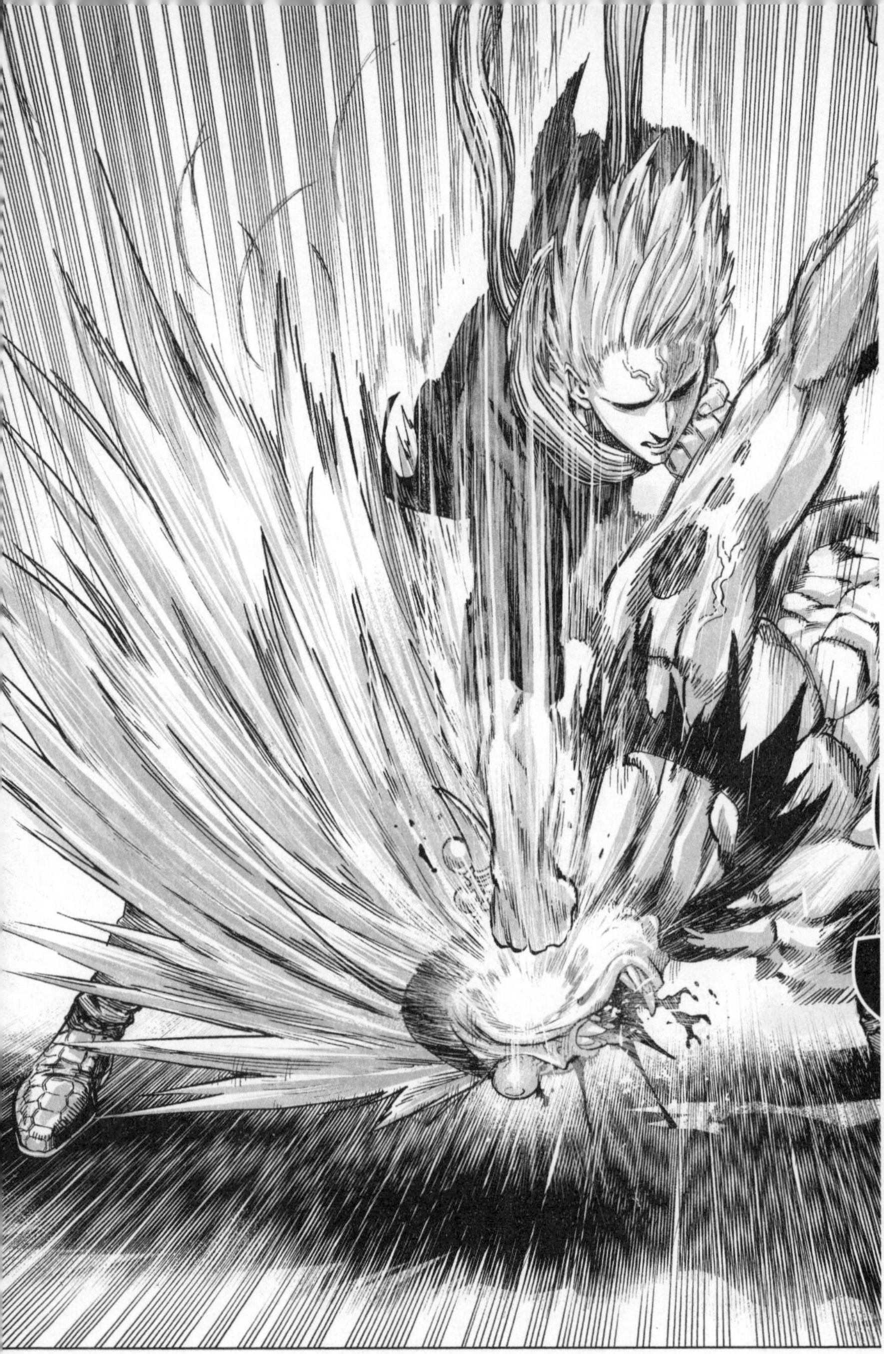

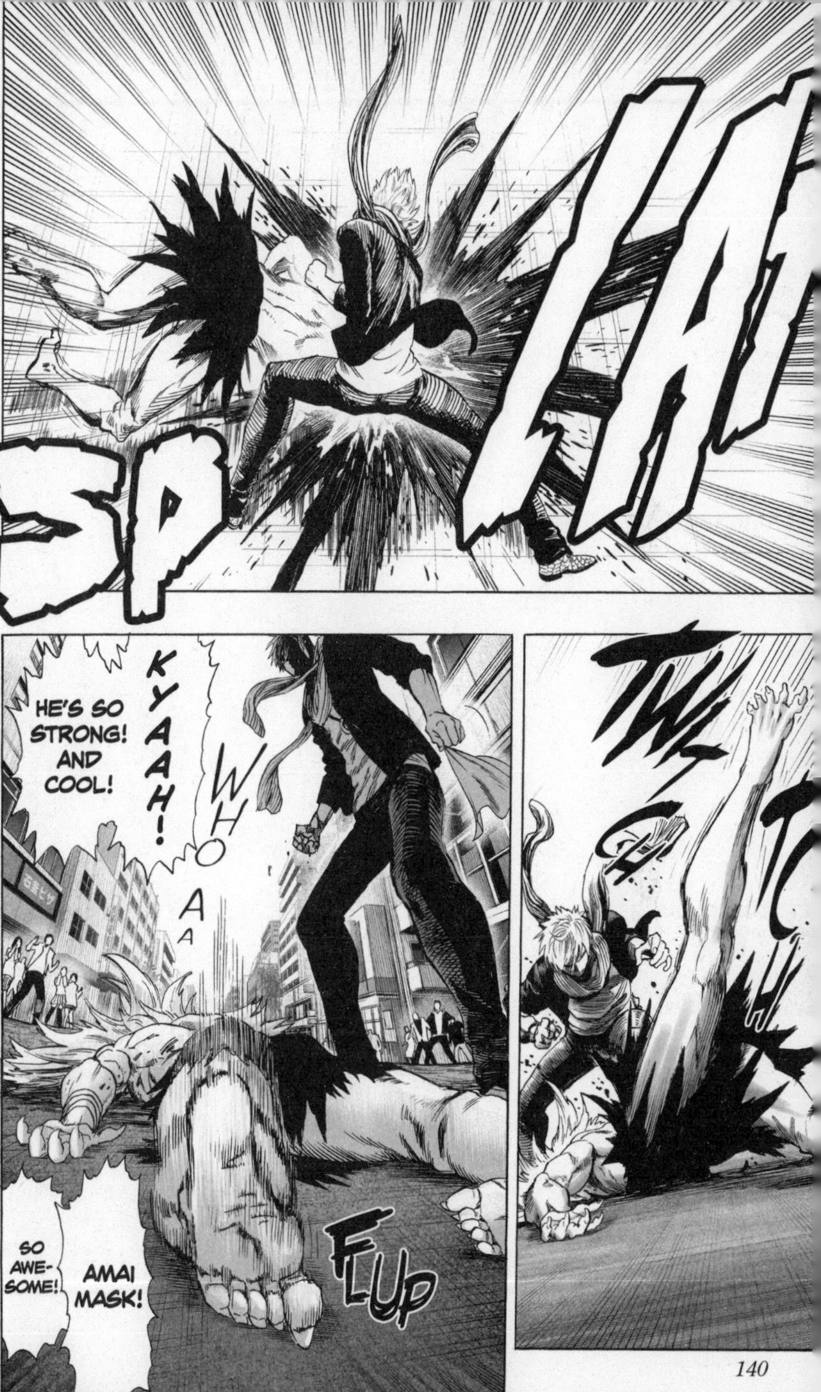
SP
WHOAA
KYAAAH!
HE'S SO STRONG! AND COOL!
AMAI MASK!
SO AWE-SOME!
FLUP

LOOK OVER HERE!

HANDSOME KAMEN! HANDSOME KAMEN!

...DEFY COMMON UNDER-STANDING.

SOME MONSTERS...

AND THEN THERE ARE MONSTERS AMONG MONSTERS! LIKE KING, THE STRONGEST MAN! AND BLAST, WHO STANDS ATOP THE HERO WORLD!

YOU'RE MONSTROUS, BUT NOT LIKE HANDSOME KAMEN AND MY SISTER!

WHAT'S WRONG WITH FORMING A FACTION?

IT'S DIFFICULT TO MOVE UP ALONE!

BUT I WON'T JOIN YOU.

NOTHING.

DING DONG

YOU'LL NEVER REACH THE TOP!

...JUST BECAUSE YOU'RE A LITTLE STRONG?

HMPH! REFUSE MY INVITATION...

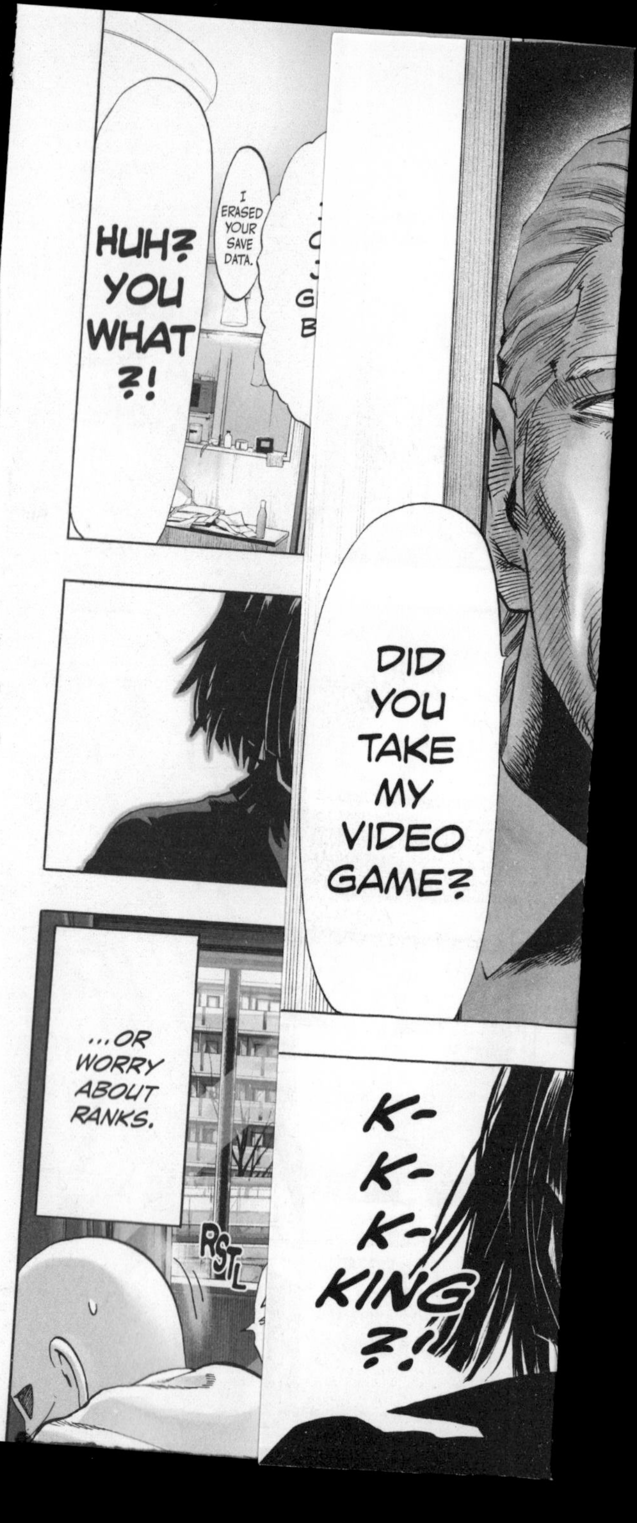
DID YOU TAKE MY VIDEO GAME?
I ERASED YOUR SAVE DATA.
HUH? YOU WHAT?!
...OR WORRY ABOUT RANKS.
RSTL
K-K-K-KING?!

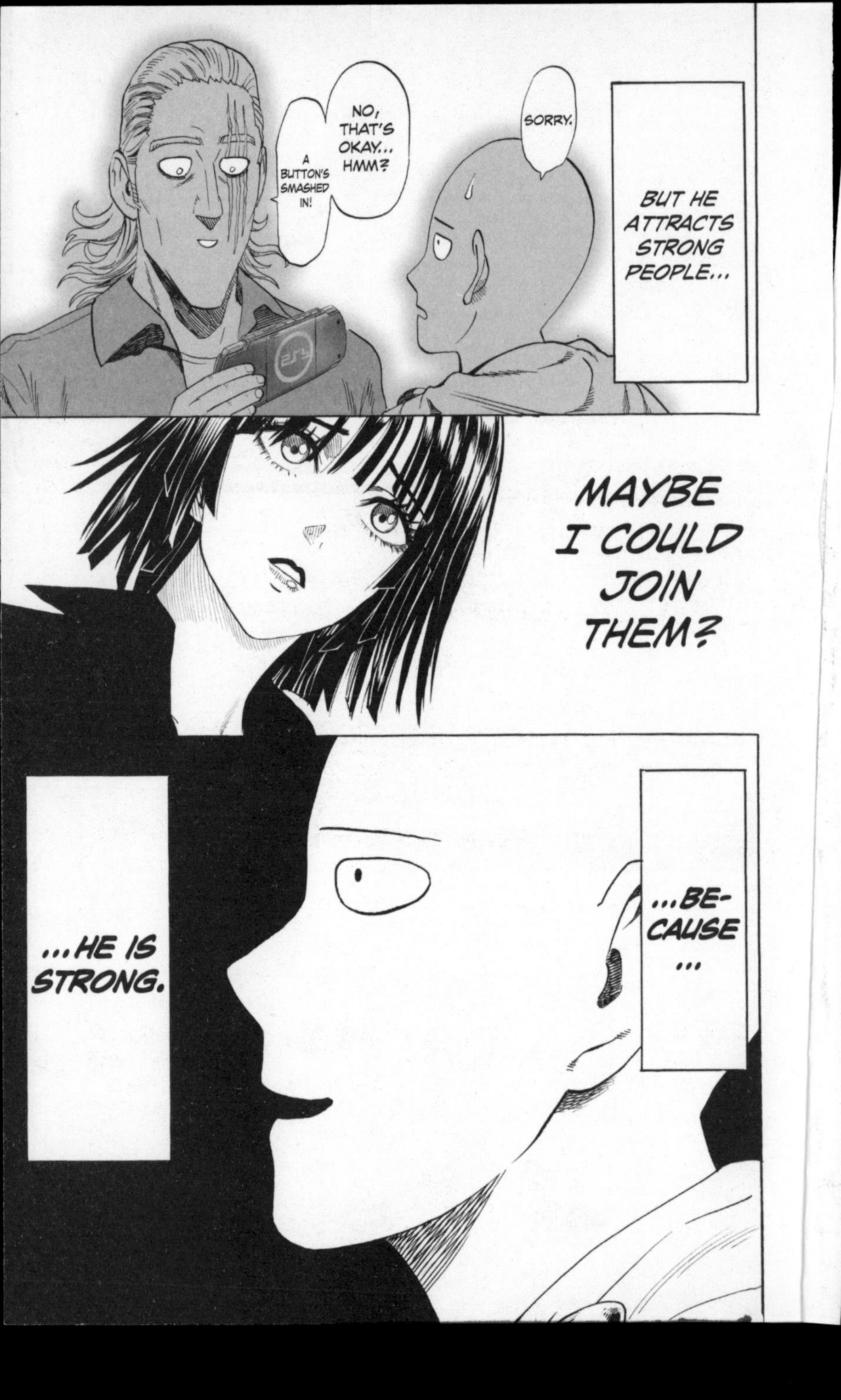
BUT HE ATTRACTS STRONG PEOPLE...
SORRY.
NO, THAT'S OKAY... HMM?
A BUTTON'S SMASHED IN!
MAYBE I COULD JOIN THEM?
...BE-CAUSE...
...HE IS STRONG.

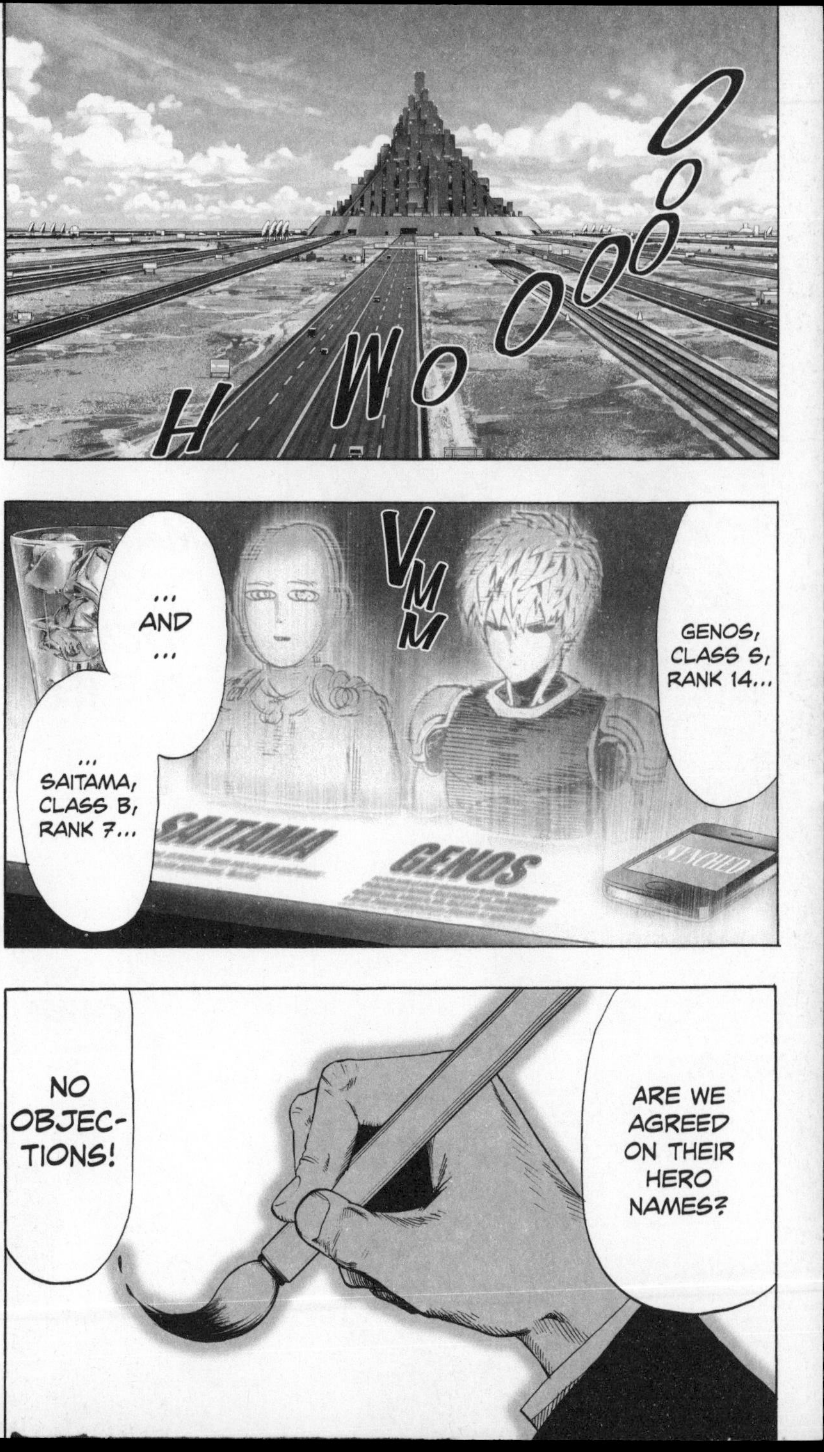
HWOOOOOOO
GENOS, CLASS S, RANK 14...
VMM
...AND ...
...SAITAMA, CLASS B, RANK 7...
SAITAMA
GENOS
SYNCHED
ARE WE AGREED ON THEIR HERO NAMES?
NO OBJECTIONS!
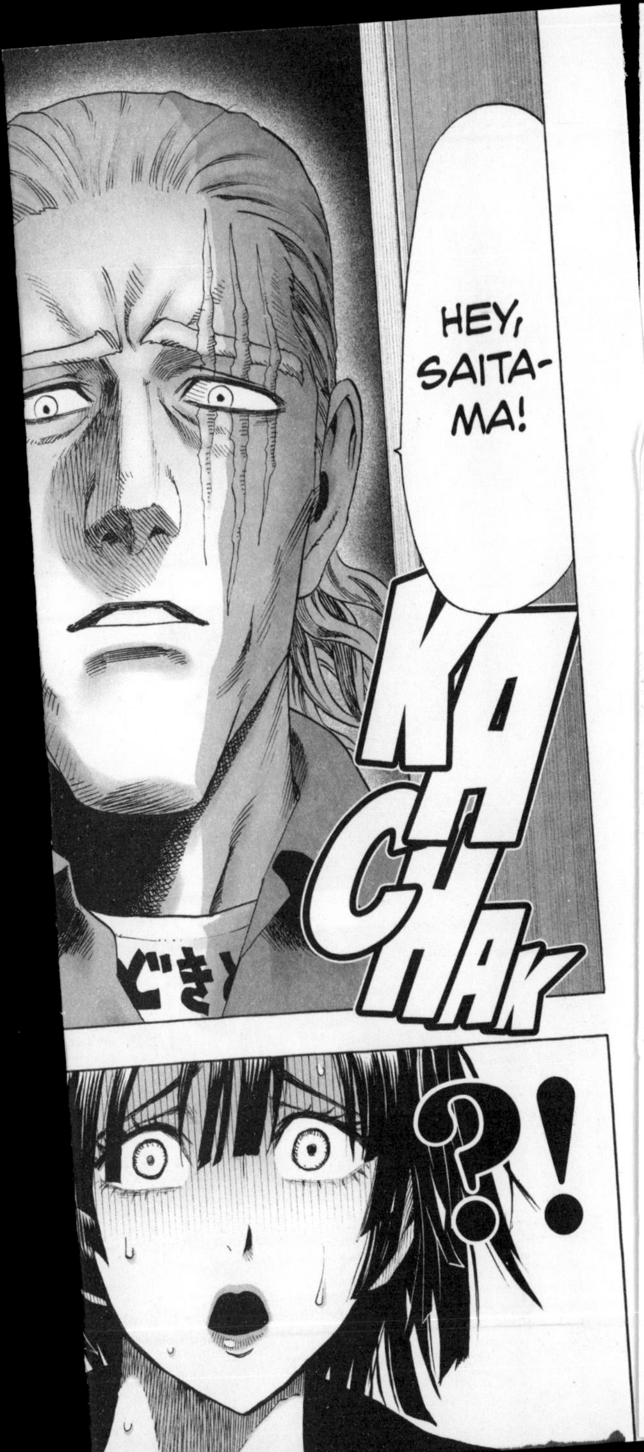
HEY, SAITAMA!
KACHAK
?!

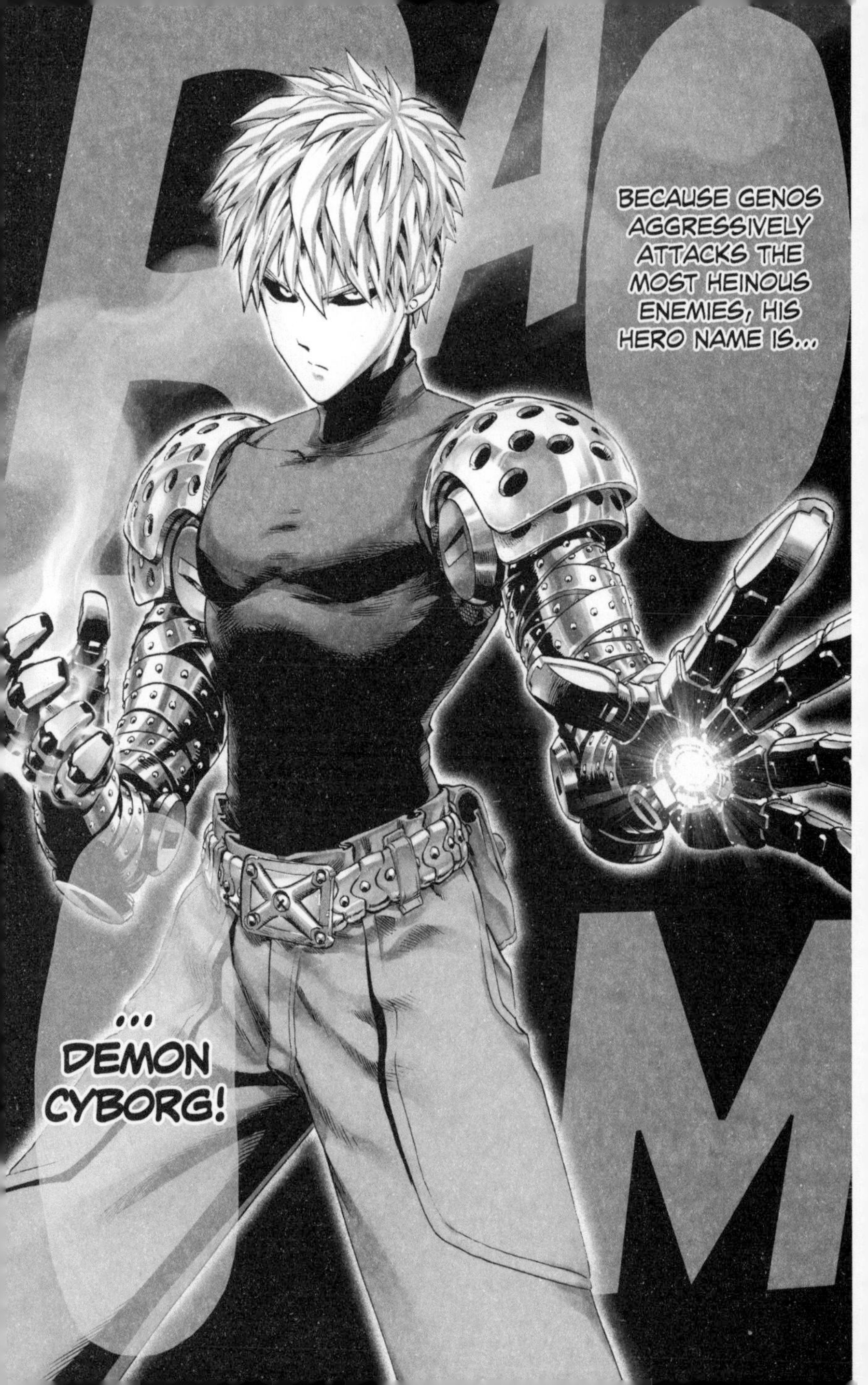
BECAUSE GENOS AGGRESSIVELY ATTACKS THE MOST HEINOUS ENEMIES, HIS HERO NAME IS...
... DEMON CYBORG!

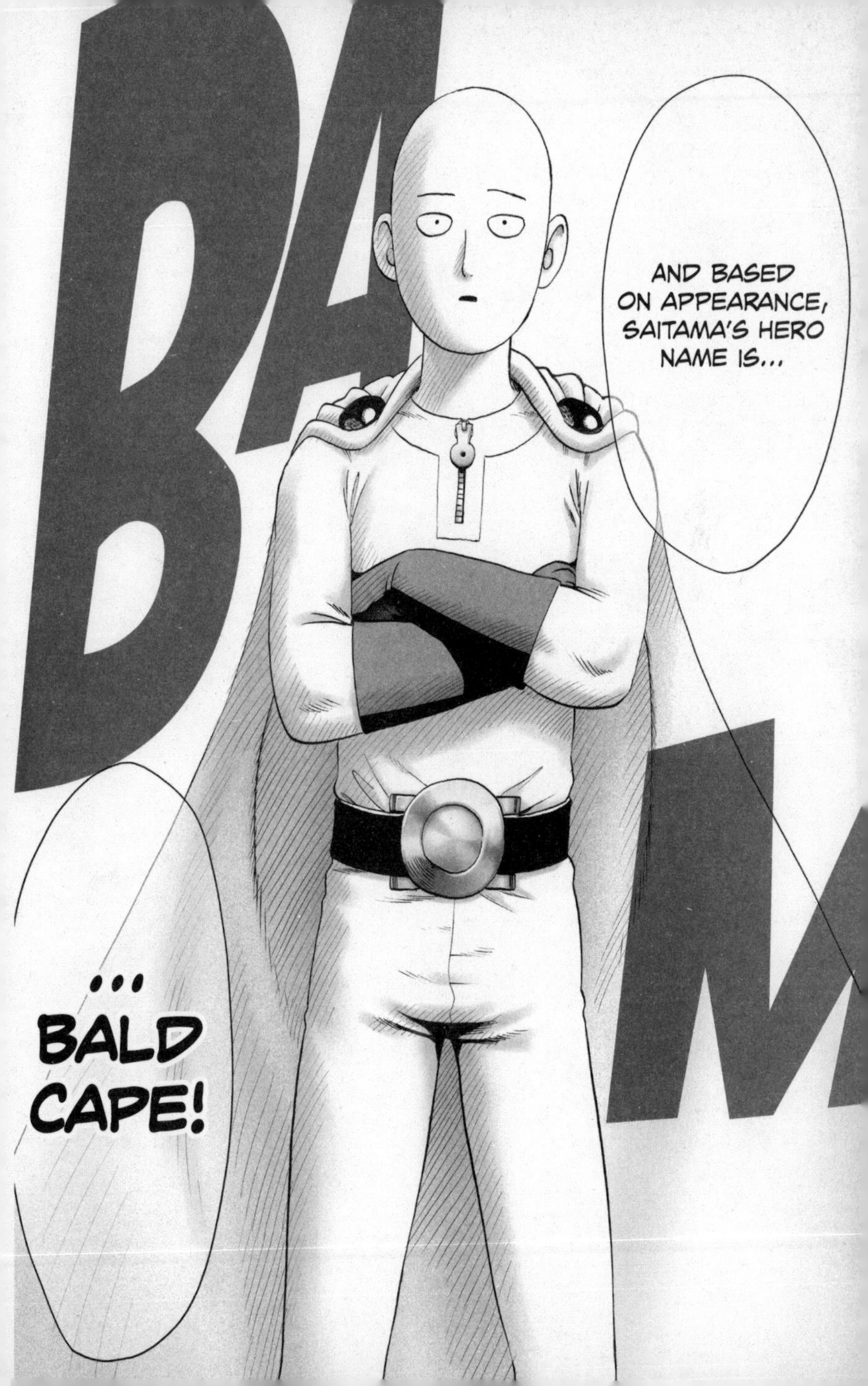
AND BASED ON APPEARANCE, SAITAMA'S HERO NAME IS...
BAM
... BALD CAPE!

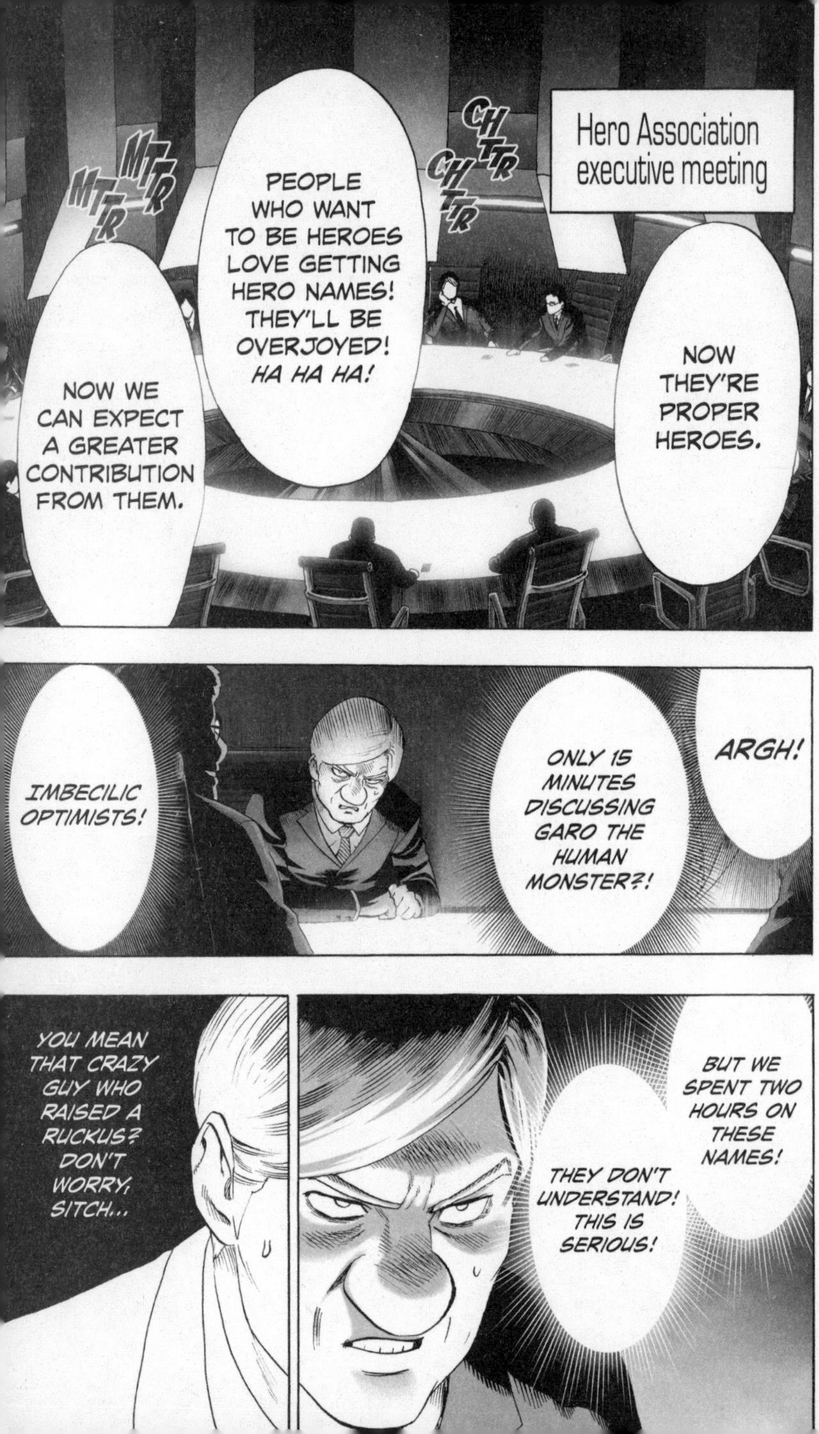
Hero Association executive meeting
CHTTR CHTTR
NOW THEY'RE PROPER HEROES.
PEOPLE WHO WANT TO BE HEROES LOVE GETTING HERO NAMES! THEY'LL BE OVERJOYED! HA HA HA!
NOW WE CAN EXPECT A GREATER CONTRIBUTION FROM THEM.
MTTR MTTR
ARGH!
ONLY 15 MINUTES DISCUSSING GARO THE HUMAN MONSTER?!
IMBECILIC OPTIMISTS!
BUT WE SPENT TWO HOURS ON THESE NAMES!
THEY DON'T UNDERSTAND! THIS IS SERIOUS!
YOU MEAN THAT CRAZY GUY WHO RAISED A RUCKUS? DON'T WORRY, SITCH...

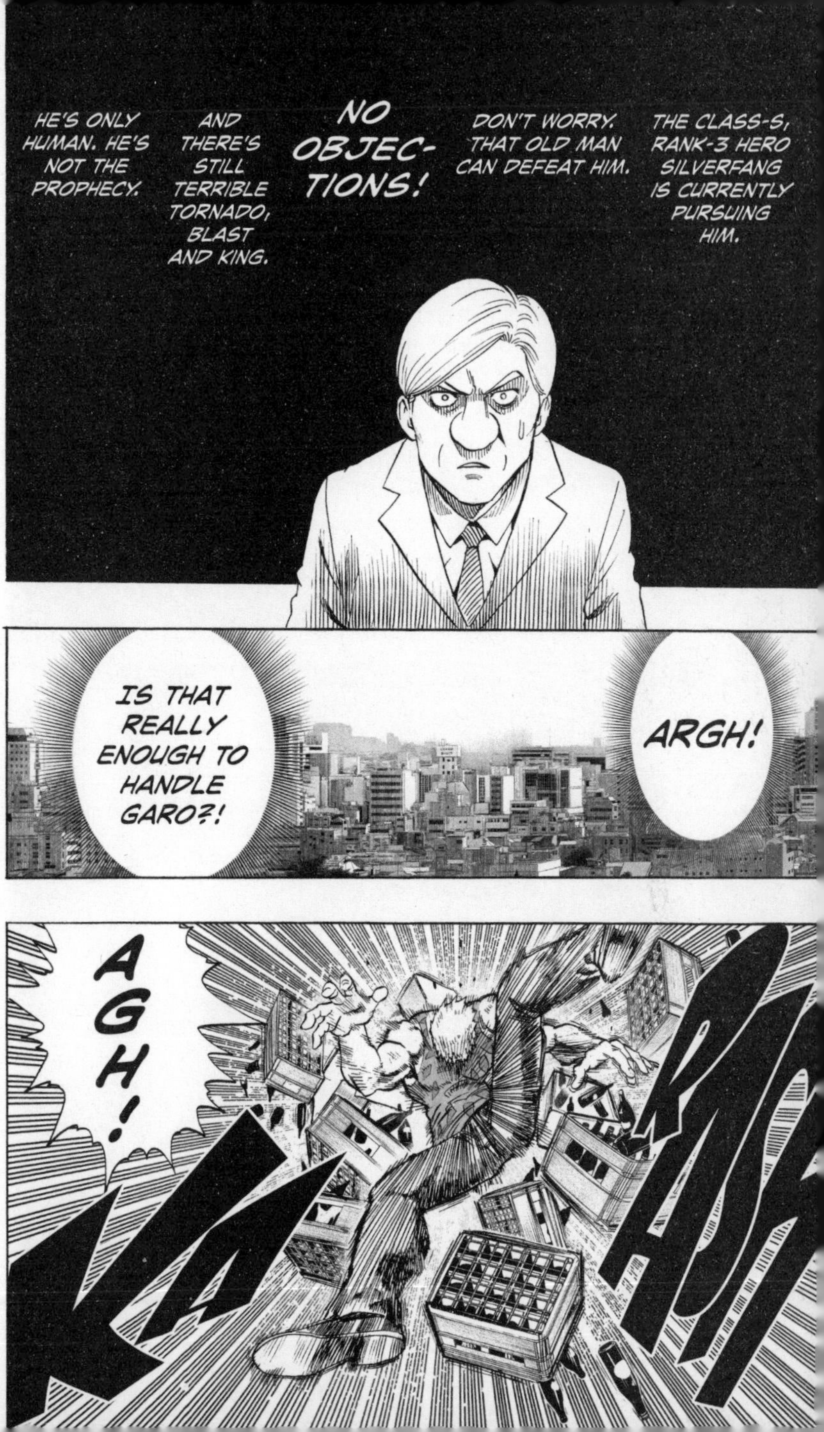
THE CLASS-S, RANK-3 HERO SILVERFANG IS CURRENTLY PURSUING HIM.
DON'T WORRY. THAT OLD MAN CAN DEFEAT HIM.
NO OBJECTIONS!
AND THERE'S STILL TERRIBLE TORNADO, BLAST AND KING.
HE'S ONLY HUMAN. HE'S NOT THE PROPHECY.
ARGH!
IS THAT REALLY ENOUGH TO HANDLE GARO?!
AGH!

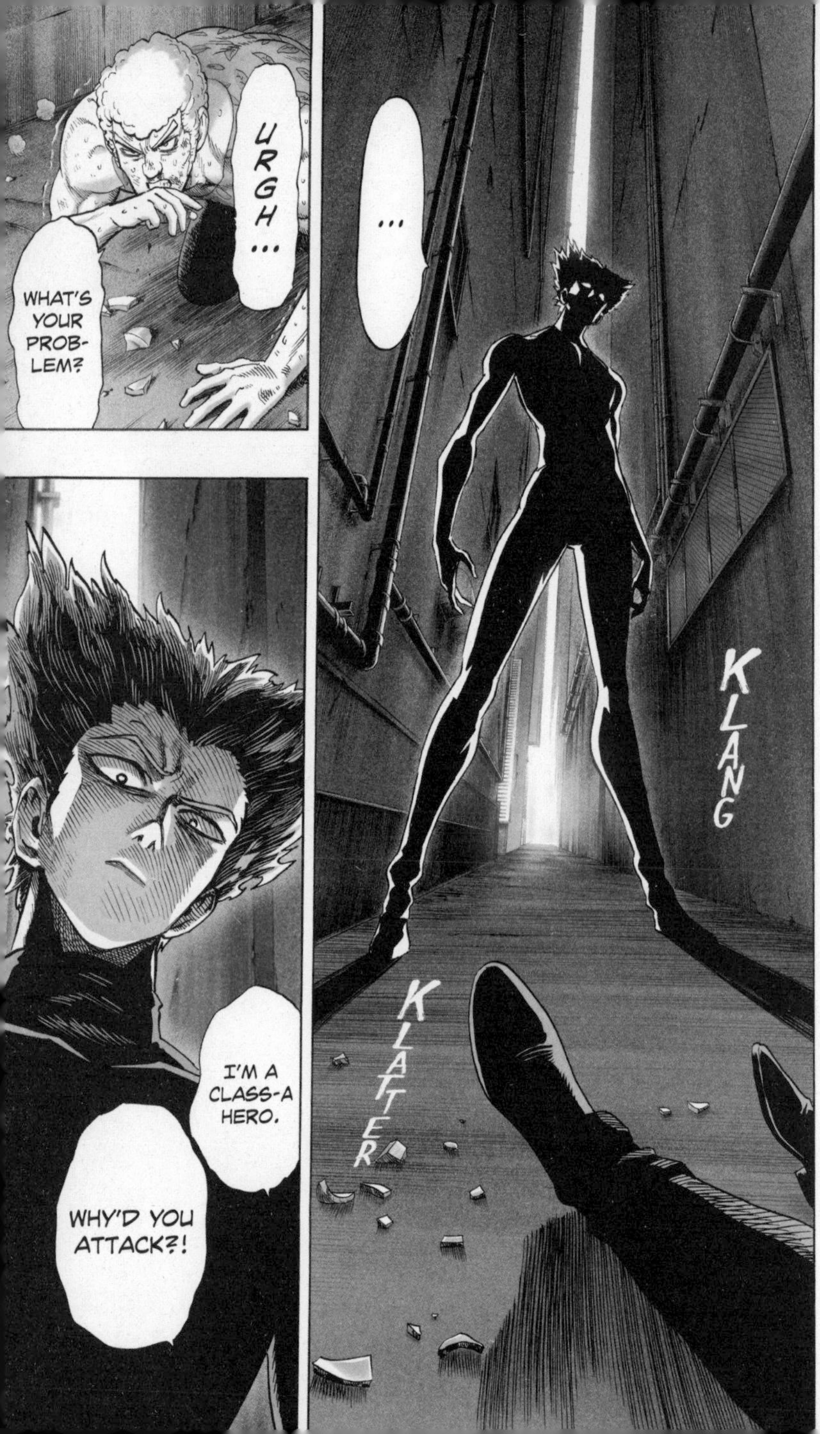
...
KLANG
KLATTER
URGH...
WHAT'S YOUR PROB-LEM?
I'M A CLASS-A HERO.
WHY'D YOU ATTACK?!

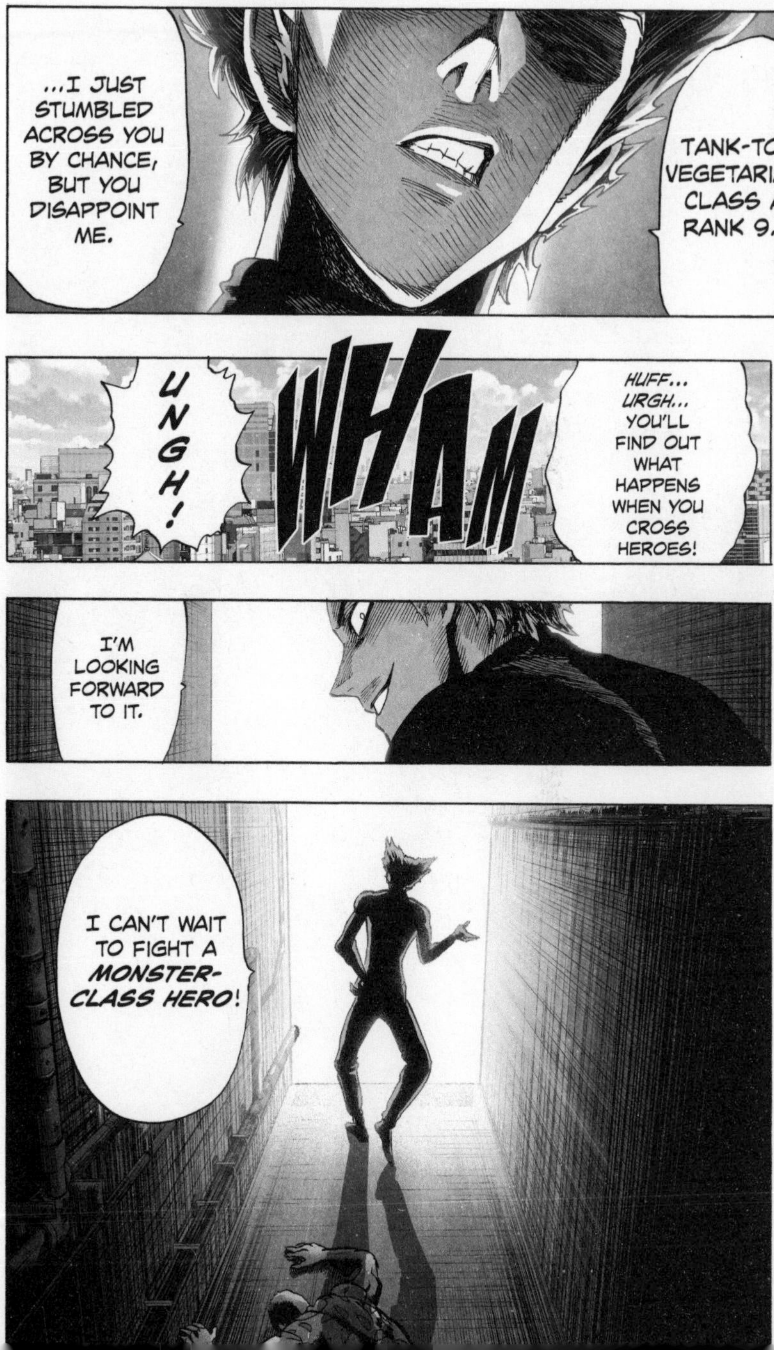
TANK-TOP VEGETARIAN, CLASS A, RANK 9...
...I JUST STUMBLED ACROSS YOU BY CHANCE, BUT YOU DISAPPOINT ME.
HUFF... URGH... YOU'LL FIND OUT WHAT HAPPENS WHEN YOU CROSS HEROES!
WHAM
UNGH!
I'M LOOKING FORWARD TO IT.
I CAN'T WAIT TO FIGHT A *MONSTER-CLASS HERO*!

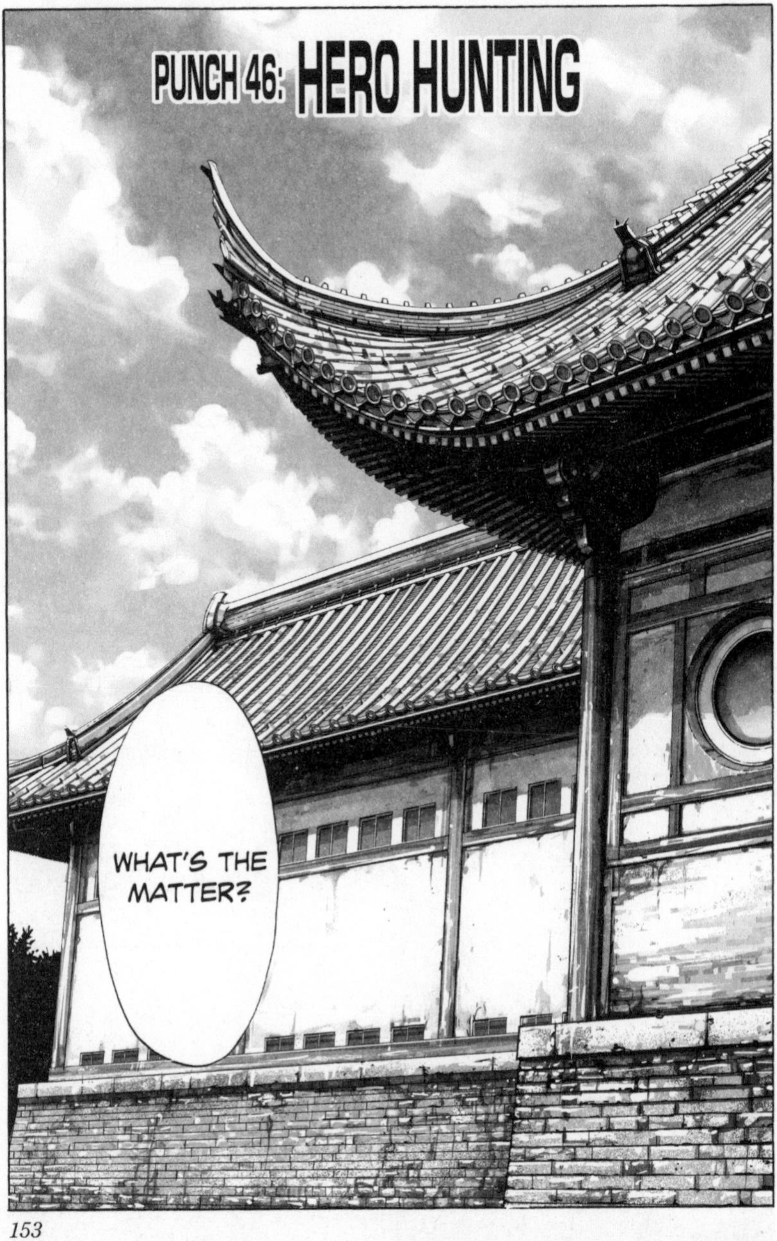
PUNCH 46: HERO HUNTING
WHAT'S THE MATTER?

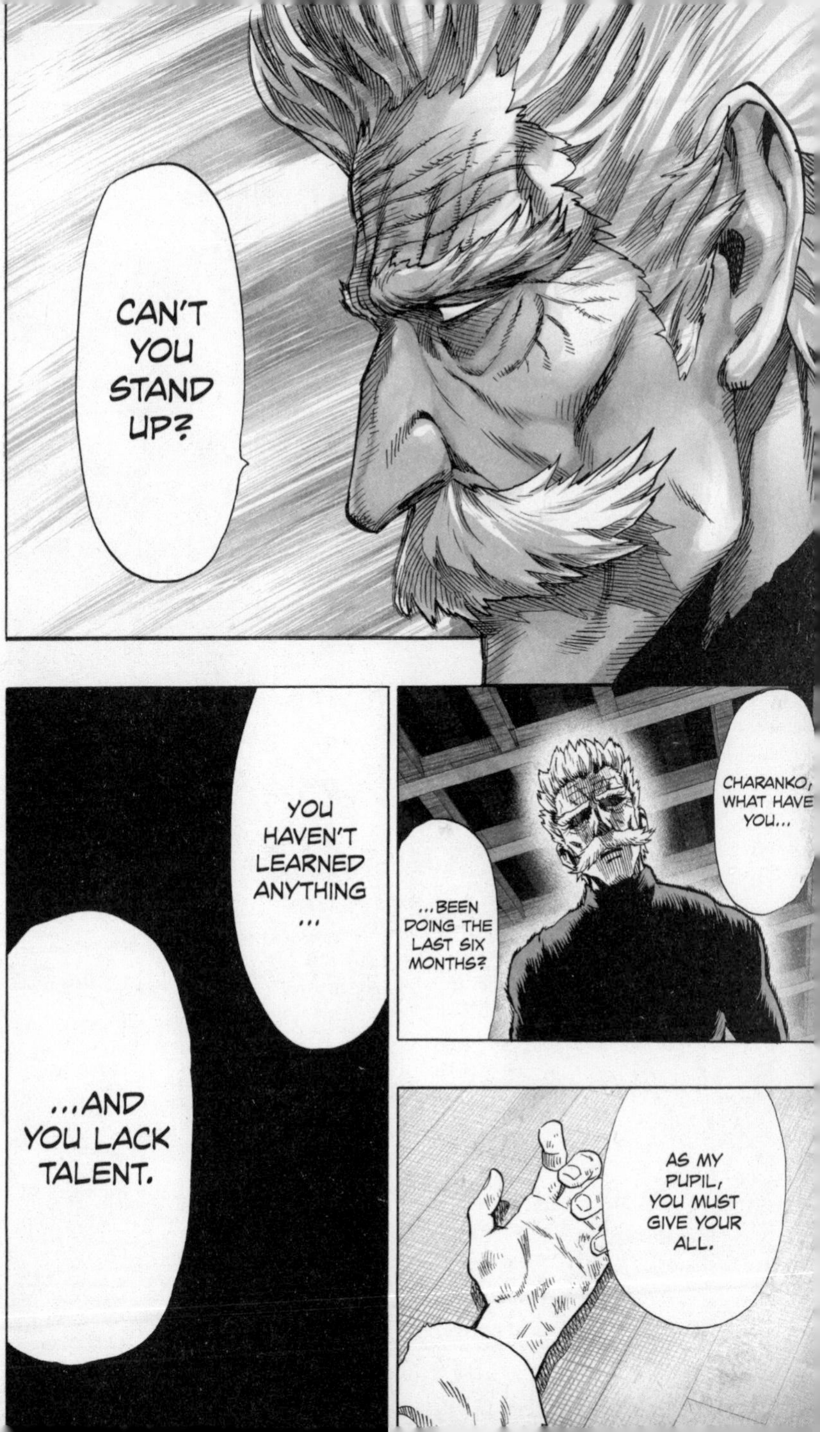
CAN'T YOU STAND UP?
CHARANKO, WHAT HAVE YOU...
...BEEN DOING THE LAST SIX MONTHS?
AS MY PUPIL, YOU MUST GIVE YOUR ALL.
YOU HAVEN'T LEARNED ANYTHING ...
...AND YOU LACK TALENT.

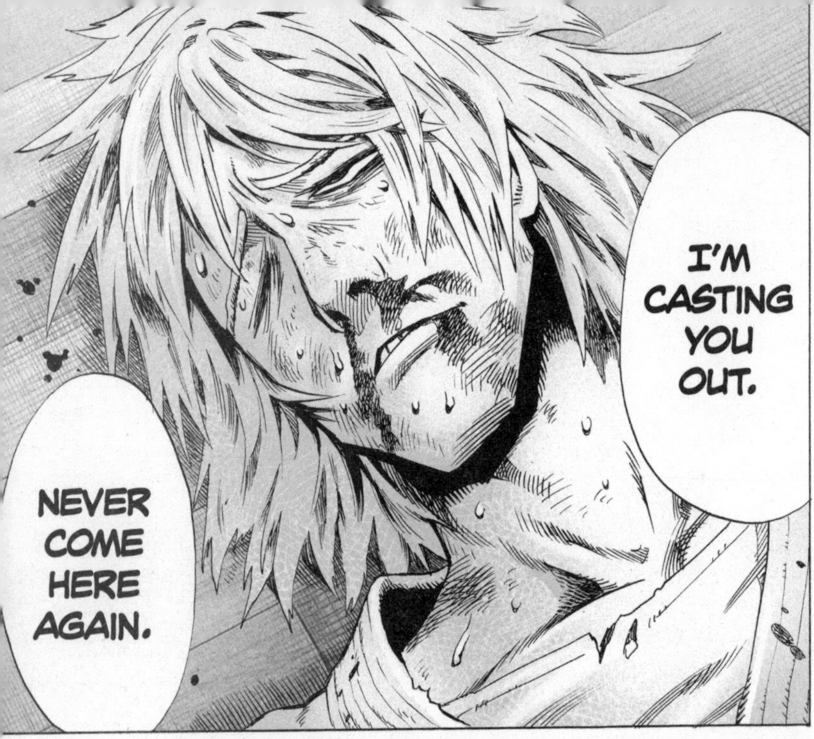
I'M CASTING YOU OUT.
NEVER COME HERE AGAIN.
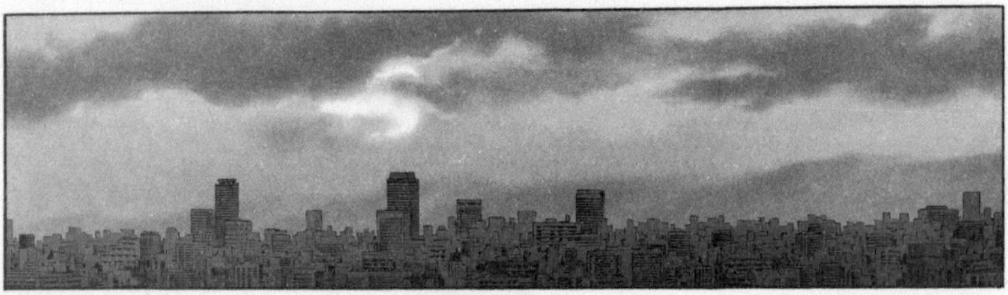
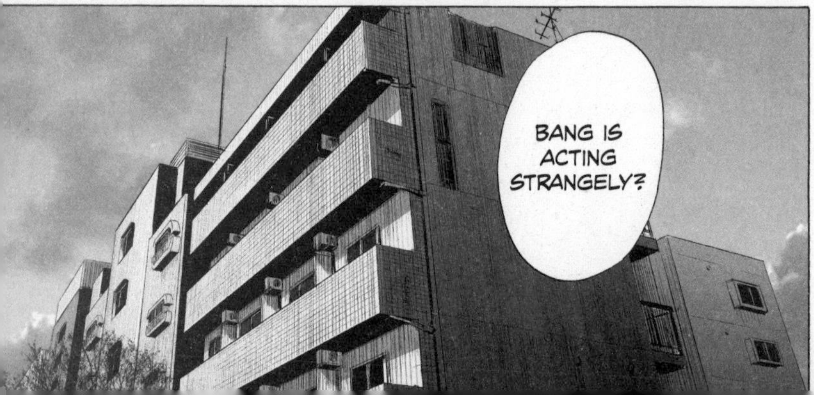
BANG IS ACTING STRANGELY?

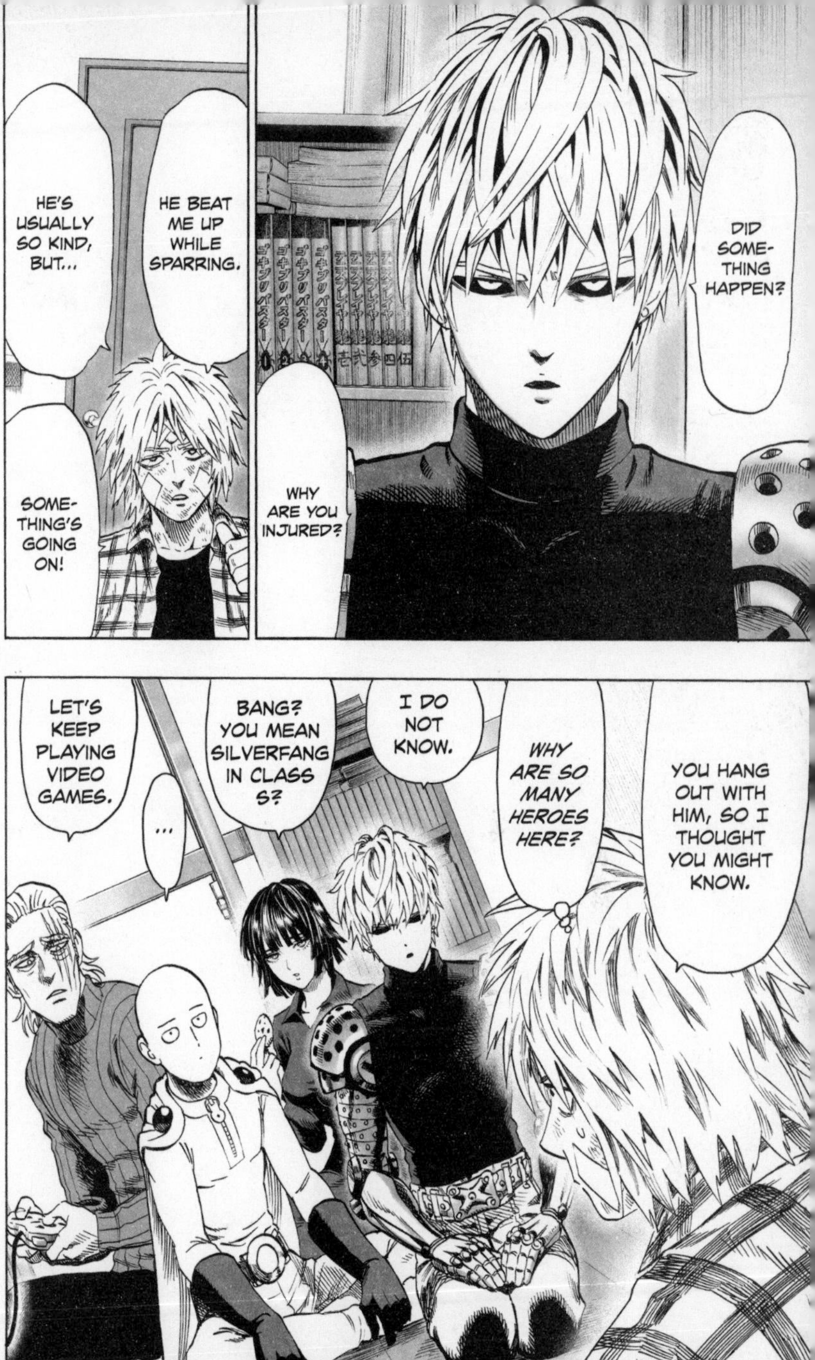
DID SOMETHING HAPPEN?
WHY ARE YOU INJURED?
HE BEAT ME UP WHILE SPARRING.
HE'S USUALLY SO KIND, BUT...
SOMETHING'S GOING ON!
YOU HANG OUT WITH HIM, SO I THOUGHT YOU MIGHT KNOW.
WHY ARE SO MANY HEROES HERE?
I DO NOT KNOW.
BANG? YOU MEAN SILVERFANG IN CLASS S?
...
LET'S KEEP PLAYING VIDEO GAMES.

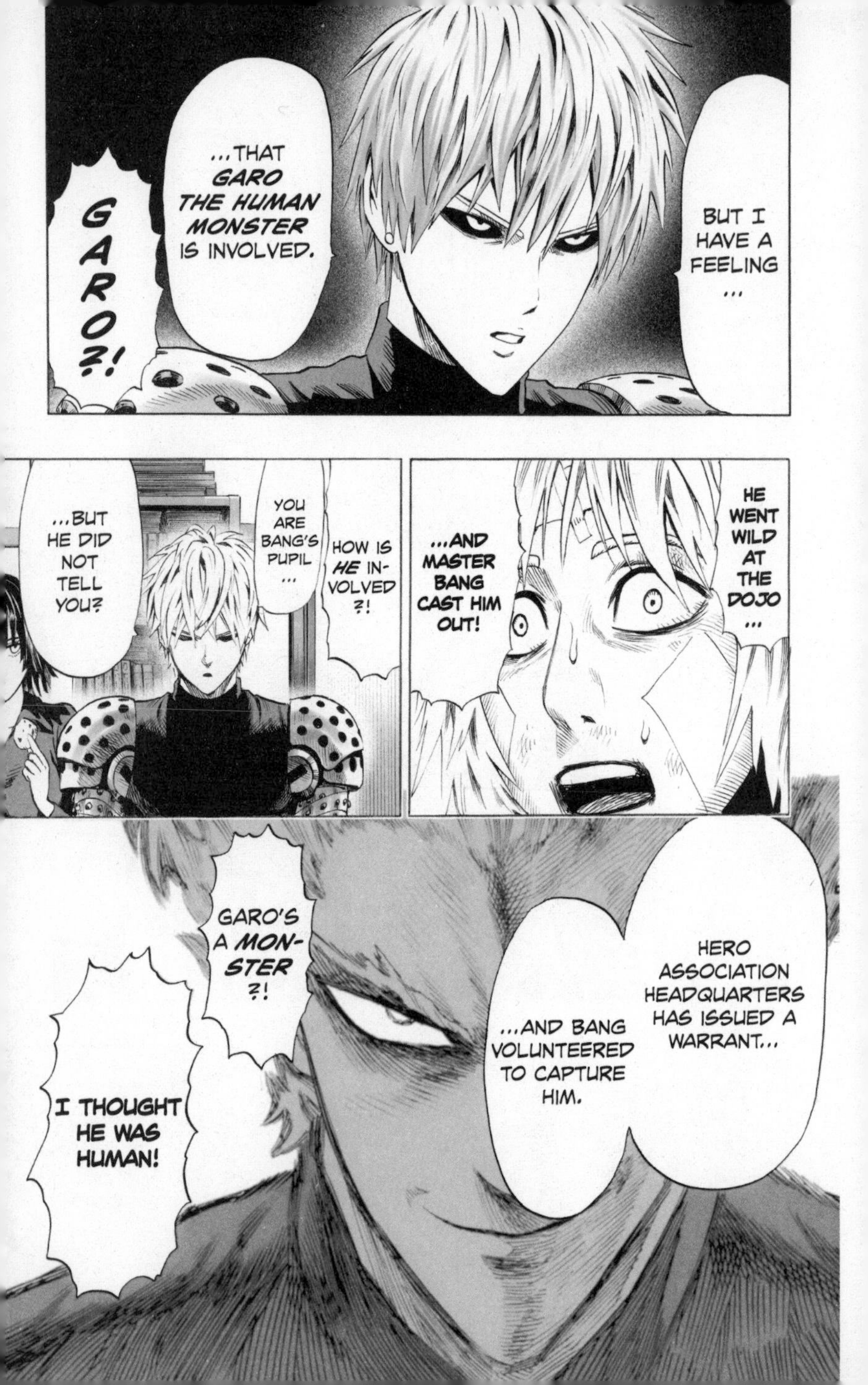
BUT I HAVE A FEELING ...
...THAT GARO THE HUMAN MONSTER IS INVOLVED.
GARO?!
HE WENT WILD AT THE DOJO ...
...AND MASTER BANG CAST HIM OUT!
HOW IS HE INVOLVED?!
YOU ARE BANG'S PUPIL ...
...BUT HE DID NOT TELL YOU?
HERO ASSOCIATION HEADQUARTERS HAS ISSUED A WARRANT...
...AND BANG VOLUNTEERED TO CAPTURE HIM.
GARO'S A MONSTER?!
I THOUGHT HE WAS HUMAN!

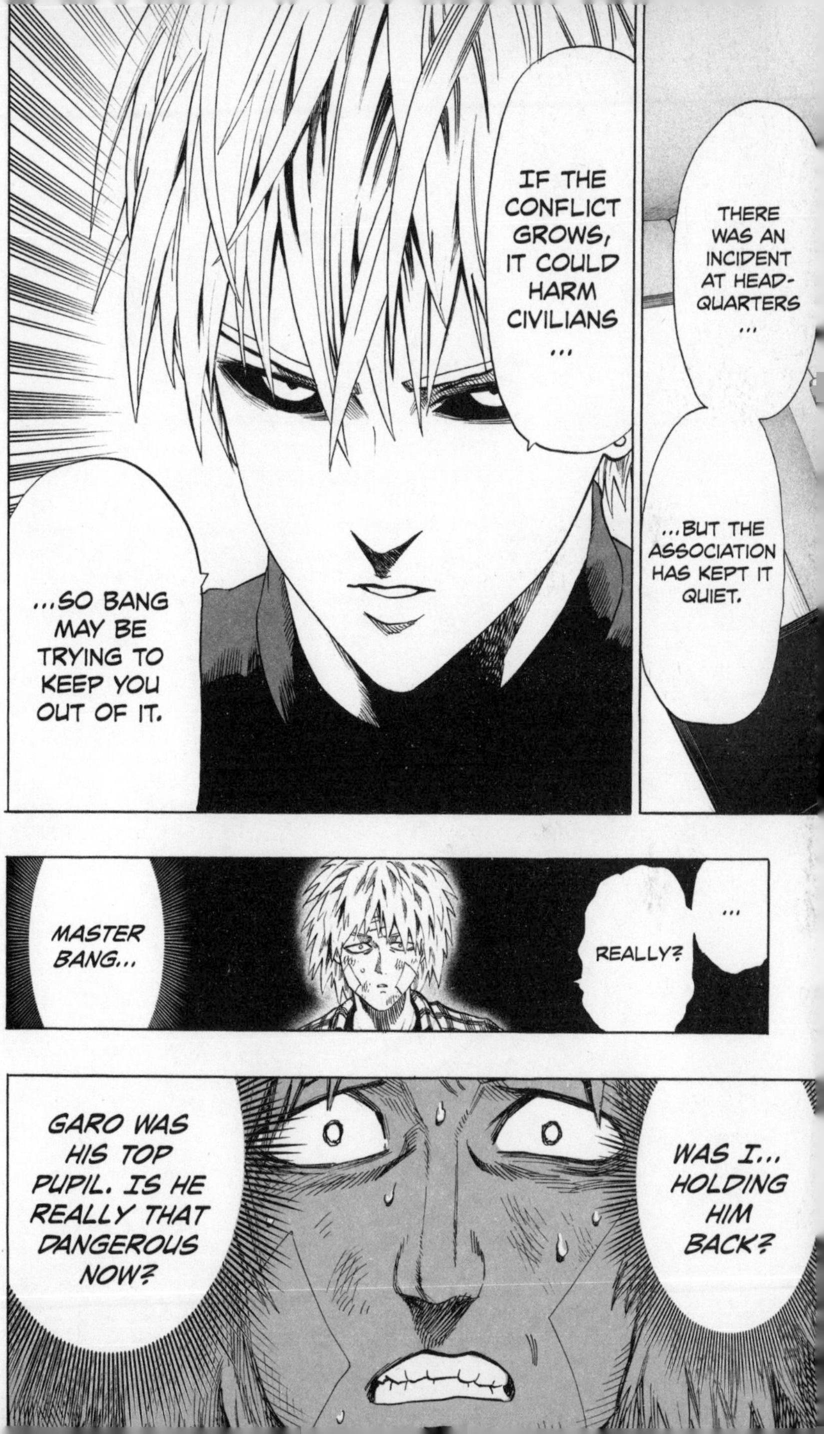
THERE WAS AN INCIDENT AT HEAD-QUARTERS...
...BUT THE ASSOCIATION HAS KEPT IT QUIET.
IF THE CONFLICT GROWS, IT COULD HARM CIVILIANS...
...SO BANG MAY BE TRYING TO KEEP YOU OUT OF IT.
...
REALLY?
MASTER BANG...
WAS I... HOLDING HIM BACK?
GARO WAS HIS TOP PUPIL. IS HE REALLY THAT DANGEROUS NOW?

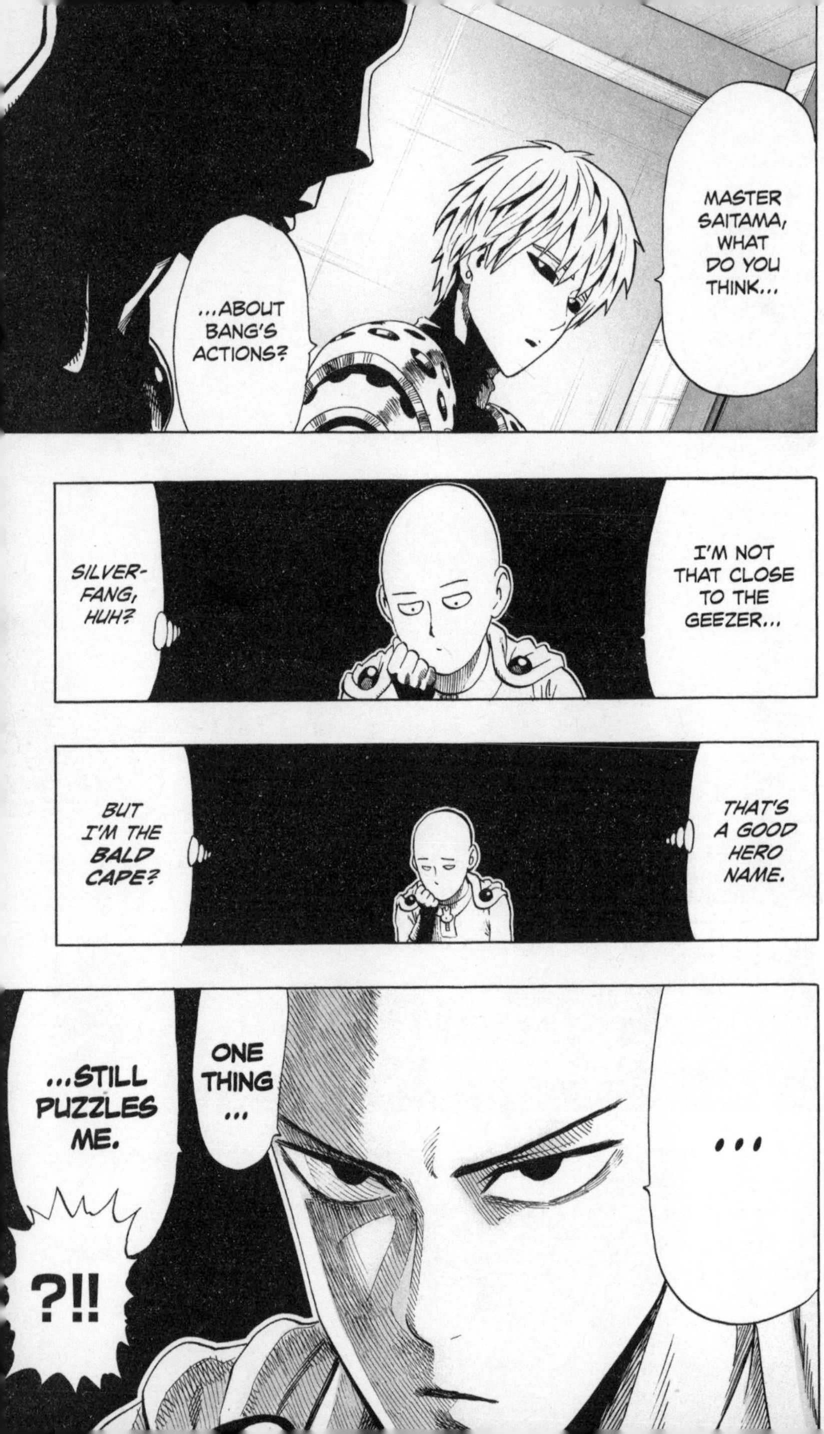
MASTER SAITAMA, WHAT DO YOU THINK...
...ABOUT BANG'S ACTIONS?
I'M NOT THAT CLOSE TO THE GEEZER...
SILVER-FANG, HUH?
THAT'S A GOOD HERO NAME.
BUT I'M THE BALD CAPE?
...
ONE THING ...
...STILL PUZZLES ME.
?!!

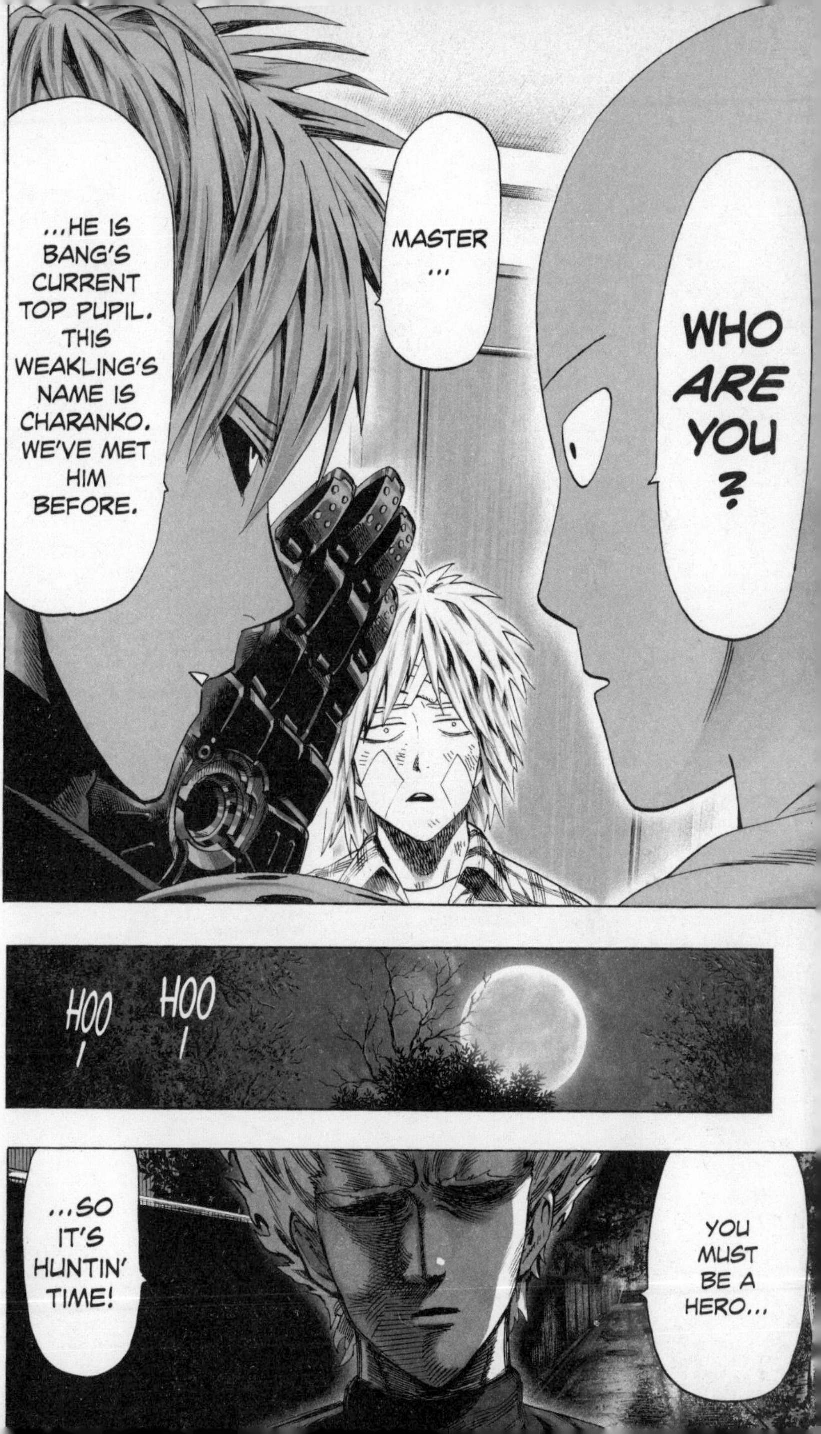
WHO ARE YOU?
MASTER...
...HE IS BANG'S CURRENT TOP PUPIL. THIS WEAKLING'S NAME IS CHARANKO. WE'VE MET HIM BEFORE.
HOO!
HOO!
YOU MUST BE A HERO...
...SO IT'S HUNTIN' TIME!

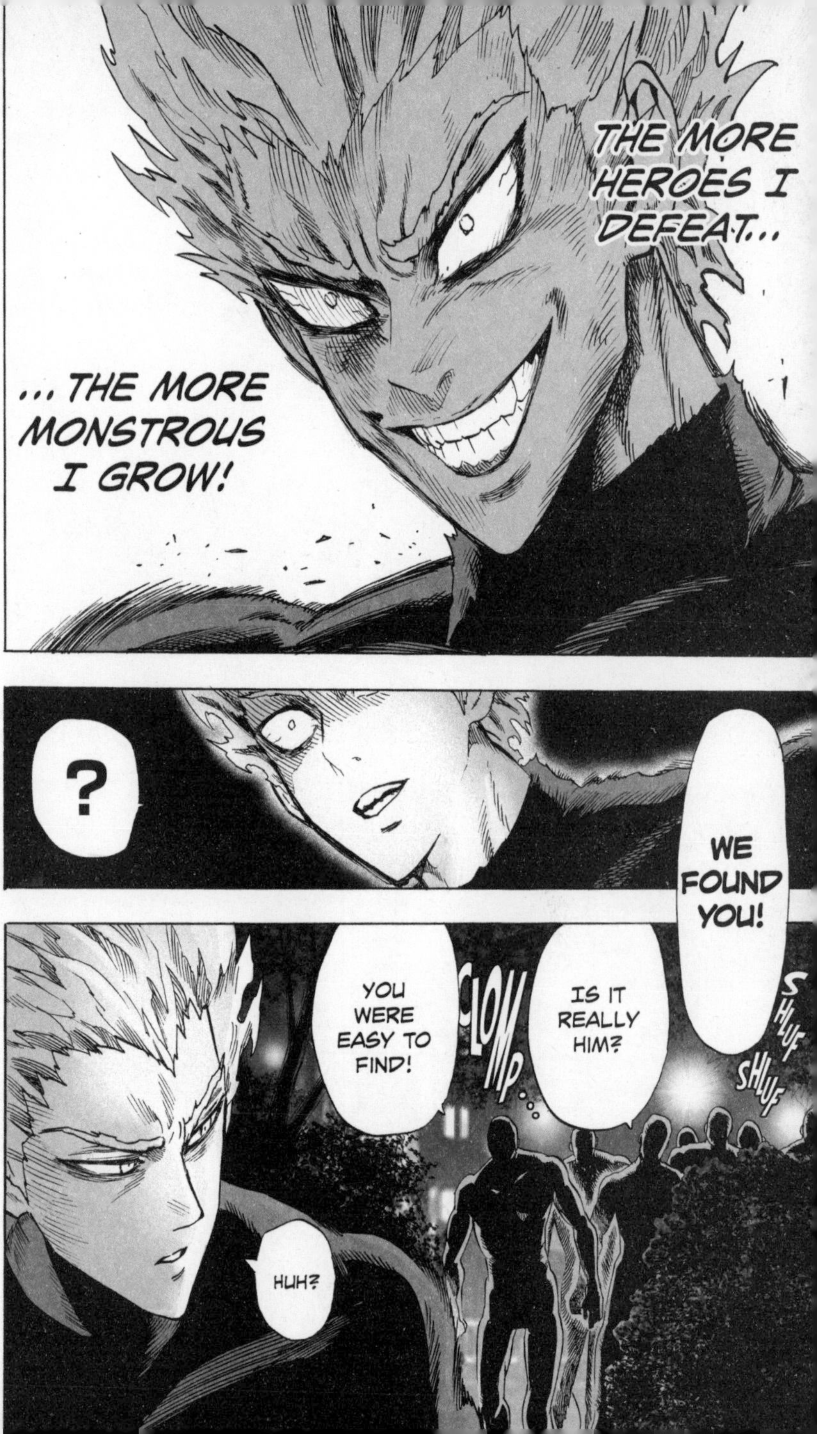
THE MORE HEROES I DEFEAT...
...THE MORE MONSTROUS I GROW!
?
WE FOUND YOU!
SHLUF SHLUF
IS IT REALLY HIM?
CLOMP
YOU WERE EASY TO FIND!
HUH?

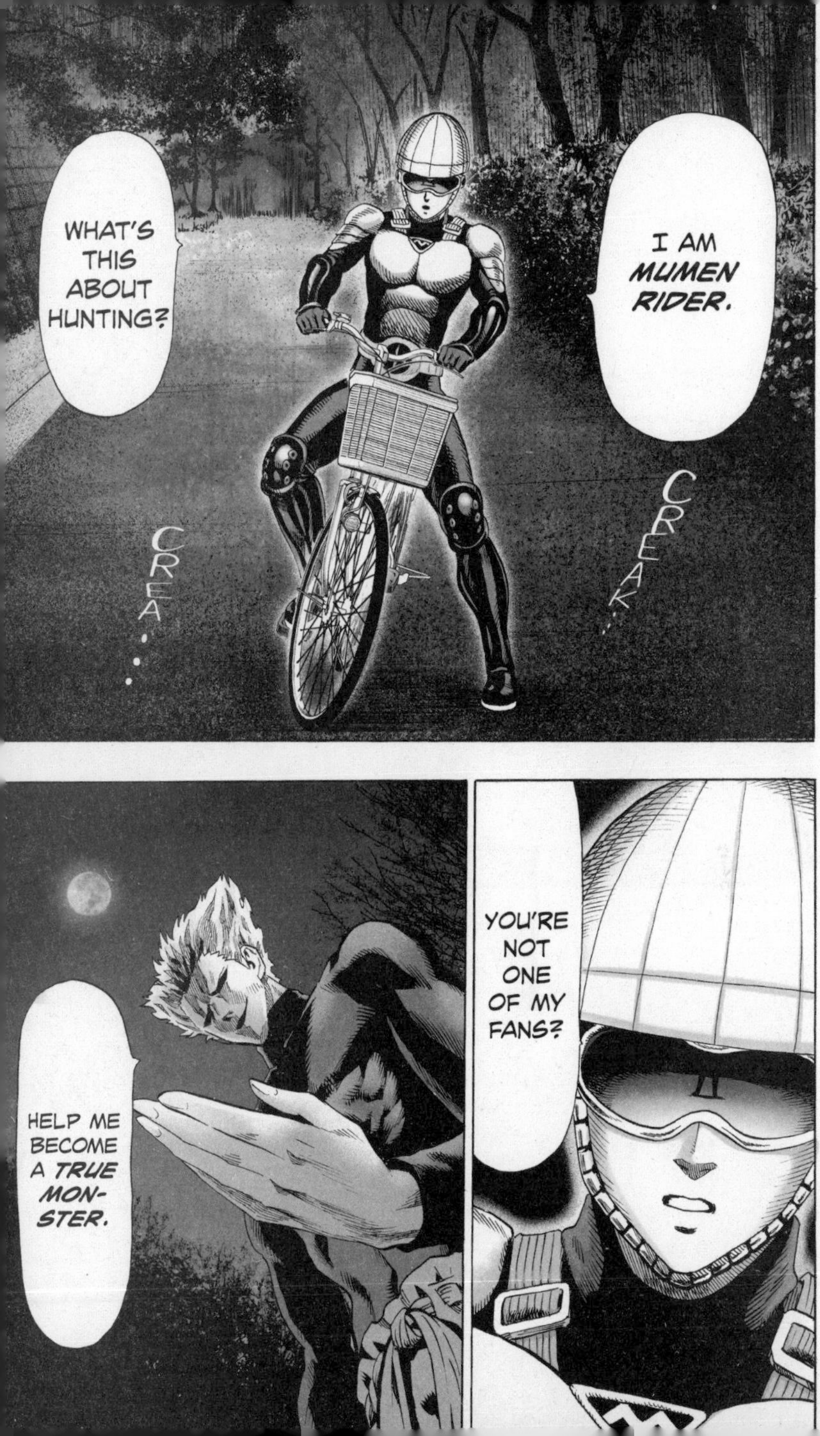
I AM *MUMEN RIDER.*
WHAT'S THIS ABOUT HUNTING?
CREAK...
CREA...
YOU'RE NOT ONE OF MY FANS?
HELP ME BECOME A *TRUE MONSTER.*

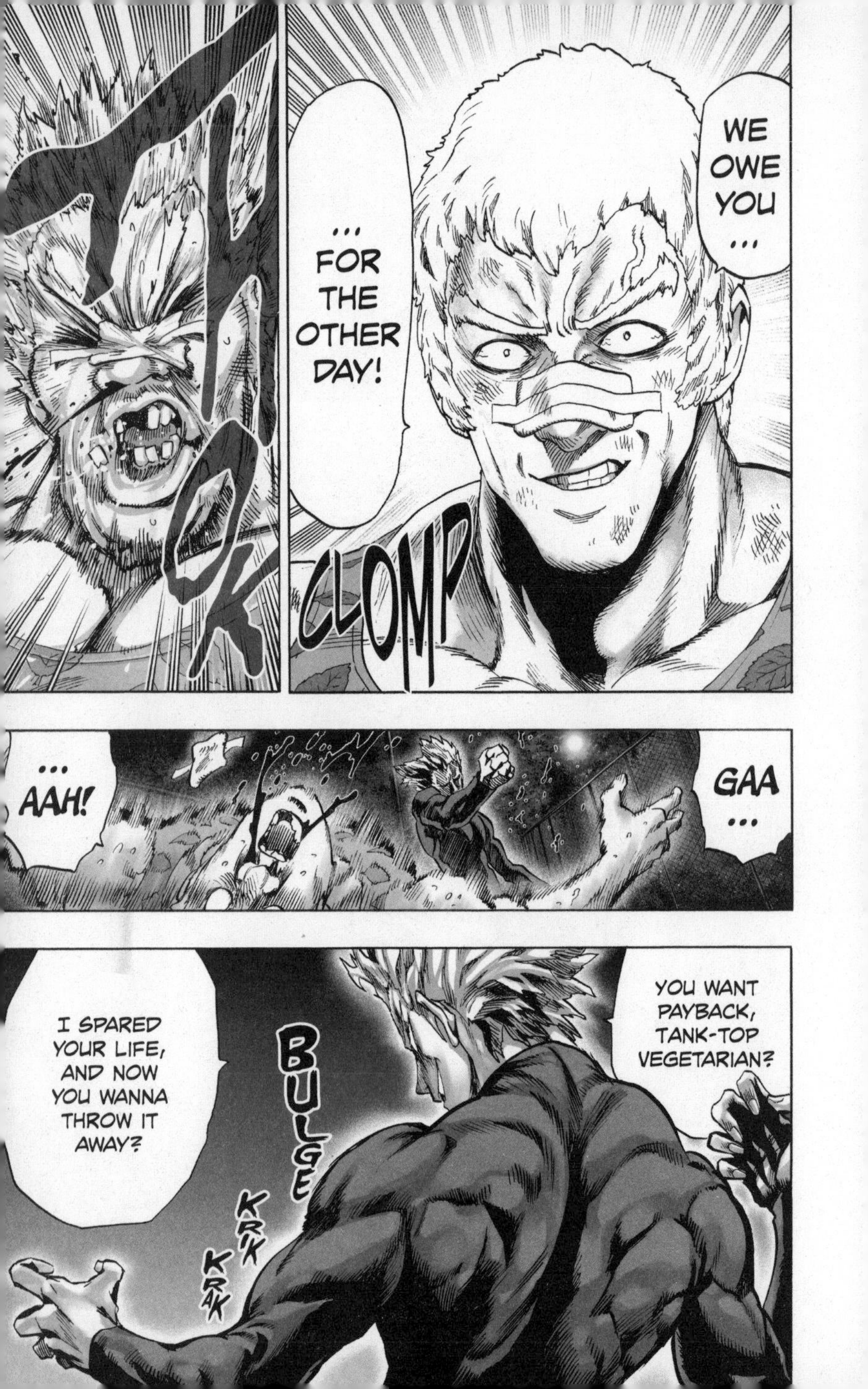
WE OWE YOU ...
... FOR THE OTHER DAY!
CLOMP
GAA ...
... AAH!
YOU WANT PAYBACK, TANK-TOP VEGETARIAN?
BULGE
KRIK
KRAK
I SPARED YOUR LIFE, AND NOW YOU WANNA THROW IT AWAY?

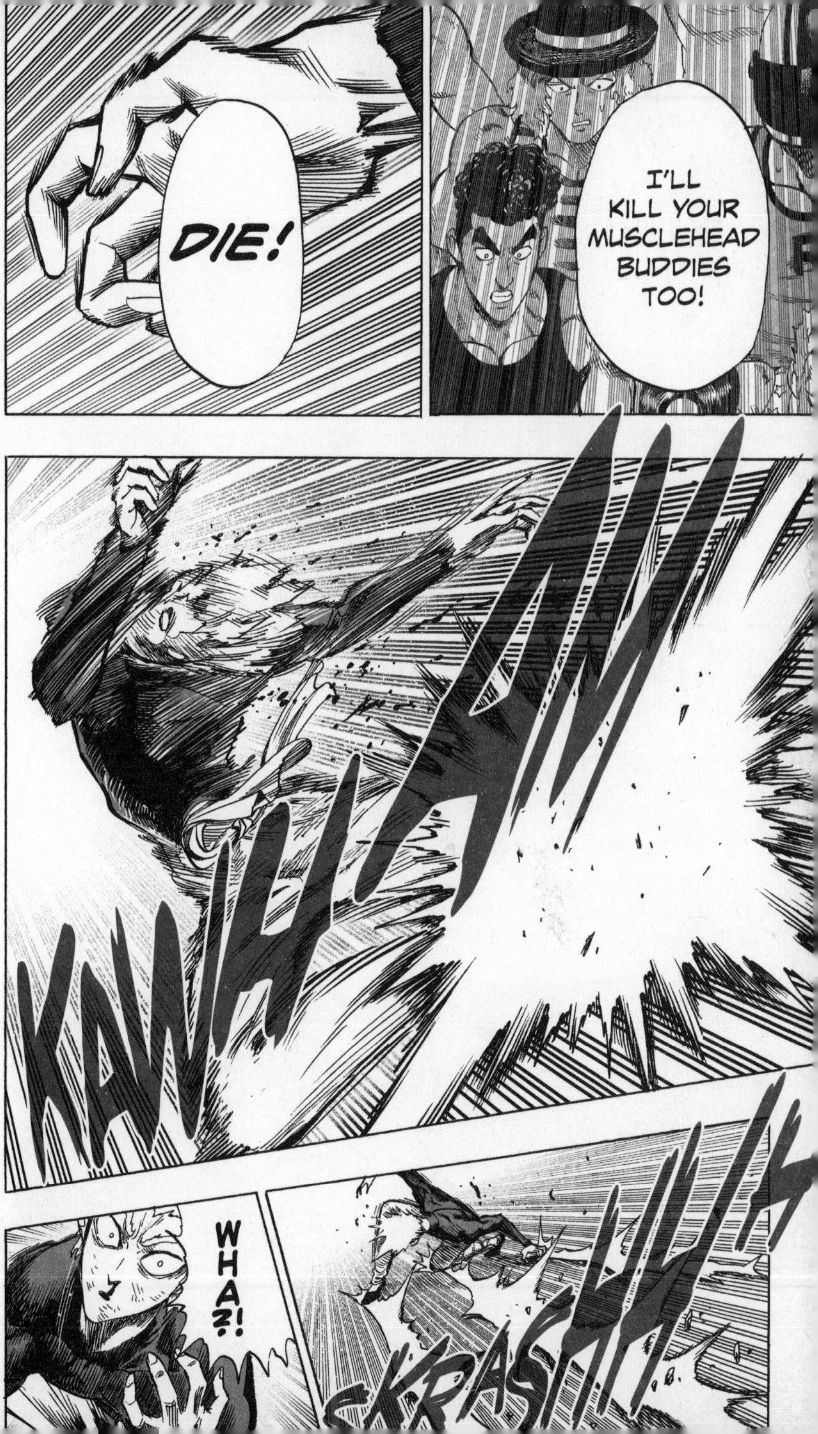
I'LL KILL YOUR MUSCLEHEAD BUDDIES TOO!
DIE!
WHA?!

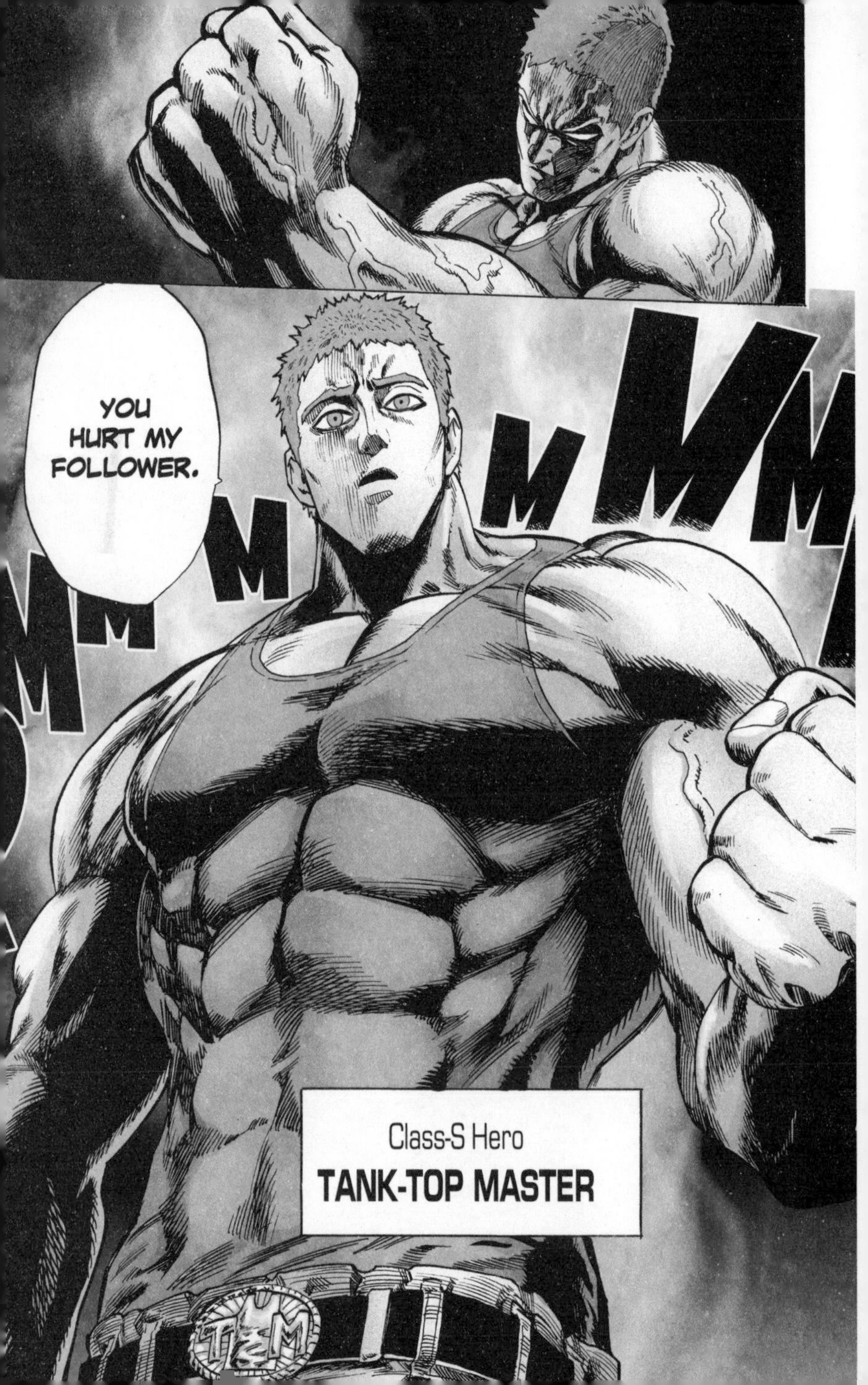
YOU HURT MY FOLLOWER.
MMMMMMMMM
Class-S Hero
TANK-TOP MASTER
TM

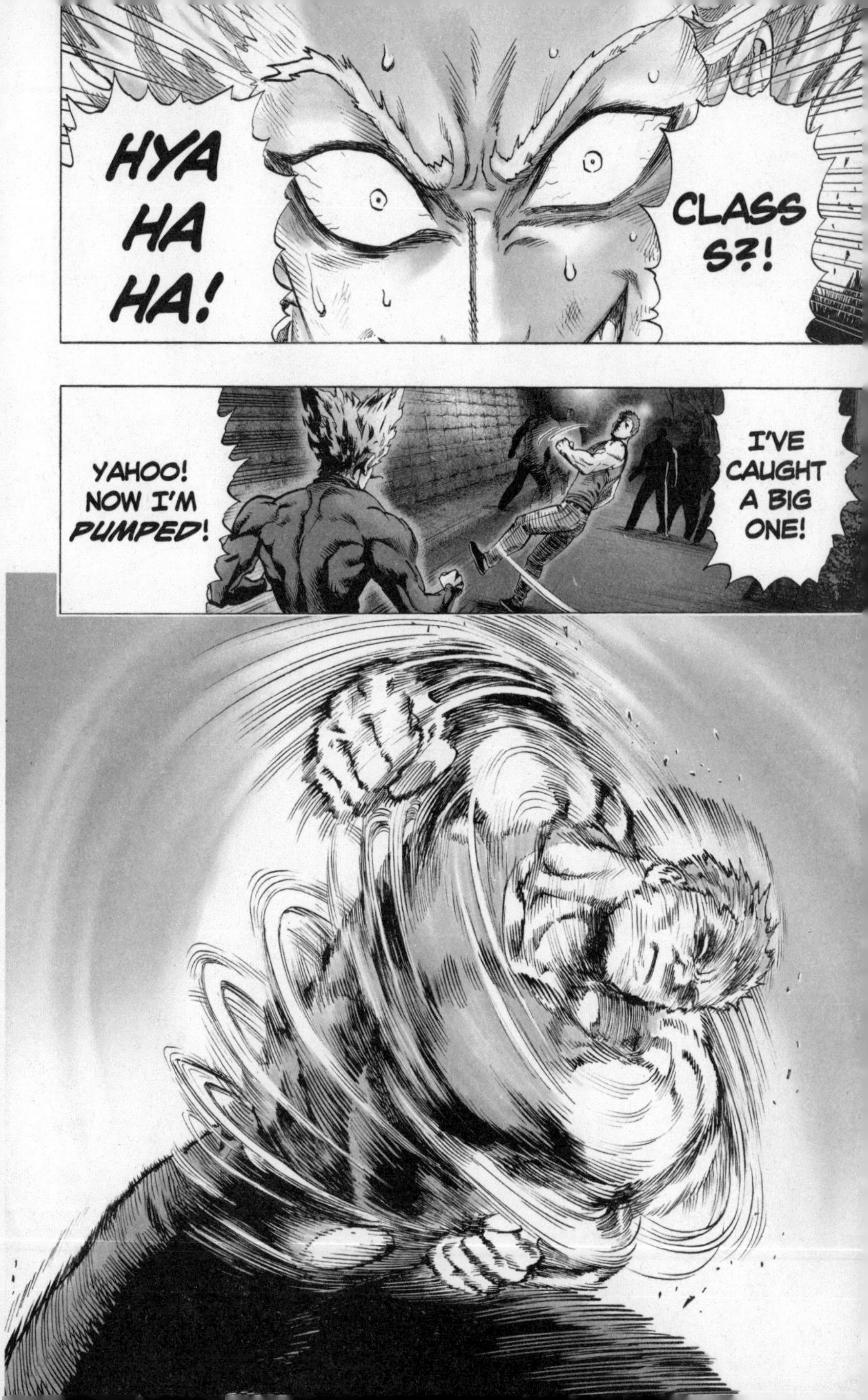
CLASS S?!
HYA HA HA!
I'VE CAUGHT A BIG ONE!
YAHOO! NOW I'M *PUMPED*!

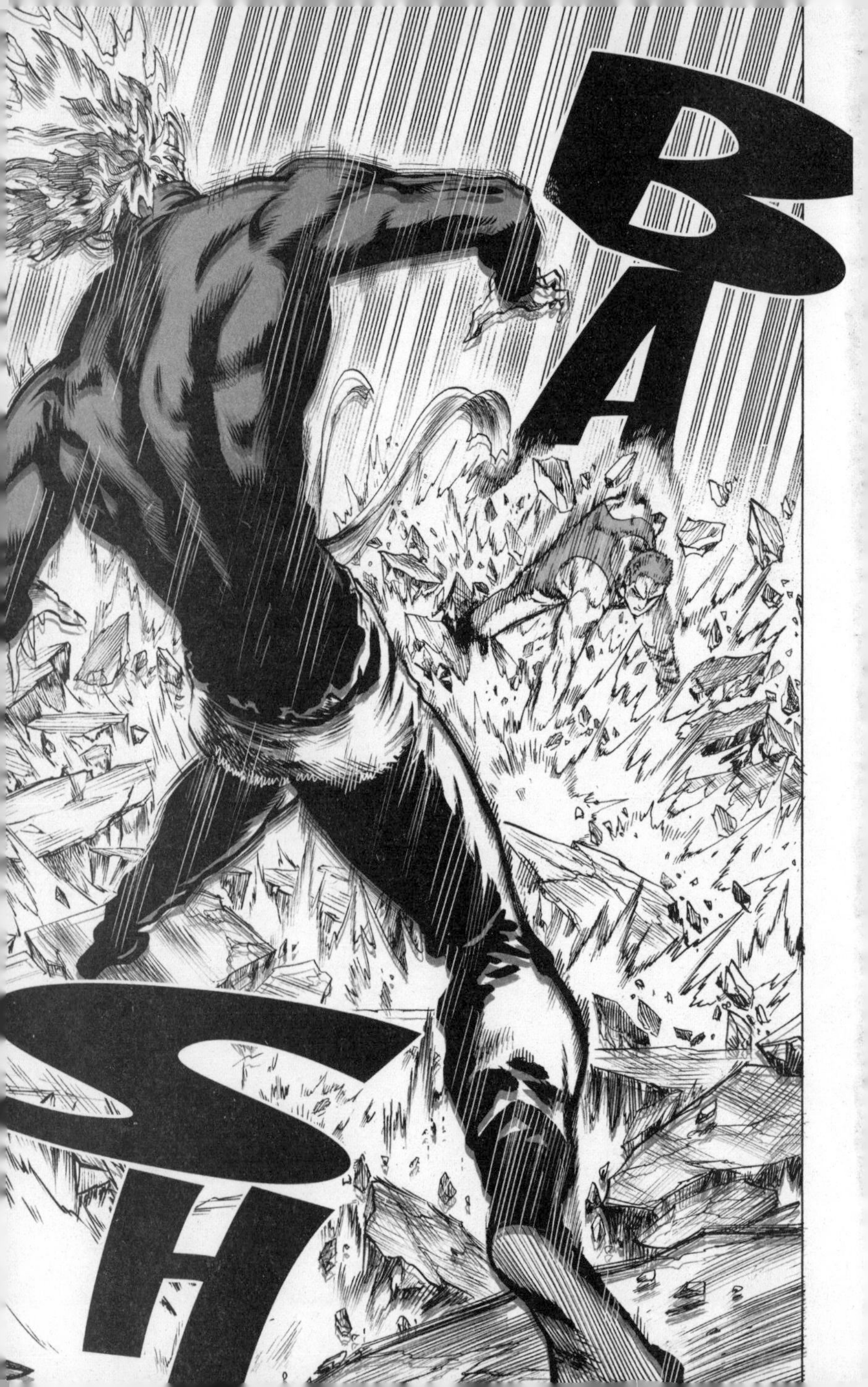
BASH

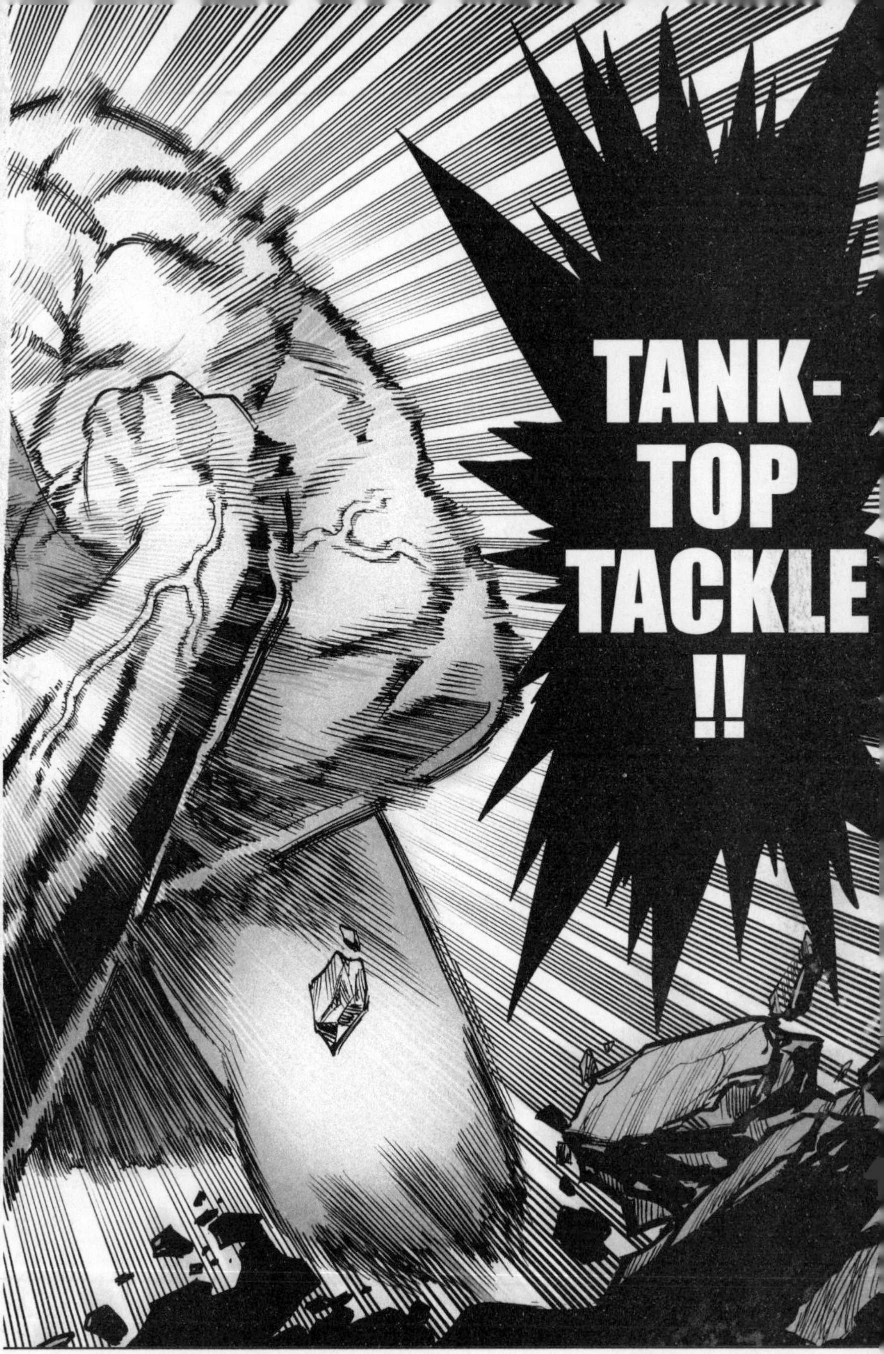
TANK-
TOP
TACKLE
!!

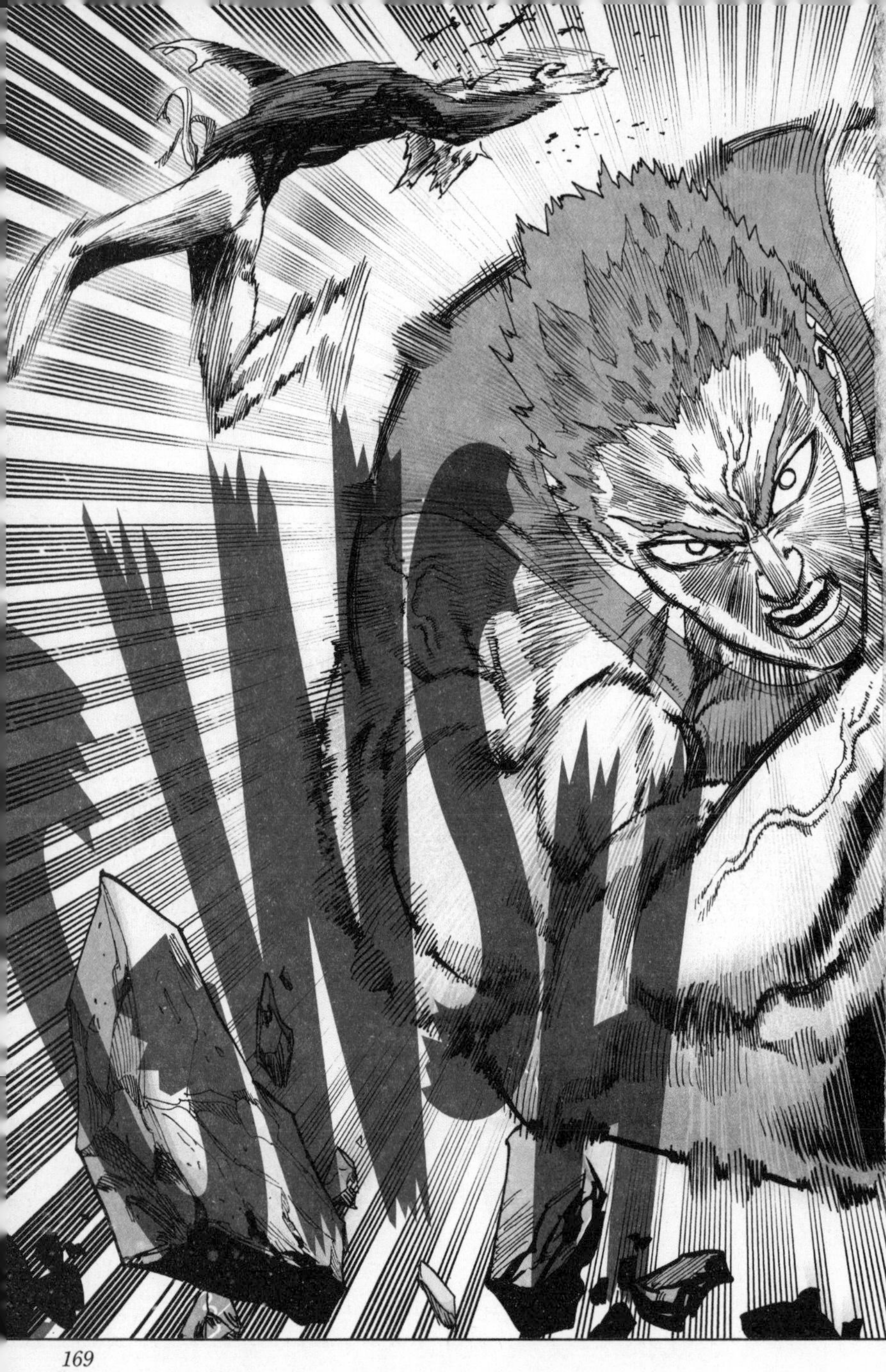

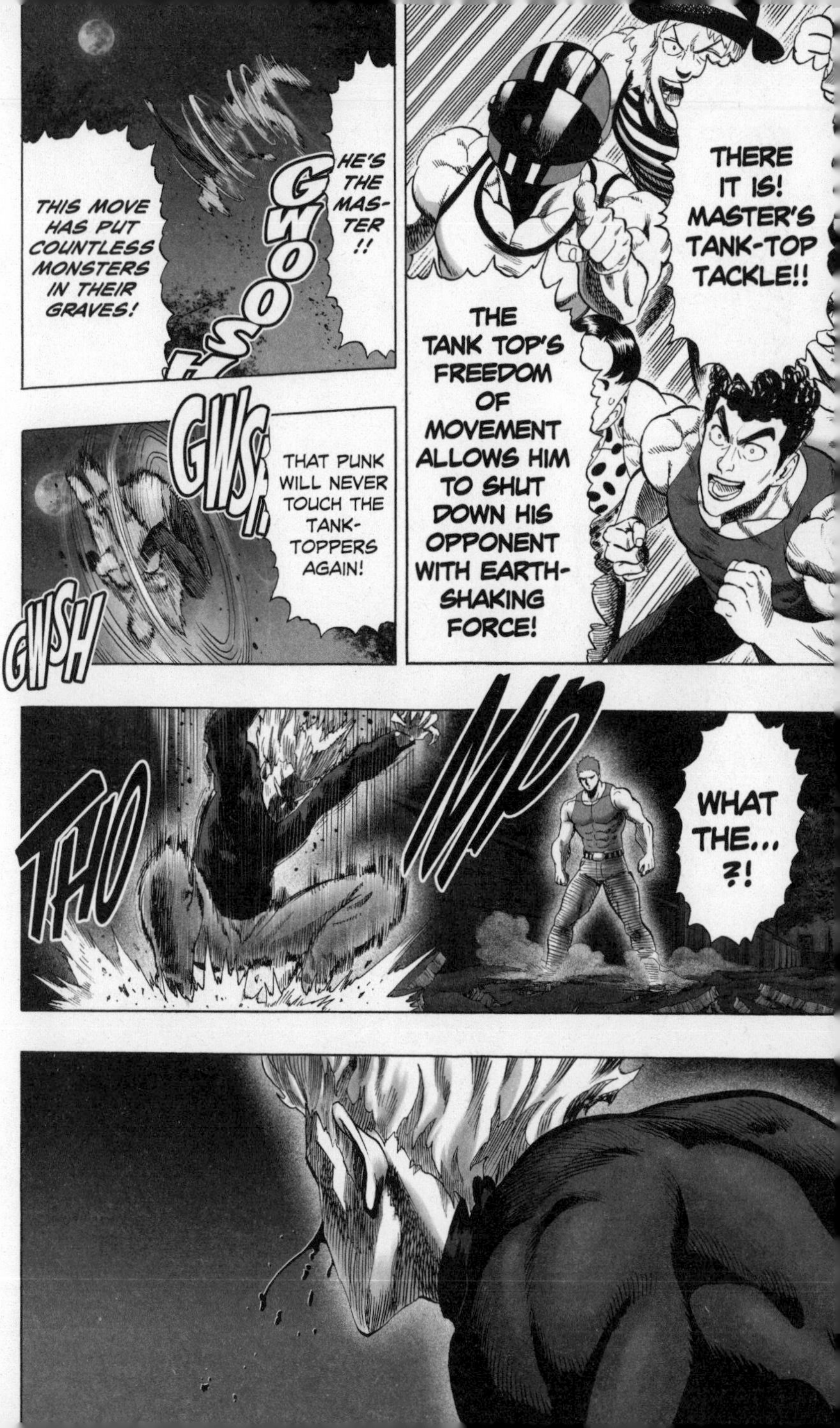
THERE IT IS! MASTER'S TANK-TOP TACKLE!!
THE TANK TOP'S FREEDOM OF MOVEMENT ALLOWS HIM TO SHUT DOWN HIS OPPONENT WITH EARTH-SHAKING FORCE!
HE'S THE MASTER!!
THIS MOVE HAS PUT COUNTLESS MONSTERS IN THEIR GRAVES!
GWSH
THAT PUNK WILL NEVER TOUCH THE TANK-TOPPERS AGAIN!
GWSH
WHAT THE...?!

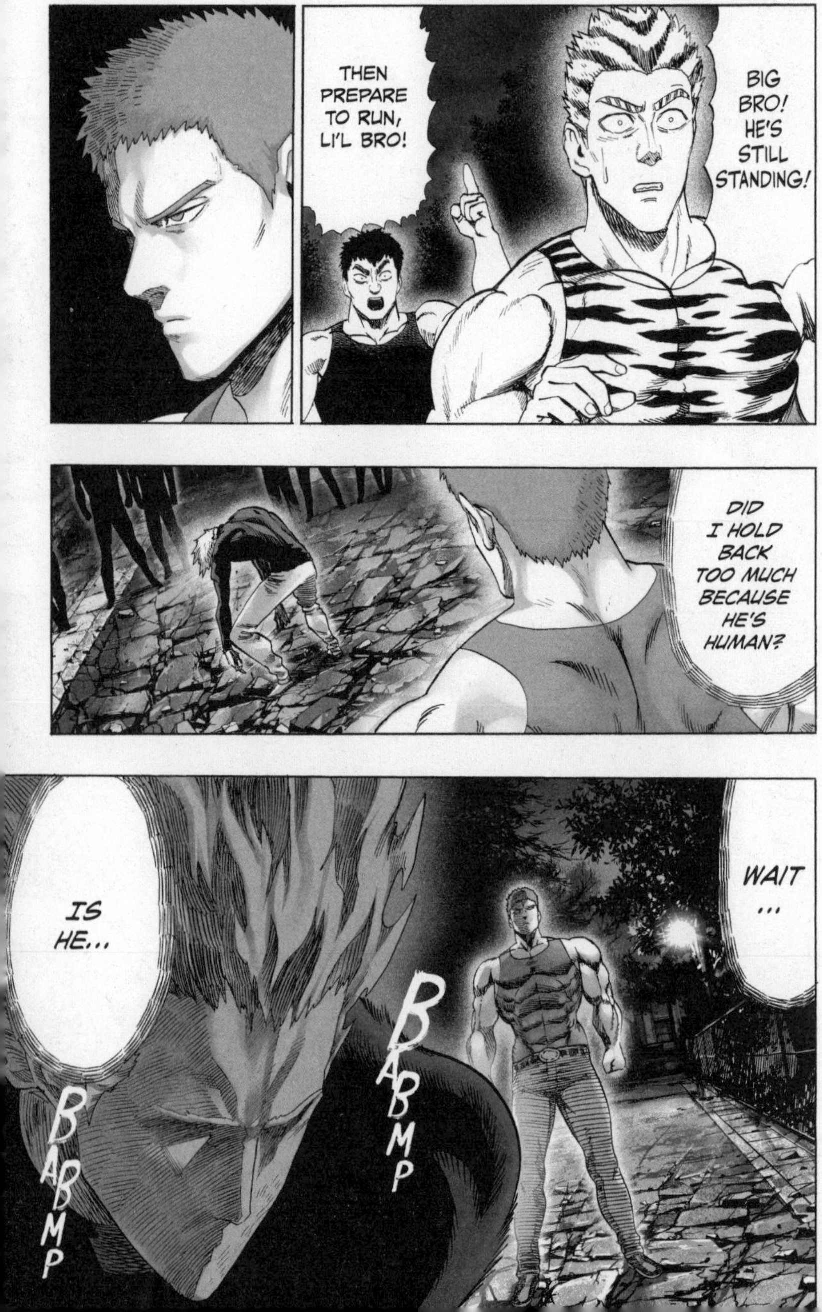

BIG BRO! HE'S STILL STANDING!
THEN PREPARE TO RUN, LI'L BRO!
DID I HOLD BACK TOO MUCH BECAUSE HE'S HUMAN?
WAIT ...
BABMP
IS HE...
BABMP

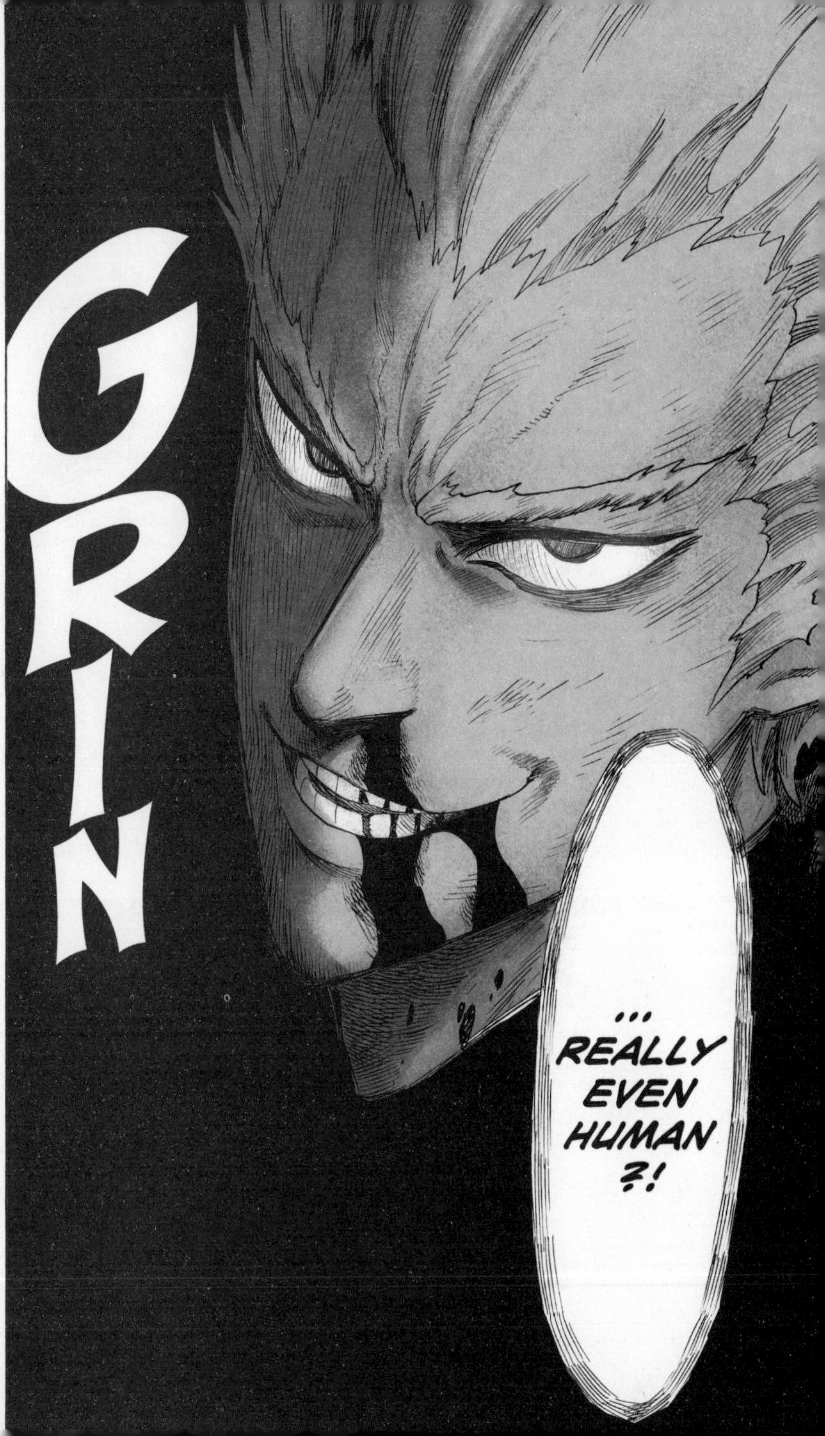
GRIN
... REALLY EVEN HUMAN ?!

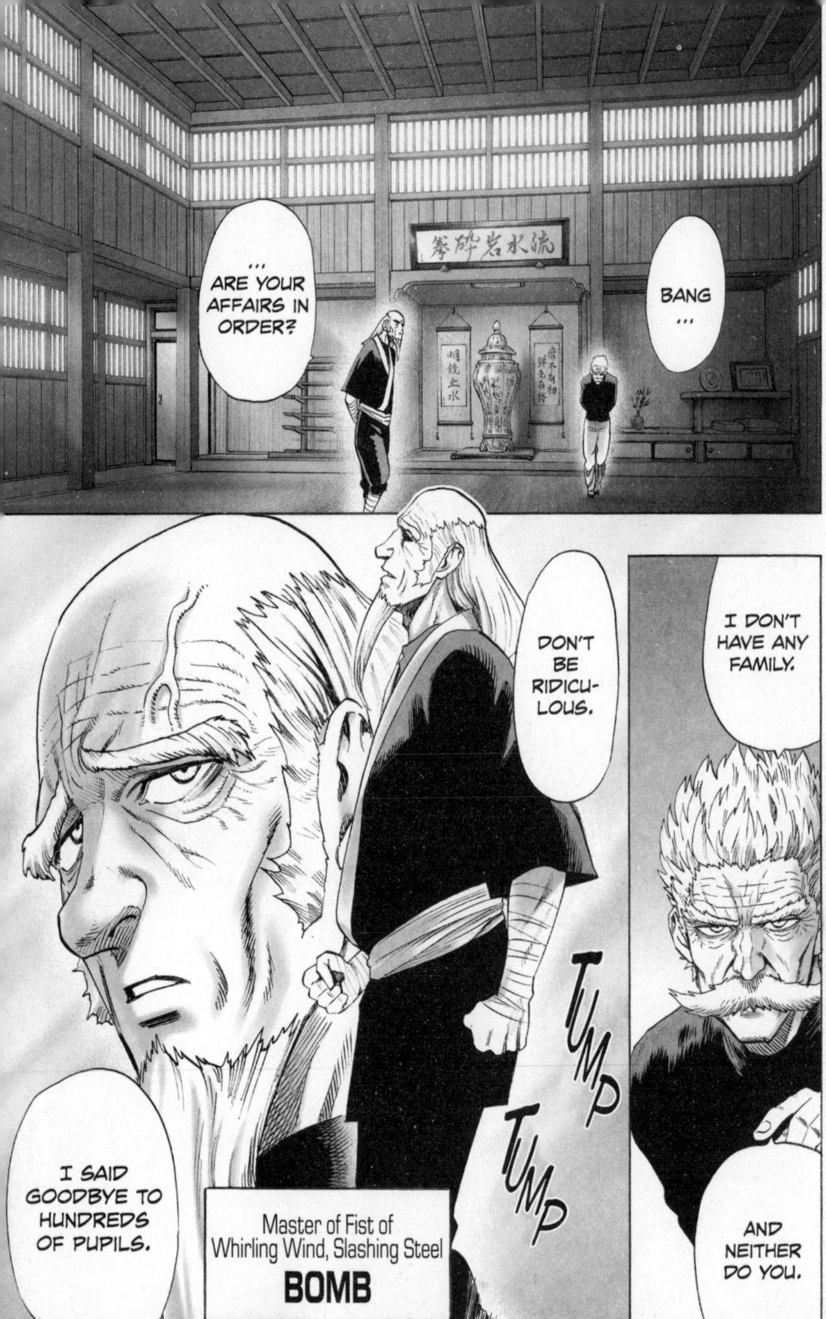
流水岩砕拳
BANG ...
... ARE YOUR AFFAIRS IN ORDER?
I DON'T HAVE ANY FAMILY.
AND NEITHER DO YOU.
DON'T BE RIDICULOUS.
TUMP TUMP
Master of Fist of Whirling Wind, Slashing Steel
BOMB
I SAID GOODBYE TO HUNDREDS OF PUPILS.

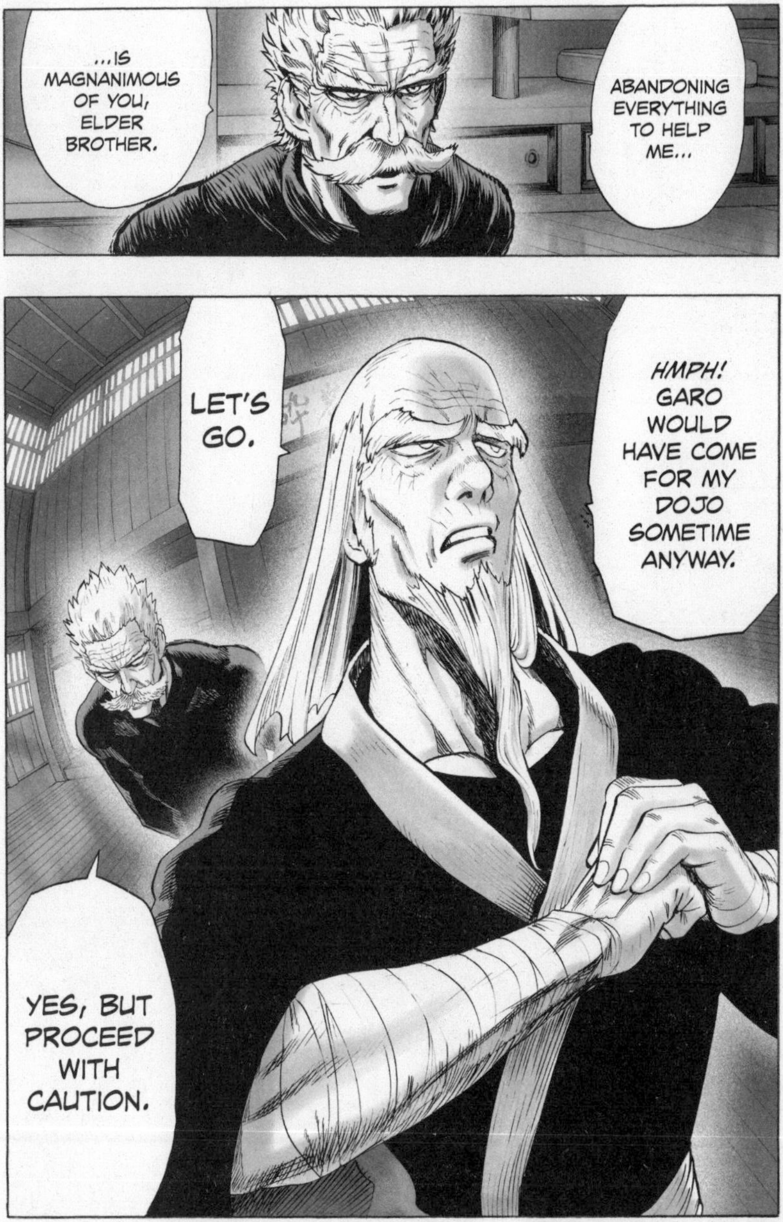
ABANDONING EVERYTHING TO HELP ME...
...IS MAGNANIMOUS OF YOU, ELDER BROTHER.
HMPH! GARO WOULD HAVE COME FOR MY DOJO SOMETIME ANYWAY.
LET'S GO.
YES, BUT PROCEED WITH CAUTION.

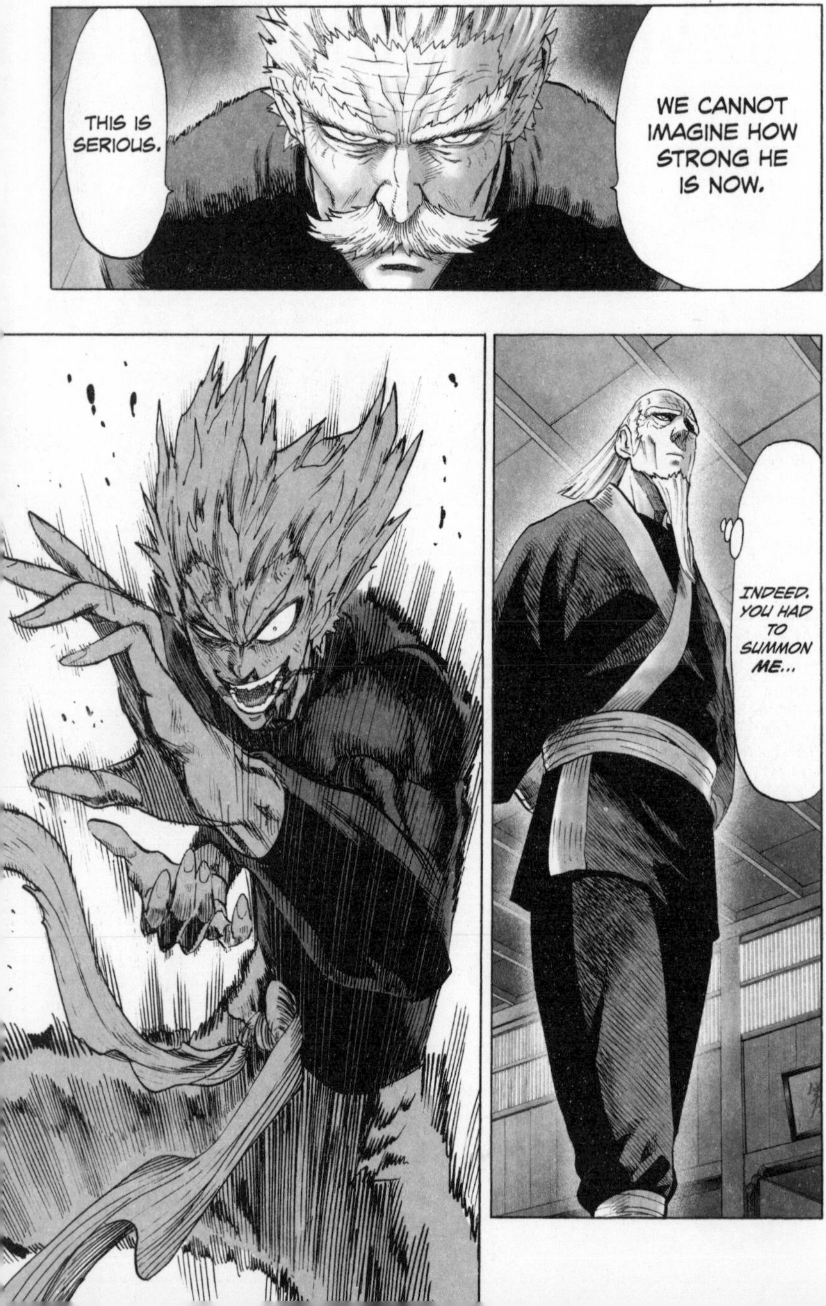
WE CANNOT IMAGINE HOW STRONG HE IS NOW.
THIS IS SERIOUS.
INDEED. YOU HAD TO SUMMON ME...

TANK-TOPPER ILLUSTRATED GUIDE

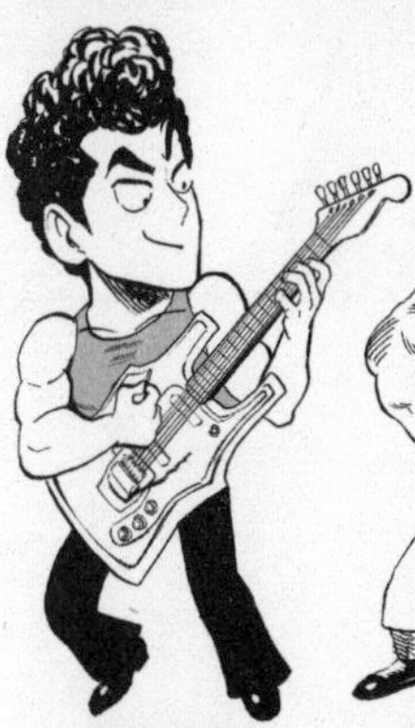

TANK-TOP ROCKABILLY

Plays guitar on the side. His favorite guitar is shaped like a tank top.

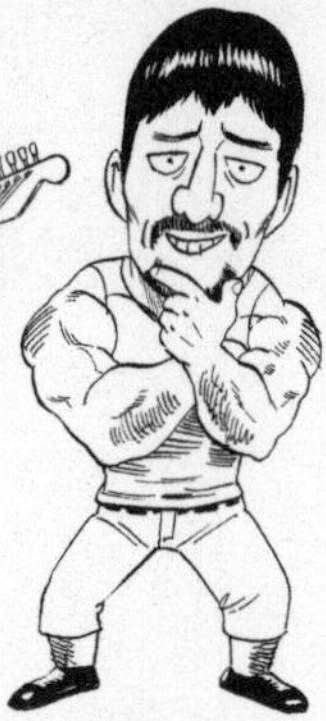

TANK-TOP JUNGLE

Hairy.

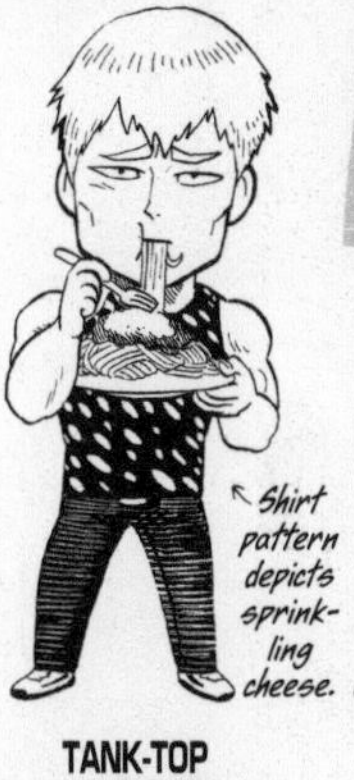
Shirt pattern depicts sprinkling cheese.

TANK-TOP AL DENTE

Often has pasta for breakfast. Puts on too much grated cheese.

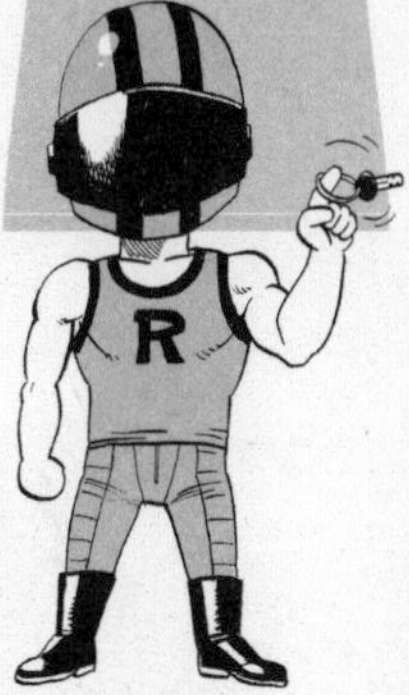
R

TANK-TOP RACER

Has a license for 50cc.

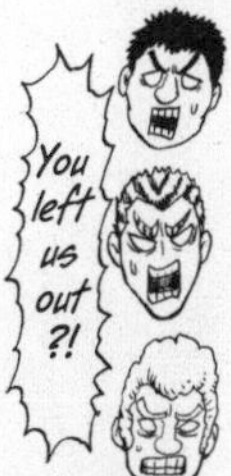
You left us out?!

TANK-TOP BLACKHOLE

TANK-TOP TIGER

TANK-TOP VEGETARIAN

Read the manga.

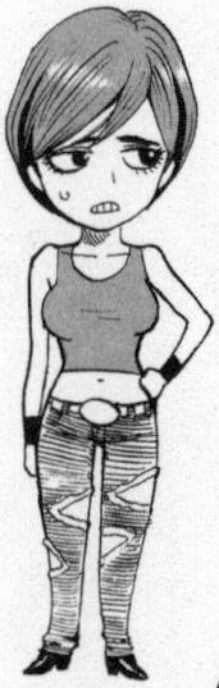

TANK-TOP GIRL

Respects Tank-Top Master but rarely participates because the others are all weird.

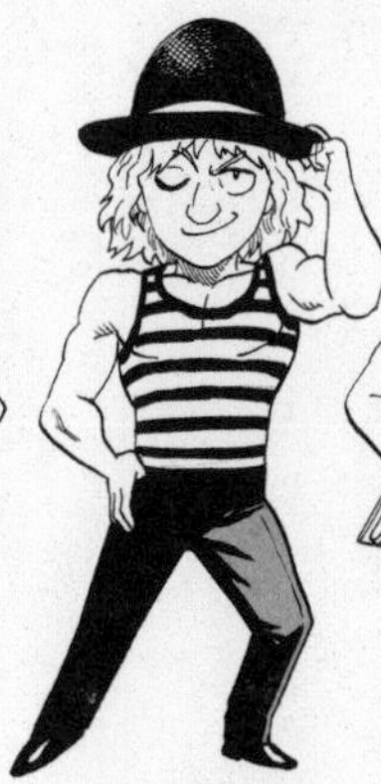

TANK-TOP HATTER

Wears hats because his fortune once said they're his lucky item, but he's never had good luck.

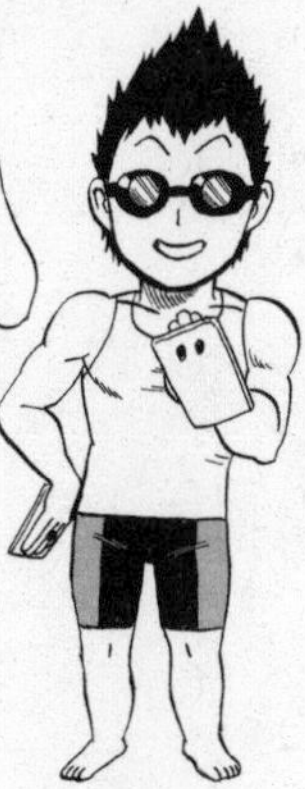

TANK-TOP SWIMMER

Good at the crawl but still can't move his legs the right way for the breaststroke.

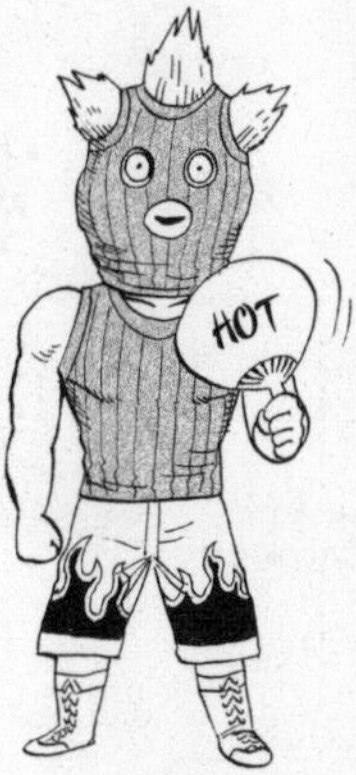
HOT

TANK-TOP MASK

Wears a child's tank top on his head. He says it's hot.

AND MANY MORE!

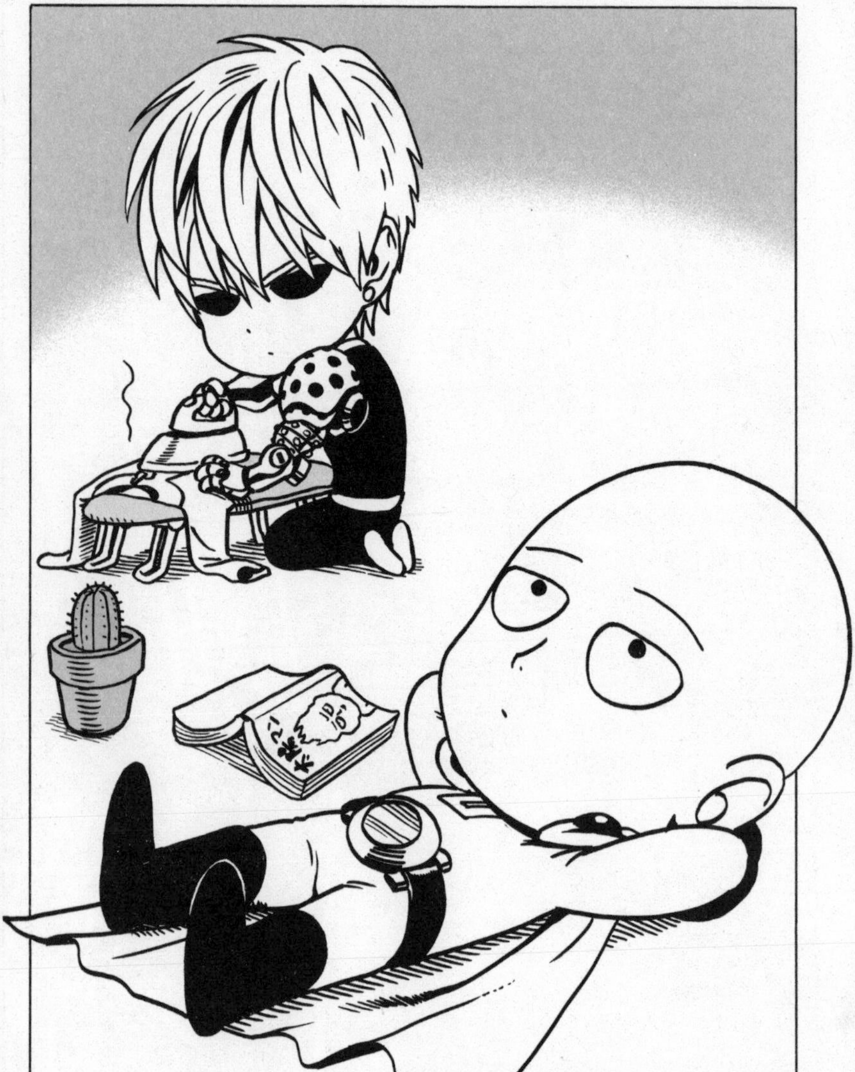

PUNCH 47: TECHNIQUE

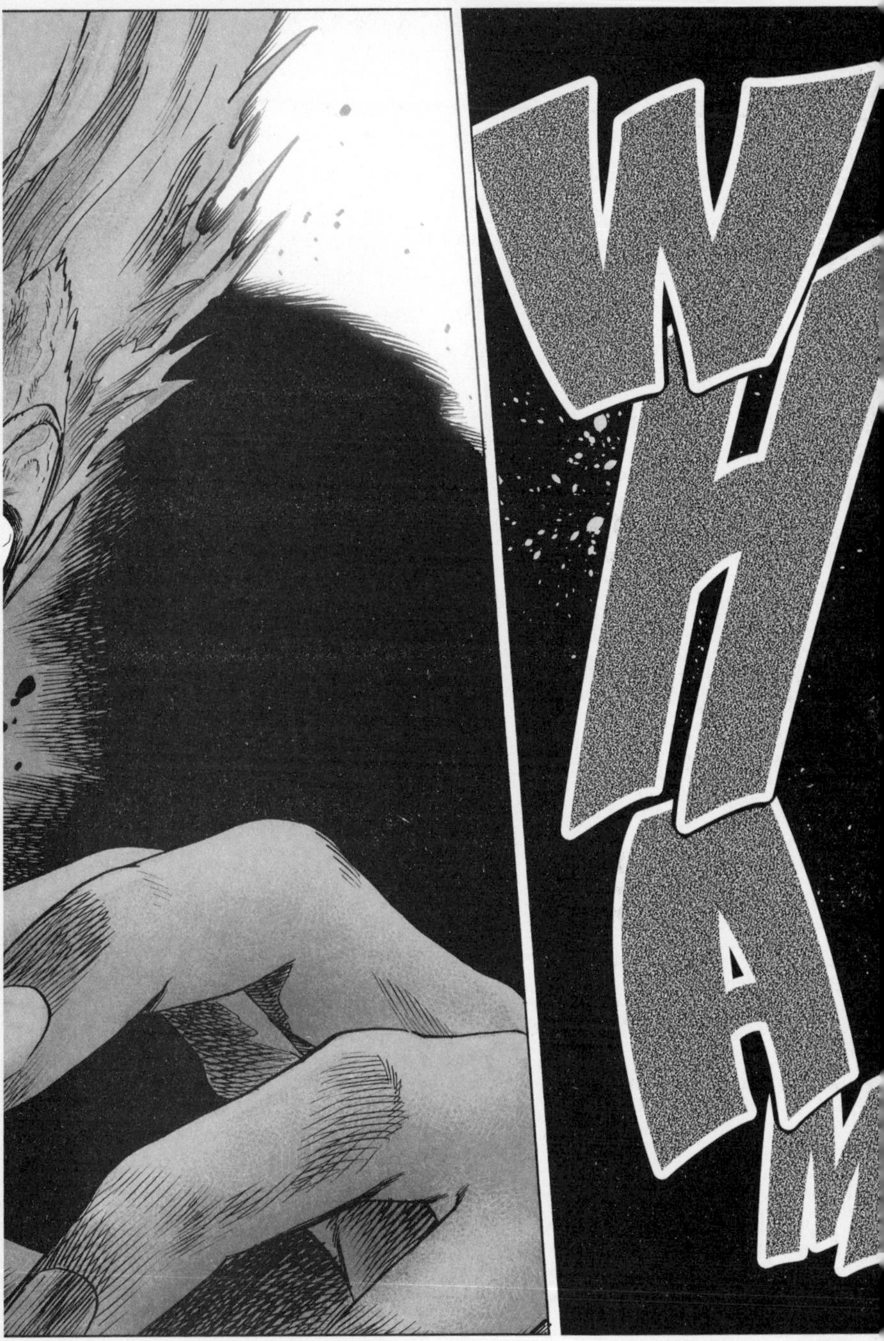
WHAM

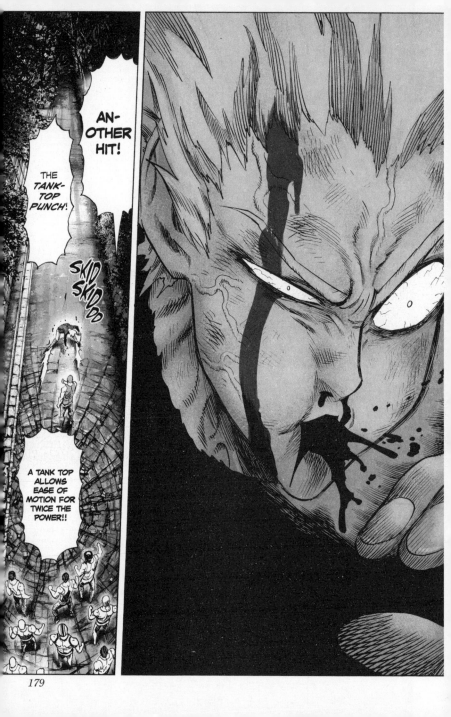

AN- OTHER HIT!

THE *TANK- TOP PUNCH!*

SKID SKID DD

A TANK TOP ALLOWS EASE OF MOTION FOR TWICE THE POWER!!

179

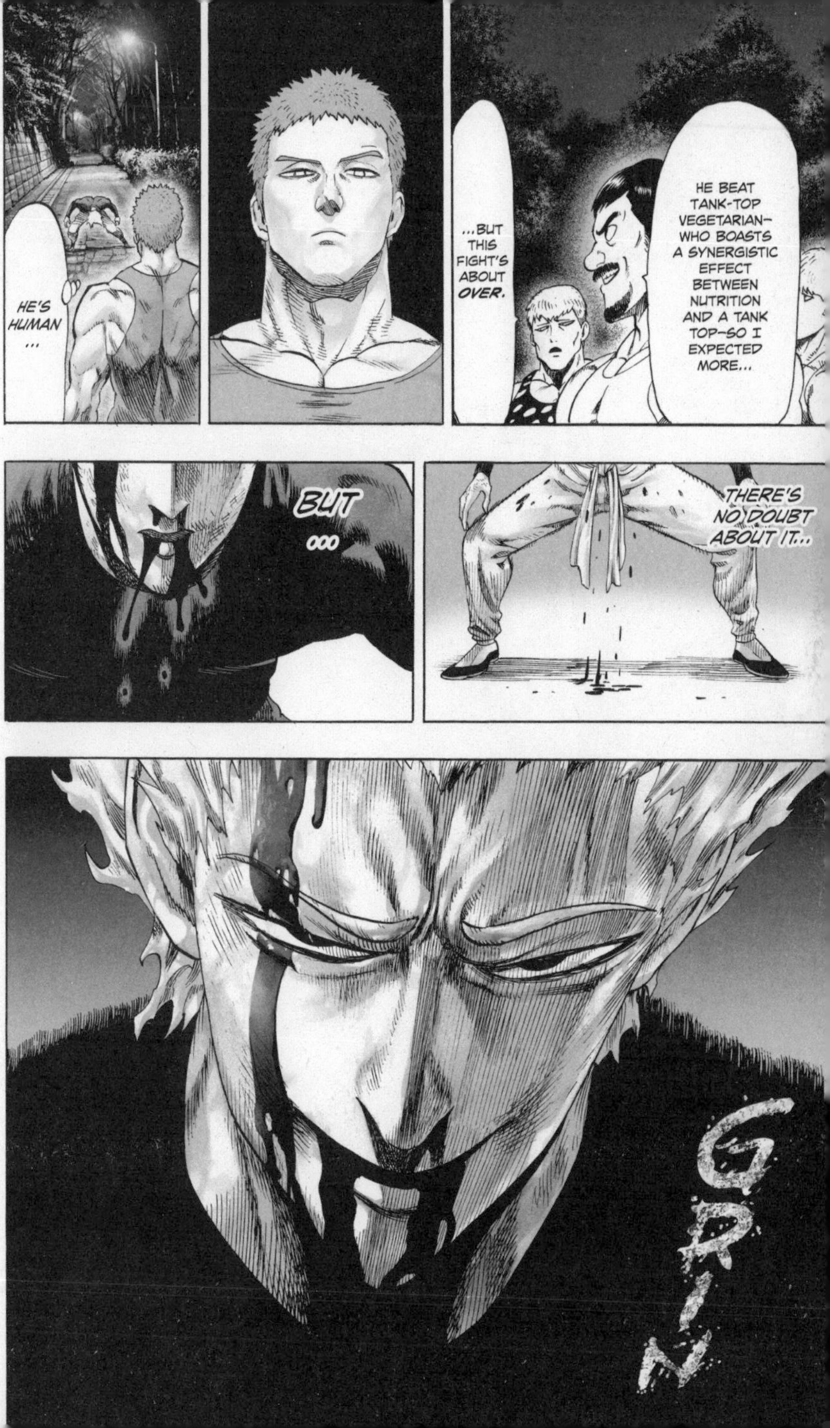
HE BEAT TANK-TOP VEGETARIAN—WHO BOASTS A SYNERGISTIC EFFECT BETWEEN NUTRITION AND A TANK TOP—SO I EXPECTED MORE...
...BUT THIS FIGHT'S ABOUT *OVER*.
HE'S HUMAN ...
THERE'S NO DOUBT ABOUT IT...
BUT ...
GRIN

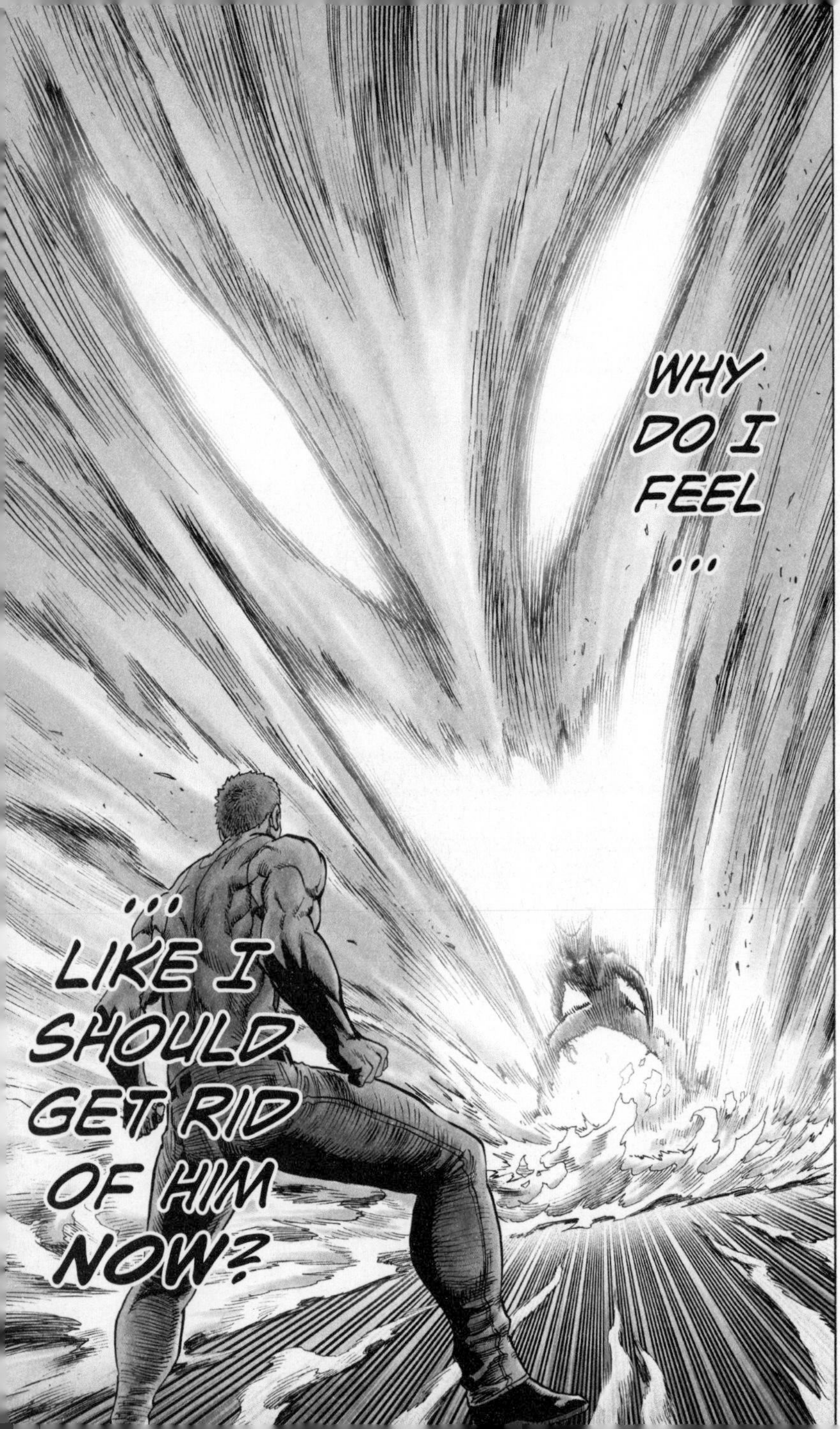
WHY DO I FEEL ...
... LIKE I SHOULD GET RID OF HIM NOW?

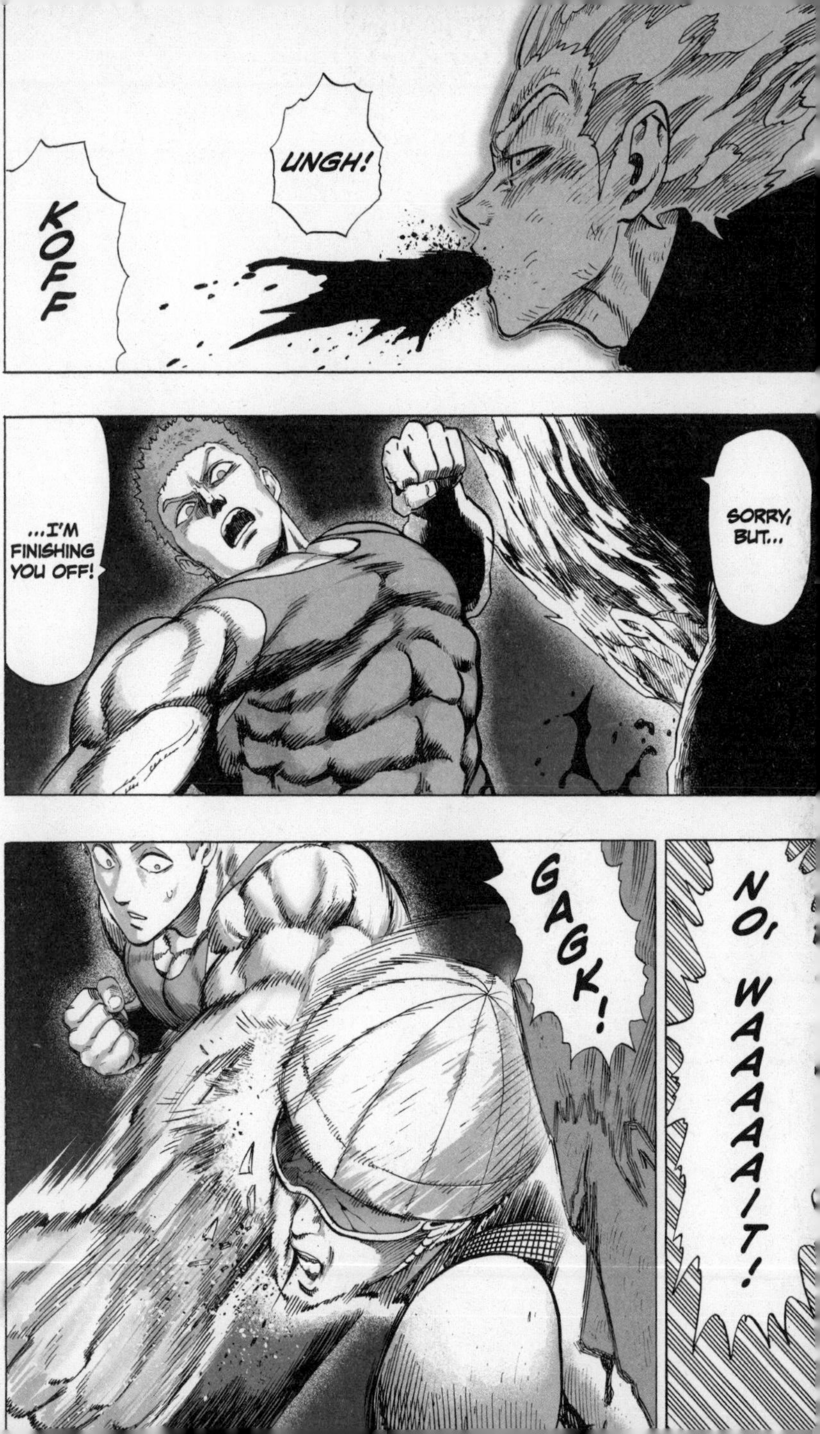
UNGH!
KOFF
SORRY, BUT...
...I'M FINISHING YOU OFF!
NO, WAAAAAIT!
GAGK!

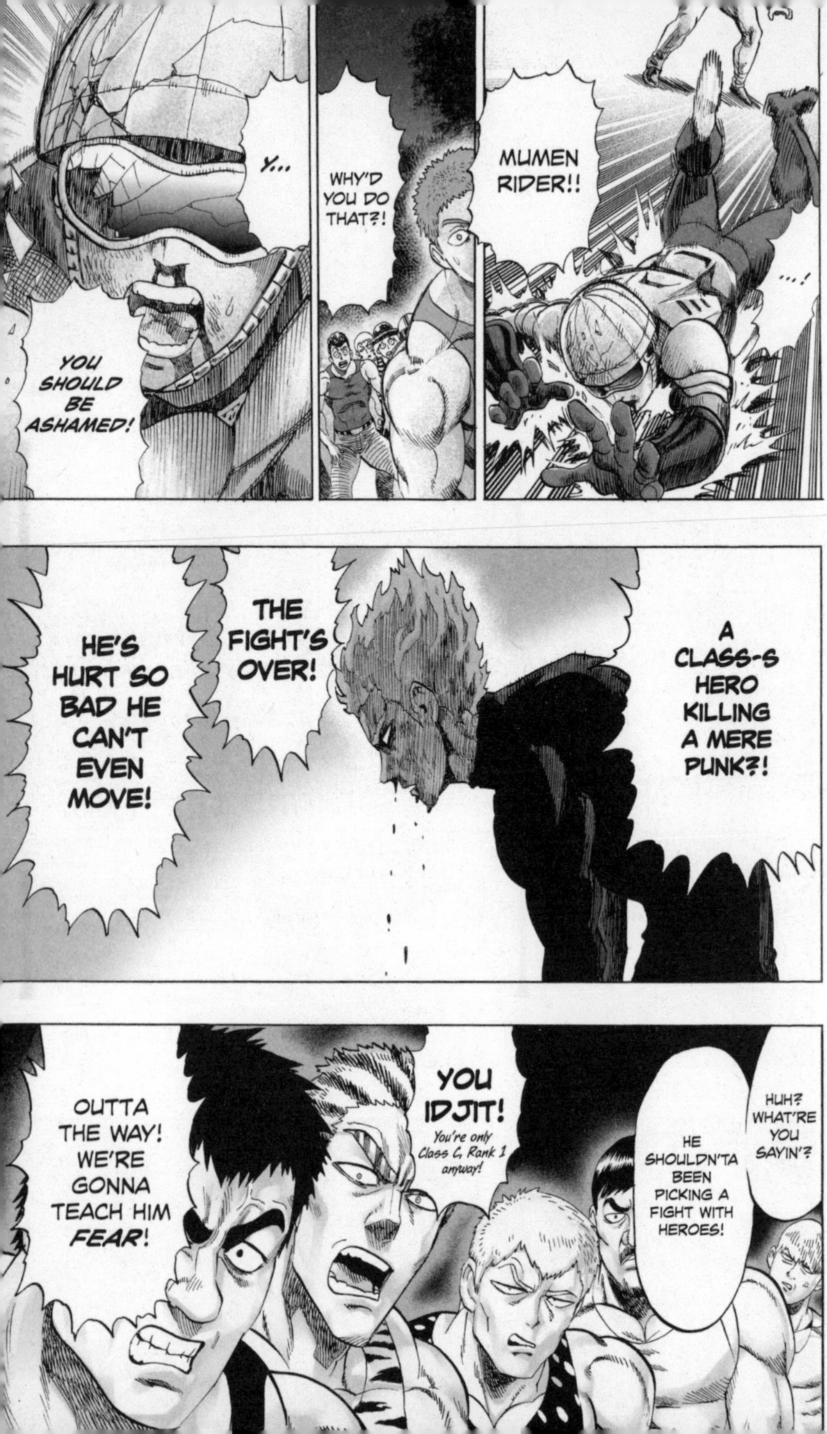
MUMEN RIDER!!
...!
WHY'D YOU DO THAT?!
Y...
YOU SHOULD BE ASHAMED!
A CLASS-S HERO KILLING A MERE PUNK?!
THE FIGHT'S OVER!
HE'S HURT SO BAD HE CAN'T EVEN MOVE!
HUH? WHAT'RE YOU SAYIN'?
HE SHOULDN'TA BEEN PICKING A FIGHT WITH HEROES!
YOU IDJIT!
You're only Class C, Rank 1 anyway!
OUTTA THE WAY! WE'RE GONNA TEACH HIM FEAR!

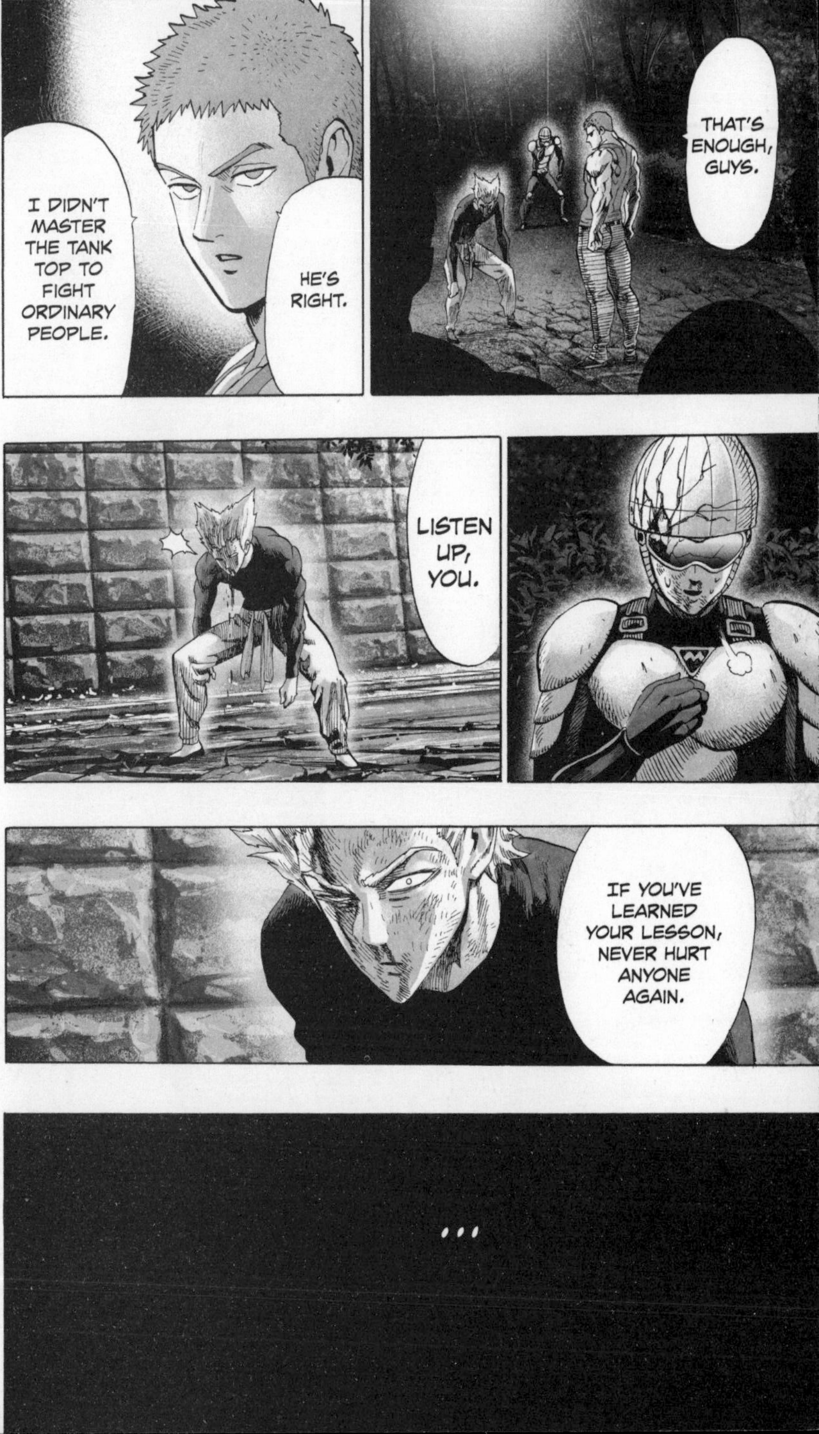
THAT'S ENOUGH, GUYS.
HE'S RIGHT.
I DIDN'T MASTER THE TANK TOP TO FIGHT ORDINARY PEOPLE.
LISTEN UP, YOU.
IF YOU'VE LEARNED YOUR LESSON, NEVER HURT ANYONE AGAIN.
...

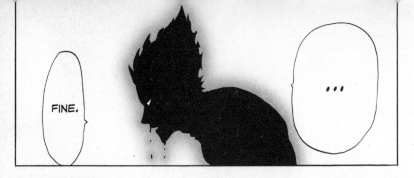

FINE.

...

I'M LEAVING NOW.

SORRY FOR CAUSING TROUBLE.

STAGGER

I'M STILL GONNA KILL ALL OF YOU!

NOT!

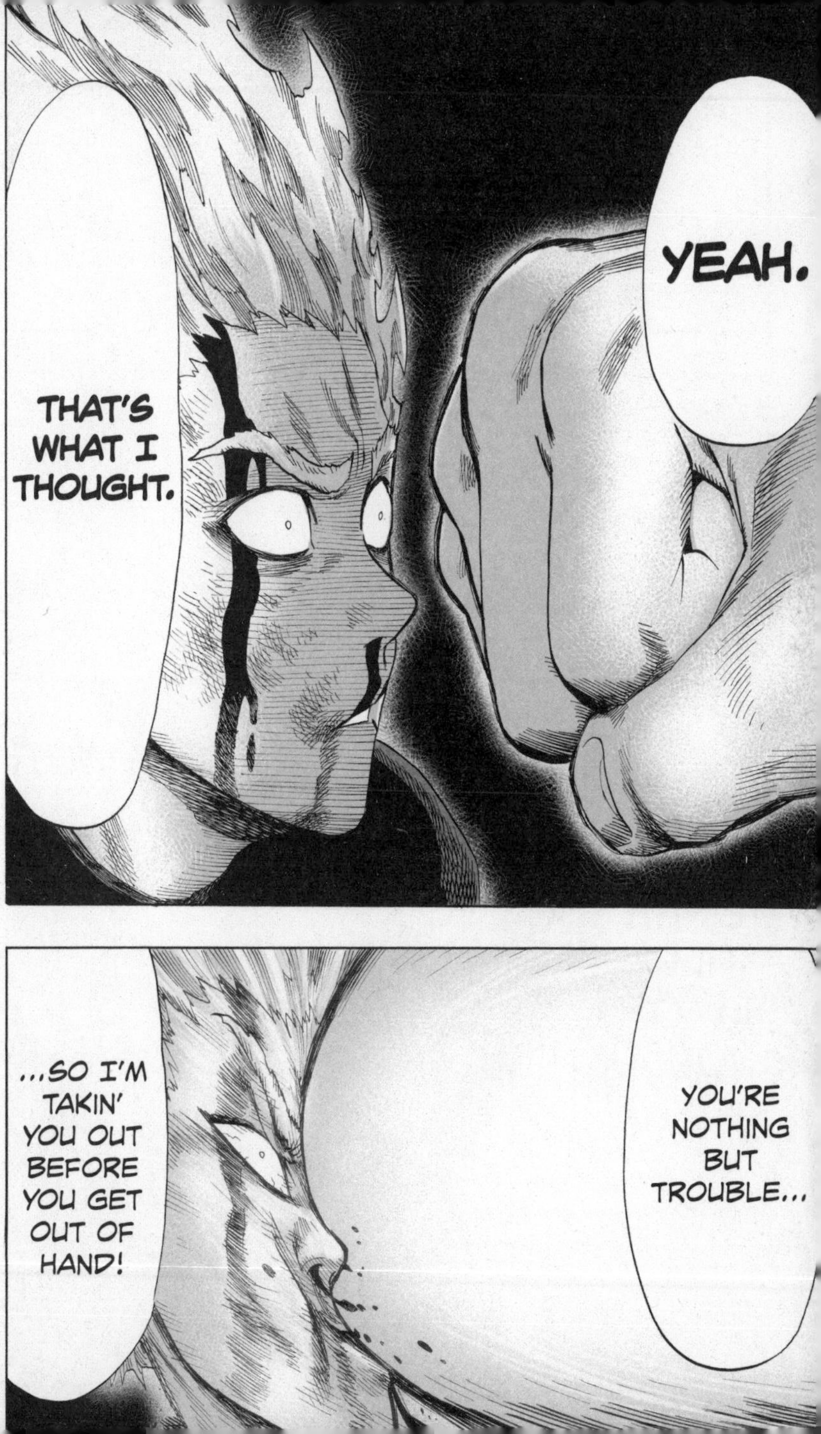
YEAH.
THAT'S WHAT I THOUGHT.
YOU'RE NOTHING BUT TROUBLE...
...SO I'M TAKIN' YOU OUT BEFORE YOU GET OUT OF HAND!

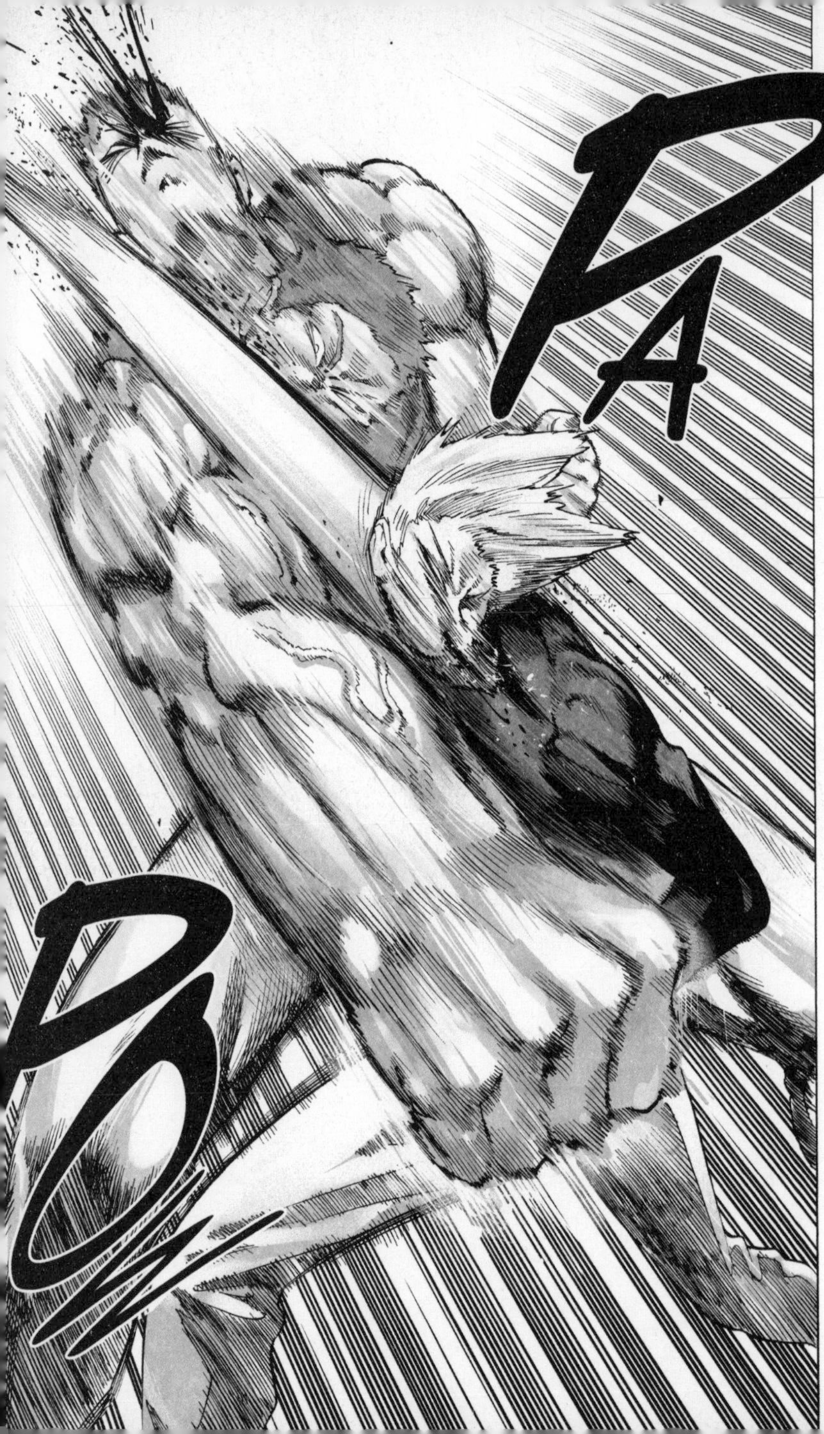
DA

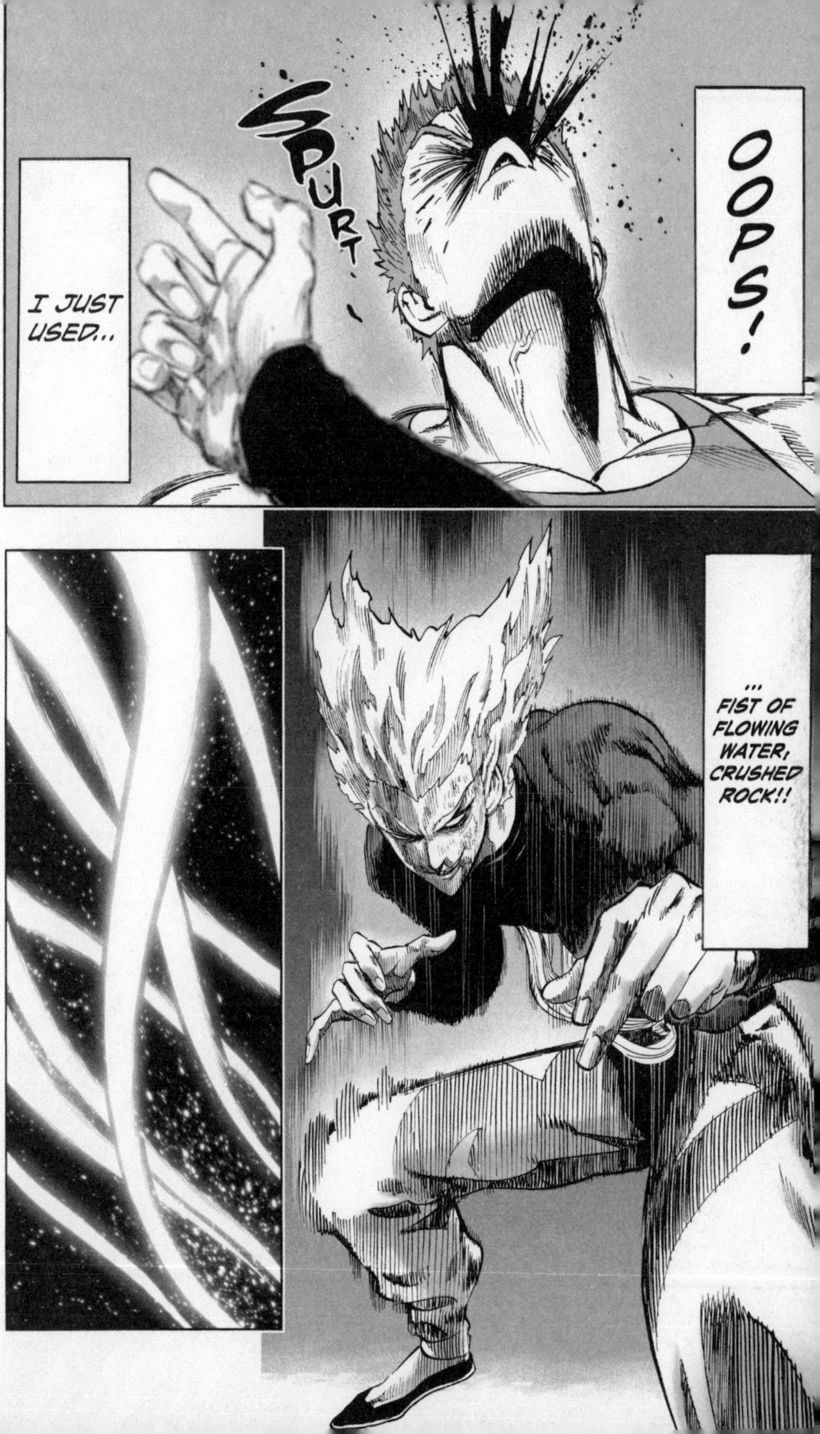
OOPS!
SPURT
I JUST USED...
... FIST OF FLOWING WATER, CRUSHED ROCK!!

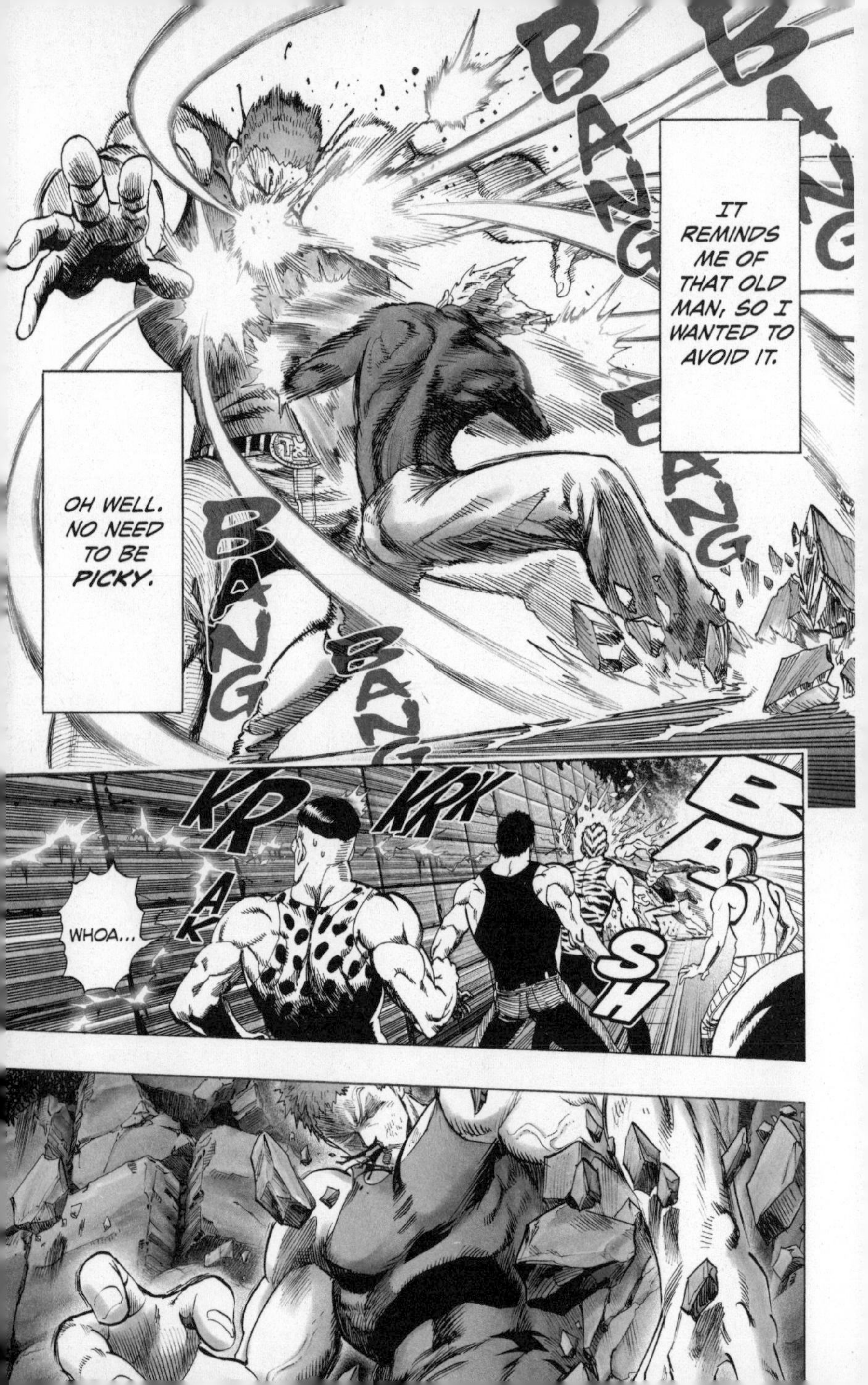
BANG
BANG
IT REMINDS ME OF THAT OLD MAN, SO I WANTED TO AVOID IT.
BANG
BANG
BANG
OH WELL. NO NEED TO BE PICKY.
BA
SH
KRK
KR
AK
WHOA...

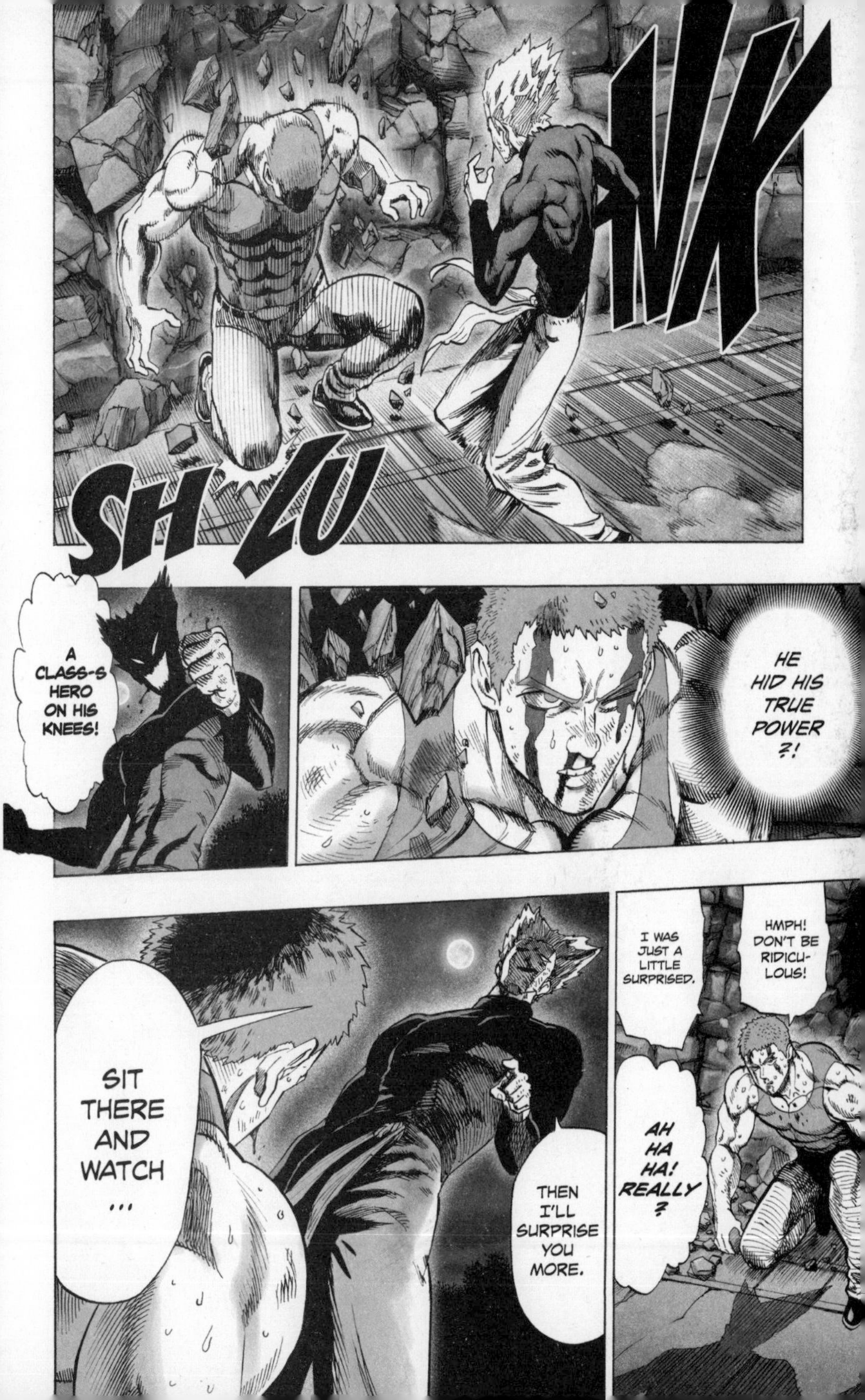
SH LU NK
HE HID HIS TRUE POWER ?!
A CLASS-S HERO ON HIS KNEES!
HMPH! DON'T BE RIDICU-LOUS!
I WAS JUST A LITTLE SURPRISED.
AH HA HA! REALLY?
THEN I'LL SURPRISE YOU MORE.
SIT THERE AND WATCH ...

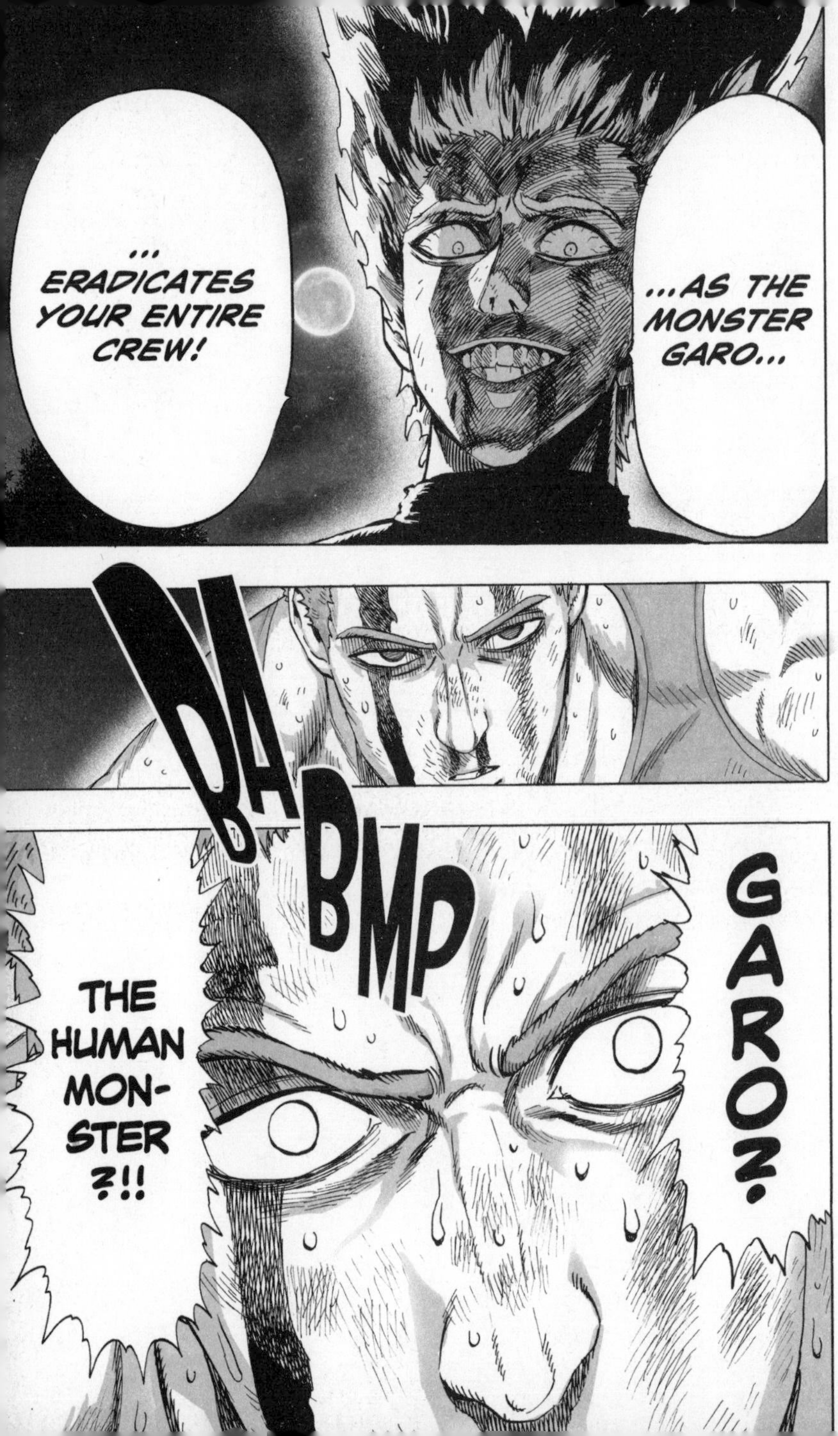
...AS THE MONSTER GARO...
... ERADICATES YOUR ENTIRE CREW!
BA BMP
GARO?
THE HUMAN MON-STER ?!!

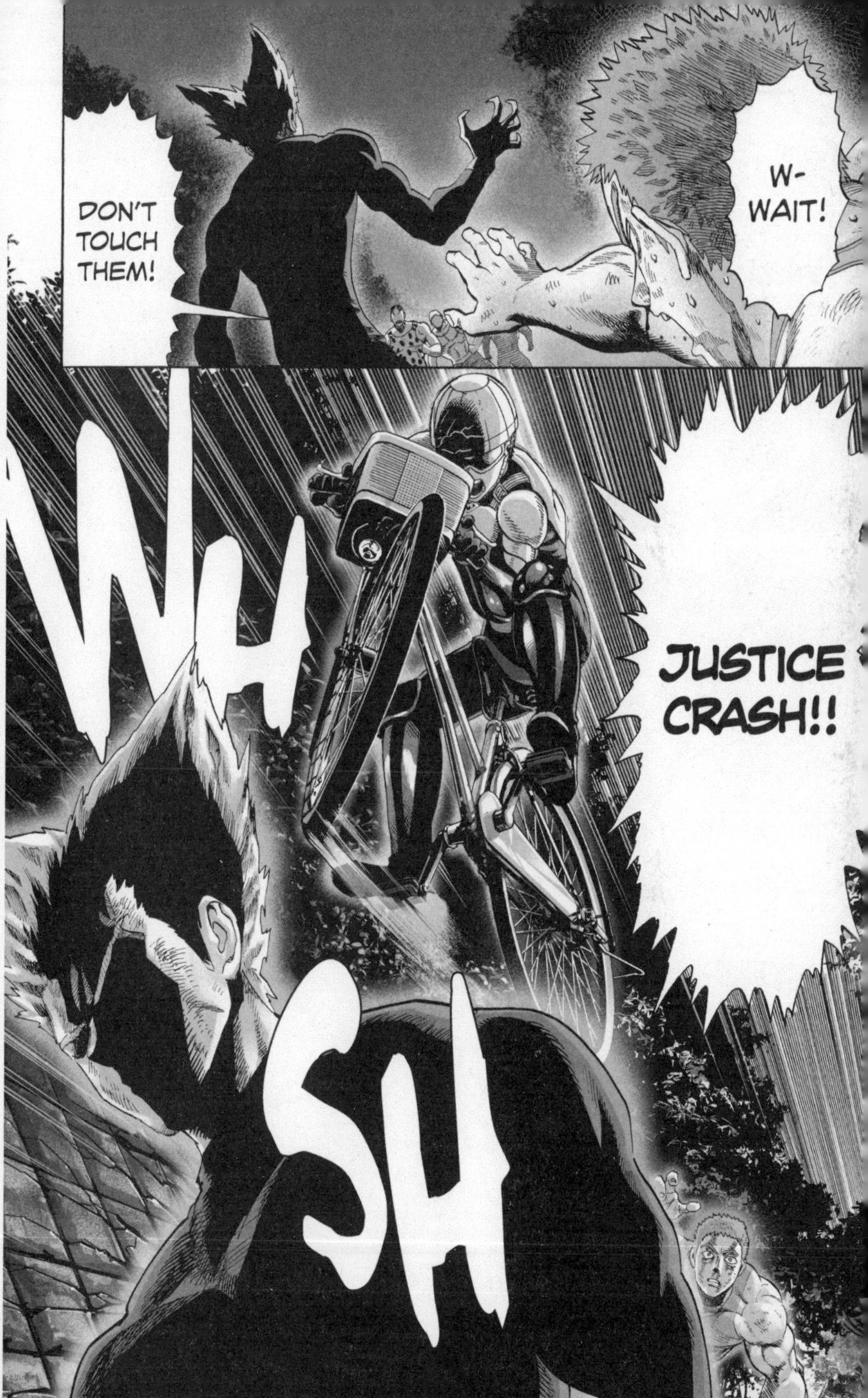
W-WAIT!
DON'T TOUCH THEM!
JUSTICE CRASH!!
WH
SH

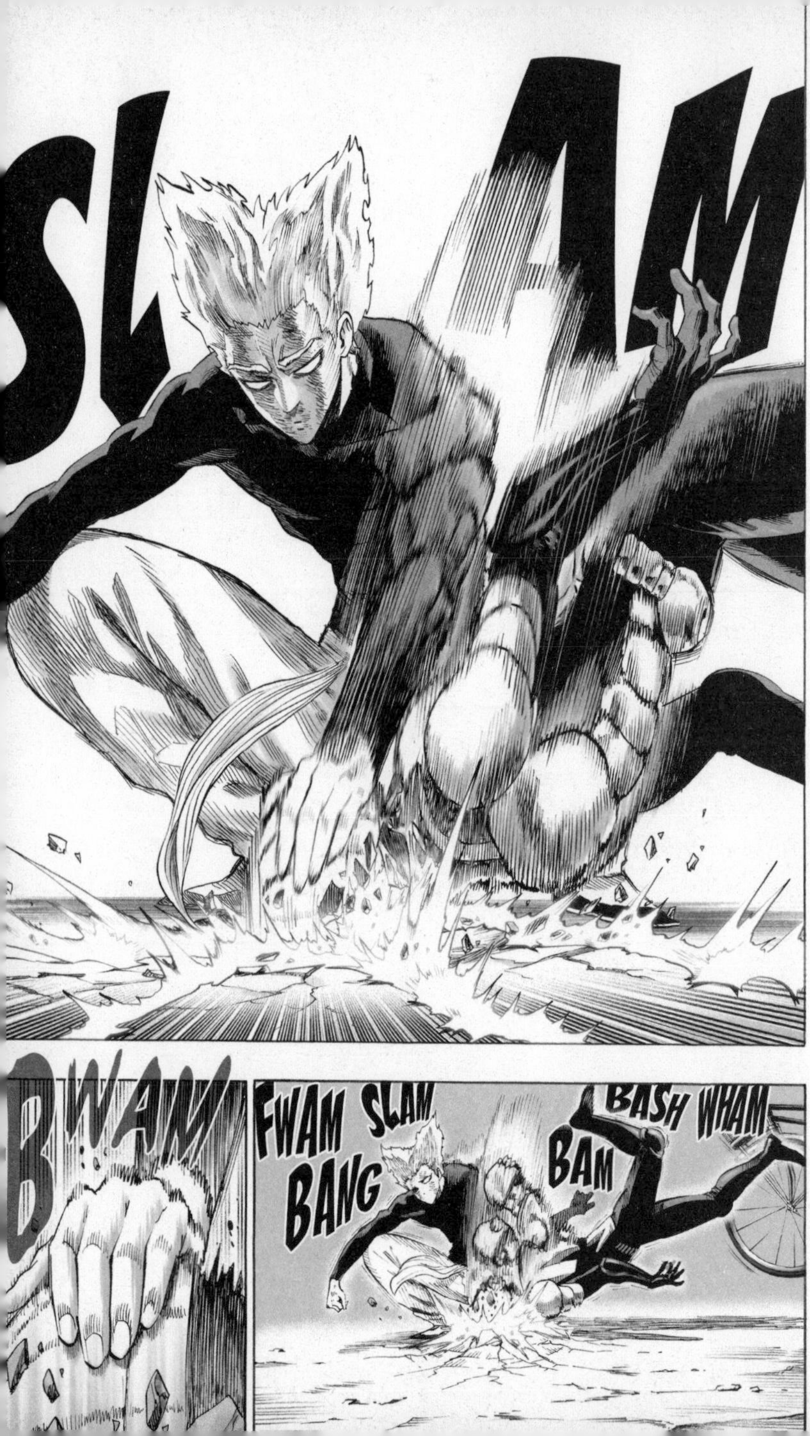
SLAM
BASH
WHAM
BAM
SLAM
FWAM
BANG
BWAM

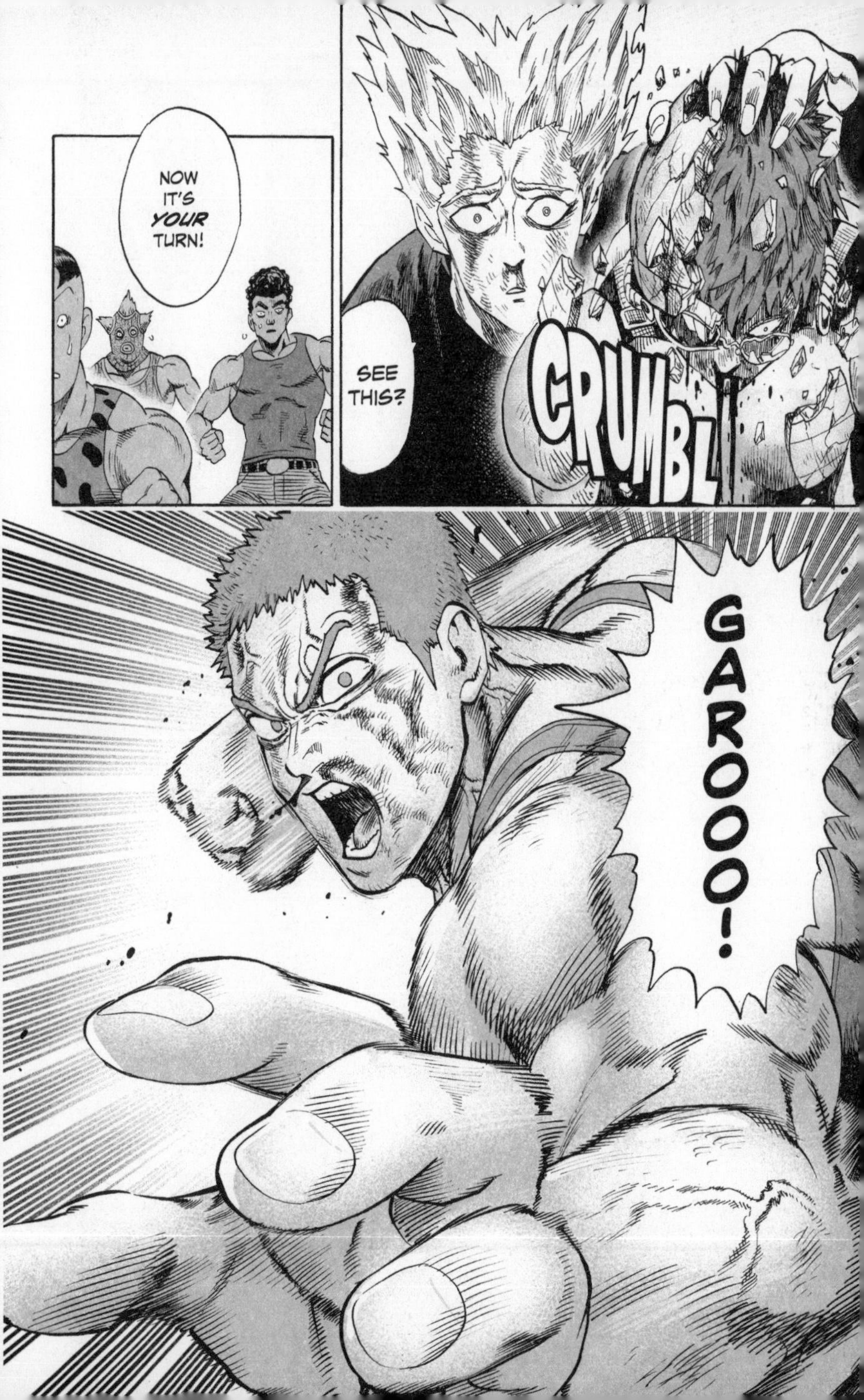
SEE THIS?
CRUMBL
NOW IT'S *YOUR* TURN!
GAROOOO!

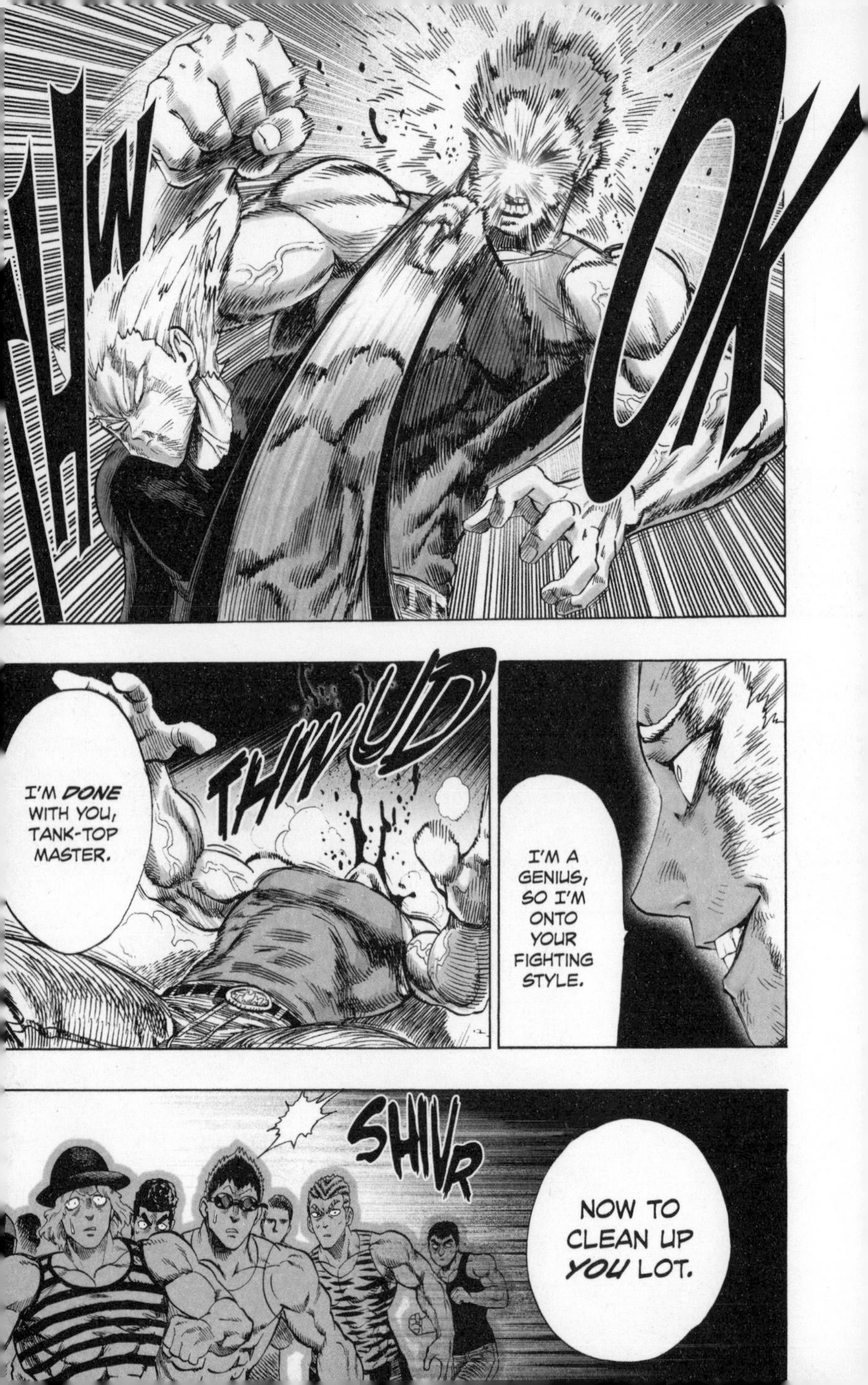
SHWOCK
I'M A GENIUS, SO I'M ONTO YOUR FIGHTING STYLE.
THWUD
I'M *DONE* WITH YOU, TANK-TOP MASTER.
SHIVR
NOW TO CLEAN UP *YOU* LOT.

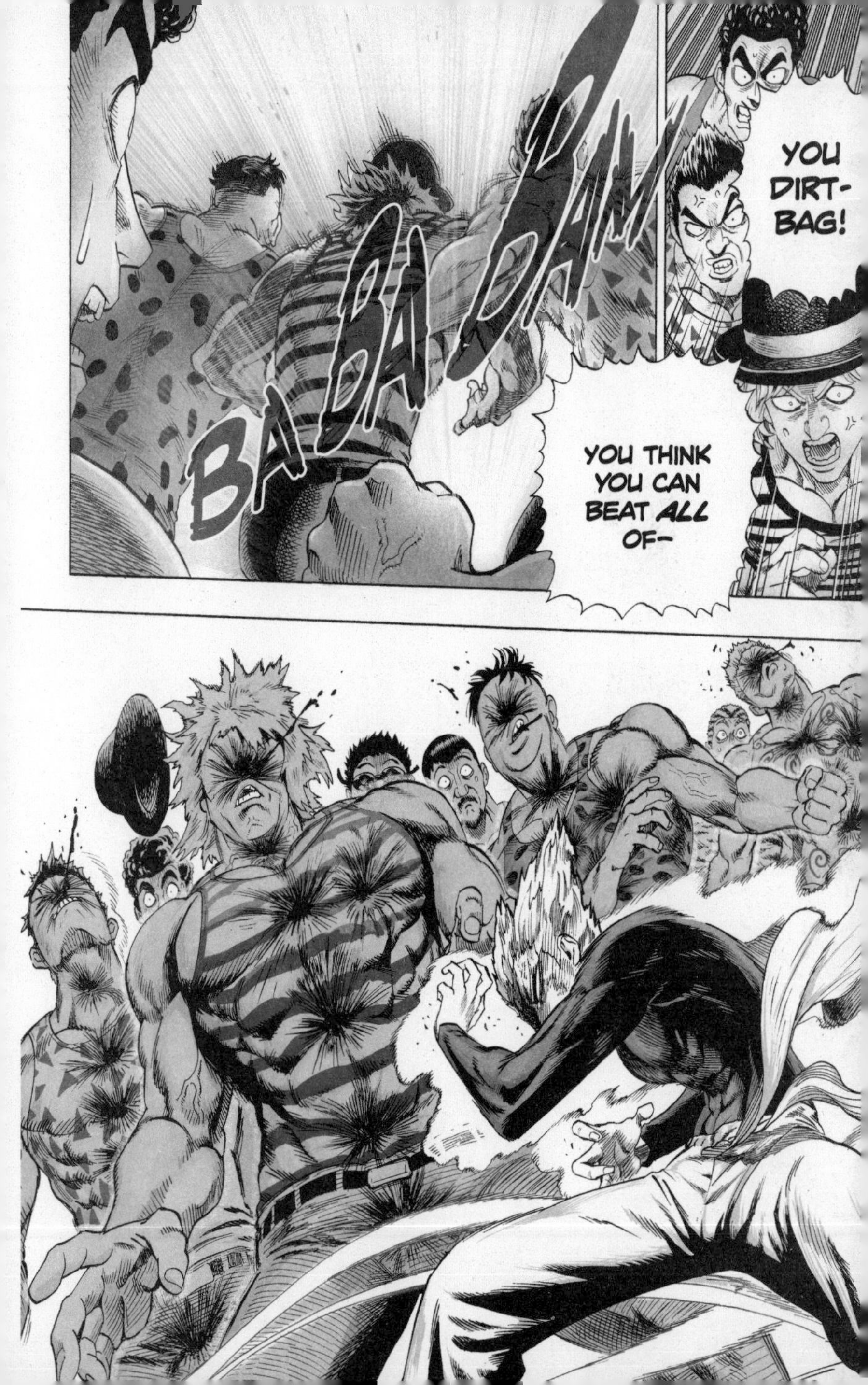
YOU DIRT-BAG!
BA BA BA BAM
YOU THINK YOU CAN BEAT ALL OF-

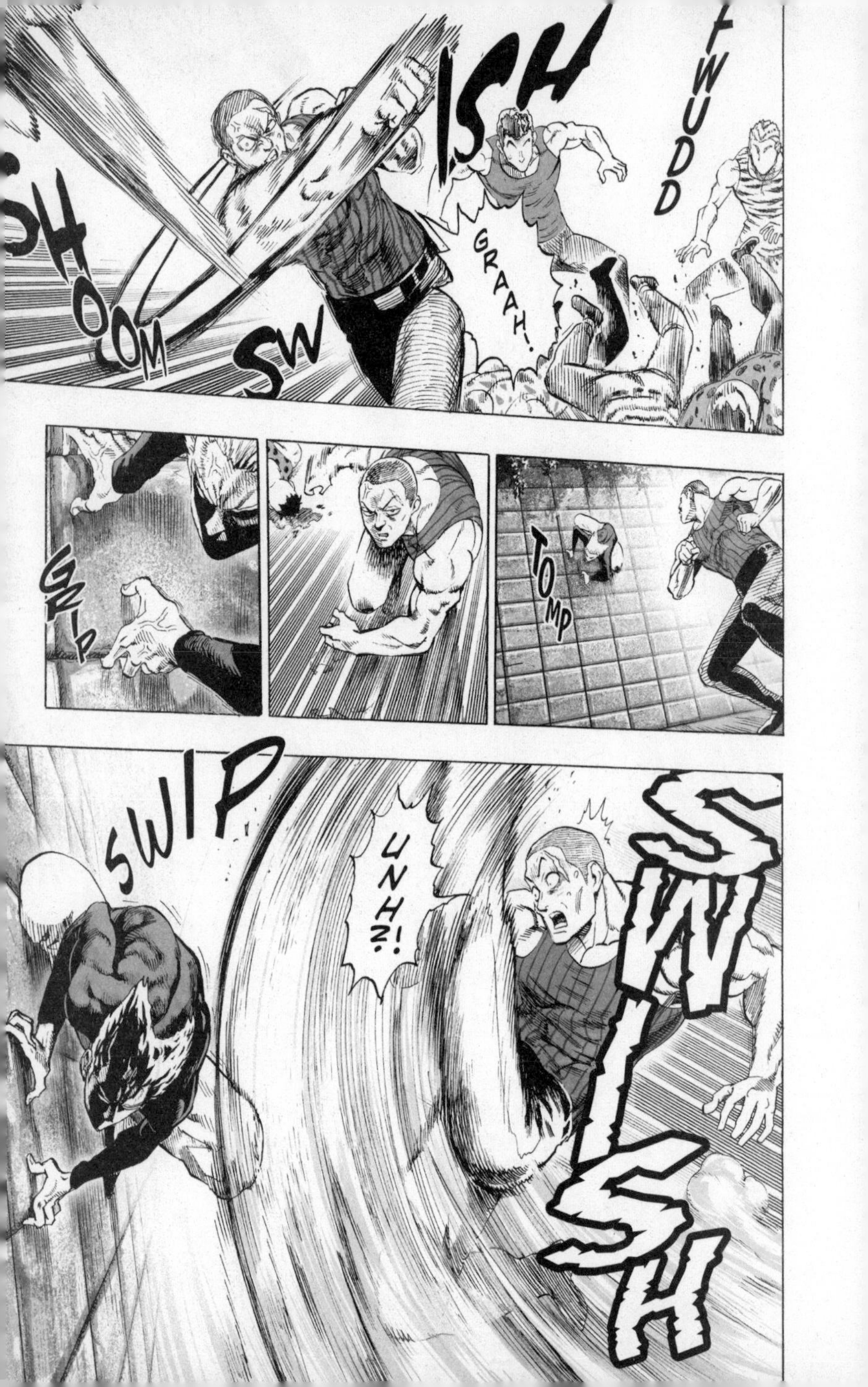

TWUDD
SWISH
GRAAH!
SHOOM
TOMP
GRIP
SWISH
UNH?!
SWIP

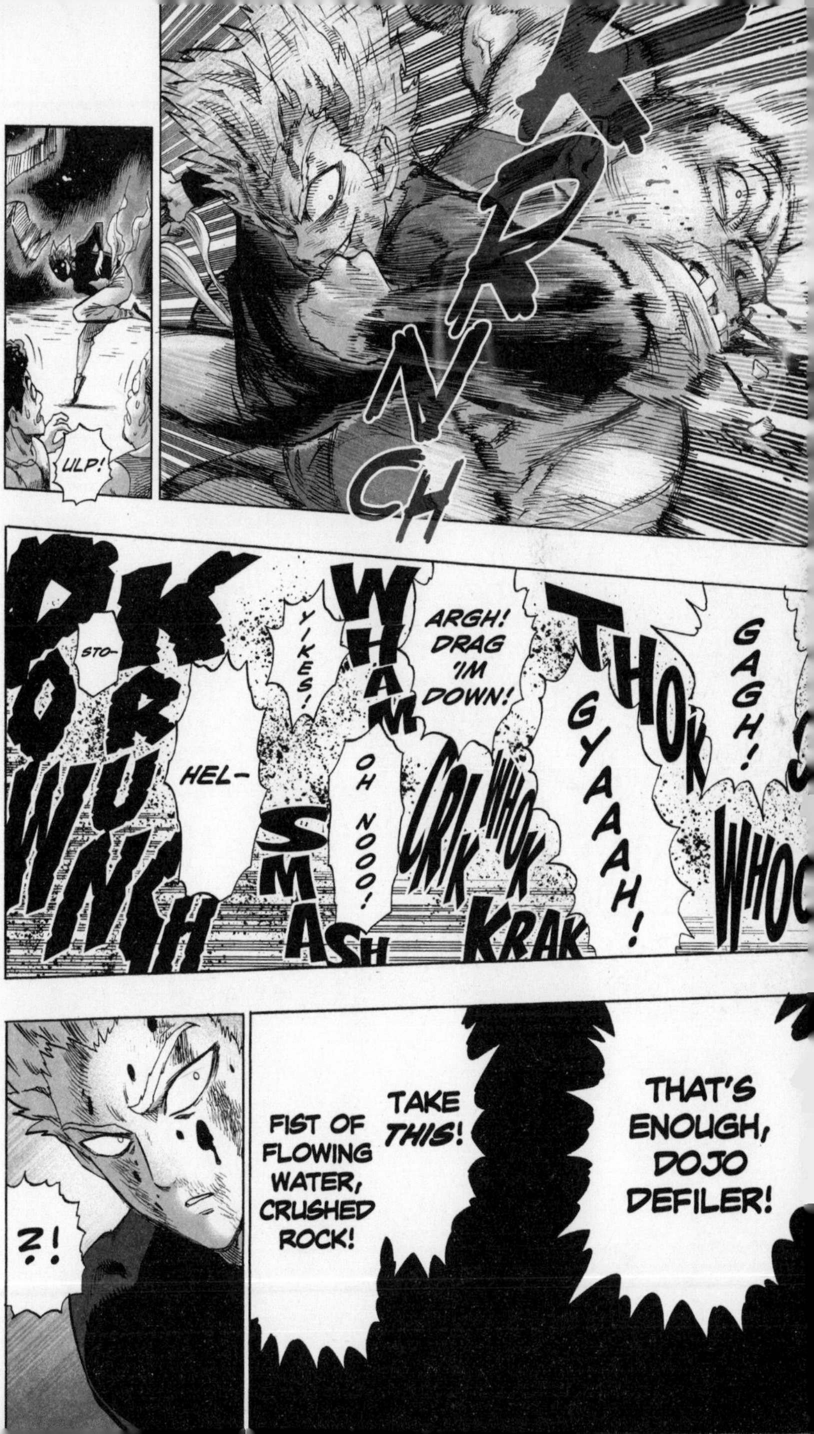
KRRNNCH
ULP!
GAGH!
THOK
GYAAAH!
WHOK
KRAK
CRIK
ARGH! DRAG 'IM DOWN!
WHAM
OH NOOO!
SMASH
YIKES!
STO-
HEL-
THAT'S ENOUGH, DOJO DEFILER!
TAKE THIS!
FIST OF FLOWING WATER, CRUSHED ROCK!
?!

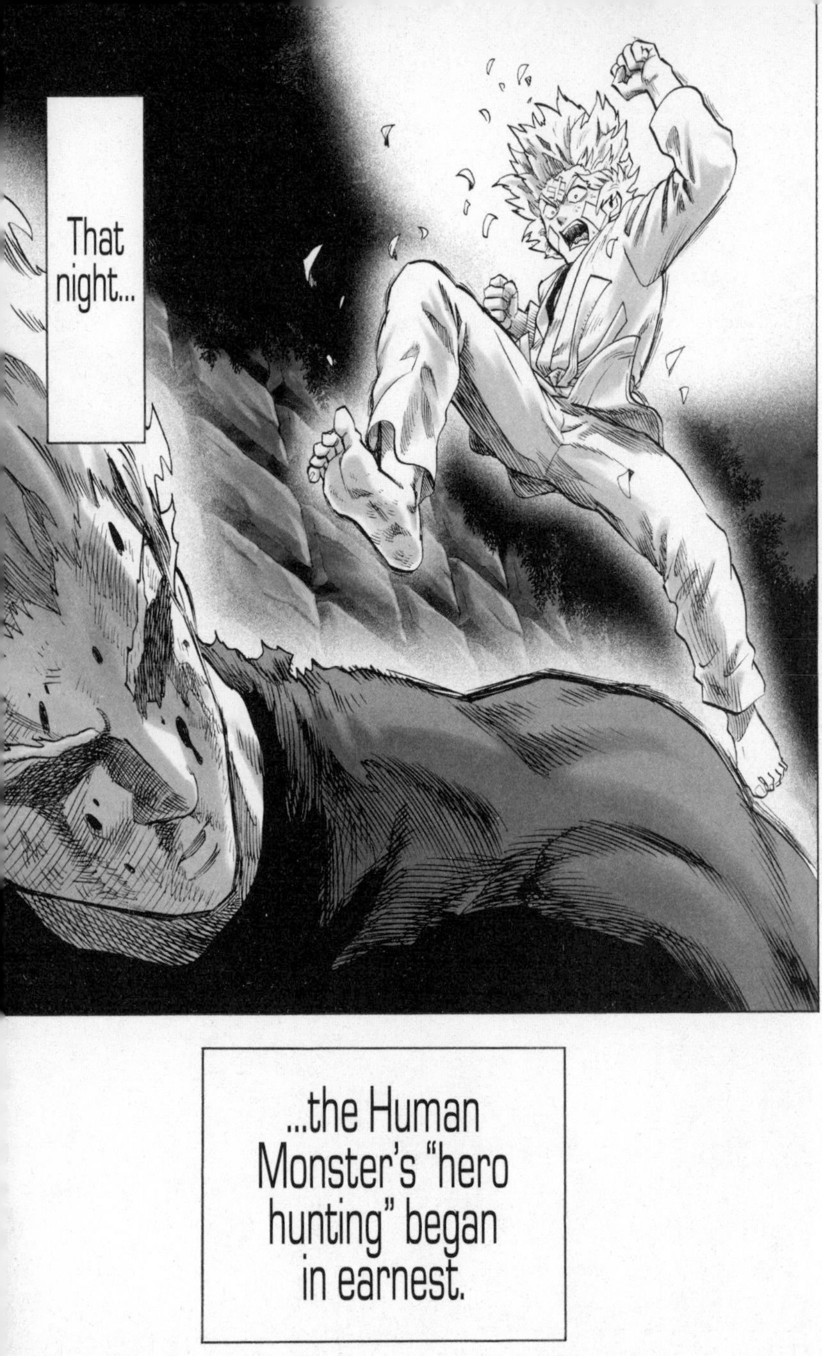
That night...

...the Human Monster's "hero hunting" began in earnest.

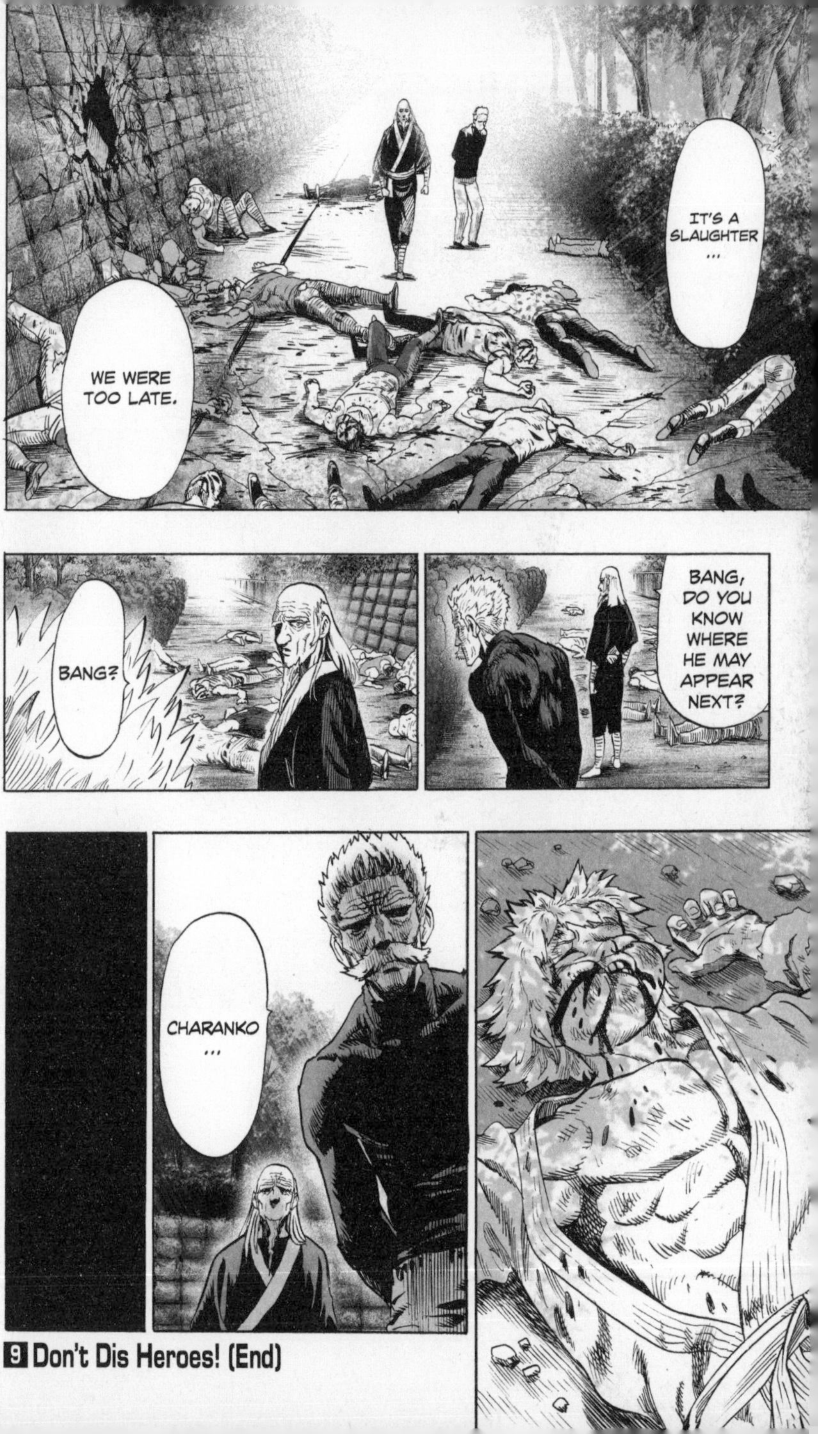
IT'S A SLAUGHTER ...
WE WERE TOO LATE.
BANG, DO YOU KNOW WHERE HE MAY APPEAR NEXT?
BANG?
CHARANKO ...

9 Don't Dis Heroes! (End)

BONUS MANGA: THE BLIZZARD BUNCH IN HARD TIMES

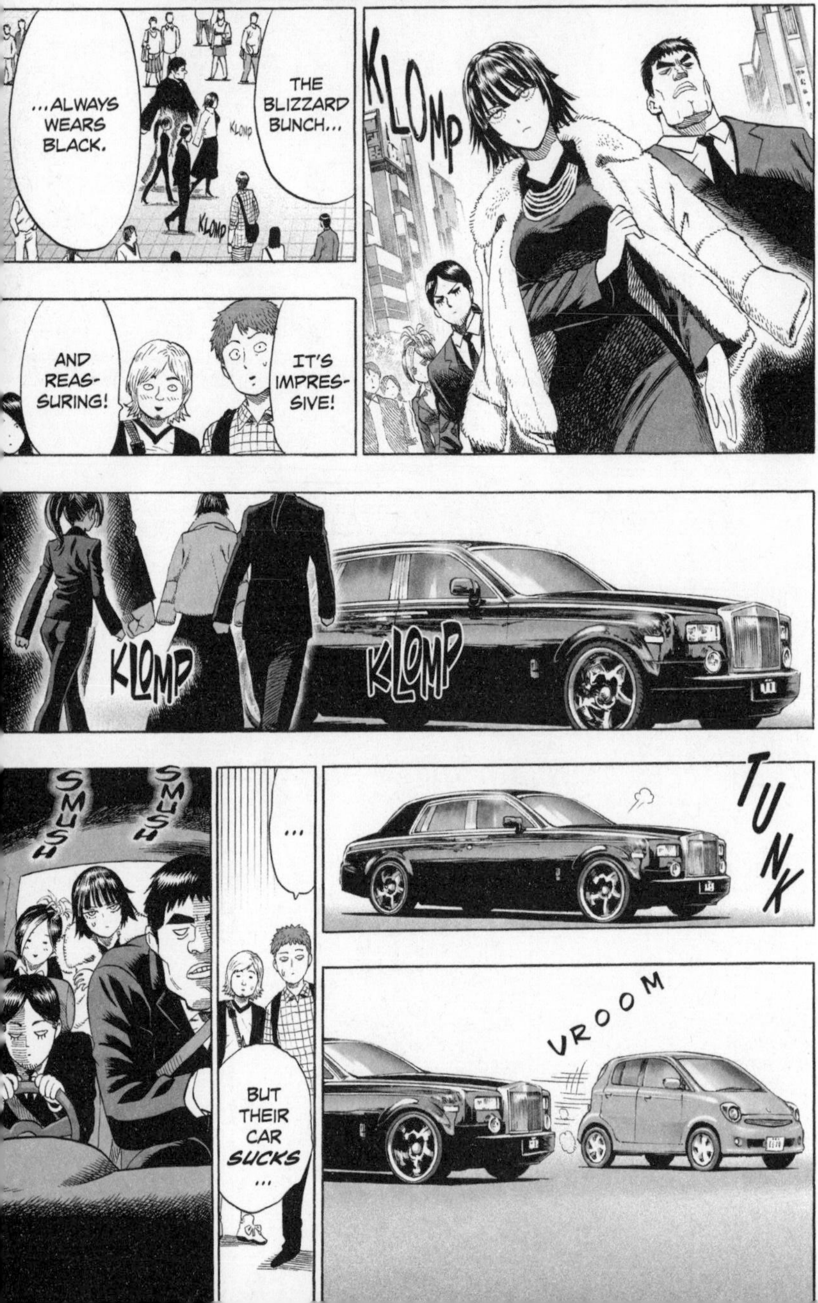
KLOMP
THE BLIZZARD BUNCH...
KLOMP
KLOMP
...ALWAYS WEARS BLACK.
IT'S IMPRESSIVE!
AND REASSURING!
KLOMP
KLOMP
TUNK
VROOM
...
BUT THEIR CAR SUCKS ...
SMUSH
SMUSH

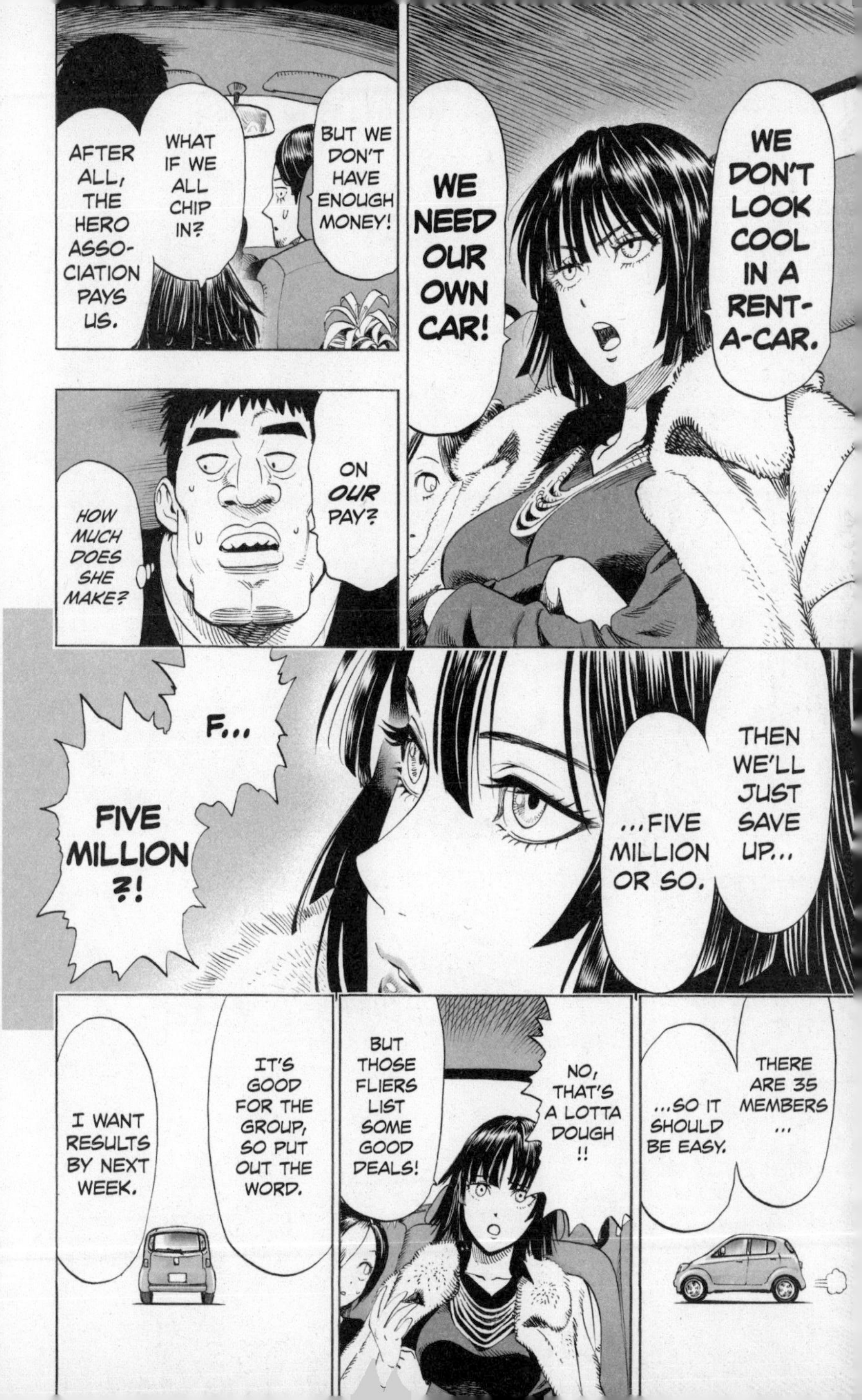
WE DON'T LOOK COOL IN A RENT-A-CAR.
WE NEED OUR OWN CAR!
BUT WE DON'T HAVE ENOUGH MONEY!
WHAT IF WE ALL CHIP IN?
AFTER ALL, THE HERO ASSOCIATION PAYS US.
ON *OUR* PAY?
HOW MUCH DOES SHE MAKE?
THEN WE'LL JUST SAVE UP...
...FIVE MILLION OR SO.
F...
FIVE MILLION ?!
THERE ARE 35 MEMBERS...
...SO IT SHOULD BE EASY.
NO, THAT'S A LOTTA DOUGH !!
BUT THOSE FLIERS LIST SOME GOOD DEALS!
IT'S GOOD FOR THE GROUP, SO PUT OUT THE WORD.
I WANT RESULTS BY NEXT WEEK.

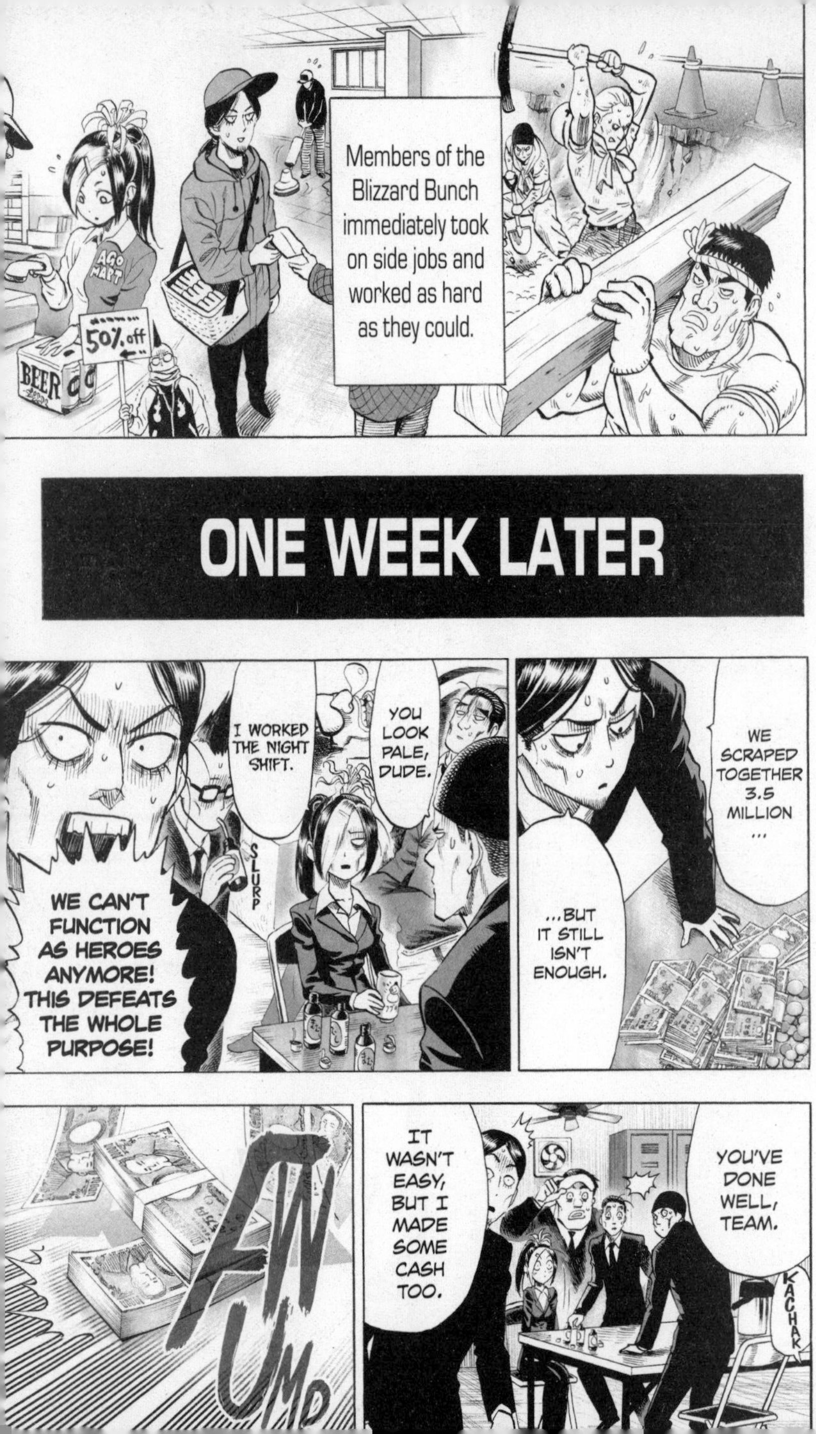
Members of the Blizzard Bunch immediately took on side jobs and worked as hard as they could.
AGO MART
50% off
BEER
ONE WEEK LATER
WE SCRAPED TOGETHER 3.5 MILLION ...
...BUT IT STILL ISN'T ENOUGH.
YOU LOOK PALE, DUDE.
I WORKED THE NIGHT SHIFT.
SLURP
WE CAN'T FUNCTION AS HEROES ANYMORE! THIS DEFEATS THE WHOLE PURPOSE!
YOU'VE DONE WELL, TEAM.
KACHAK
IT WASN'T EASY, BUT I MADE SOME CASH TOO.
FWUMP

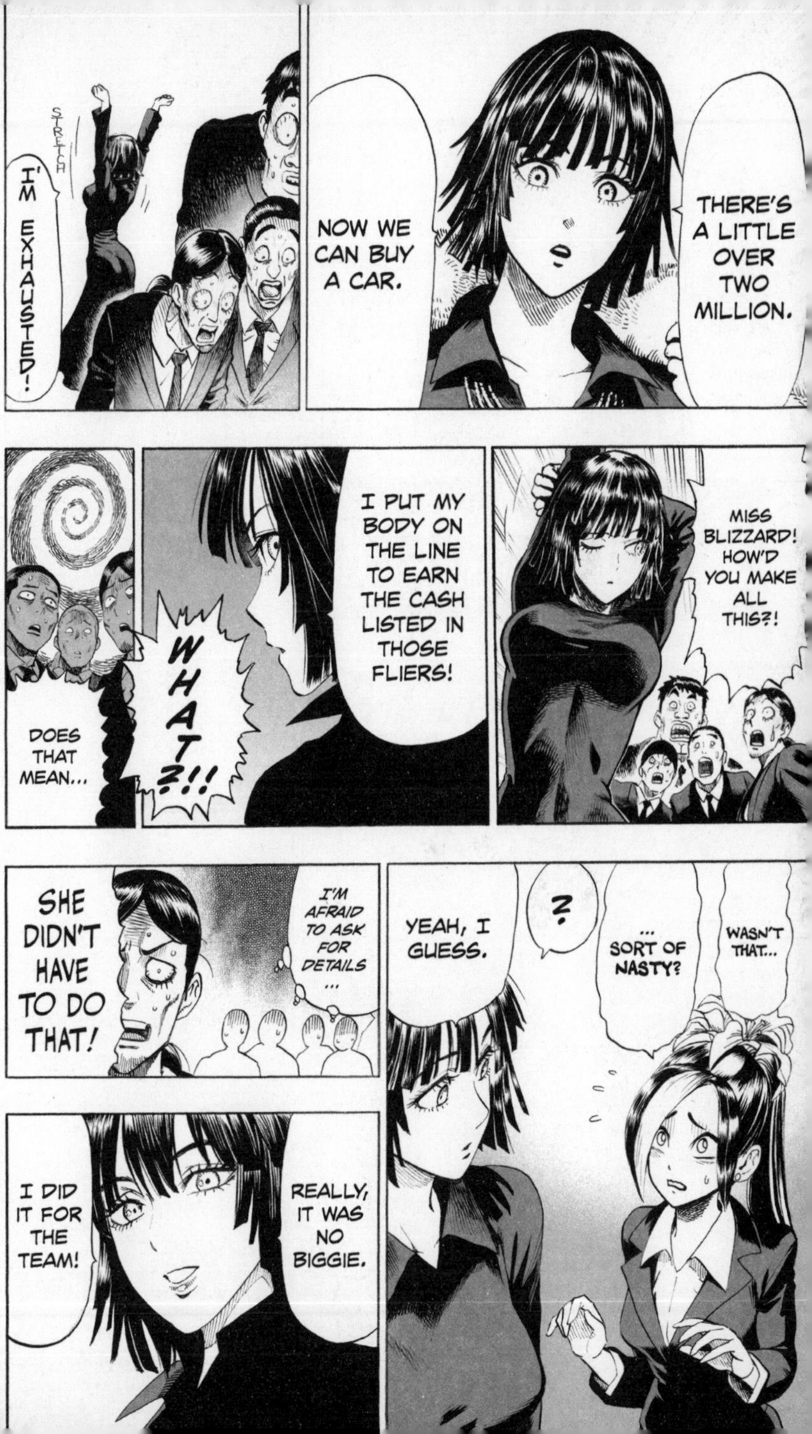
THERE'S A LITTLE OVER TWO MILLION.
NOW WE CAN BUY A CAR.
STRETCH
I'M EXHAUSTED!
MISS BLIZZARD! HOW'D YOU MAKE ALL THIS?!
I PUT MY BODY ON THE LINE TO EARN THE CASH LISTED IN THOSE FLIERS!
WHAT?!!
DOES THAT MEAN...
WASN'T THAT...
...SORT OF NASTY?
?
YEAH, I GUESS.
I'M AFRAID TO ASK FOR DETAILS...
SHE DIDN'T HAVE TO DO THAT!
REALLY, IT WAS NO BIGGIE.
I DID IT FOR THE TEAM!

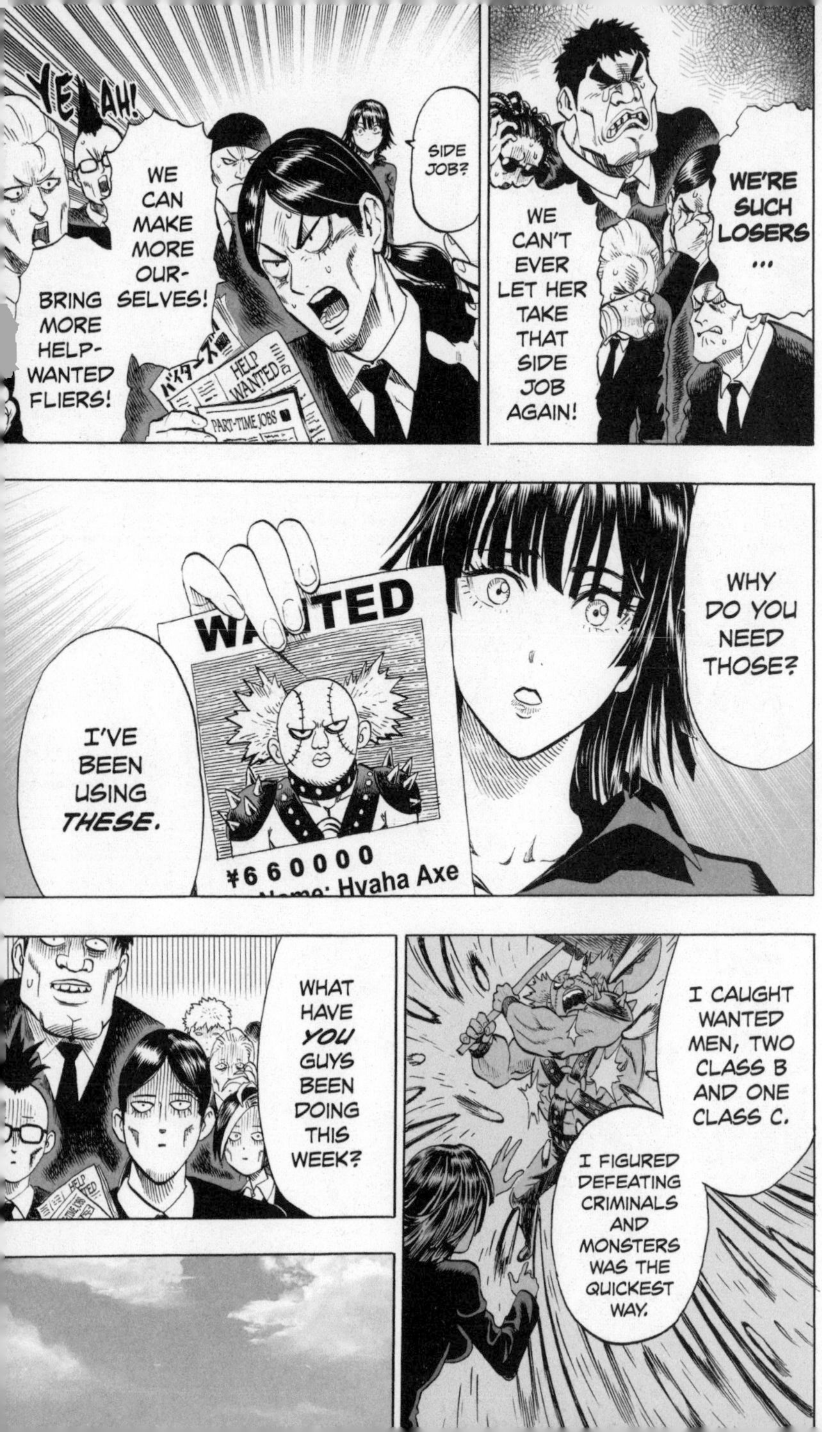
WE'RE SUCH LOSERS ...
WE CAN'T EVER LET HER TAKE THAT SIDE JOB AGAIN!
SIDE JOB?
WE CAN MAKE MORE OURSELVES!
BRING MORE HELP-WANTED FLIERS!
YEAH!
HELP WANTED
PART-TIME JOBS
WHY DO YOU NEED THOSE?
I'VE BEEN USING *THESE*.
WA TED
¥660000
Hyaha Axe
I CAUGHT WANTED MEN, TWO CLASS B AND ONE CLASS C.
I FIGURED DEFEATING CRIMINALS AND MONSTERS WAS THE QUICKEST WAY.
WHAT HAVE *YOU* GUYS BEEN DOING THIS WEEK?

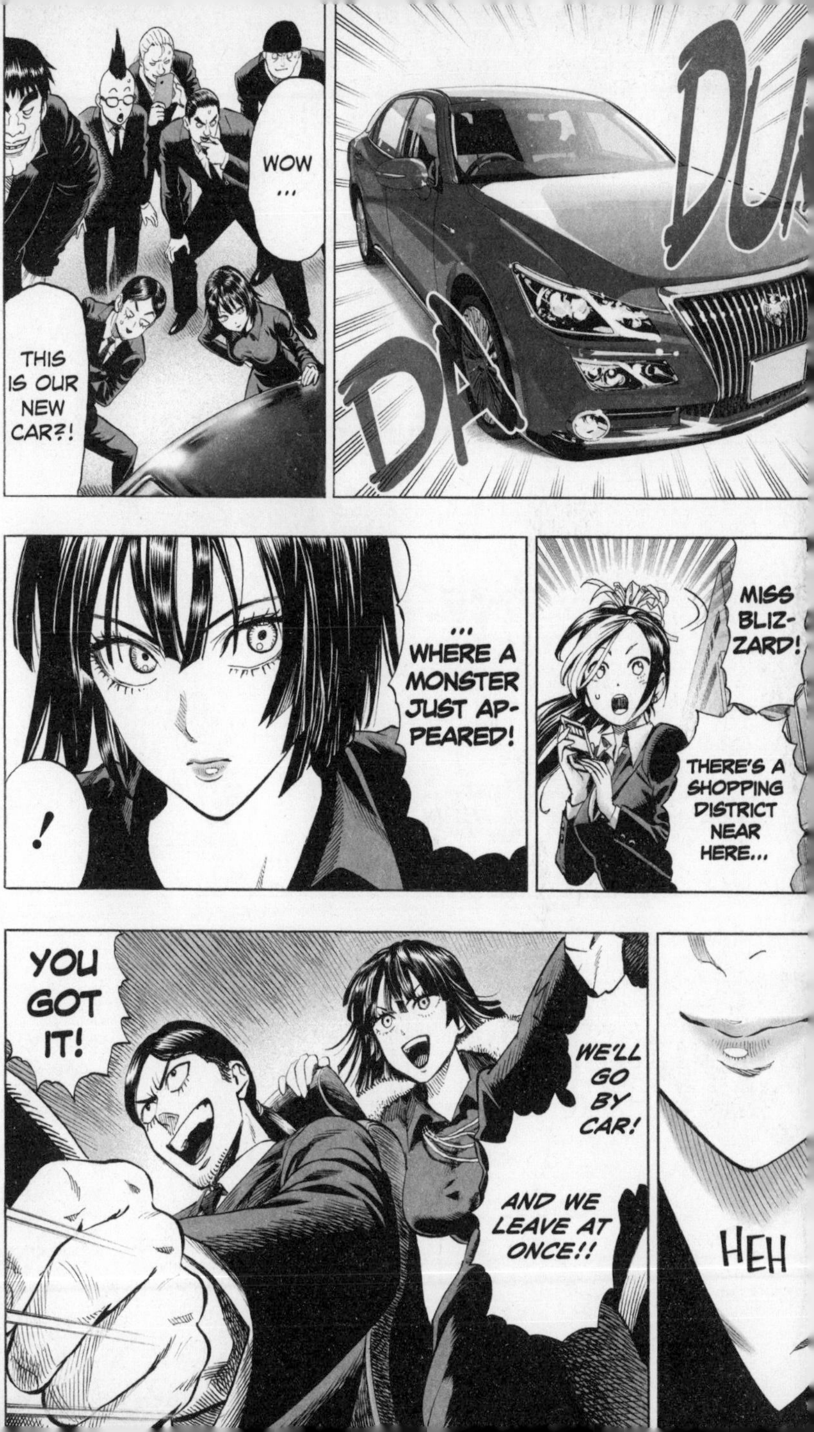
DU
DA
WOW ...
THIS IS OUR NEW CAR?!
MISS BLIZ-ZARD!
THERE'S A SHOPPING DISTRICT NEAR HERE...
... WHERE A MONSTER JUST AP-PEARED!
!
HEH
WE'LL GO BY CAR!
AND WE LEAVE AT ONCE!!
YOU GOT IT!

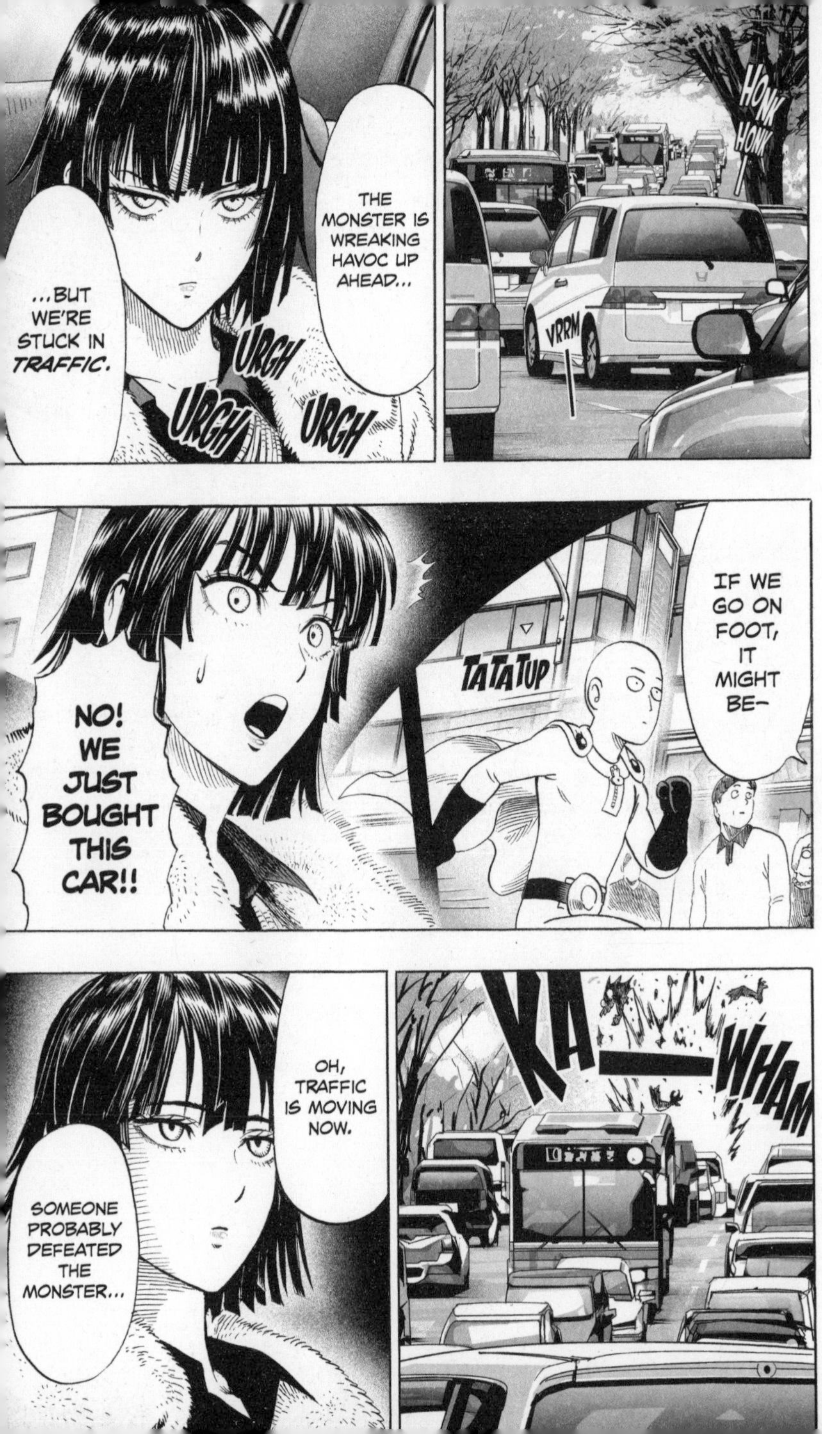
HONK HONK
VRRM
THE MONSTER IS WREAKING HAVOC UP AHEAD...
URGH URGH URGH
...BUT WE'RE STUCK IN *TRAFFIC*.
IF WE GO ON FOOT, IT MIGHT BE—
TATATUP
NO! WE JUST BOUGHT THIS CAR!!
KA—WHAM
OH, TRAFFIC IS MOVING NOW.
SOMEONE PROBABLY DEFEATED THE MONSTER...

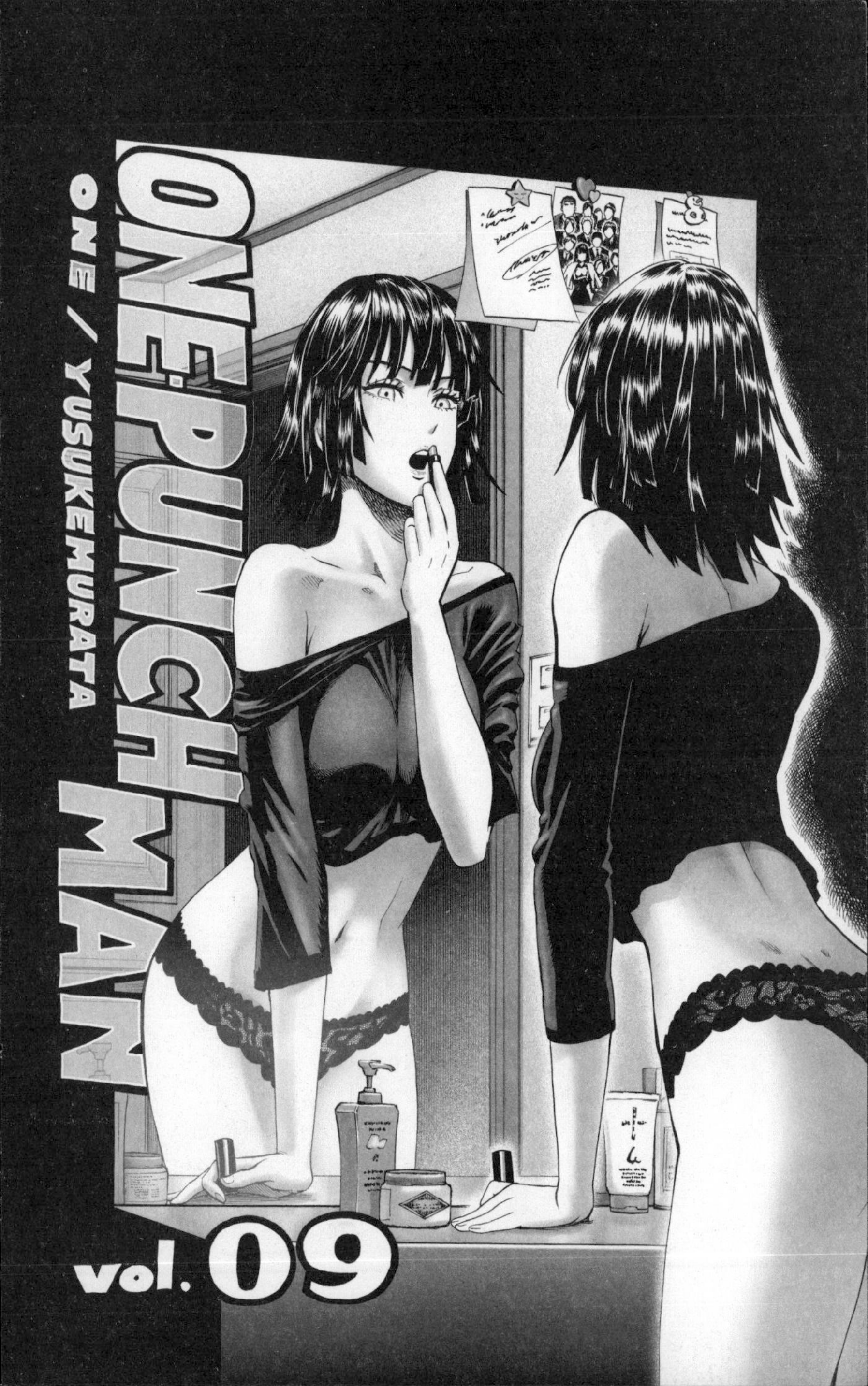
ONE-PUNCH MAN
ONE / YUSUKE MURATA
vol. 09

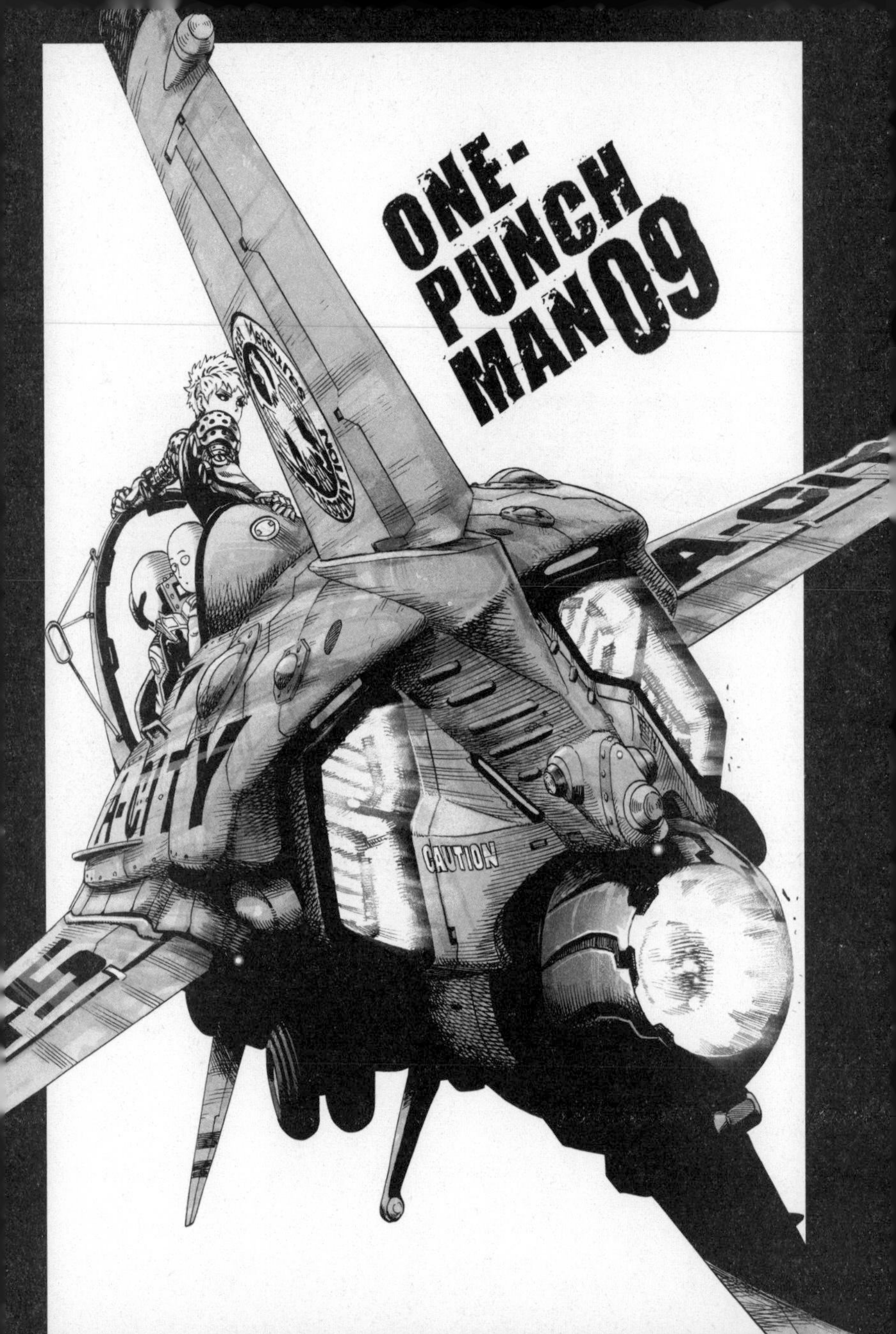
ONE-PUNCH MAN 09
A-CITY
CAUTION

END NOTES

PAGE 143, PANEL 1:
The T-shirt peeking out from King's shirt has *doki doki* on it in Japanese. This could be referencing his secret love of the *Doki Doki Sisters* (Heartthrob Sisters) video game.

PAGE 173, PANEL 1:
The sign says *Fist of Flowing Water, Crushed Rock.*

PAGE 177:
The title of the manga is *Sun Man*, which is a story ONE drew in his teens.

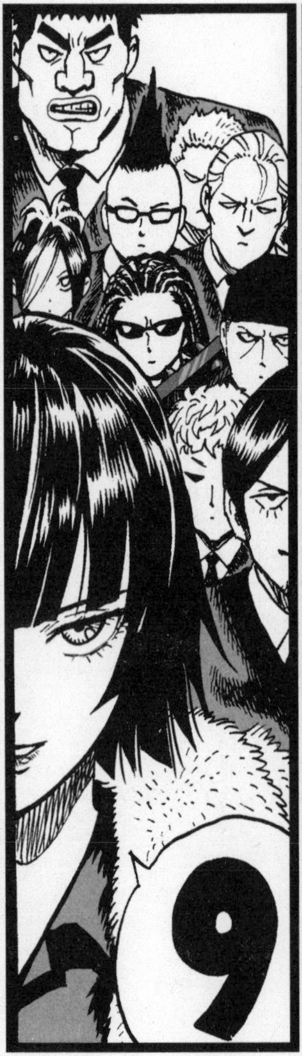
9

ONE-PUNCH MAN

VOLUME 9

SHONEN JUMP MANGA EDITION

STORY BY | ONE
ART BY | YUSUKE MURATA

TRANSLATION | JOHN WERRY
TOUCH-UP ART AND LETTERING | JAMES GAUBATZ
DESIGN | FAWN LAU
SHONEN JUMP SERIES EDITOR | JOHN BAE
GRAPHIC NOVEL EDITOR | JENNIFER LEBLANC

First published in Japan in 2012 by SHUEISHA Inc., Tokyo.
English translation rights arranged by SHUEISHA Inc.

Printed in the U.S.A.

Published by VIZ Media, LLC
P.O. Box 77010
San Francisco, CA 94107

VIZ MEDIA
viz.com

SHONEN JUMP

10 9 8 7 6 5 4 3
First printing, November 2016
Third printing, March 2021

ratings.viz.com RATED T TEEN

PARENTAL ADVISORY
ONE-PUNCH MAN is rated T for Teen and is recommended for ages 13 and up. This volume contains realistic and fantasy violence.

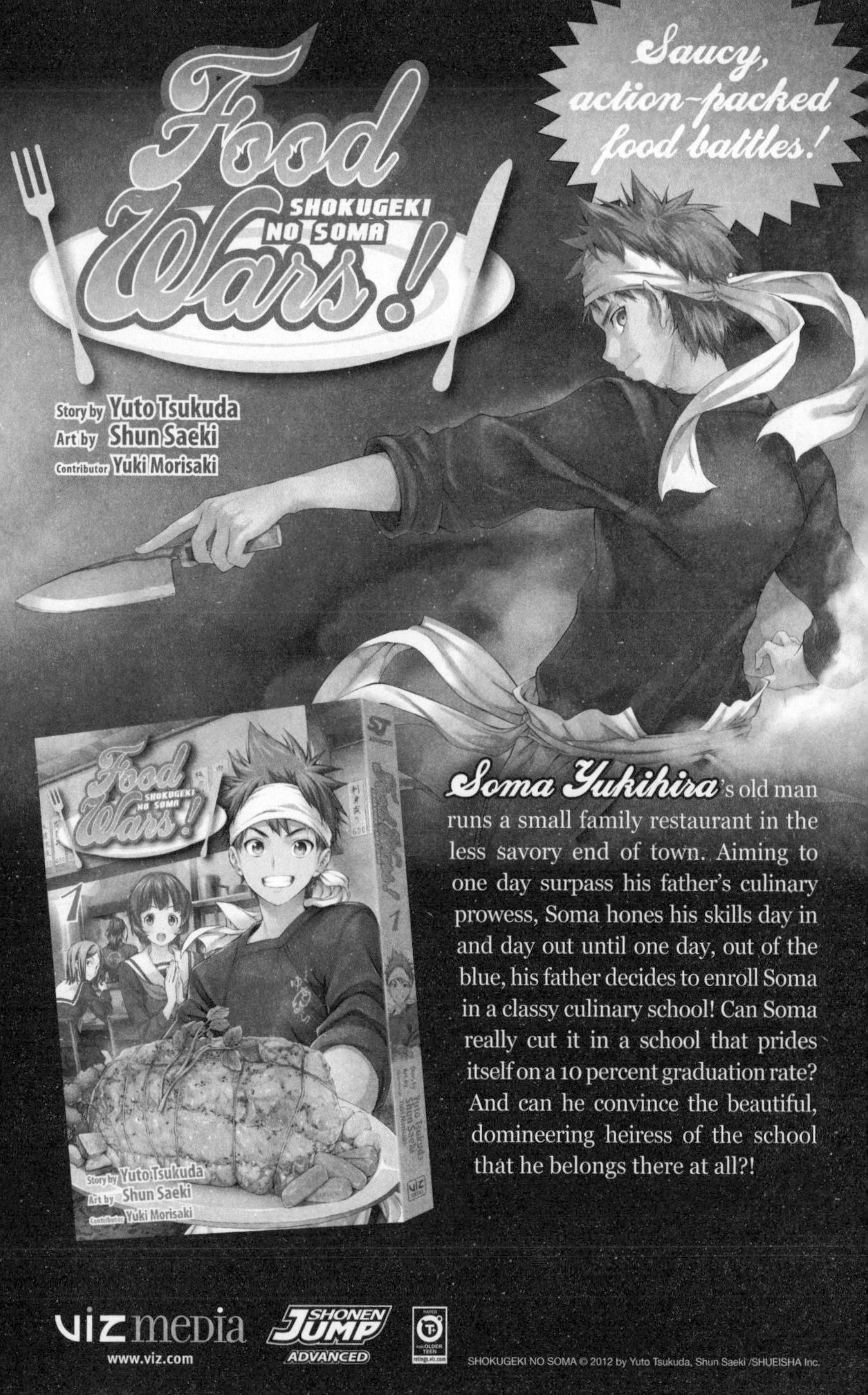
Food Wars!
SHOKUGEKI NO SOMA
Saucy, action-packed food battles!
Story by Yuto Tsukuda
Art by Shun Saeki
Contributor Yuki Morisaki
Soma Yukihira's old man runs a small family restaurant in the less savory end of town. Aiming to one day surpass his father's culinary prowess, Soma hones his skills day in and day out until one day, out of the blue, his father decides to enroll Soma in a classy culinary school! Can Soma really cut it in a school that prides itself on a 10 percent graduation rate? And can he convince the beautiful, domineering heiress of the school that he belongs there at all?!
viz media
www.viz.com
SHONEN JUMP ADVANCED
RATED T+ FOR OLDER TEEN ratings.viz.com
SHOKUGEKI NO SOMA © 2012 by Yuto Tsukuda, Shun Saeki /SHUEISHA Inc.

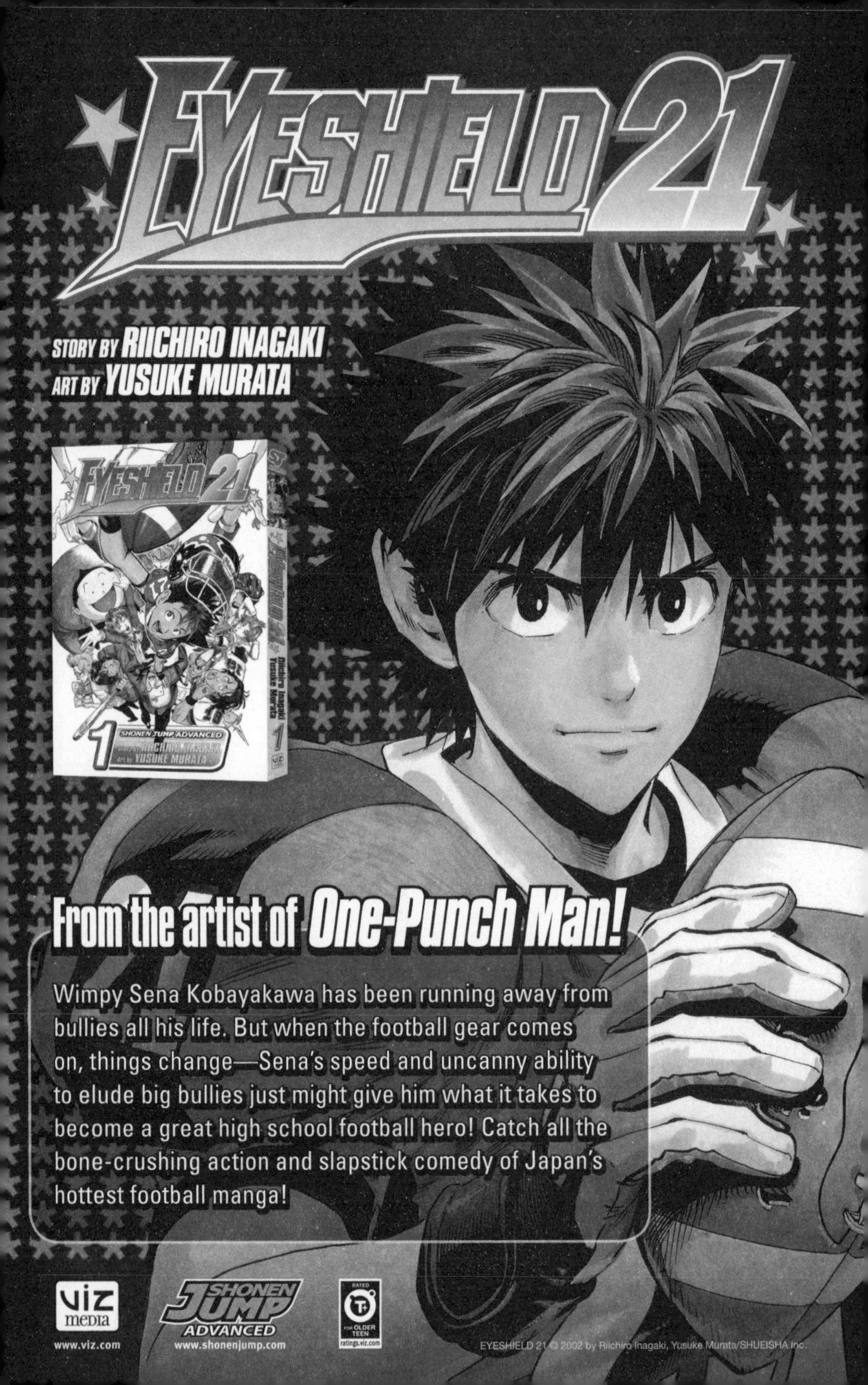
EYESHIELD 21
STORY BY RIICHIRO INAGAKI
ART BY YUSUKE MURATA
EYESHIELD 21
1
SHONEN JUMP ADVANCED
Story by RIICHIRO INAGAKI
Art by YUSUKE MURATA
From the artist of One-Punch Man!
Wimpy Sena Kobayakawa has been running away from bullies all his life. But when the football gear comes on, things change—Sena's speed and uncanny ability to elude big bullies just might give him what it takes to become a great high school football hero! Catch all the bone-crushing action and slapstick comedy of Japan's hottest football manga!
viz media
www.viz.com
SHONEN JUMP ADVANCED
www.shonenjump.com
RATED T+ FOR OLDER TEEN
ratings.viz.com
EYESHIELD 21 © 2002 by Riichiro Inagaki, Yusuke Murata/SHUEISHA Inc.

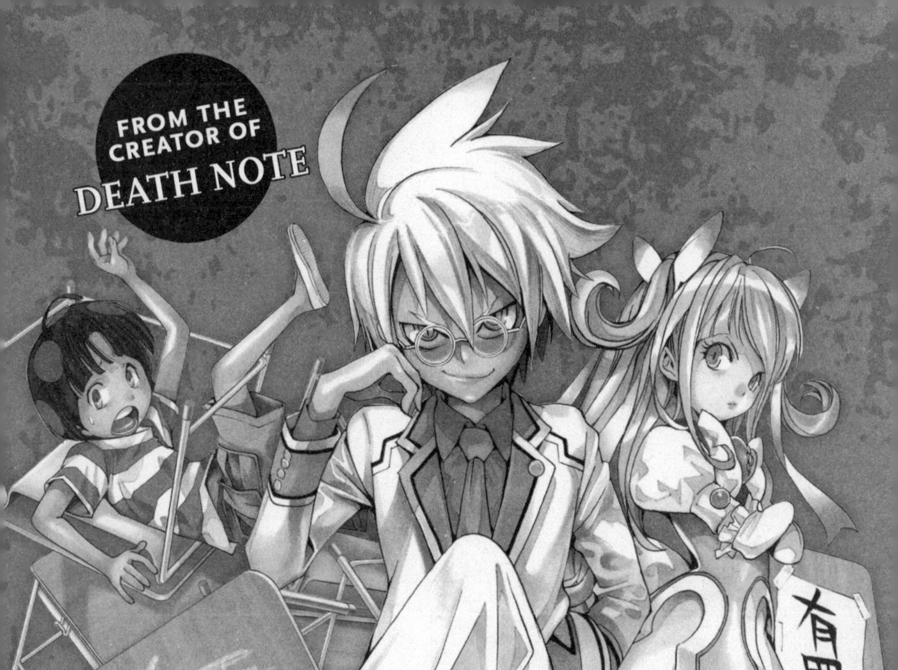
FROM THE CREATOR OF DEATH NOTE
無罪
有罪

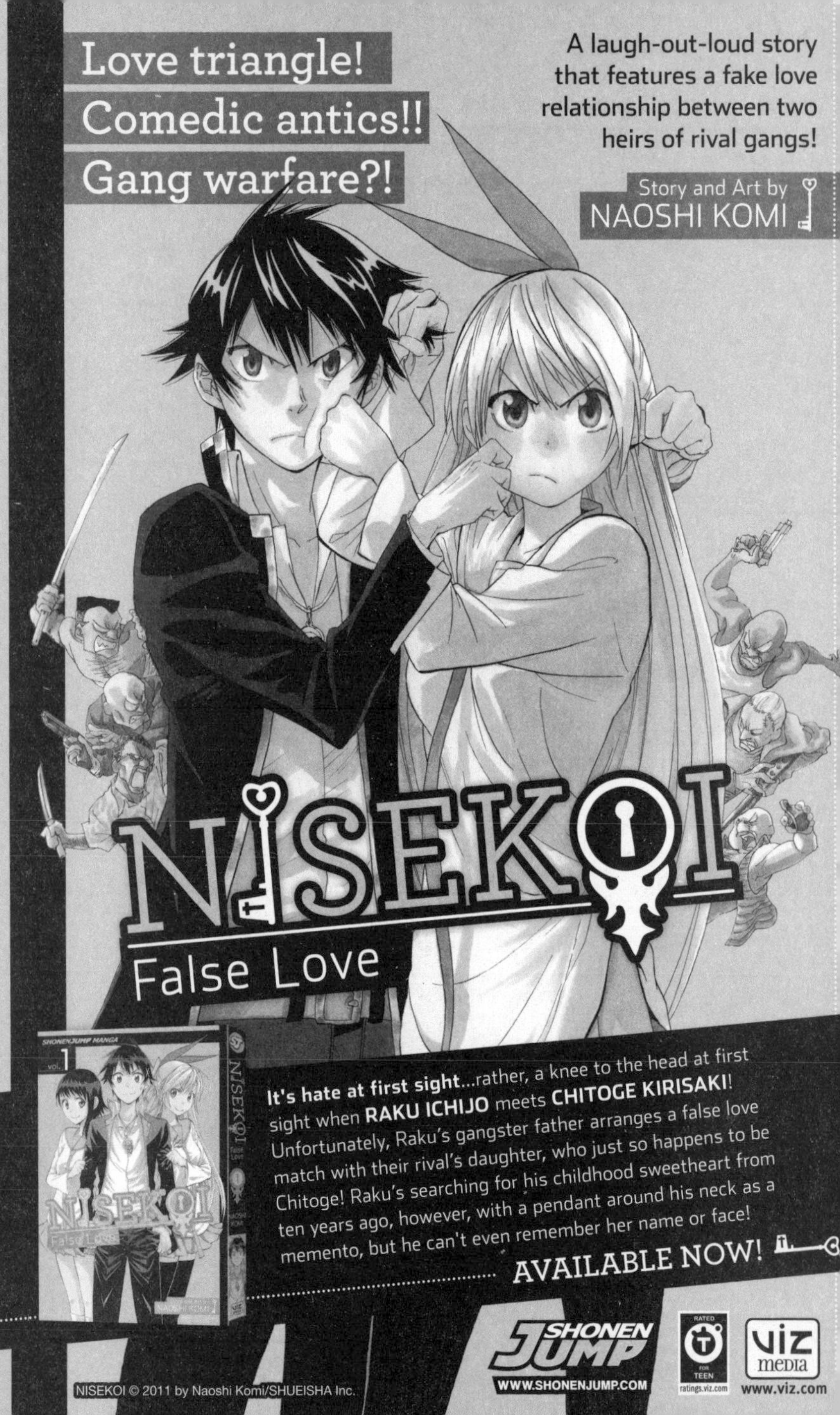
Love triangle!
Comedic antics!!
Gang warfare?!
A laugh-out-loud story that features a fake love relationship between two heirs of rival gangs!
Story and Art by
NAOSHI KOMI
NISEKOI
False Love
SHONENJUMP MANGA
vol. 1
NISEKOI False Love
It's hate at first sight...rather, a knee to the head at first sight when RAKU ICHIJO meets CHITOGE KIRISAKI! Unfortunately, Raku's gangster father arranges a false love match with their rival's daughter, who just so happens to be Chitoge! Raku's searching for his childhood sweetheart from ten years ago, however, with a pendant around his neck as a memento, but he can't even remember her name or face!
AVAILABLE NOW!
SHONEN JUMP
WWW.SHONENJUMP.COM
RATED T FOR TEEN
ratings.viz.com
VIZ media
www.viz.com
NISEKOI © 2011 by Naoshi Komi/SHUEISHA Inc.

STOP!

YOU'RE READING THE WRONG WAY!

✦ ONE-PUNCH MAN READS FROM RIGHT TO LEFT, STARTING IN THE UPPER-RIGHT CORNER. JAPANESE IS READ FROM RIGHT TO LEFT, MEANING THAT ACTION, SOUND EFFECTS, AND WORD-BALLOON ORDER ARE COMPLETELY REVERSED FROM ENGLISH ORDER.

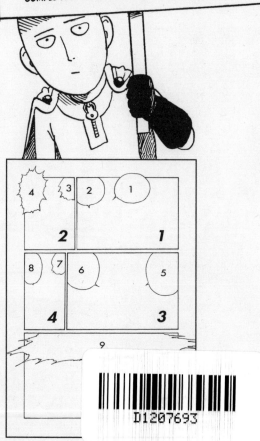